The Resource Handbook for Academic Deans

The Resource Handbook for Academic Deans

THIRD EDITION

LAURA L. BEHLING, EDITOR

Sponsored by the
American Conference
of Academic Deans (ACAD)

ACAD
AMERICAN CONFERENCE
OF ACADEMIC DEANS

JB JOSSEY-BASS™
A Wiley Brand

Cover design: Michael Cook

Cover image: © Vectorig/iStockphoto

Published by Jossey-Bass
A Wiley Brand
One Montgomery Street, Suite 1200, San Francisco, CA 94104-4594—www.josseybass.com/highereducation

Jossey-Bass books and products are available through most bookstores. To contact Jossey-Bass directly call our Customer Care Department within the U.S. at 800-956-7739, outside the U.S. at 317-572-3986, or fax 317-572-4002.

Wiley publishes in a variety of print and electronic formats and by print-on-demand. Some material included with standard print versions of this book may not be included in e-books or in print-on-demand. If this book refers to media such as a CD or DVD that is not included in the version you purchased, you may download this material at http://booksupport.wiley.com. For more information about Wiley products, visit www.wiley.com.

Library of Congress Cataloging-in-Publication Data

Library of Congress Cataloging-in-Publication Data has been applied for and is on file at the Library of Congress.

ISBN 978-1-118-72042-4 (cloth);
ISBN 978-1-118-72051-6 (ebk.);
ISBN 978-1-118-72040-0 (ebk.)

Printed in the United States of America
THIRD EDITION

HB Printing 10 9 8 7 6 5 4 3 2 1

The Jossey-Bass Higher and Adult Education Series

CONTENTS

THE AMERICAN CONFERENCE OF ACADEMIC DEANS

The mission of the American Conference of Academic Deans (ACAD) is to provide academic leaders who share a commitment to student learning and to the ideals of liberal education with networking and professional development opportunities and to support them in their work as educational leaders.

ACAD is committed to the ideals of a liberal education and supports academic leaders in their work.

ACAD supports academic administrators as they strive to promote and support the ideals of a liberal education.

ACAD is a membership-driven organization that provides academic leaders with the resources they need to excel in their field.

http://www.acad-edu.org/

PREFACE

A few years ago, literally on the eve of becoming the chair of ACAD's board of directors, I had coffee and a chat with Joseph Subbiondo. Joe is currently the president of the California Institute of Integral Studies, but in the 1980s, he served a term as the ACAD board chair. In our conversation, he shared a thought that resonated powerfully. All of us who serve as academic administrators first completed advanced degrees and climbed up the professorial ranks. After spending years mastering the work of teaching and researching in our first disciplines, we were called to work for which we were mostly unprepared. We became academic administrators, and then, Joe explained, we had to master a second discipline.

The parallel really is striking. The process of earning a doctoral degree involves tremendous focus and, even today, does not commonly include purposeful preparation for college teaching. Rewards are the fruits of narrowing our field of view and excluding distractions. Even as part of a team, the doctoral student must demonstrate the ability to make and defend original contributions, and the doctoral degree becomes, in a sense, a license to do autonomous research. When we begin faculty work—teaching, doing research, contributing to campus governance, and serving the profession—we quickly learn that doctoral study really only prepares us for part of the job, and we must learn from our colleagues and from trial and error how to do the other parts. After several years, we might come to feel that we have achieved some degree of mastery of the first discipline.

When making the transition from faculty work to academic administration, we discover that there is little in faculty work that prepares us for administrative work. The community of colleagues on our campus that supported our mastery of the first discipline isn't there to support mastery of the second discipline. The mission of ACAD is to provide academic leaders who share a commitment to student learning and the ideals of liberal education with networking and professional development opportunities and to support them in their work as educational leaders. Joe Subbiondo put that mission in perspective for me: ACAD exists to help deans, provosts, and other senior academic leaders master their second discipline.

ACAD was founded in 1945. At that time, the college president leaders of the American Association of Colleges, the forerunner of today's American Association of Colleges and Universities (AAC&U), recognized the need for an organization to support academic deans in their work. ACAD and AAC&U have remained closely linked and jointly sponsor an annual meeting. For the past two years, ACAD has offered a highly successful Dean's Institute, an all-day workshop on the day before the annual meeting. ACAD also provides workshops at some of AAC&U's Network for Academic Renewal meetings.

In addition to its connection to AAC&U, ACAD enjoys a productive relationship with the Phi Beta Kappa Society, jointly sponsoring a biennial conference in odd-numbered falls. The first joint ACAD-PBK conference was on the topic of leadership for the liberal arts, and the subsequent conferences have explored liberal arts themes relating to global liberal education, science and the liberal education, and the humanities.

Online, ACAD provides its members a very active discussion list on which deans and provosts discuss issues and get advice from their colleagues. In fact, one of the most significant benefits of ACAD membership is the fellowship of other academic leaders. ACAD remains a "conference" of individuals, as opposed to an association of institutions, reflecting its long-standing commitment to networking and professional development.

One of ACAD's most important resources is *The Resource Handbook for Academic Deans*, and we are very pleased to introduce this third edition. In this significantly expanded and updated version of the *Handbook*, academic leaders speak to academic leaders, covering more than fifty topics organized in reference style. I have every confidence that experienced and new leaders alike will find this *Handbook* a valuable source of information and, I hope at least occasionally, inspiration.

Previous editions of the *Handbook* were published and distributed by ACAD, but we are happy to celebrate a new partnership with Jossey-Bass in publishing this edition. I am very grateful to my board colleagues for helping to nurture the partnership, especially Linda Cabe Halpern (James Madison

University), my predecessor as chair, and Marc Roy (Goucher College), the current chair. Our gratitude is also extended to Sheryl Fullerton, executive editor at Jossey-Bass for her commitment to building a relationship with ACAD. Laura Rzepka, ACAD's executive director, makes everything happen at ACAD, and her dedication to ACAD's mission is immensely appreciated. Finally, many thanks to Laura Behling (Knox College) for selflessly assuming the editorship of the *Handbook* and wrangling dozens of contributors.

Carl O. Moses
Susquehanna University
Past chair, ACAD board of directors

EDITOR'S INTRODUCTION

The roles and responsibilities of college and university senior academic leaders—deans and provosts, and their associate and assistant deans and provosts—are many and diverse. From faculty hiring and evaluation to curriculum development and review, from working with presidents and other colleagues across campuses, to responding to external constituencies, including those who are involved in fundraising—the work of the college and campus academic leaders is not easy, and is becoming even more complex.

This third edition of *The Resource Handbook for Academic Deans* intends to provide valuable perspective and support on the challenges and opportunities senior academic leaders encounter, both deans of colleges within larger universities and deans or provosts who serve as an institution's chief academic officer (including those associate and assistant deans and provosts who work closely with such leaders). ACAD, partially through this *Resource Handbook*, provides support for a variety of senior academic leaders because the position of "dean" requires different roles and responsibilities depending on the type of institution. Such a diversity of experiences provides a diversity of perspectives, some of which may be more relevant to your particular position, but all of which provide valuable insight. As the major publication of the American Conference of Academic Deans (ACAD), the national association providing connection among academic leaders at senior leadership levels, this *Resource Handbook*, written by academic leaders and ACAD members from across the country, delivers that diverse perspective. Topics and approaches to each topic have been suggested and written by these leaders who are drawing on their own experiences—senior academic leaders who have provided leadership for general education programs, who have understood the cycles of their own careers, and who have engaged in strategic planning, to name just a few of the more than fifty topics covered in the *Resource Handbook*.

You'll find a multitude of topics, many of which point to the new work that now takes an academic leader's attention, such as developing online courses and curriculum. You'll find entries that speak to the unique work of deans at different kinds of institutions, two- and four-year colleges, as well as universities, public and private. And you'll find that many of the topics are the ones to which senior academic leaders always must be attentive—faculty development, curriculum development, evaluation, teamwork, and, not surprisingly to those who have done or aspire to the work of a senior academic leader, the challenges of personnel and personalities on campuses.

Each entry has been written by an academic leader and reflects her or his own views and perspectives, based on personal experience. You'll find that brief scenarios begin each entry, allowing you to imagine the type of experience that you may encounter (or to find comfort in the similarities of the work we all do); entries then explore the issues raised in each scenario so as to provide you with ways particular concerns may be addressed. Each entry closes with several points of advice, including questions to ask when dealing with particular issues, perspectives to take, points to remember, or clear suggestions to help you in your work.

More than forty-five contributors from around the country and from a range of types of institutions contributed to the volume, underscoring the importance of collaboration, conversation, and collegiality. As many deans and other academic leaders will confess, this can often be lonely work, with few, if any, people to talk with on campus about the issues detailed in this volume. ACAD's *Resource Handbook for Academic Deans* understands that, and thus, offers readers a collection of perspectives on issues common to all of us. Thanks to the contributors for their willingness to share their wisdom and experiences, and to Lisa Ijiri, Mariangela Maguire, Pete Skoner, and two anonymous reviewers for their careful and thoughtful critiques of the *Handbook*. Just as ACAD remains true to its mission as a conference of academic leaders and colleagues, so too does ACAD's *Resource Handbook* provide a tangible resource for senior academic leaders to be thoughtfully effective for the good of their colleges and universities.

October 2013

Laura L. Behling
Knox College

The Resource Handbook
for Academic Deans

PART ONE

BECOMING A DEAN

CHAPTER ONE

Preparing for a Successful Career in Academic Leadership

Understanding Your Role

Marc M. Roy
Goucher College

July 1, 2012. Charles Sessions approached his office and inwardly smiled. There was his name on the door: Dean Sessions. He could not help but feel some pride as he opened the door, set down his briefcase, and sat in the executive chair behind a beautiful desk, complete with a new computer, tablet, and smartphone. The moment did not last long. Dean Sessions felt a sinking feeling rapidly replacing the pride of a few moments ago when he noticed the piles of folders left by his predecessor. As his assistant knocked on the door and said, "The president would like to see you in five minutes, and you have an appointment with the dean of students at 9:30," Dean Sessions had just one thought. "What have I gotten myself into?"

The feeling of being overwhelmed as a new dean is quite common. Because most deans start as faculty, very few deans have had formal leadership training. Instead, deans have risen through the ranks, all the while engaging in campus service and leadership, such as chairing committees, or directing departments, programs, or special centers on their campuses. Because they have knowledge of the institution, and the respect of the faculty, often these faculty leaders are tapped to serve as assistant or associate deans, giving them some chance to learn by watching their deans. However, there is not a "dean's school" for aspiring deans, and many deans learn their roles and responsibilities as they begin their jobs. The learning curve can be especially steep if the dean has moved to a new institution.

The roles of deans vary considerably from one institution to another, but there are similarities. In small colleges, the dean is usually the chief academic officer and may also have the title of vice president for academic affairs or provost. In larger universities, the dean is the head of a college and, along with the deans of other colleges, reports to the provost. Regardless of their scope of responsibilities and their type of institution, people who serve as senior academic leaders at the dean, provost, or associate or assistant levels, will encounter similar scenarios, challenges, and opportunities.

Metaphorically, deans work between a rock and a hard place, and the best way to move in that tight space is to realize that good relationships are essential for success. On the one hand, deans are champions for the academic division, especially for the faculty. On the other hand, they are administrative officers and must keep the best interests of the college in mind. These positions inevitably come into conflict. For example, the faculty may want larger departmental budgets, and there may be good reasons for increases. However, the college or university may not have the financial resources necessary to increase the budgets of some or all departments. What should be the highest priority? Should all departments be treated the same? Can the dean try to get additional funds? Any decision is likely to be met with criticism from one corner or another. Therefore, decisions about all matters need to be presented clearly so that faculty members can understand the rationale, even if they do not agree with the outcome. Even then, there is no escaping the position between the rock and the hard place.

Deans are first and foremost academic leaders working with faculty members to shape the curriculum and provide educational opportunities that are consistent with the college's mission and values. The dean needs to articulate an overarching vision while refraining from simply imposing this vision on the faculty. Along with the college or university mission and strategic plan, the vision should guide decisions about curricular changes, hiring of faculty and staff, and budgeting. There is a natural tension between serving as an academic leader and participating in shared governance. The faculty are responsible for most curricular decisions, and the dean must lead, often from behind. To walk between this rock and a hard place, a dean must be an excellent communicator.

The quality and timing of one's oral and written communication skills can lead to success or sink a dean's career. Seemingly small mistakes, such as typographical errors, can be interpreted as sloppiness or a lack of caring. Faculty members want to read high-quality academic prose, but vice presidents and staff members often prefer clear, brief messages. The faculty and staff want as much transparency as possible. Although some issues are necessarily confidential, openness helps to build trust and effective working relationships. How things are said is often as important as what is said. Unfortunately, electronic communication is limited in its ability to convey the feelings and intentions behind our words. This frequently leads to misunderstandings. Many successful deans invite faculty and staff members to speak on the phone or in person rather than engage in lengthy e-mail exchanges. A quick way to choose a medium is to ask yourself: "Will it take more than a brief paragraph to explain the situation?" If the answer is yes, pick up the phone or call a meeting. Another useful guide comes from a question posed by a president: "Do you want your words to appear on the front page of the local newspaper?" In the age of nearly instant electronic communication, what we say, whether in writing or orally, can be shared around campus and across the country in moments, so choose your medium of communication as carefully as you choose your words.

Deans look forward to the opportunities to wrestle with big ideas and provide visionary leadership, and this is an important role. New deans can be surprised to learn that much of a dean's daily work is management. At times, managing situations, people, and budgets interferes with the time necessary for "big picture" thinking and leadership. However, careful management and appropriate attention to detail are also important in being a successful dean. One must clearly articulate expectations and hold faculty and staff members accountable for their responsibilities. At the same time, the dean needs to empower individuals to carry out their duties. Department chairs in particular often feel as though they have very little power and influence, making their jobs quite difficult. Deans can help those individuals understand the influence that they do have. When the dean supports decisions made by chairs (and assistant or associate deans), this empowers those individuals and helps them to be effective leaders.

Being an effective manager and leader requires that deans be careful listeners, seeking out multiple points of view. Repeating back to another individual allows the dean to confirm that she has listened carefully: "What I hear you saying is that . . ." Some individuals will come to speak to the dean wanting little more than to be heard. They are not necessarily asking for the dean to solve a problem. After listening to a person air concerns, it can be helpful to ask what he would like to see done to resolve the problem and then guide the individual to find his own good solution.

Another role of an academic dean is problem solving when others are not able to do so or when it is not appropriate for them to solve the particular problem. This too can involve moving between a rock and a hard place. If the dean imposes a solution without careful listening and consultation, there will inevitably be pushback because the solution was handed down from "the administration." Engaging faculty and staff members in problem solving allows the dean to suggest possible solutions and work with the individuals to find a solution that is acceptable to all parties. However, there are times when policy issues come into play and the dean must make decisions and impose solutions. Using careful communication to convey the decisions can mitigate any pushback that might arise.

Budget management is a critical part of a dean's responsibilities. The chief financial officer can be the dean's best friend or worst enemy. Building a good relationship with the CFO is important to success in managing budgets. Details are important. When seeking additions to the budget (or defending against cuts), clear, brief arguments are often the best way to make your case. Many college officers, unlike faculty, do not want to wade through lengthy arguments and justifications. The dean is also responsible for ensuring that departments and offices manage their budgets appropriately. A history of good management and balanced budgets is quite helpful when the dean is seeking increases in the budget. In contrast, frequent overspending will work against requests for additions to the budget.

Another important role of the dean is to hire (or oversee hiring of) the best individuals possible. One must build a strong team of assistant or associate deans and administrative support individuals. A team that you can trust and rely on in all situations is priceless. It should go without saying that overseeing the hiring of new faculty will have long-term implications for the college or university. Bad decisions can lead to difficult tenure cases, or worse. Faculty members who are good teachers and scholars but who do not get along with their colleagues can cause years of frustration and difficulty. If those individuals are tenured, it can hurt a department for decades. In contrast, hiring individuals who work well with their colleagues leads to strong departments. When the dean hires faculty members who are excellent teachers, scholars, and department citizens, and when those faculty members are supported and mentored and perform to their best ability, tenure cases can be a "slam dunk." Those individuals often become future leaders of the faculty who will work well with the dean's successors. However, search committees are not always in agreement (amongst themselves or with the dean) about the best candidate, providing the dean with another opportunity to glide between a rock and a hard place.

Many day-to-day responsibilities of the dean involve faculty and staff members, but the dean must work carefully also with other deans or vice presidents and the president. These relationships are also crucial to the success of a dean. In particular, a good working relationship with the dean of students can help to blend the boundaries between learning in and out of the classroom. Collectively, the senior leaders must support and protect the president, at least publicly. Making disagreements public can shorten a dean's tenure dramatically. Supporting the president publicly, even when disagreeing privately, requires deft movements. The communications skills mentioned above are essential in these situations.

Deans are also mentors and talent scouts. Deans need to mentor faculty, especially new department chairs, to help them develop the leadership skills necessary for them to be successful in their jobs. Fortunately, there are workshops and webinars to help department chairs. Search firms frequently send deans job advertisements and ask for recommendations of possible candidates. Deans should mentor associate deans so that they might someday move into a deanship themselves.

Being a dean is a difficult job. There are numerous roles and responsibilities, and there is never enough time. Working with the faculty is often compared to herding cats. Although this can be a nearly impossible task, you can put out cat food. Publicly celebrating the success of others, giving credit to faculty and staff members where it is due (and criticizing only in private), allows a dean to guide individualistic and disparate faculty and to build the relationships that will lead to a successful and rewarding deanship.

June 1, 2013. A week after graduation the campus was fairly quiet. Dean Sessions leaned back in his chair and sighed deeply. What a year it had been! There were plenty of challenges, some successes, and some things that he wished he had handled differently. He was reminded of the wise words he had heard at the ACAD annual meeting:

- Being a dean is not much different from being a scholar. One must learn to ask good questions, the right questions. One must learn to find good answers and help others find good answers.
- Perhaps most important, one must persuade others that the answers are well thought out and the conclusions are justified.
- And in the end, good relationships and good communication make it much easier to move between the rocks and the hard places.

CHAPTER TWO

A President's Perspective on Serving as a Dean

Philip A. Glotzbach
Skidmore College

Dear Colleague,

Congratulations on your appointment as dean! I hope any feelings of uncertainty or trepidation associated with this new phase of your life are balanced by the promise of new opportunities now before you. Above all, I hope you are eager to do all you can to help make your college or university a better place for its students, faculty, and alumni.

Your life now has changed—at least for the duration of your administrative tenure and, most probably, for the remainder of your academic career. From this point forward, you will view the world from a different perspective, and you must not be surprised when others cast you in an unfamiliar light. This certainly will be true if you have just arrived at a new school. But even if you are continuing at your current institution, you will notice a change in the attitudes of at least some faculty colleagues (even among those you have known for some time). Above all, people will expect new things of you. It is your job to live up to those expectations that are reasonable and challenge the ones that are not.

As a dean, you are in a wonderful leadership position to advance the mission of your institution. If you work effectively with others, you can

- direct resources where they can be used most strategically;
- articulate, affirm, and if necessary raise academic standards;
- strengthen curriculum and pedagogy;
- support your faculty in achieving your school's primary learning outcomes for your students; and
- through hiring and tenure decisions, shape your faculty for the next twenty to thirty years.

Along the way, you will face obstacles that will challenge your intellect and test your spirit. In short, the position of academic dean can be, at once, a most demanding and a most rewarding administrative post.

Versions of this article have appeared in previous editions of ACAD's *Resource Handbook for Academic Deans*; it has been revised and expanded for this edition.

Leadership is the art of helping people accomplish together what they cannot do individually. Easily said, not always so easy to do. Your president is the overall leader of your institution. He or she expects *you* to be the leader of your faculty. So you now need to think more seriously about leadership than ever before: to become a student of leadership, actively develop your own leadership abilities, and work intentionally to cultivate leadership within the faculty (especially among department and committee chairs but also among both new and established faculty members). You will need to know what the faculty is thinking. You must care what the faculty is saying. You will be the administrative point-person in dealing with problems that arise within the faculty so your president does not have to play that role. At the same time, you must be the primary cheerleader for your faculty, its principal advocate within the administration, and a leading proponent of the intellectual life of your school.

Following are some more specific suggestions to consider as you begin making the dean's job your own. Even though this list includes fifteen entries, it does not begin to exhaust the inventory of your responsibilities. The range of topics covered in this third edition of the ACAD *Resource Handbook for Academic Deans* will give you a better sense of the scope of your new portfolio, along with sound advice about managing it. Still, writing as one who experienced this transition himself twenty years ago, and more recently as a president with specific expectations for his own academic administrators, I do hope the reflections offered here may prove helpful as you embark on this new and exciting stage of your professional life.

1. Focus on doing what is best for your college or university, and your career will take care of itself.

Be guided, above all else, by the mission of your college or university. Always place your institution first, other people second, and yourself third. If you focus, instead, on advancing your career, you will make decisions that will adversely affect your institution (and ultimately your professional prospects as well). Be assured that people will discover your real agenda, and they will judge you accordingly.

This job is not about you; so check your ego at the door. Do not expect people to appreciate your, no doubt, admirable virtues; instead, focus on appreciating theirs. And if their virtues are not readily apparent, look harder until you find them.

Maintain your humility. More deans fail from hubris than from lack of intelligence or administrative ability. Share the credit; take the blame. The great football coach Bear Bryant used to say, "If it's good, we did it. If it's really good, you did it. If it's bad, I did it." Write lots of thank-you notes. People will appreciate them, and it's a great way to reinforce good behavior.

Sometimes people will let you know when they appreciate something you've done. Keep a file of thank-you notes you receive—they will help to remind you that some people do, in fact, appreciate what you are doing. Just don't take everything you read there at face value. Take satisfaction ultimately from the results of your efforts, not from the recognition of others.

2. Internalize the following mantra: "I am never not the dean."

Every word you speak always comes from the dean. There are no throwaway lines in your script. As a faculty member you could brainstorm with colleagues, try out crazy ideas, and make immodest proposals with relative impunity. In your new role and especially at the beginning of your deanship, you will need to do that kind of "blue-sky" thinking most often with other administrators and much less frequently—in fact, seldom—with faculty colleagues. Remember that the half-baked thought you toss off and immediately forget may be remembered by someone else as a promise (or threat!) and repeated to others. Prepare to have your most benign, innocuous, or well-intentioned statements and actions scrutinized, overinterpreted, sometimes misinterpreted, or blown out of all proportion. It goes with the territory.

In short, pay close attention to what you say. Always.

3. Good administrative work is fundamentally about relationships, not transactions.

Good relationships enable people to work together. No matter how well-intentioned you are or how brilliant your ideas, you will fail as a leader if people refuse to work with you. Even if you are not the smartest person in the room, or the one with all the good ideas (and no one has *all* the good ideas), you will succeed as a leader if you facilitate effective collaboration and shared decision making. To do so, you must work effectively with others, and they must be willing to work with you.

Relationships ultimately stand or fall on the basis of trust. Be generous in offering trust to others; withhold it only when someone has proven that he or she will abuse it. This does not mean that you should be naive. Ronald Reagan was right to say, "Trust but verify."[1] But always open by offering trust.

People must know they can trust you with extremely sensitive information. As a dean, you will come to possess information most people in your institution do not and cannot know—including details about some of your colleagues that you would rather not know. Dealing with this burden of confidential information is an inescapable dimension of your job. Be known as someone who is absolutely reliable in keeping confidences. And understand that some of your most significant achievements as a dean will involve matters that can never be discussed, much less celebrated, beyond a very small inner administrative circle.

Keep your promises. Nothing builds trust more effectively than keeping promises. If people know that you will follow through on commitments you make, they will rely on you. The inverse is equally true. Remind yourself that it takes much longer to build trust than to lose it.

Develop a reputation for fairness, honesty, and consistency, and trust will follow. Your college or university (indeed, the academic world as a whole) is a very small village. Assume that what you say about someone will get back to her. In fact, when talking about a third party, a good heuristic is to imagine him to be present in the conversation. Never play favorites. Be especially transparent and clear in your reasoning when you need to make an exception to a rule. Always consider the way an action or decision will look from the perspective of those it will most directly affect. Ask yourself how you would feel if *you* were in their situation. Consider, as well, how your decision will look to others who cannot know all the inner details.

Build relationships that can survive disagreement. As Stephen Covey (1989) has written, "seek first to understand, then to be understood." Demonstrate to people that you will listen to them—*actively* listen. You need not always agree, but acknowledge and credit what others are saying before you articulate a contrary position.

Be impatient with yourself but patient with others. Paradoxically, some of the very strengths you cultivated as a faculty member and that brought you to this juncture—especially mental quickness and, perhaps, impatience in moving things forward—can undermine your success as a dean. Your position gives you access to information and institutional perspectives not readily available to those outside the administration. So, when sharing that information, give people a chance to catch up and process what has become familiar to you but will be new to them. Work on giving others the time they need to think through a problem at their own pace, not yours. Let them finish their thoughts, even when it seems clear to you where they are heading. (Besides, they sometimes will surprise you.) Value their participation; honor their contributions to the process.

Be mindful of your own fallibility. You may be wrong—even when you are convinced you are right. (Descartes to the contrary, very strong feelings of certainty never guarantee that one actually knows something.) Displaying a willingness to change your mind when faced with new facts or superior arguments also builds credibility. Be tolerant of disagreement and strive to create a climate in which contrasting views can be explored constructively. Be grateful when someone shows you a better way to think about an issue.

Even if your thinking is correct as far as it goes, someone else may have a still-better idea or one that takes the conversation in a different direction. Be open to those possibilities. There are many worthy goals and even more paths to achieving them. Develop the art of encouraging others to collaborate with you in thinking through problems, and earn a reputation for valuing their ideas. Show that you have a tough skin, can tolerate criticism, enjoy vigorous discussion, and can hold your own in debate.

Maintain your sense of humor. Being able to laugh at your own foibles shows that you are not overly impressed with yourself and encourages others to relate to you as a human being—not as someone defined entirely by his or her position.

No one expects a dean to be perfect. So be willing to admit your mistakes; just try not to have to do so too often.

4. Above all, people want to know who you are and what you stand for.

Following Machiavelli, understand that it is far more important for a dean to be respected than to be liked—or loved.[2] There will be times when you need to make and *own* a difficult decision or take a tough or unpopular action. If you do so with integrity, others will respect you. One way you establish your values is to say no. Be clear about what you are not prepared to accept. Others will notice. Call people on unacceptable behavior (it is, of course, better to do this privately, but sometimes it needs to happen in public), and then forgive them. We all need "a shot at redemption" (Simon, 1986) from time to time. Develop a long memory for the good deeds of others and a short memory for slights and transgressions. In addition to your decisions and actions, you establish your values by what you praise. So be careful what you applaud and how much you do so. It's much easier to step up your praise later on, if it is merited, than to take back praise once you've gone too far.

If you really want to be loved, get a dog.

5. Be willing to fight when necessary, and when you must fight, fight to win.

As noted earlier, the ability to foster collaboration is crucial to your success as a leader. Even so, upon very rare occasions, collaboration will be impossible and you will need to invoke alternative strategies. Sun Tzu was right to say that the best general is one who wins the war without ever having to fight a battle. The truly strategic thinker is able to diffuse problems in advance or neutralize opposition before it can coalesce into an effective force. But, alas, even the most competent leader cannot always meet this high standard.

Therefore, first of all, it is important to know what you are willing to fight for—what you are prepared to do to preserve a core value or support a key initiative. Next, pick your battles carefully—even if you are in the right, some battles are just not worth the collateral damage. Deciding when to do battle and when to let something go is always an act of judgment. There is no algorithm to help you make such a decision—other than to say that one must never compromise on basic values. Third, when you must fight, *always* fight to win. As "Viper," the commander of the training squadron in *Top Gun* informs his new class of hotshot pilots, in combat "there are no points for second place." Finally, when it's over, remember you're all on the same team; do everything you can to repair relationships and return to collaboration (Simpson & Bruckheimer, 1988).

6. It is far better to complete a few high priority projects than to work on many and finish none.

It is important to have some early successes, even if they are mostly symbolic. So as you begin your first year, pick one or two objectives you can accomplish that will be perceived as making an immediate difference, even if they do not represent the highest strategic priorities on your long-term list.

Similar advice applies later on, as well. Identify those strategic initiatives that will make the most progress toward realizing long-term institutional goals. Then focus on those that are most readily achievable. Remember the slogan of the Navy Seabees: "The difficult we do immediately; the impossible takes a bit longer." An objective may be extremely important but unrealizable at a given moment. If so, defer it. Do what is possible first. You can always put something back on your list later on—when people are more ready to consider it and to help achieve it, or when the necessary resources are in place.

Finish what you start.

7. Efficiency matters.

Administrators, faculty members, and others will judge your effectiveness, in part, in terms of the efficiency of your office. In other words, they will ascribe the efficiency—or lack of efficiency—of your staff and subordinates to *you.*

They also will judge you by how well you manage your staff—and by how effectively your people move work along. As you transition from the faculty to administration, your effectiveness will be determined in no small part by how well you *turn over to others* much of the paperwork and other tasks that for so long, as a faculty member, you did for yourself.

Be intentional about sharing authority and power. Develop strong working relationships with your subordinates (e.g., associate deans). Help them earn your trust and expand their sphere of autonomy. Delegate the authority they need to do their jobs, but be aware that you cannot delegate responsibility—ultimately, responsibility in your division flows up to you.

Resist upward delegation. Don't assume you have to solve every problem someone brings into your office. Most problems belong to someone else—usually those who are trying to give them to you! Therefore, your first task is to identify the right person or group to address the issue. Then coach that person or those people to resolve it. *Always* ask, "Whose problem is it—who owns it?" *Always* stop before you commit to doing something and ask yourself, "Is this something I *can* or *should* do—and, if so, by when?" It is much easier to explain, in advance, why you cannot (or should not) do what someone wants than it is, after the fact, to explain why you failed to fulfill a commitment. Once you've made it clear whose problem it is, identify the next step(s) in the process, and encourage the owner to return later and report on progress.[3]

Ensure that information flows effectively in and out of your office and is managed well in between. Never let your office become an institutional black hole into which communications vanish never to be seen again. See to it that your office employs an effective paper-management and filing system—one that is organized according to the central ongoing tasks that you oversee (curriculum, faculty reviews, student matters, board matters, departmental issues, accreditation, assessment, and so on). You may find it helpful to distinguish the various categories through color-coding your office files. Make sure your principal assistant understands the importance of having an effective system, collaborate with her or him to design one, and see that it is implemented. Do it in whatever way makes best sense to you and your team. But do it.

The worst possible use of your time is searching for a misplaced piece of paper. Discipline yourself to touch a piece of paper (or e-mail!) once: *respond* to it, *refer* it to a file, to your assistant, or to someone else, or *relegate* it to the trash. Think "OHIO": only handle it once.

Decide how to manage the notes from all those meetings that now will occupy such a large portion of your time. As you take your notes, delineate follow-up items to which you must attend personally and distinguish them from those you will delegate to others.[4] Develop a system for your assistant to create and manage your project follow-up list, ensure that nothing gets lost, and keep you on track in following through on your commitments. Your assistant then can inform others as to the progress of key tasks, letting people know that you haven't forgotten about their concerns.

Give your executive assistant the guidelines he or she needs to manage your calendar and your day (rules for prioritizing meetings, scheduling desk time for you in addition to meetings, and so on). Try to reserve some time in each day to deal with the unexpected and unplanned problems that inevitably will crop up. Make sure your assistant communicates with those outside your office clearly and in ways that reflect your values. Remember that everything she or he says—and *how* it is said—will be attributed directly to you. Help your assistant learn to guard your time without walling you off from those who need to see you, and most especially without making people who do not gain immediate access to you feel unimportant.

8. You are still a teacher.

In your administrative role, instead of students, you now are teaching members of your faculty (especially department chairs, program directors, and committee chairs), other administrators, and even members of the board of trustees. Think of yourself as running an extended graduate seminar on shared governance, curriculum, pedagogy, institutional history, and leadership, along with other key dimensions of your portfolio. As a dean, you must advocate for the academic programs in your college or university, but this advocacy can never go in just one direction. You also must help the members of your faculty understand the larger institutional context in which they operate, just as you must help other administrators understand the academic perspective.[5] Similarly, you must help department chairs themselves learn to function as mediators between their departments and the larger school or college. Effective mediation requires understanding both sides of the relationship and the willingness to advocate in both directions.

9. Administrative privilege entails corresponding responsibilities.

Your administrative position gives you access to the highest levels of institutional decision making, and with that access comes a capacity to influence policy that no one on the faculty can possess. But this access to administrative decision making comes with a price. As a dean, you relinquish any right to complain to the faculty about administrative matters—for example, about not carrying the day in a budget or policy decision or the bad behavior of an administrative colleague. You now have three—and *only* three—options as you participate in administrative deliberations: (a) persuade others that your position is right, be persuaded by them of the merit of their views, or collaborate in crafting a compromise that you can embrace; (b) accept and implement a decision with which you disagree without communicating your disagreement beyond the administration; or (c) resign your position. There is no legitimate fourth option of going back to the faculty (or any other group outside the administration) to continue fighting a lost battle.

In short, *never* bring an administrative conflict back to the faculty or position yourself with the faculty in opposition to your president (or provost or vice president for academic affairs). Doing so may provide you a short-term advantage with some constituency, but in the long run it can only fragment the faculty itself or divide the faculty as a whole from the administration. No president (or provost) worth his or her salt will countenance such behavior.

10. Be proactive in managing your boss.

Anticipate the information he is likely to need from you and provide it before you are asked. Make sure she hears bad news from you first. Never bring him a problem without suggesting at least one or two possible solutions. Regardless of whether you report directly to your president, never surprise him or her in a meeting where others are present—and most especially, *never* do so in front of the board of trustees. Remember that just as your primary constituency is the faculty, your president's is the board.

11. Prepare a yearly written plan of goals and major projects and assess your progress annually.

Review your plan with your immediate superior, and refer to it throughout the year. Track your progress in achieving your goals. Keep a file of accomplishments. This file will be useful when you revise your CV and when you prepare your annual report to your boss, which you should do whether you are asked for one or not.

12. Don't sacrifice your body to your job.

Unlike a faculty position, in which the year is broken up by academic terms and breaks that give one time to recover and shift focus, administrative jobs are relentless and ongoing. Discipline yourself to eat well and to remain physically active. Take vacations that get you out of the office for blocks of time during which you can reconnect with yourself and the significant others in your life. As Vince Lombardi frequently remarked, "Fatigue makes cowards of us all."

13. Don't sacrifice your mind to your job.

Reserve time regularly in your schedule to plan and to reflect. Make it a point always to be reading something that interests you that is not directly related to your administrative job. If possible, keep your hand in teaching, and stay connected to your academic discipline. But if it proves impossible to do so—and it frequently is impossible, in these jobs—you still can (and must!) stay connected to current developments in the world of ideas in general. It is important that the members of your faculty continue to respect the ideas you bring to discussions.

14. Don't sacrifice your spirit to your job.

Deans face relentless demands. Issues will arise without warning, and without your ability to control them. Facing these challenges year in and year out can wear you down. Your position calls on you to be at your best when the stakes are highest and a misstep could prove to be most costly. It is easy to feel isolated and even fearful. In the end you have to find the resources to overcome your anxiety. But in doing so you are never alone. You should be able to seek counsel from your administrative colleagues and superiors. It is a sign of respect to ask them for help, and they should be more than willing to offer advice and support. Admitting your difficulties also helps you remain humble.

The problems you face will be familiar to your counterparts at other institutions. So be intentional in building relationships with professional colleagues; develop a network of deans at other schools whom you respect and trust. Seek their advice. Create opportunities for mutual professional support and renewal. Join ACAD. Attend professional meetings regularly. Discuss your most difficult challenges, and share success stories as well.

15. Always remember why you entered the academy in the first place—presumably, for a love of learning and the other intrinsic values you found there.

A college or university should be a place that nurtures a flourishing life of the mind and spirit, and its ultimate success is measured in the educational and personal development of its students. Your job is to help make it so.

Therefore, always consider the following questions when deliberating a course of action: "Will this decision serve to enhance or diminish my institution's values and its capacity to fulfill its fundamental educational mission?" and, more specifically, "How will this decision affect our students?"

To be an excellent dean, you need to respect and, yes, *love* both your institution and the members of your faculty. No one expects either a school or a faculty to be perfect. But these relationships should be marked by love all the same—even if you're sometimes called on to provide some "tough love." So if you cannot develop such a profound level of caring and affection for your faculty and institution, you need to find another job.

In sum, as an academic dean, you are called on to be efficient, patient, ethical, courageous, visionary, and wise—certainly a daunting list of attributes. But if others did not see these traits in you, you would not have been appointed to your deanship in the first place. So even as you remain cognizant of your own limitations and practice humility, be honest as well in affirming your strengths. Just as you must know your faculty, follow the Socratic imperative and make sure that you know yourself best of all.

In the final analysis, no one can tell you how to make the key decisions that will shape your deanship. You have to develop your own capacities for judgment and trust your instincts. Approach them as experiments, whose success or failure will be determined not *a priori* but after the fact—by the results they produce. But in making these inductive decisions, an abiding commitment to the core values of your college or university and a steadfast focus on the important work you have taken on will remain your most important assets. If you persist in that commitment and maintain such a focus throughout your tenure in office, you will have a profound influence over the direction of your institution. Virtually all of our schools are feeling the challenges of these times—financial, regulatory, political, ideological, and other trials that place in question not only our institutions' core values but, in some cases, their very survival. But moments of great adversity also present great opportunities. It is a good bet that you have within you the capacity to provide the leadership your school requires to identify and capitalize on the opportunities that are present. Even if those opportunities are not obvious, it is your job to help bring them to light.

Over time, realizing the difference you have made for your school will provide an enormous sense of professional and personal satisfaction. Indeed, many people who have moved from a deanship to other positions (e.g., a presidency) will tell you they enjoyed their time in the dean's office more than in any other administrative position. My fondest hope is that you will have just such an experience.

All best wishes for your success!

Notes

1. Reagan repeated this phrase frequently—especially in the context of arms negotiations with the Soviet Union. Ironically, as he was aware, Reagan was quoting a Russian proverb that was a favorite of Lenin.
2. Discerning readers will note that I have taken a liberty here. In *The Prince*, Machiavelli considers the merits of a prince's being loved versus his being *feared*—probably the right contrast for sixteenth-century Italy, but certainly not the right one for the twenty-first-century dean's office. Today a dean who is feared by the faculty (or others) is most likely dysfunctional and destined for a short term of office. On the other hand, a dean who is respected can lead effectively and remain in office long enough to accomplish important work. See Niccolò Machiavelli, *The Prince*, in *The Portable Machiavelli*, trans. and ed. Peter Bondanella and Mark Musa (New York: Penguin Books, 1979), chapter XVII, pp. 130–33.
3. A very helpful (short) book on this topic, which should be required reading for any new dean, is *The One Minute Manager Meets the Monkey*, by Kenneth Blanchard, William Oncken Jr. and Hal Burrows (New York: Harper Collins, 1989).
4. Levenger's "Annotation Ruled" notepads (an example of one commercial product) make it easy to differentiate a to-do list from informational notes. There certainly are other options, including creating your own unique structure within your notes. But it really is worth the effort to decide how you want to do this. So create an effective strategy and then employ it consistently over time.
5. See Richard Morrow, *Strategic Leadership: Integrating Strategy and Leadership in Colleges and Universities* (Praeger Publishers: Westport, CT, 2007).

References

Covey, S. (1989). *The seven habits of highly effective people*. New York: Simon and Schuster. Chapter 5.

Simon, P. (1986). You can call me Al. *Graceland*. Burbank, CA: Warner Bros.

Simpson, D. & Bruckheimer, J. (Producers) & Scott, T., (Director). (1988). *Top gun* [Motion Picture]. United States: Paramount Pictures.

CHAPTER THREE

The Qualities of Effective Senior Academic Leadership

Robert Holyer
AGB Search

The dean or chief academic officer has arguably the most demanding job on campus—in many ways, more demanding than the president's. The hours are long, the tasks are many and varied, the necessary skill-set is extensive, much of the work is on the front line, mistakes are often very public and may affect colleagues' careers and well-being, resources are always constrained, and faculty are not easily led and certainly not "managed." However, for the right kind of person, it can be the most rewarding job in higher education.

Those who enjoy their work as a dean or a chief academic officer (CAO) and do it well find it satisfying in many ways. They enjoy working with a broad range of talented colleagues—faculty, student-life staff, the president's cabinet, the academic deans and academic affairs staff, board members, and the president. They find that administrative work is intellectually engaging and challenging. However, the deepest satisfactions come from the opportunity to improve education and to be of service to colleagues. Effective senior academic leaders are deeply committed to educational values, and they know that their position provides them with a unique opportunity to collaborate with colleagues to improve higher education. They are also committed to the personal and professional growth of their colleagues, and they are the kind of people who take personal pleasure in the accomplishments and success of others. What is more, they have the ability to see potential in their colleagues and understand that part of their work is providing the context and the opportunities for faculty to develop their abilities—possibly even to enter academic administration.

Thanks to members of the American Conference of Academic Deans for their suggestions, via the Discussion List, about important qualities and characteristics of senior academic leaders.

Effective deans or chief academic officers are both leaders and managers. As leaders they must understand the "big picture" and bring a vision to their work. Indeed, it falls to them as to no one else to articulate and defend the institution's mission and values and to bring them to bear on institutional discussions and decisions. At the same time, they must be good managers of both finances and people. They must be effective at budgeting and financial management, able to bring both into the service of larger goals and institutional values. They must also be good at handling administrative detail. There is much of it, and without the skills to handle it effectively, the dean or CAO is easily overwhelmed and loses valuable opportunities. Deans and CAOs also come to realize that their role is not just to work with colleagues, but also to manage staff—and they are comfortable doing so. As good managers, they know the line between managing and micromanaging and realize that talented people flourish when they receive the same trust and freedom that they themselves would like to receive from the president. Senior academic leaders also must be able to see the potential in others and provide the opportunities for it to develop, readily recognize the good work of others, and be eager to express praise and gratitude. At the same time, they are able to deliver the honest but possibly painful evaluation and counsel necessary for good colleagues, even good friends, to become better. In all of this, effective deans or CAOs are good at aligning administrative detail and managerial practice with the bigger issues. They know that they lead in part by managing and administering well and that how they do both types of work sets a powerful example for colleagues and helps set the tone for the institution as a whole.

The vision out of which deans or CAOs work is rooted in fundamental moral, educational, and institutional values. Good deans and CAOs are mission-focused, and they regard their work as a calling. They have the wisdom to know when these values are better advanced by their own direct support and advocacy and when they are better entrusted to others. In either case, though, the vision that guides their work is inclusive in the sense that it has room for—indeed, requires—the creative contributions of others. While adhering strongly to underlying values, effective senior academic leaders are appropriately flexible in how these values are implemented. Indeed, they are always ready and eager to give ownership to others, delegating important tasks to those able and willing to take them on. To a unique degree, deans or CAOs have the opportunity and obligation to live out in a public way their institution's basic moral and educational values.

As clichéd as it may sound, the heart of the dean's or CAO's work is effective communication, and a good dean or CAO needs to be skilled in the communicative arts. They must communicate instructions and decisions clearly; they must also be able to explain educational issues and policies to wider audiences—faculty, students, parents, trustees, the community at large—in clear and compelling ways. They must be effective and empathetic listeners, able to listen equally to all parties in a dispute, able to listen to criticism of themselves without becoming defensive, and able to listen patiently to irrational requests. What is more, they must have a certain level of comfort with confrontation. Not only is it unavoidable, but if embraced productively, it is necessary for making progress on difficult issues. Equally, deans or CAOs must practice the discipline of silence, keeping private information private and waiting until the appropriate time and place to offer productive criticism, to confront inappropriate behavior, and to voice and pursue disagreements.

The soil from which effective communication grows is the person of the dean or CAO. Effective deans or CAOs are easily approachable, comfortable with peers, and able to establish rapport easily even with those who are very different from them. They are also able to inspire trust through honest communication and forthright action, by their ability to keep confidences and measure their remarks, and, most important, by their willingness to trust others as they would like to be trusted. Effective deans or CAOs also must convey a comfort with public disagreement and a high degree of public scrutiny of their work.

Additionally, such senior academic leaders also must possess a certain intellectual character and certain intellectual skills. They are bright. Not only does this help with the work, but because institutions of higher education are full of other bright people, it also helps to establish and maintain trust and credibility. Faculty colleagues will naturally assume that administrative mistakes are conspiracies, and the fewer mistakes, the less opportunity there is for mistrust to develop. Effective deans or CAOs also have the habit of working hard to get things right, whether by doing sufficient background reading or by mastering the relevant facts, histories, and documents or by understanding the processes that most reliably lead to good decisions and effective planning. Conversely, they must be comfortable admitting that they don't know or are in error and be welcoming of those who can offer instruction, guidance, and correction. Good leaders also are patient with ambiguity and see its value as part of a larger process. It is disastrous for deans or CAOs to believe that they are the source of all good ideas, decisions, and plans; they must have the wisdom to recognize good ideas, decisions, and plans. Increasingly, academic administration has a quantitative dimension. The effective dean or CAO must be good with budgets, quantitative assessment of programs and learning outcomes, and data-driven planning. Good deans or CAOs also must have broad intellectual and artistic interests and an eagerness to learn things outside their own academic disciplines. Faculty expect their senior academic leader to value and exemplify the life of the mind as well as to understand and appreciate their respective disciplines. Effective deans or CAOs must also be very good at reading institutional culture and understanding how differences of power affect human relationships. Perhaps most important, they know themselves. They are almost always part of the equation, and to know how and in what ways is invaluable. Although some of these skills and dispositions can be acquired and all of them improved, a natural disinclination with respect to any one of them may be a serious obstacle to effectiveness.

Effective senior academic leaders also must have a certain temperament. To a very high degree, they must be persistent—on occasions, even courageous. Most things will not require the dean's or CAO's direct involvement, but they will require persistence in the face of setbacks, failures, opposition, perplexities, doubt, and waning support. What is more, they must have the resilience not to be worn down by very demanding work and a brutal schedule. The mood and temperament of the dean or CAO exercises a significant influence on faculty and staff. So they must naturally project a sense of humble confidence and be able to handle adversity calmly. They are also able to move easily and quickly from situations that evoke very different emotional responses without letting the emotions natural to one bleed into the other—celebrating a faculty accomplishment, meeting immediately thereafter with the parents of a student expelled for repeated academic failure, followed by a meeting with the cabinet to deal with a major budget shortfall. Perhaps most challenging is that almost all of this has to be accomplished without the usual support provided by faculty colleagues. In short, senior academic leaders must have formidable emotional resources that do not require much emotional support from others.

Certainly one of the greatest gifts a dean or CAO can give to colleagues of any description is a sense of humor. It brightens the gloomiest of days; it helps disarm tense situations and leads to productive outcomes; it helps to establish rapport; and it can be the best way of communicating one's humanity and humility.

If you are considering moving into senior academic leadership positions or are already there, it may be helpful to consider the following questions:

- What are your personal strengths and weaknesses, and how well do they match up with the qualities and characteristics of successful leadership?
- Why does serving as a senior academic leader appeal to you professionally? What areas of such a position give you pause?
- What are the qualities that you most admire in senior academic leaders with whom you have worked? How might you incorporate such qualities into your own practices?

CHAPTER FOUR

The Role of the Academic Dean in a Community College

Thomas W. Meyer
Broward College

Despite the afternoon heat, Dean Palmer scurries out of the student union and across the hot cement courtyard to the administration building. He's a little worse for wear but on a day like this, he doesn't have time for a stroll through the air-conditioned corridor that connects the two buildings. In addition to the regular run of late spring meetings, he has called an emergency meeting of the academic leadership team to discuss pending Florida legislation that would drastically alter state funding of college preparatory courses. One version in the House of Representatives would eliminate funding for all such courses, while the Senate version would eliminate the lowest level of these courses. Community colleges would still be permitted to offer college preparatory courses, but would face two challenges: they would not receive any funding from the state to cover the costs, and students would not be able to count such courses toward credits earned or use them to qualify for student financial aid.

All the campus presidents, academic and student deans, and the associate deans responsible for college preparatory math, English, and reading are gathered together to discuss the ramifications and possible solutions. The legislators have been talking about this for a long time, but now it may finally be a reality. After years of questioning the dismal success rates of students in college readiness courses, and after years of trying new methods and approaches to teaching students in these courses, everyone is disappointed but not surprised.

Hundreds of sections would be affected, leading to a possible reduction in workforce (full-time and part-time faculty, as well as lab staff). Thousands of students would no longer have the opportunity to improve their basic knowledge in order to take college-level courses. The college stands to lose millions of dollars. Once again, legislation, student success, and access to education are at the forefront of items confronting Dean Palmer at his community college.

Deans at community colleges share many of the responsibilities and challenges that their contemporaries at other institutions of higher education face. Simply put, the dean of any institution is the leader of the faculty; that is, it is the dean's job to set forth a vision with respect to academic programming and student success, gain faculty buy in, monitor tasks required to implement the vision, and eventually, through successful execution, bring the vision to life.

However, given the unique role that community colleges play in preparing students for transfer to four-year institutions or to enter the workforce, academic deans at our nation's community colleges often focus on items specific to two-year public institutions. The role of deans in this specific setting differs in many ways from that of their counterparts at public and private four-year institutions. This is due in large part to the increasingly important role two-year colleges play in the American higher education system. The White House briefing "Building American Skills through Community Colleges" accurately describes the unique characteristics of the two-year college:

> As the largest part of the nation's higher education system, community colleges enroll more than six million and are growing rapidly. They feature affordable tuition, open admission policies, flexible course schedules, and convenient locations. Community colleges are particularly important for students who are older, working, or need remedial classes. Community colleges work with businesses, industry and government to create tailored training programs to meet economic needs like nursing, health information technology, advanced manufacturing, and green jobs. (White House, 2010)

Community colleges serve a growing demographic of mature students and specialize in enhancing employability through affordable technical and workforce education. Therefore, deans at two-year colleges often find themselves supporting interdisciplinary discussions, working with faculty senates and unions, promoting student success and access, and forging relationships that stretch far beyond the confines of the campus.

DEAN AS GENERALIST

When I introduce myself to others as a dean, I am often questioned as to what exactly I am dean of. I find myself having to explain that at community colleges, deans are often interdisciplinary academic leaders due to the structure of the two-year educational institution. In four-year colleges there are deans of schools of nursing, arts and letters, engineering, social science, or education, to name a few. And although some community colleges subscribe to a similar structure, the majority require deans to oversee all academic areas or academic departments. In this type of setting, the dean is not an expert in every area of study; instead the dean is a generalist, given the task of hiring subject matter experts to be associate deans, directors, or chairs to work with the faculty in their respective academic disciplines. Larger schools might have their own deans, but overwhelmingly the dean at the community college is responsible for ensuring that all academic programming campus-wide is distributed fairly and appropriately so that students can complete their general education courses and degree requirements in a timely and cost-effective fashion.

FACULTY UNIONS

Community colleges are often unionized, requiring the dean to possess a unique complement of skills. As dean, you will inevitably set forth an academic vision or new initiative. Faculty unions can sometimes create challenging obstacles and at other times, they can prove quite helpful. It is the dean's job to work with the union as they would with any faculty or any faculty senate, with an understanding that certain nuances exist. Fortunately, the faculty contract spells out most responsibilities as well as governance, and a successful dean will make it a point to read the contract in full and become familiar with it. It is vital to know what is and what is not permitted under the contract and then work with union colleagues to more clearly define gray areas. Avoid statements such as, "the contract doesn't allow for that" or "that's not in the contract" because this may lead the faculty to believe you are being too rigid or don't wish to help them. Even though faculty may quote the contract, deans should use caution citing contractual obligations. Forge a good working relationship with union colleagues and ask them for assistance in ensuring the success of your vision and college initiatives. Unions are present to protect faculty, and once their leaders see that you wish to work with them to ensure faculty success and well-being, they will often prove a valuable ally.

TEACHING FOCUS

Another unique feature of community colleges is the expectation that faculty are experts at *teaching* the materials in the area in which they are credentialed. Community colleges certainly encourage publication and research, but such research is usually more classroom-based and oriented toward student success, and it is not a requirement for tenure. "Publish or perish" is not the mantra at two-year colleges. Professors at two-year colleges are expected to be and typically are good *teachers*. Community college professors are grounded in student learning, and deans at community colleges promote excellence in classroom teaching and the best practices related to student success. Good community college deans solicit feedback from faculty on best classroom practices, find innovative ways of institutionalizing them, and provide the resources faculty members need to help their students succeed.

THE COMMUNITY COLLEGE STUDENT POPULATION

Certain nuances exist in the student population of two-year colleges as well, stemming from our inherent core mission. First, community colleges remain open enrollment. As such, the community college remains the only option or opportunity for those students with a high school diploma who initially lack a definitive vision of their future. Deans at community colleges encourage the creation of programs that prepare college-ready students for careers (the focus of the Associate in Science degree) or transfer to a four-year institution (the focus of the Associate in Arts degree). As a result, there are three important considerations to keep in mind about students at two-year colleges that most likely will affect your work as dean.

Less Likely to Be Prepared

Unfortunately, having a high school diploma does not necessarily mean a student is college-ready. The fact that any student with a high school diploma is welcome to study at the community college means that deans at two-year institutions must also familiarize themselves with the challenges of developmental education. Deans at two-year colleges often find themselves managing programs that help students learn the knowledge they should have acquired in high school, or that help returning students relearn the foundational education they have forgotten over the years. Many community college deans forge partnerships with their local high schools in the creation of such programs in order to align curricula with the goal of graduating more high school students who are college-ready.

More Likely to Study Part-Time

Many community college students are more likely to study part-time due to the fact that they are working part-time or full-time jobs. Additionally, many of them are often taking care of family members or are in the process of raising a family. This means that a significant percentage of community college students' schedules do not fit into the traditional college schedule. Because of this, community colleges offer classes in a variety of flexible schedules to help accommodate the lifestyles of commuting students. Classes are offered in sessions of varying length and are taught from early morning to late into the evening. Online or blended formats are gaining momentum to ease the burden of travel time to and from campus. It is the dean's role at the community college to see that innovative schedules are fostered to serve the local community.

Less Likely to Be Privileged

Another key difference of the community college is affordability. Without this, many disadvantaged Americans would not otherwise be able to attend college and pursue a higher degree. Community colleges pride themselves on providing quality education at a relatively inexpensive price thus providing opportunity to students who would not otherwise be able to afford the cost of higher education. It is the dean's role at a community college to ensure and maintain educational opportunities at reasonable costs by keeping lab fees low, resisting unnecessary tuition increases, and maintaining seat limits that promote productivity and discourage waste.

PUBLIC FUNDING

Funding is another distinction with which deans at community colleges must contend. There is a depressing saying in the two-year college community that goes something like this: "We used to be publicly funded; now we are barely publicly supported." According to the US Department of Education, state and local appropriations for basic operations fell from 70 percent of total revenues in 1980 to 50 percent in 1996 (Merisotis & Wolanin, 1999). Although on the decline, the amount of money that community colleges receive from public funding still consists of a sizeable portion of the community college budget.

> Community colleges are highly dependent on state funding since, unlike four-year, public schools, they do not have diversified revenue sources such as hospitals, endowments, or research grants. While enrollments have been increasing, state support per student has remained relatively flat. (Kingkade, 2012)

Were such funding to evaporate, many two-year colleges would likely close or be forced to implement sharp cuts in services. Moreover, in today's political climate and with the increasing politicization of education, the management of funds in public institutions of higher education is more closely scrutinized than in the past. Deans at two-year colleges have varying degrees of involvement in managing public funds, but with respect to key decisions on how funds are allocated for growth, construction, and program development, the dean is often included.

To help your institution stay financially sound, you can use strategies such as monitoring enrollment, developing private-public partnerships, and seeking out alternative funding sources.

Monitor Enrollment

As a community college dean, it is important to monitor enrollment closely and supervise chairs and associate deans to ensure that courses have sufficient enrollment and programs remain viable and relevant. Maintaining an adequate balance of larger general education lectures and smaller boutique programs with lower enrollment is critical at the community college. This is the dreaded business aspect of community colleges that so many academicians loathe; however, it is the dean's managerial role to see to efficient classroom operations. At larger two-year institutions this can pose challenges because many of the academic departments operate in silos and classroom allocations roll over from term to term. A review of the enrollment reports often reflects oversights such as a class with a seat limit of fifteen scheduled in a classroom that seats twenty-five, or a program that has been operating at 50 percent capacity for years yet still remains in the catalog of offerings. By monitoring enrollment, ensuring productive use of classrooms and labs, and eliminating obsolete programs, the dean at a community college plays a critical role in saving the institution money.

Develop Public-Private Partnerships

Another way that community college deans can boost their institutions' income is by partnering with local businesses and industries to create innovative two-year degree programs or career-enhancing certificates. In such cases, the dean seeks out partnerships in which the college offers the academic training and the business provides funding for facilities, internships for students, or equipment for classrooms and labs. For example, when a south Florida power company realized that many of its employees were retiring, two community college systems were tapped to help provide additional workforce training. Courses were created for a viable degree, and instead of a commencement ceremony, successful graduates attended a hiring ceremony and began working at the power plant immediately.

Another example of a public-private partnership can be found in the development of a culinary program. A private partner may equip and operate a restaurant where college students complete their lab hours, serve as interns, and gain valuable real-life experience prior to graduation. The opportunities in this area are endless, and imaginative deans can help their institutions earn or save money while preparing students for lucrative careers.

Seek Alternative Modes of Funding

Because public funding is on the decline, deans at community colleges find an increasing percentage of their responsibility becoming the identification and management of alternative modes of funding, such as grants. Although this part of the job may not be entirely new or unique to a community college dean, the increased expectation is, and in a two-year setting fundraising does have its differences. Grants that community college deans pursue are more likely to be related to student success initiatives or transfer to a four-year institution. Because deans are generalists at community colleges, the dean is more likely to work with associate deans, chairpersons, and faculty to provide support and leadership in the writing of the grants. For example, a dean at a two-year college might pull together a team of experts from the various STEM disciplines to partner on writing grants related to recruitment, retention, and success of underserved populations in the STEM fields. Once again, deans are not necessarily the experts; they simply lend assistance and guidance to the group. Community college deans promote and support grant-writing endeavors, recognizing those who try and lauding those who succeed.

As a community college dean, you should remember the following:

- Capitalize on the strengths and talents of your discipline experts. Deans at community colleges wear many different hats. You are the leader of the faculty from a multitude of disciplines and must work with colleagues across the college to implement innovations as well as daily functions.
- Be an ambassador for access to education and educate others about the important role of the community college in the US higher education system.
- Create opportunities for students. Think innovatively about new programs that will lead students to transfer to a four-year degree program or to enter the workforce.
- Find creative ways to raise funds for the college. Public-private partnerships are great ways to help new programs get started and to prepare valuable hands-on training experiences for students.
- Find ways to serve the community through partnerships with local industries or through sponsorship of educational events for local residents.

With the recent increased awareness of the important role that community colleges play in the US higher education system, deans at two-year institutions will have a huge impact on the workforce of the twenty-first century. “In the coming years,” President Barack Obama has noted, “jobs requiring at least an associate degree are projected to grow twice as fast as jobs requiring no college experience. We will not fill those jobs—or keep those jobs on our shores—without the training offered by community colleges” (Obama, 2009).

By ensuring access to education through open enrollment and low-cost innovative programming, community college deans remain integral to getting people started on the path to the American Dream.

References

Kingkade, T. (2012, December 26). Community college funding shrinks, for-profit enrollment grows: Treasury report. *The Huffington Post*. Retrieved from http://www.huffingtonpost.com/2012/12/26/community-college-for-profit_n_2340958.html

Merisotis, J. P. & T. R. Wolanin. (1999). *Community college financing: Strategies and challenges*. Washington, DC: The Institute for Higher Education Policy.

Obama, B. (2009, July 14). Excerpt from remarks on the American Graduation Initiative delivered in Warren, MI.

White House. (2010, October 4). Building American skills through community colleges. Retrieved from http://www.whitehouse.gov/issues/education/higher-education/building-american-skills-through-community-colleges

CHAPTER FIVE

A Successful Career as an Online Dean

Pamela Monaco
Southwestern College of Professional Studies

Now that online education has become an educational option at most colleges and universities, your college has given some serious consideration to how to brand online education more effectively in the market. The arrival of massive open online courses (MOOCs) showed potential students worldwide what could be done to make an online course more visually appealing, to provide instant feedback on some types of exercises, and to bring the sense of the professor's presence into the asynchronous experience. Your provost was one of the thousands who signed up for a MOOC; she kept reading about this "disruption" and wanted to see what it was all about. She is convinced your college should not miss this opportunity to participate in this new kind of online course. The IT department is a bit concerned that should such a course be delivered, the department wouldn't be ready to handle all the support it might need to offer; currently, online has been growing slowly but steadily and the IT department has been able to accommodate the demands.

However, the IT department has wondered if now might be the time to change learning management systems (LMS), or at least consider a different hosting option. If the LMS changes, all the current courses may have to be revised. Staff in the Center for Teaching and Learning (CTL) are intrigued by the MOOC possibility, but no one has used the level of technology required, and there is concern that the production resources are just not available for this kind of project. You have looked at the courses presently being offered online and the faculty involved. Most tenured faculty have been reluctant about developing and delivering an online course. They discovered the extra time requirements to teach this kind of course and think faculty loads need to be adjusted to reflect online teaching assignments. Your university has been fortunate to have developed some very fine contingent faculty who teach most of these courses, and although the full-time faculty are happy someone else is doing the online teaching in their discipline, they are not convinced the courses are as rigorous as an on-the-ground course. You know some of the part-time faculty are doing a great job and they understand how to engage with students online. You find all of this conversation about online education in general, and MOOCs in particular, intriguing, and a good thing, too: your provost has tasked you with being the dean who will serve as point person as your university makes its way into online education. What do you need to think about as you get this initiative ready?

Online course and program delivery began in the mid-1990s and quickly replaced or supplemented various kinds of distance education options offered by colleges and universities whose primary target was working adults and degree completion students. Residential colleges saw little reason to embrace online education, both because of a high level of skepticism about the quality of the teaching and learning experience in online education and because of the belief that students attended a traditional or residential university in order to experience life on a college campus. Some large land-grant universities started to offer online courses through their continuing or extended education offices, and some even offered full degrees online. After the financial problems of 2008–2009, many colleges, particularly state college systems that have continued to operate with lower state funding levels, realized that online offerings provided a revenue stream and opened the possibility to new markets of students. Today, it is the rare college or university that does not offer some online courses.

The role of dean of online learning can take many permutations. Sometimes the job title is very clear, sometimes not. Frequently, the well-defined position of leadership for online learning occurs within schools or colleges of continuing education. In other cases, being dean of online learning means providing leadership for a traditional disciplinary-defined school or college, and part of the course offerings include some, or perhaps mostly, online courses or programs. The difference between these two types of deanships has more to do with reporting structure, the amount of time devoted to concerns about online learning, differing divisions of revenue sharing, and the kind of networking required than with anything else. Most important, no matter where situated in a college or university, the dean whose portfolio includes online instruction will have to be focused on assuring a quality program to an often skeptical audience, both internally and externally.

If the online dean is situated in a school or college of professional or continuing education, or as a separate university within a state system, the online dean will be actively engaged with the leadership of the other colleges or universities in the college or system. Often, in these circumstances, the online dean negotiates with other existing degree programs to migrate courses or programs to online delivery. *Negotiate* is the appropriate term for these discussions. The dean will want to work out agreements about intellectual property for courses developed for online delivery. Will a particular course be taught only by the person who was involved with the original course? If so, for how long? Can the particular course be taught by others in the original design? Part of the appeal of online learning, in addition to the potential for new student populations, is the ability to standardize a course and replicate it many times without additional investment in design.

Another point of discussion is the disbursements of the revenue return. In many institutions, there is a revenue share agreement between the online office or college and the department, school, or college that manages the curriculum. The online dean's office will want to develop the policies to regulate this process. It will be important to outline who pays for the instructor, whether teaching online is part of a teaching load or overload, what oversight of delivery the online dean maintains, and what percentage of net revenue is shared, and with which office. In these circumstances, it also is wise to have clear policies in place about staffing decisions, about who does what with teaching evaluations, about the support and training offered and by whom, and about the scheduling decisions, including when and under what circumstances to no longer schedule a course or program.

The traditional method of teaching, often referred to as face-to-face instruction, seems fairly simple in retrospect. Departments know how many sections to offer, the time in a classroom is universally calculated with exceptions for lab, studio, or practicum courses, and faculty are expected to bring scholarship into the class, stay current in the field, and provide a quality learning experience. Online learning requires rethinking everything one knows about teaching and learning. In a traditional class, the professor is expected to bring to his or her lectures, readings, and assignments the latest theory and development, as appropriate in the field. In the online environment, updated curriculum must be supported by updated technology. The dean will be involved in discussions about updates to the learning management system, new technology tools, and the rapid evolution of defining the qualities of a good online course.

Accrediting bodies want the online class to meet the standards of the on-the-ground class. What does the Carnegie unit mean when students can log in to class whenever it is convenient for them? How do we calculate the amount of time a student is engaged in the class? Is this important? With a host of options available for synchronous components of an online class, many colleges encourage this, but distance learners may be in different time zones or have working hours or obligations that prevent this level of engagement. Ongoing concerns about student authentication have resulted in retina scans, cameras that record who is taking an exam, remote disabling of the Internet during a test and even recognition of typing patterns. These solutions carry a price, including responsibility of managing the process. Depending on to whom one is marketing online courses or programs, the mechanisms that answer the critics' concerns about online integrity can be viewed as impediments by students. With the high competition in the online market and the push on many campuses to use online education for a revenue stream, balance must be a goal.

Teaching online courses well takes dedicated, innovative professors. Teaching online requires considerably more time than traditional teaching. The level of faculty involvement in the online class matters, which means an online instructor should try to be in the online class daily. More and more colleges are mandating instructor engagement a set number of times during the week. The instructor will have to devote considerable time developing the course and maintaining the course. The more technologically sophisticated a course or the more a class relies on materials or experiences other than the traditional printed text, the greater the need to make sure the course remains current and up-to-date.

Although full-time faculty may enjoy teaching the specialized courses in their discipline, many colleges rely on contingent faculty to teach service and lower-level courses online. Both of these populations, full-time and part-time faculty, will need training in how to teach online and then monitoring, to ensure the quality of the course and the teaching. Service and lower-level courses may be standardized because the investment in the course development and the alignment with the face-to-face course are best realized through replication. Expect to have some discussions about the competing desires for standardized courses and academic freedom.

The wise dean has to think about workload issues and compensation of the faculty who teach online because the time commitment is different from a traditionally offered course. If there is a centralized center for teaching and learning, each college or university will want to make sure part-time faculty are receiving appropriate training and support for online instruction, and this, too, must be calculated with respect to contingent employee contracts. Will an adjunct be paid for training, or will the training be considered an opportunity for professional development?

Much of the ongoing training that online teaching now requires, from upgrades to the learning management system to the use of new tools, should be offered through a center for teaching and learning, but the dean's office will want to provide input into the setting of standards and expectations. Who will perform quality checks to make sure the course is ready for online delivery each semester? Who will perform a peer review, and during what time frame of observation and during what point in the semester? Does a peer review even need to occur during the active semester, or should the review occur after the semester so the entire teaching experience can be reviewed? If contingent faculty will not be widely used, the dean needs to develop policies about who teaches online, what the balance between traditional and online courses may be, and consider how policies, such as office hour requirements, might need to be weighed.

Student behavior in an online course has become of increasing interest. The impact of social media and the erasure of boundaries in electronic communication mean that not all students are well prepared for academic discourse, tolerance of differing points of view, or social interaction in online communities. Netiquette policies set expectations, but problems may still occur. Increasingly, the mental and emotional health of online students is receiving attention. In many online environments, the college, the instructor, and the students all can be in different locations, even different states or countries. A faculty member confronting a student in crisis needs to know whom to call or consult, and the solution is not to wait until someone returns to work during normal business hours on the campus. Gray areas will continue to deepen. What kind of protection does the college need to provide an instructor or another student against aggressive or bullying behavior that occurs because of the online environment? The online dean wants to consider these situations before a need for intervention occurs.

As a dean of online education, your will bear responsibility for increasing enrollments. You will be responsible for ensuring the online offerings have the same rigor as the traditional offerings, and you will work closely with the admissions office to guide policies and standards regarding those seeking online offerings. It will be important also to work closely with the recruitment and marketing offices, because the regulations of "distance education" at the state and federal levels must be closely understood and monitored. Many, if not most, colleges and universities have a staff position responsible for "state authorization." States have long regulated institutions offering education within their boundaries, but the explosion of online instruction has brought nuances to the definition of "presence" in another state.

Each state's regulations must be carefully studied. For example, if your college employs contingent faculty at a distance, some states consider the hiring of their residents as having a presence in that state. If your college's online programs or courses include practicums or internship requirements, placing students in these experiences in other states could also signal presence in those other states. The strategies for marketing and for requirements that are used to generate online enrollments must be viewed in light of state authorization rules. Some states impose very high fees to operate in their boundaries, even if "operate" means only enrolling students in an online program. If a state's fees or requirements to operate are too high or stringent, it will be essential to make clear to prospective applicants that they cannot enroll in your online program if they reside in certain states. As of 2010, the federal government issued new regulations with regard to "program integrity" that enforce the need to seek authorization to operate in another state if students of other states are to receive federal financial aid. As online education continues to evolve, one should expect that regulations will do so too.

Higher education is no longer a predicable business for those in academic administration. Online education is just one of the ways our evolving global world and technological advances have changed what it means to "go" to college. As on online dean, or one who is considering this career option, keep in mind the following questions:

- What is the responsibility of the online dean's office with respect to enrollment goals for the entire college and university? An online dean must be comfortable thinking beyond academic concerns and considering and understanding the role of enrollment management.
- Does this college have the resources—financial, instructional, and technological—to be competitive in the online market?
- How comfortable are you, as an academic administrator, in a world without carefully defined boundaries? Maintaining work-life balance is challenging for any academic administrator, but the online world is always awake and always looking for more attention.

CHAPTER SIX

Moving from Professor to Dean

Bonnie D. Irwin
Eastern Illinois University

After serving a term as chair of the faculty senate, a professor found herself increasingly frustrated with the narrow view of her departmental colleagues and why they did not see the bigger picture of the university that she had become accustomed to seeing. When the position of graduate dean became open, she decided to apply. She had taught many graduate courses, had served on the graduate council, and believed she had some unique skills to bring to the position, a combination of experiences that, when coupled with her admirable campus and departmental service, made her a well-qualified candidate. When she became a finalist for the position, some of her longtime colleagues and friends questioned her loyalty to her department and her discipline. Knowing she would control budget decisions, graduate assistant assignments, and a host of other resources, some friends worried that their relationship would change and that they could no longer trust her once she was on the "dark side." More than one colleague approached her with the words "I hope we can still be friends." Did this mean that they expected favors from her or that they feared they would not be able to go out to dinner anymore?

Even if a dean believes that she is the same person as she was as a faculty member, others will think differently. Jokes about the dark side aside, administrators have a different relationship with their institution and their faculty than they had before joining the administrative team. Imagine wearing a neon side above your head that reads "Dean." You may not be able to see it, but others certainly will.

ATTENDING SOCIAL AND CEREMONIAL OCCASIONS

Many deans find the first few months an awkward transition, especially if they have become dean on a campus where they have spent significant time as a faculty member. Invitations to regular informal social occasions may dwindle because your friends are unsure if you can or will associate with them on the same level. Faculty friends imagine that your day is chock full of all manner of busywork, and that you no longer have time for lunch. There is some truth to that assumption, as your calendar becomes something that can control you if you do not control it. You may find that you must reach out to those who harbor doubts about your availability if you indeed want to see them.

There will be no lack of invitations, however—to receptions, ceremonies, dinners, and luncheons. These are less social occasions than working ones. The dean becomes accustomed to standing and waving as others applaud her mere presence. Often your seat will be assigned, and often that assignment is at a head table, meaning that you are on display throughout the event. If you are not naturally a gregarious person, you will learn to become one, making small talk with whomever is at your table or in your company at such events.

At these ceremonial occasions, you will often be asked to give welcoming or concluding remarks, and on some days, particularly in the months of April or May, you may have several different such occasions stacked up. Preparing a stock of core messages with specific talking points for each audience will help streamline the preparation process until these sorts of events become second nature. It is essential to learn who the audience will be and what kinds of remarks are expected before setting off to the next reception. You also may be buttonholed at such events by those who have specific questions for you. Some of these questions are easily answered, but others will entail research. Faculty can just show up at events; deans need to prepare and always carry a pad or smartphone on which to jot a couple of notes.

INTERACTING WITH FACULTY

It is often said that when one becomes an administrator, one learns who one's real friends are. You will find a way to continue long-standing relationships, but it is important to remember that newer faculty will see you first as dean rather than colleague. Remember that neon sign above your head. A piece of advice may appear to be a criticism, regardless of how well it was meant. New faculty may not even know your departmental affiliation or your research area; they will not know that you were a union officer or served on the curriculum committee as a faculty member. Making connections with new faculty on that level will help humanize you in their eyes.

Some deans teach; many deans still conduct research, albeit on a smaller scale. Just because one still does faculty work, however, does not mean that one is still a member of the faculty. Faculty expect their dean to stay current in his academic field, but at the same time may doubt that he does. At the same time, you will have much, much more outside your field with which to keep abreast: enrollment reports, budgets, articles and books on higher education. Finding a balance between one's discipline and the discipline of higher education is key to maintaining the respect of the faculty while also doing one's new job well. You may also find that a limited research agenda provides you with a mental refuge from the day-to-day demands of academic administration.

BECOMING ACCUSTOMED TO HANDLERS

Depending on the size of the staff, as dean you may find yourself more isolated and catered to than you are accustomed to. Typically there will be at least one person, and perhaps more people, between you and the front door to your office. Among your staff and to all outside audiences, you will be referred to as "the dean," no matter how many times you ask to be called by your first name. Respect for the office generally permeates the staff, even with the most informal or laid-back of deans. Someone will open (and often prioritize) your mail, keep your calendar, book your appointments, and generally stand guard over your time and space. Others will keep many of your files, make your photocopies, and even prepare your reports. Someone will offer to book your travel, prepare your vouchers, and type your correspondence. If you continue to teach, your staff might also prepare syllabi, schedule student conferences, and run off your exams.

If you are coming from an environment in which faculty members manage their own logistics for professional obligations, the environment of the dean's office may feel a little rarified at first. It may seem impersonal to ask another to make a phone call for you, but in this age of caller identification, the dean may not want her direct line to show up on the caller ID of a parent or disgruntled faculty member. Typically your staff has more experience in the dean's office than you will. Setting clear expectations for them and then letting them do their jobs generally will help ease the transition on both sides.

SHARING ONE'S VIEWS

Faculty fiercely protect their academic freedom and their freedom of speech, and rightly so. A dean gives up these rights to a degree because she now also speaks for the college. When a dean offers an opinion, faculty wonder how soon it will be before the opinion becomes policy. One is also part of a hierarchy in which it is generally bad form to criticize the college or any of its offices publicly. "Praise publicly, criticize privately" is the rule by which most deans operate. In this sense *privately* also carries a special meaning, the zone of privacy generally being limited to one's closest staff or peers. A careless word, even among friends, can have repercussions across the campus; many define breach of confidentiality as telling only one other person. This is not to say, however, that you should not speak up when you see misconduct; you can usually find inside channels to report wrongdoing, and most people have a clear enough sense of right and wrong to distinguish between honest mistakes and actual malfeasance. One learns to protect the reputation of one's institution from the former while firmly dealing with the latter, even if one has to do so publicly.

A dean's speech may also be limited on any number of issues that have no direct relationship with the job. Even when you speak on your own time, you are a representative of the university, and you will find yourself needing to work with community members and alumni who may have political and social opinions much different from your own. You may find yourself taking a less visible role in any political organizations that you belong to.

LEARNING TO FIND REWARD IN THE ACCOMPLISHMENTS OF OTHERS

It is not about you. Rarely will you be honored or thanked for doing your job well; you *will* be criticized for doing so. You will quickly learn that even in a culture of mutual respect and shared governance, some will not be happy with your decisions. Just as your words take on greater significance in this new role, so do your opinions. College constituents will always listen to what you say, providing you with both great opportunity and great responsibility.

You will be in a position to praise the work of others, and you will need to do so often and publicly. You may create a new, successful initiative for the campus, but the faculty needs to take ownership of it for it to succeed. Sharing the praise and putting faculty and staff in the limelight reminds the campus community that your number one job is to facilitate the success of others.

ESTABLISHING NEW NETWORKS

Because as a dean your relationship to faculty on your home campus changes, it is important to establish both social and professional relationships with other deans and vice presidents. You will find that you will need a confidant at times, a sounding board at others, and that one's old friends may not be appropriate in that role. Many academic leaders also have partners working on the same campus, and a dean cannot take the job home in the same way a faculty member can. Attending higher education meetings or meetings expressly designed for deans will provide important connections. Most of these professional organizations also have e-mail lists where one can seek advice and become a member of a new community.

The person sitting behind the dean's desk may have a broader perspective of higher education and a deeper investment in the logistics of running the university, but she is still the same person she was while sitting in a faculty office.

Remembering the values that are shared across the campus—the education and welfare of students, creating new knowledge, serving the greater community—will keep you thriving and comfortable in your own skin, even on the dark side. Here are some keys to making the transition:

- Find your circle of trust.
- Let your staff do their jobs.
- Keep a connection with your discipline.
- Think before you speak, and say *thank you* often.
- Establish a network of colleagues.
- Keep the broader perspective of higher education in sight.

CHAPTER SEVEN

Understanding the Social Roles of a Dean

Jeffrey R. Breese
Rockhurst University

It is a late December afternoon and time for the last school-wide faculty meeting of the semester. The main agenda item is to review and provide feedback on the emerging strategic plan for the school of business. In "new dean school" last summer, I learned how important it is for deans to lead this process and to take a prominent role in creating and communicating the vision and strategic directions for the future. As an "internal" dean who rose from within the school, I look around the meeting room and see colleagues I know very well.

The meeting concludes; we have unanimously approved a new strategic plan that will guide us for the next five years. After the meeting, several colleagues speak privately to me about the transition I have made from being a faculty member to a dean. One of the management professors even tells me he has been analyzing my transition as a case study of how someone moves from management to leadership. Although the comment was meant to be positive (I think), it made me reflect upon the transition of an internal dean: "Am I prepared to be a case study? Am I prepared to receive comments on my dress, my hair, and my demeanor? Am I prepared to grow up in a fishbowl?"[1]

As a sociologist, I was interested in understanding the path(s) one could take into the world of academic affairs administration. In my work as a sociologist, I have previously applied the "role exit" theory developed by Helen Rose Ebaugh (1988) to the study of individuals in the midst of a significant transition. Ebaugh's theoretical framework focuses on leaving behind a major role or incorporating the ex-role into a new identity. Ebaugh contends that, regardless of the types of roles being departed, there are underlying similarities that make role exit unique and definable as a social process. One of the core elements of her theory is the "voluntary" and "involuntary" type of life transitions individuals can experience. In one study, for example, I identified homeless women and their children as experiencing an involuntary life transition; I also identified adult women and other nontraditional students completing their college educations due to some life events that resulted from both voluntary and involuntary role exits. In applying role exit theory to academic administrators, I sought to understand the transition into administrator. I wanted to study individuals engaged in a career trajectory that would lead to significant levels of stress, role conflict, and role residual. The role residual or "hangover identity" quality of a role exit emphasizes how aspects of one's previous work and central sense of self carry over into the new role a person has taken.

With this research interest established and as a member of ACAD, there was a natural sample in mind for my embarking on this line of inquiry. In 2009, with the approval of the organization, a request was placed on the ACAD e-mail list to respond to a survey of seventeen primarily open-ended questions. Most of the questions were based on items drawn from existing research instruments using role exit theory and key themes identified in previous research on the role of a dean in higher education; 62 ACAD members completed the online survey.

Of the respondents, 35 in the sample were female, 57 held a PhD (English, writing, or literature being the most common field, represented by 20 in the sample), and only 3 in the sample were non-white. The positions held by these individuals at the time of the study reflect the reality that not all ACAD members are deans, exclusively:

23 academic deans

11 associate/assistant provosts or VPAA

10 associate deans

9 provosts and/or VPAA and dean of faculty

8 provosts or VPAA

1 director

Fifty of these individuals had been in their current position for less than five years (27 of them for less than two years). Clearly, the majority of the sample were in the midst of a significant career transition when they completed the survey. An unanticipated theme that emerged from the data was the clear difference in experience for these individuals based on whether they took on their role as an "insider" or "outsider." Did they become an administrator at the institution at which they were already employed, or did they make a physical move in concert with a career transition?

There are both pros and cons to making the move into administration within one's current institution or to exiting one institution as a faculty member and entering a different one as an administrator. As an example, four individuals in my study who moved into an administrative role where they had served as a faculty member used the expression "moving to the dark side" when reflecting on colleagues' perceptions of their change in status. In this sample, there is a fairly even split between the types of moves: 32 achieved their current position as the result of an external search, and the other 30 were serving as an administrator as a result of being an internal candidate, filling an interim appointment, or converting from an interim to a permanent appointment.

The internal and external candidates shared a profound sense of how their previous work and experiences lingered into and affected their current work. As Ebaugh's theory describes, this hangover identity affected their present position in two ways: the link to their experience as a faculty member and the connection, training, and grounding from their specific academic discipline. As a dean who was a trained nurse put it: "How did they ever manage without a nurse in this position? I do problem solving, behavior modification, therapeutic listening, assessment, tracking and monitoring, counseling of students and faculty, and check the president's blood pressure." The balancing act for all academic administrators is departing from a role that lingers into their present work and from their sense of identity as a faculty member. Yet the faculty they had once worked with, quite literally in the cases of administrators who stayed at the same institution, now could be the very individuals one must meet on the other side of the dean's desk.

Like any new social role that requires resocialization and a significant change to one's sense of self, individuals who have exited the faculty role, along with its degree of autonomy over one's work schedule and productivity, face a very different work life with new patterns and rhythms to how their days are spent. Any career or job change carries with it surprises or disappointments, or perceived positive and negative elements of the new position. Because of the all-consuming work that tends to be the norm in higher education administration, the impact of the transition on others in one's social network can be important in making a successful career change. However, all these factors and experiences also are affected by whether it was a career change within the same campus community or entailed moving to a new institution with all new individuals and expectations.

In my sample, 38 respondents indicated that they had received feedback from others indicating a change to themselves that was noticeable (major categories were clothing, personality, and how they spent their time), with this feedback being more pronounced for the internal deans. One woman who moved to a different institution indicated that she did not get such feedback because "[she] came to a new institution and people who knew [her] well were not in a position to judge." On the positive side, administrators who remained at their home institutions expressed the encouragement received on their campuses, including the intent of helping their institution and in some instances "being tapped" for the new role.

The administrators in my research represent the unique changes implicit and explicit in moving from faculty member to administrator. However, the key difference is the ways the transition can vary, depending on whether one assumes the role of administrator at a different institution or moves into administration at the same institution.

The residual or hangover identity of faculty colleagues tends to be less pronounced for persons who are new to an institution. The "calling" into administrative work for faculty to a new institution was more likely based on thoughts of seeking new challenges and engaging in a natural career progression. Those situated at a new campus as administrator could have been wrestling with such outward signals and markers of change as much as internal deans, yet these would not be considered changes by individuals encountering the new administrator as a "blank slate."

Taking on the responsibilities of an administrator, whether internal or external, is not easy. Each responsibility calls for a new orientation to the life and work of the institution, requires learning about a given institution's sense of being and cultural attributes, and identifying where the land mines are. I was hired as an external dean and now currently serve as an interim vice president for academic affairs at the same institution. What I had learned as the new external dean now needed to be refined, expanded upon, and rethought because the responsibilities, priorities, personalities, and relationships I had come to know were altered because of my newer role.

One important question I consider as a critical initial benchmark is: what is the first thing shared with me by an individual when I am new to a role? Does the colleague, subordinate, or superior use that first substantive encounter to crow about strengths and successes in their respective area? Does the person complain about limited resources, budget shortfalls, or perceptions that "we are headed to hell in a handbasket at this place?" Do they play up *or* tear down colleagues in their office or department? For an external dean new to a campus, these first encounters can provide much context in understanding individuals' priorities and mind-sets. For the internal dean, that first conversation after the appointment sheds a rather interesting light on colleagues who are not new to you.

A final thought for those of you who are new to your campus in the role of administrator: be careful with what and how you share from the previous institutions where you have worked. As Glick (2006) succinctly states, "It is natural but deadly for new administrators to refer back to their previous university. Nothing alienates colleagues more, and it leads them to wonder why you did not stay there" (p. 92). Odds are you were selected for your post from the outside because of your experiences and the fresh ideas you would introduce to your new campus community. But tread lightly, and don't use that hammer too often.

I have spent the bulk of my career in Catholic higher education, but the following prayer can serve as beneficial advice to any administrator, external or internal, at a private or public institution. In my first faculty meeting as a new dean, I shared a copy of it with my new colleagues to set a tone for how I hoped to ideally approach my way of proceeding. I keep a copy of it hanging in my office:

> Lord, thou knowest better than I know myself that I am growing older and will someday be old. Keep me from the fatal habit of thinking I must say something on every subject and on every occasion.
>
> Release me from craving to straighten out everybody's affairs. Make me thoughtful but not moody; helpful but not bossy. With my vast store of wisdom it seems a pity not to use it all, but thou knowest, Lord, that I want a few friends in the end.
>
> Keep my mind free from the recital of endless details; give me wings to get to the point. Seal my lips on my aches and pains. They are increasing and the love of rehearsing them is becoming sweeter as the years go by. I dare not ask for grace enough to enjoy the tales of others' pains, but help me to endure them with patience.
>
> I dare not ask for improved memory, but for a growing humility and a lessening cocksureness when my memory seems to clash with the memories of others. Teach me the glorious lesson that occasionally I may be mistaken.
>
> Keep me reasonably sweet; I do not want to be a saint—some of them are so hard to live with—but a sour old person is one of the crowning works of the devil. Give me the ability to see good things in unexpected places, and talents in unexpected people. And, give me, O Lord, the grace to tell them so. Amen.
>
> **—Anonymous**

As you work in higher education administration consider the following questions:

- How would my approach to work in my current role be different if I had the opposite of my actual experience? For example, if internal, would I be tackling or perceiving various aspects of my job differently if I were an external hire?
- How am I navigating learning a new institution's people and culture as an outsider? As an insider?
- How am I reordering my thinking on issues and personalities, as an insider, because I now deal with colleagues differently in my new role on a campus already familiar to me?
- What have been the pros and cons to my work in this administrative role? Am I doing my work as the result of being tapped from the inside to move up, or as the product of a search, now new to the institution?

Note

1. Thanks to Cheryl McConnell, dean of the Helzberg School of Management, Rockhurst University, for providing the opening scenario.

References

Ebaugh, H. R. (1988). *Becoming an ex: The process of role exit*. Chicago: University of Chicago Press.

Glick, M. D. (2006). Becoming "one of them" or "moving to the dark side." In R. J. Henry (Ed.), *New Directions for Higher Education*: Number 134. *Transitions between faculty and administrative careers* (pp. 87–96). San Francisco: Jossey-Bass.

CHAPTER EIGHT

Working with a Former Dean

Karen Ryan
Stetson University

> As a new dean brought in to lead the university's College of Arts and Sciences, you are doing multiple searches across the college, and candidates are arriving thick and fast for interviews. A few weeks into the hiring season, you are told that the former dean always attended job candidates' research presentations and engaged in departmental conversations to rank the candidates. The former dean—now returned to the faculty—also always attended meetings of the curriculum committee, appended personal notes to letters suspending students, and knew all the names of the children and grandchildren of members of the advisory board.

Assuming a position as a new dean, you are inevitably replacing a dean who is stepping out of that role. The former dean may have left to accept a position at another institution, in which case his or her reputation, policies, and leadership style will be present only in memory (however powerful). Alternately, he or she may have become provost or president at the same institution and is present, but in a higher leadership role. These first two scenarios can be relatively simple for a new dean to navigate in that both situations have presumably resulted from a successful deanship because the former dean has moved—either externally or internally—into another leadership role. A new dean will likely be able to express genuine respect, admiration, and gratitude for the former dean's strong and able leadership.

In a third scenario, however, the former dean may have returned to the faculty; he remains a part of the institution but is no longer in a major leadership position. This is more complicated and requires a nuanced approach. Of course, a former dean's returning to the faculty of the home institution does not imply an unsuccessful deanship. His tenure as dean may have been brilliant and advanced the college in important ways; he may be returning to the faculty for a well-earned respite from administration, heeding the siren call of research and teaching. Or the former dean may have been encouraged to step down by a new provost or president looking for a different leadership style or a different vision. Particularly if the former dean was well liked and appreciated by the faculty, this is a delicate situation for a new dean. In addition to learning a new institutional culture, getting to know faculty and departments, building relationships with advisory board members, and so on, one needs to take into consideration the former dean's presence and (more or less) vocal advice and judgment.

The faculty, your major internal constituency, tends to evaluate your performance as dean vis-à-vis your predecessor's performance, especially if the former dean served in that role for many years. This may seem unfair, but it is human nature. Moreover, comparison may be an effective tool of leverage, if managed thoughtfully. It is important—and would be important even if the former dean had departed—to acknowledge her accomplishments and to praise the solidity of the foundation you have inherited. The faculty is the core of the college you now lead, and the former dean had some role in shaping the faculty. Expressing appreciation for the work of the former dean implies respect for the faculty and its programs, curricula, teaching, and scholarship. In addition, acknowledging the former dean's strengths as an administrator can disarm faculty members who remain loyal to her vision and style and are skeptical of new leadership. The college you now lead has a rich and variegated past; there is much to be gained by understanding, accepting, and recognizing that past and positioning oneself in the historical landscape.

It is equally important to establish the ways in which your deanship is different from that of your predecessor. Having acknowledged the past, you can move on to more creative endeavors. (The possibility of building something new, after all, is probably why you accepted the position.) Thus, as a new dean you need to make clear your agenda for the college, though it may be very different from the former dean's. Indeed, you must ensure that faculty members understand that change has occurred and is occurring, that things are being done differently. This need not involve explicit or even implicit criticism of the former dean; it is simply expressing your own leadership style, your values, and your vision. It is important that the reason for change be articulated because otherwise faculty may conclude that you are changing policies and processes solely for the sake of change. If you decide, for example, not to attend every job candidate's research presentation as your predecessor did, it is worthwhile to address that change in a faculty meeting or a department chairs' meeting. Rather than disrespecting the faculty and the importance of the hiring process, you might explain, you are allowing departments to make decisions about candidates based on their disciplinary expertise. Your not attending is a demonstration of confidence in the faculty to make a reasoned judgment in ranking the candidates for the position.

Working with staff whom you have inherited from a former dean also has pros and cons. On the one hand, staff members who have been in the Dean's Office for some years will likely have deep institutional knowledge; they will know people across the college and will know policies and procedures. Their support can be invaluable, especially during transition into a new deanship. On the other hand, loyalty and even devotion to a former dean can complicate your working relationship with staff. They may be resistant to change and hope that you will continue to manage the office in the same way that your predecessor did. Almost inevitably, that will not be true, especially if you are coming in as a creative change agent. Explicitly appreciating the expertise and knowledge offered by staff members goes a long way toward easing transition. Bringing in new members of your office staff, however, also offers many advantages. Although "insider" knowledge is helpful, the fresh "outsider" perspective brought by a new administrative assistant or executive assistant can be enormously useful. There is much to be said for inviting a new pair of eyes to look objectively at processes specifically and at the culture of the Dean's Office generally. A good assistant can help a new dean in eliminating redundancies, streamlining stale processes, and using technology more effectively. Overcoming the inertia of doing things the way they have been done for years is remarkably challenging, but good will, acknowledgement of tradition, and the support of new or flexible staff members are strong arrows in one's quiver.

Presumably, you have accepted your position as dean because you believed other administrators at the institution—provost, president, vice presidents—would be excellent colleagues. Moreover, those administrators hired you, confident that you would make positive changes and lead the college forward. More than likely, however, you inherited one or more associate or assistant deans from your predecessor. As with members of your staff, your associate deans may have strong ties to the former dean and see change as betrayal. This can be problematic, as trust and confidentiality are fundamental to the work of the Dean's Office. A transitional period will shed light on this dynamic and give you a chance to assess the working relationship: are your associate deans the best people to help you move the college forward, or are they invested in the status quo? The institutional knowledge of associate deans who have been in their roles for some time can be a tremendous asset. If they are to continue in their roles, it is crucial that they recognize and support key differences in leadership style, extent of delegation of authority, and vision of the future of the college.

Finally, as a college within a larger university, you may have inherited an advisory board of alumni and friends of the college from your predecessor.

Indeed, it is quite possible that all the members of this college advisory board were recruited by the former dean. Because your predecessor remains on the faculty, they will probably continue to maintain a relationship with him or her. This can create awkwardness; whether board members stay or depart, it is important that the advisory board become *your* board in short order. As alumni and friends of the institution, they will probably strongly value the history and traditions of the college. Of course, you will want to emphasize the ways in which your leadership expresses continuity with those traditions. And to the extent that the former dean represented those traditions and the storied past of the institution, his or her legacy and achievements should be acknowledged. It is often useful to openly address concerns your board members may have about your agenda: Do you intend to change the nature or mission of the college? Do you want to shape the college in the mold of your own previous institution? Does your leadership mark a radical departure from that of the previous dean? It will probably pay to be explicit in addressing these questions, even if they are not posed directly.

Your arrival and a period of transition present an opportunity to review the membership of the board and offer a chance to recruit new members. Most terms on advisory boards are two or three years, so turnover can be fairly rapid. Your development officer will be of help in recommending whether members should remain on the board or step off. Although the previous dean may have strong opinions (and may express them) on this point, it is crucial that you be comfortable with the board's membership. There will be board members whom you definitely want to retain and reappoint, that is, those who are supportive of your vision of the college's future and your priorities. In recruiting new board members, it may be advantageous to seek alumni who have interest and capacity to support those initiatives that will be the signature programs of your deanship.

With all these various constituencies, both internal and external, the presence of a former dean can present complications. It is important to recognize and acknowledge his or her accomplishments and legacy, but it is even more important not to lose momentum. As new dean you need to establish your identity, leadership style, and vision for the institution. Loyalties and friendships are not insignificant and to the extent that they are transferable to your efforts to promote the community as a whole, they are assets. In other words, it will sometimes make sense to capitalize on continuity by stressing your connection with the former dean. In other situations, it will be strategically wiser to emphasize the differences in your approaches to the deanship. Knowing which tack to take requires sensitivity and shrewdness, just like most other situations that you confront as dean.

Here are some useful questions to ask yourself as you consider your role as dean:

- To advance your vision of the future of the institution, is it strategically useful in a given situation to emphasize continuity with the former dean's work or to stress ways in which your leadership is different? Or both?
- Have you been as clear as possible about your reasons for doing things differently from your predecessor?
- To what extent does loyalty to the former dean or to the status quo inhibit various constituencies (faculty, staff, administrators, advisory board members) from supporting and helping to advance your vision? How can you address this in a given situation?

CHAPTER NINE

Understanding Institutional Climate

Frank Eyetsemitan
Roger Williams University

> Dean Alexander has recently been hired at Milton College, and among faculty expectations are running high because the place is in a mess. Coming in with dazzling credentials and having previously served as dean at a comparably sized institution, Dean Alexander was expected to move quickly. And quickly he moved. Faculty morale had never been lower in the history of the college. Dean Alexander was acutely aware of this and decided to institute changes right away. With eleven years of experience as a dean under his belt he knows how to do the job, after all! He knows what action to take.
>
> But the actions he has taken can only be likened to a knee-jerk reaction to the situation at hand. In sports metaphor, it resulted from "muscle memory"; more correctly, it came from mental or behavior memory. As a result, there is a problem: what worked at Dean Alexander's previous institution is failing to work at Milton. Although the symptoms appeared the same, the causes and contexts were different. In fact, his actions have worsened matters; it hasn't taken long for the "savior dean" to become a bust!

LEADERSHIP STYLE AND SITUATION

Academic leaders, typically, are expected to lead through collaboration and consultation—at least, this is what is expected from faculty members whom they lead. Collaboration and consultation are viewed as core characteristics, or "core-quisites," of academic leadership within an academic culture. Usually the precept of "shared governance" is understood within this context.

But given that each institution is unique, other demonstrable leadership traits are necessary. A college or university's uniqueness may stem from its past or recent history, tradition, expectations of the faculty, and vision for the future. And for each institution, an effective leadership style has to embrace both the needs of those being led and the needs of the institution at that particular point in time. Therefore, a one-style-fits-all approach to leadership may not cut it; in other words, as the saying goes, a successful leader in wartime may not be successful in peacetime. Success at one college may not make for successful leadership at another; success at one time is no guarantee of success at another.

Leadership is a behavior, measured in terms of actions taken by the leader. But the leader's behavior and the leader's personality and value system cannot be entirely separated. They are intertwined. A leader with an authoritarian personality or mind-set may be challenged by collaborating and consulting with others, even if these are required behaviors on the job. If a conflict should arise between the leader's personality and the behaviors required by the job, the tendency is for the leader to approach the job in ways that are congruent with his or her personality; it is easier to change the demands of the job than to change one's personality. Simply put, it is easier for an academic leader to compromise how the job should be done for the sake of preserving one's personality.

Although the fictional Dean Alexander may have had transferable skills, he needed to understand the underlying issues that were responsible for low morale at his new institution. Dean Alexander chalked up the low morale to raise freezes, as was the case at his previous institution. But the problem at Milton College had a different origin: it had at its core a lack of transparency by the administration. Because low morale was a symptom that was similar to what Dean Alexander had experienced at his previous institution, on assuming his new position he worked assiduously to unfreeze raises in order to improve morale. However, he and the president were in agreement that raises would go to some faculty as increases to base pay, and other faculty would receive additional money only as a bonus. The algorithm for this decision was never shared. Unfortunately this lack of transparency further fueled the gripe of the faculty. In focusing on the symptom and failing to confront its root cause, Dean Alexander added to the problem.

A MODEL FOR LEADER EFFECTIVENESS

The IMPACT leadership theory of Geier, Downey, and Johnson (1980) provides a framework for understanding how a leader's behavioral style should mesh with the organizational climate. The authors identified six behavioral styles and organizational climates that complement each other:

- *Informational style.* This behavioral style is effective in a situation where the leader brings expertise into an area that the organization is lacking in at that particular time, for example, enhancing transparency, diversity, or fundraising.
- *Magnetic style.* The leader brings in energy and optimism in a climate that is marked by despondency, despair, and low morale.

- *Position style.* In a climate of instability the leader emphasizes or exerts his or her position in order to ensure stability. This could happen, for example, in departmental mergers or when a new organizational structure is being created from existing ones.
- *Affiliation style.* The affiliation style works best when anxiety is the order of the day and people want a leader who feels and identifies with their "pain."
- *Coercive style.* This style is needed in a climate of crisis.
- *Tactical style.* In a climate of disorganization the leader provides a purposeful and strategic approach to leadership.

The IMPACT theory, however, has two assumptions: (1) that leaders find a climate that fits their behavioral style, or (2) that leaders change their behavioral style to fit the climate.

The first assumption requires that the leader be selective, patient, or just plain lucky in finding a climate that's a good fit for his or her behavioral style. Dean Alexander might have noticed Milton College's problem with low morale when he interviewed for the job and thought that was a good fit. He lacked due diligence, however, in determining the source of the program. On the other hand, if he knew that the president he would be working for was not transparent in style, he should have evaluated his persuasive skills before accepting the job.

The second assumption requires that the leader be flexible in learning the style that is appropriate and suitable for the organization. The leader also should try to change the followers' perception of the climate in order to align with his or her style. Dean Alexander would have had to earn the trust and respect of the faculty to have a chance at changing the faculty's perception of a lack of transparency. But he needed time to prove himself and to earn trust.

There are many instances in which a leader's vision for the institution is not shared by the faculty. Leaders may have to adopt a behavioral style, such as a lack of transparency, that they hope will help to accomplish this vision, believing that faculty members will come along with time. Perhaps that was the case at Milton College. The question then is, should the leader proceed with his or her behavioral style and vision in the hope that faculty members will come around to accept it? There are two answers: yes, but only if faculty members have a reason for understanding this behavior; and, no, especially if there's a strong belief that transparency (or any other behavior) is a "core-quisite" for effective leadership in academia.

The rush by colleges and universities to adopt a "business model"—another way of suggesting that leadership has to quickly respond to the market in order to survive—creates an interesting scenario in which the concept of shared governance may have to take a backseat. Leadership often argues that with dwindling revenues faculty jobs are in jeopardy; faculty might counter by asking the administration to do more fundraising. Thus, when tradition and culture are pitched against financial survival, which one should prevail? Can both coexist? Culture and tradition are internalized and therefore become part of an individual's perceptual set. As a cultural norm, shared governance becomes part of the perceptual set of faculty members. In trying to change this norm, leaders can run against this deep-seated orientation. Therefore, it behooves leaders to gauge first how strong this norm is in the perceptions of faculty before attempting to institute changes. But, as trust and confidence in the leader grow, such changes to cultural norms and traditions will become easier.

Here are some questions to ponder as you consider your deanship:

- As a new leader do you really know the prevailing needs of your new institution?
- As a leader are you flexible to meet the prevailing needs of your institution?
- How deeply does your faculty care about shared governance and transparency?
- As a leader, what do you do to earn the trust of your faculty colleagues?

Reference

Geier, J. G., Downey, D. E., & Johnson, J. B. (1980). *Climate impact profile.* Minneapolis: Performax Systems International.

CHAPTER TEN

Balancing Management and Leadership

Mary L. Lo Re
Wagner College

Despite your competing responsibilities, you rush in to an 8 a.m. meeting called by a senior administrator only to observe that the person calling the meeting seems to have no agenda and, after a moment, looks around the long conference table, takes a pause, and asks, "So, what's new?" After a moment of silence contemplating what that question really meant, you hear your colleagues either singing their own praises or complaining. An hour later, after listening to endless *uh-hums* from the senior administrator, you find your brain racing with questions such as: What is the point or goal of this meeting? What is being accomplished? Why are no answers or suggestions being given to my colleagues' questions? Is this leadership? Is this the senior administrator's style of management—or should I be concerned about why the "the leader" does not seem to be leading?

Or, in a different scenario, imagine that it's 10 a.m. on the first Tuesday of the month, then this must be "the meeting that drives you crazy," more formally known as the Dean's Council. Once a month you and the dean's other direct reports gather in a library conference room to . . . well it's difficult to say. The group has no formal role in the college's decision-making structure so it never makes any decisions. The purpose may be to act as an advisory group for the dean, but he rarely introduces topics or seeks feedback. The goal may be information sharing among group members, and there is "once around the table to see who has something to share" at the start of the meeting, but most information is shared among participants through electronic means and in smaller, focused meetings. Efforts to discuss pressing issues or resolve common problems are routinely met with silence from the dean and too frequently result in squabbling among the participants. You spend much of the meeting doodling, making to-do lists, and wondering how the dean can justify wasting everyone's time this way month in and month out.

In order to effectively manage a group, every senior academic leader should understand both his management and his leadership style, and work to understand the distinction as expressed by colleagues. Too often we observe leaders not leading, or to the other extreme, not allowing any input. Too often, we see colleagues confuse management with leadership, and we may even commit the same error ourselves. How do you best express yourself as a manager? How do you choose your leadership style? Can you identify when you're managing and when you're leading? Does it matter? Should you use different styles depending on the situation at hand? Which styles do most people prefer in a dean? And what are the behaviors and qualities that campus constituencies want and need in order to willingly and enthusiastically follow senior academic leaders?

From the literature on management, we can borrow a few leadership-style models that can be evaluated and applied to the leadership position of the dean or any academic leader. According to Blake and Mouton's Management Grid (Blake & Mouton, n.d.), people fall into four leadership categories: Country Club, Impoverished, Team, or Authoritarian, depending upon their concerns for people compared to their concerns for tasks. Other models of leadership weigh the benefits of a Democratic versus an Autocratic style of leadership (see Blanchard & Johnson, 1982; Eagly & Johnson, 1990; Hollinger, 2001; Jago & Vroom, 1982; Luthar, 1996). Still others (Bass, 1990; Cherry, n.d.; Homrig, 2001; Riggio, 2009) believe the Transformational style of leadership, supportively challenging people to be creative and innovative, is the style leaders should adopt.

Understanding management and leadership styles and your predominant style will not only identify your strengths and weaknesses as a senior academic leader but also will help you establish your own effective style for goal setting and for motivating, developing, praising, and refocusing faculty members.

MANAGEMENT AND LEADERSHIP STYLES

By applying the construct of Blake and Mouton's Leadership Grid to leaders' concern for people or tasks, a leader can be categorized under one of four leadership styles: Impoverished, Country Club, Authoritarian, or Team Leader.[1]

The figure summarizes the four distinct leadership styles on a two-dimensional graph-like scale where the y-axis measures the concern for people, and the x-axis measures the concern for tasks along a score of 1 to 9.

The most desirable place on the Blake and Mouton Management Grid is to be a Team Leader along the two axes—a score of 9 on tasks and a score of 9 on people. However, this style cannot be effectively achieved unless there is a great degree of trust, understanding, open communication, and respect among the faculty members, other academic leaders, and the dean.

Even if you have successfully reached this level, you should not entirely dismiss the other styles of leadership because certain situations may require the need for one of the other styles to be used. For example, by adopting the Impoverished Leader style, you allow your team to gain self-reliance. If your faculty members are self-motivated, effective, and knowledgeable of

y-axis = *Concern for People*		
9	***Country Club***	***Team***
	• high concern for people • low concern for tasks/productivity • non-confrontational • opposite of Authoritarian style • all too eager to please • keep the peace at all costs Premise: If faculty members are kept happy, then they will produce. Results in: very relaxed atmosphere with minimal output, foresight, and little direction/control from the dean.	• high concern for people • high concern for tasks/productivity • dedicated and inspires dedication • opposite of Improverished style • faculty input required • faculty ownership of tasks/decisions Premise: If faculty members fully invested and needs met, then needs = wants and productivity rises. Results in: team spirit, members and team are effective, reach goals and achieve highest potential.
5	***Impoverished***	***Authoritarian***
	• low concern for people • low concern for tasks/productivity • a minimalist • opposite of Team style • exerts little effort for relationships and tasks; "hands-off" Premise: Faculty members need not be managed; just delegate and allow faculty to do what they wish. Results in: stagnant, unfulfilling, apathetic, possibly unhappy faculty and power struggles.	• low concern for people • high concern for tasks/productivity • all-controlling • opposite of Country Club style • publish-or-perish mentality Premise: Faculty members are a means to an end; only efficiency and productivity matter; leader knows best. Results in: a great deal of production, suppressed conflicts, low morale, minimal communication.
1	1 2 3 4 5	6 7 8 9

x-axis = *Concern for Tasks*

Figure 10.1 Blake and Mouton Management Grid

their tasks, they may prefer this type of laissez-faire approach. By adopting an Authoritarian leadership style, you will instill a sense of discipline in an unmotivated worker. Hollinger (2001) notes that "governance works best when there is some actual governing going on" (p. 30). But, Blanchard and Johnson (1982) caution that very little will be accomplished if managers assume that only their ideas are the best.

Aside from these five classifications of leadership, other studies categorize leadership as either Autocratic or Democratic. In light of Blake and Mouton's leadership styles, the Autocratic style would most approximate the Authoritarian Leader, and the Democratic style would most approximate the Team Leader. But is one style preferred to the other? Many studies, including Eagly and Johnson (1990), Eagly, Makhijani, and Klonsky (1992), and Jago and Vroom (1982), find that subordinates prefer Democratic-style leaders as opposed to Autocratic-style leaders. As argued by Luthar (1996), this may be because: "In North America . . . people live in a democratic society, are embedded in democratic institutions and expect to participate in decisions that may affect them. People cannot put away these values simply because they enter into the workplace, so it follows that they would tend to favorably evaluate democratic managers relative to autocratic managers" (p. 339).

Additionally, Luthar (1996) posits that "democratic managers are perceived to be much higher performers and superior leaders when compared to autocratic managers" (p. 337). Does this imply that a leader should adopt only one style—the Democratic style of leadership? Blanchard and Johnson (1982) argue that if a leader is either results-oriented (i.e., Autocratic) or people-oriented (i.e., Democratic), then he is only "half" a leader; an effective leader needs to be both. "Effective managers manage themselves and the people they work with so that both the organization and the people profit from their presence" (Blanchard & Johnson, 1982, p. 15).

According to Riggio (2009), the most popular theory of leadership today is Transformational Leadership. The term *transformational leader* was introduced by James MacGregor Burns in 1978. The four essential components to Transformational leadership, as cited by Bernard Bass (1990) and others (Homrig, 2001; Riggio, 2009; Cherry, n.d.), are Idealized Influence, Inspirational Motivation, Individualized Consideration, and Intellectual Stimulation. A Transformational Leader must serve as a role model, inspire and motivate followers, show genuine concern for the needs and feelings of followers, and challenge followers to be innovative and creative and to achieve higher performance levels in turn.[2] Homrig (2001) states the premise of this style of leadership:

> People who think on their feet, are creative, come up with the best solutions, don't need to be closely supervised and do what is necessary just because it is

> the right thing to do. All their energy is focused to achieve maximum results with less oversight because the leader has articulated the target goal so everyone understands the direction to move toward. (p. 8)

With this style of leadership, followers integrate the leader's goals and values, and share the same culture and loyalty to the organization.

However, although the strengths of Transformational leaders include consensus and innovation even when the organizations they lead are generally successful, this style also has drawbacks:

- Passion and confidence can be misconstrued for truth and reality.
- Overabundance of energy can "wear out" the followers.
- Focus on the big picture may cause him or her to miss the details.
- Frustration will surface if no transformation is needed in the organization over a prolonged period of time.
- The goal of obtaining consensus for all does not bode well under emergency situations.

Regarding the final point, Homrig (2001) states, "In true consensus, the interests of all are fully considered, but the final decision reached may fail to please everyone completely. The decision is accepted as the best under the circumstances even if it means some individual members' interests may have to be sacrificed" (p. 5).

Staying true to one management and one leadership style at all times may not make you as effective as you could be. You should use different styles depending on the situation at hand. There is no magic formula or matching column listing situations and the best corresponding leadership styles. Homrig notes that "when to make the transition [from one style of leadership to another] is an art borne of experience and education" (2001, p. 2).

Initiating Goal Setting

Although most deans will agree that faculty members have to perform well in three categories—teaching, research, and service—goal setting will differ depending on a faculty member's personal situation, educational attainment, years in the academy, title or position, type of institution, and the current needs of the school and department.

In order to aid the faculty in setting goals, the dean will need to have a vision of the entire school and department so that the individualized faculty goals support the overarching school and departmental goals. As stated by Homrig, "One important characteristic of a great leader is his/her ability to make sound judgments and good decisions based on their internalized vision" (2001, p. 7). The leadership styles best suited to help the faculty in setting goals are the styles that are skewed toward valuing people—Country Club, Team, Democratic, and Transformational.

Motivating Faculty Members

Motivation can be defined as "the process that initiates, guides and maintains goal-oriented behaviors . . . motivation is what causes us to act" (Cherry, n.d., p. 1). So, how do deans or academic leaders motivate faculty members in the three performance areas?

Burns claims that leaders could have the greatest impact in motivating their workers if they appealed to their shared values (a characteristic of a Transformational Leader) and if the leaders could satisfy the workers' higher-order needs, such as aspirations and expectations, and could cultivate a shared sense of what is important, worth doing well, and expending energy on (Riggio, 2009).

Brewer and Brewer (1990) posit that what motivates faculty members in doing research is monetary rewards, tenure, promotion, retention, and research support. Honeycutt, Thelen, and Ford's study (2010) found that financial incentives (in terms of merit pay, awards, travel funding, and grants for databases and software) were the most reported methods that leaders used to motivate research. Less reported methods were course release, collaboration, and faculty mentoring; and least reported methods were threats and penalties (mainly evidenced by Authoritarian or Autocratic styles of leadership).

The most prevalent motivating tools to increase teaching effectiveness are financial incentives (e.g., travel funds to attend teaching conferences, teaching excellence merit awards, and training programs) and nonfinancial incentives of reduced course loads or preparation. Likewise, Honeycutt, Thelen and Ford (2010) found that only a few deans used financial incentives to motivate faculty members to do service and that the predominant motivations employed were cajoling or begging, creating a sense of shared service commitment, and the threat that service is required for tenure and promotion.

In addition to rewards, threats, and penalties, two additional motivators can be used: praise and reprimands.

Even though a dean may observe faculty members who have gone beyond the call of duty, the act of openly expressing approval or admiration may seem awkward or difficult for him or her. Unfortunately, we usually do not take the time to articulate laudatory remarks that we have been thinking. However, faculty members need to feel they are being valued, that their work is worthy of notice; great work should be encouraged, supported, and praised. Even if you are a task-oriented leader, remember, you can catch more flies with honey!

Not all experiences between an academic leader and a faculty member are affirming. Even experienced faculty members may become complacent in their responsibilities in teaching, research, or service. To be effective, these faculty members will need to be refocused. Keep in mind that in employing the Autocratic style or Authoritarian style of leadership, morale may decrease when faculty members feel threatened if they do not perform (Hollinger, 2001). Thus, refocusing faculty members is no simple feat.

If you are stepping into this situation, here is where listening skills are key. The dean needs to listen and find out why this faculty member is no longer being involved. As articulated by Schoorman and Acker-Hocevar (2010), "when faculty input and leadership listening are highly evidenced, given time, faculty will no longer have to be persuaded to participate, the faculty will expect to be involved in the decision-making process" (p. 315).

To avoid this type of situation, you should strive to employ the Transformational style of leadership. Riggio's research (2009) showed that teams led by Transformational-style leaders had higher levels of performance and satisfaction than groups led by other types of leaders. He credits this to the fact that Transformational leaders hold positive expectations for their teams and believe that their teams will do their best. As a result, this type of leader will inspire, empower, and stimulate followers to exceed normal levels of performance; therefore refocusing should become a moot point!

WHY PEOPLE FOLLOW LEADERS

Maxwell (2011) affirms that there are five progressive reasons why people follow leaders. In order for a leader to become successful, with skill and dedication, academic leaders should strive to master these five *P*s:

- *Position*. People follow because they have to.
- *Permission*. People follow because they want to.
- *Production*. People follow because of what the leader has done for the organization.
- *People Development*. People follow because of what the leader has done for them personally.
- *Pinnacle*. People follow because of who the leader is and what he or she represents.

According to Homrig (2001), by mentoring and empowering the faculty, a dean can encourage them to develop their full potential and thereby contribute more capably to their organization.

Employing the Transformational style of leadership may work best in this situation because it has "communal aspects . . . individualized consideration, whereby leaders focus on the mentoring and development of their subordinates and pay attention to their individual needs" (Eagly & Johannesen-Schmidt, 2001, p. 790). In fact, as argued by Blanchard and Johnson (1982), a measurement of a good leader is his or her ability to develop other leaders, not other followers. As Maxwell puts it: "A leader's last value is measured by succession" (2007, p. 223). Additionally, Maxwell philosophizes that "to add growth, lead followers—to multiply, lead leaders!" (p. 220).

According to John Maxwell (2007), the true measure of leadership is influence. So, how do you become a more influential, respected, and successful leader? The literature on leadership styles is full of anecdotes. Here is a list of suggestions.[3]

- Be democratic
- Have a commitment to self-analysis
- Have constant communication; be transparent, consistent, and accountable
- Struggle to get through packed agendas without short-circuiting discussion
- Have a role model or mentor
- Be a role model
- Gain trust, build confidence in people
- Be honest, trustworthy
- Empower people and support risk taking
- State future goals and plan to achieve them
- Be attentive, considerate
- Set high standards but doable expectations
- Make decisions first on areas of consensus and then working (sometimes through a committee) toward compromise on divergent areas
- Action, follow-through, result
- Keep at it! Leadership develops daily, not in a day!

Although the models that examine these leadership principles and anecdotes may change, "leadership principles are timeless!" (Homrig, 2001, p. 1). In the end, as Simplicio (2012) argues, "When all is said and done, it comes down to the reality that leaders who respect and value those who work under them help create a nurturing environment and a culture for success" (p. 110).

Notes

1. If you would like to explore your leadership style beyond reviewing the definitions presented in this chapter, you can test yourself by completing Blake and Mouton's Leadership Questionnaire by visiting http://www.nwlink.com/ ~ donclark/leader/matrix.html
2. Should you want to test yourself as to whether you have these leadership qualities, see Riggio 2009.
3. These suggestions were compiled from the works listed in the References section of this chapter.

References

Bass, B. M. (1990, winter). From transactional to transformational leadership: Learning to share the vision. *Organizational Dynamics*, pp. 19–31.

Blake, R., & Mouton, J. (n.d.). *The Blake and Mouton managerial grid: Leadership self-assessment questionnaire* . Retrieved January 10, 2013, from The Vision Council: http://www.bumc.bu.edu/facdev-medicine/files/2010/10/Leadership-Matrix-Self-Assessment-Questionnaire.pdf

Blanchard, K. H., & Johnson, S. (1982). *The one minute manager*. New York: Blanchard Family.

Brewer, P. D., & Brewer, V. L. (1990). Promoting research productivity in colleges of business. *Journal of Education for Business, 66*(1), 52–57.

Cherry, K. (n.d.). *What is motivation?* Retrieved January 9, 2013, from http://psychology.about.com/od/mindex/g/motivation-definition.htm

Eagly, A. H., & Johannesen-Schmidt, M. C. (2001). The leadership styles of women and men. *Journal of Social Issues, 57*(4), 781–797.

Eagly, A. H., & Johnson, B. T. (1990). Gender and leadership style: A meta-analysis. *Psychological Bulletin, 108*(2), 233–256.

Eagly, A. H., Makhijani, M. G., & Klonsky, B. G. (1992). Gender and the evaluation of leaders: A meta-analysis. *Psychological Bulletin, 111*, 3–22.

Hollinger, D. A. (2001). Faculty governance, the University of California and the future of academe. *Academe, 87*(3), 30–33.

Homrig, M. A. (2001, December 21). *Transformational leadership*. Retrieved January 13, 2013, from http://leadership.au.af.mil/documents/homrig.htm

Honeycutt, E. D., Thelen, S. T., & Ford, J. B. (2010). Evaluating and motivating faculty performance: Challenges for marketing chairs. *Marketing Education Review, 20*(3), 203–214.

Jago, A. G., & Vroom, V. H. (1982). Sex differences in the incidence and evaluation of participative leader behavior. *Journal of Applied Psychology, 67*, 776–783.

Luthar, H. K. (1996). Gender differences in evaluation of performance and leadership ability: Autocratic vs. democratic. *Sex Roles, 35*(5–6), 337–361.

Maxwell, J. C. (2011). *The 5 levels of leadership: Proven steps to maximize your potential*. New York: Grand Central Publishing.

Maxwell, J. C. (2007). *The 21 irrefutable laws of leadership workbook*. Nashville, TN: Thomas Nelson.

Riggio, R. E. (2009, March 24). Are you a transformational leader? *Psychology Today*. Retrieved from http://www.psychologytoday.com/blog/cutting-edge-leadership/200903/are-you-transformational-leader

Schoorman, D., & Acker-Hocevar, M. (2010). Viewing faculty governance within a social justice framework: Struggles and possibilities for democratic decision-making in higher education. *Equity and Excellence in Education, 43*(13), 310–325.

Simplicio, J. (2012). It all starts at the top: Divergent leadership styles and their impact upon a university. *Education, 132*(1), 110–114.

PART TWO

ROLES AND RESPONSIBILITIES OF BEING A DEAN

CHAPTER ELEVEN

The Case for Servant Leadership

Peggy Rosario
Pennsylvania College of Health Sciences

> Regardless of the issue raised, Dean Stewart endeavored to approach all the questions and concerns brought to her office from a servant-leader perspective. Her first e-mail on this particular day was from a faculty member submitting his resignation as chair of the curriculum committee because he was fed up with another committee member he felt was undermining the group process. As an ad hoc member of this committee, Dean Stewart had seen the tension between these two rising. She made a note to call the chair to see what could be worked out. An e-mail from the registrar informed her that fifteen students were on the waitlist for a math course required for first-year students. Dean Stewart sent a note to the chair of the math department asking her to collaborate with math faculty and then get back to her with their ideas for a solution. Next, Dean Stewart saw an e-mail from a faculty member wondering why he hadn't received his stipend for his leadership on a major campus grant application. The last e-mail was from a faculty member providing feedback for the annual academic report, one of many who had done so at the invitation of the dean. And Dean Stewart was happy to see that her desk in-box included an update from her assistant indicating that the six faculty members invited to this week's faculty lunch meeting had confirmed their attendance.

BASIC PRINCIPLES OF SERVANT LEADERSHIP

There are innumerable philosophical, theoretical, and technical approaches to the study of effective leadership, but a philosophical perspective that is of particular value to effective leadership in higher education is Robert Greenleaf's (1970) concept "servant leadership." For Greenleaf servant leadership "begins with the natural feeling that one wants to serve, to serve *first*. Then conscious choice brings one to aspire to lead" (Greenleaf Center for Servant Leadership, 2011). Although it has proven difficult to operationalize for the purposes of systematic measurement, servant leadership continues to draw attention because servant leaders are seen to be capable of providing and encouraging organizational wisdom, applied knowledge, and informed experience in the pursuit of "optimal and altruistic choices" (Barbuto &

Wheeler, 2006). Institutions of higher learning promote bringing knowledge and practice together, making the servant-leader approach consistent with the values espoused by our colleges and universities.

Spears (1998) explored Greenleaf's conception of servant leadership and identified ten key principles of servant leadership (identified in italics) that are illustrated in how Dean Stewart dealt with her in-box messages. The first e-mail enabled Dean Stewart to use three principles of servant leadership—*listening, empathy*, and *healing* (Spears, 1998). Dean Stewart called the committee chair to hear his concerns, understand his perspective, and discuss how they could work out the problem together. She arranged to meet for coffee with the two faculty members who were at odds. Her goal was not to solve their problem but to help them hear each other's concerns in a nonthreatening environment so they could find common ground to continue to work together on the committee. She listened and demonstrated empathy for the committee chair's concerns and encouraged each faculty member to have empathy for the other's perspective.

Although it would have saved a lot of work to just reply to the registrar's e-mail about the class waitlist by telling her to overload the existing class or reminding her that the students can take it next semester, Dean Stewart considered what option best served the institution, by using the servant-leadership principle of *stewardship* (Spears, 1998). She realized that putting the section into overload would not serve either the faculty or the students well, although it would bring in needed income, and that putting the students off until next semester would not help the financial bottom line and some students might take the class elsewhere. Dean Stewart took a collaborative approach by contacting the chair of the math department to discuss what option would provide the most benefit, satisfying student, faculty, and institutional needs. The math department chair in turn collaborated with her faculty to identify the best solution. This created an opportunity for the math department chair to develop leadership skills in identifying a solution with her faculty, both *building community* and illustrating Dean Stewart's commitment to the servant leadership principle of supporting the *growth* of others (Spears, 1998). Dean Stewart also used the servant leadership principle of *persuasion* because she wanted a specific outcome but rather than dictate it, she engaged the faculty in achieving it (Spears, 1998).

The problem with the missing stipend enabled Dean Stewart to accept responsibility for her error and strive to prevent it in the future, both important aspects of servant leadership. When Dean Stewart checked her records, she realized that she had not given her assistant the final list of faculty who were to receive stipends for their work on the grant. Rather than place blame elsewhere, the Dean thanked the faculty member for bringing the matter to her attention (*listening*), accepted responsibility, apologized (*healing*), and explained how the error not only would be corrected but also avoided in the future (*foresight*) (Spears, 1998). She closed by thanking the faculty member for his important contribution to the grant process thus reinforcing his crucial role (*building community*) in the college community (Spears, 1998).

The academic report–writing process provides an excellent example of servant leadership. Sections of the report were written collaboratively by the department chairs with input from their faculty, creating a *growth* opportunity in their development as leaders (Spears, 1998). The dean then asked all faculty members for input into the draft report before finalizing the report that would be released to the college. Dean Stewart used an egalitarian (*community building*) approach to producing the report so that faculty members had a sense of ownership over it and constructive criticism was integrated into the final product (Spears, 1998). She took the time to consider the feedback and the action that would be taken because of it and communicated appreciation to the faculty for being a part of the process. When the report was released, Dean Stewart was also careful to present it as coming from the faculty rather than taking sole credit for it, modeling the humility of servant leadership.

As a servant leader, Dean Stewart scheduled informal lunch gatherings to give faculty members the opportunity to socialize, share ideas, and bring up concerns. She met with faculty members at least weekly, either informally during these lunches or in formal faculty meetings, to help *build community* among the faculty, an important servant-leadership principle (Spears, 1998). The lunchtime discussions also enabled Dean Stewart to achieve two other servant leadership principles. *Awareness* was developed by improving her understanding of herself based on what others shared with her, and she demonstrated *conceptualization* in sharing the big picture of the college in the course of their lunchtime discussions (Spears, 1998). Deans, understandably, become overwhelmed when managing the day-to-day work of the organization. A servant-leadership perspective reminds us of the critical importance of stepping back from routine work in order to examine larger issues in higher education, focus on strategic initiatives, and plan for the future needs of the institution. A servant leader is also committed to bringing many perspectives into the process of conceptualization, a goal that was well-served by Dean Stewart's weekly lunches.

BENEFITS OF SERVANT LEADERSHIP

To be sure, senior academic leaders who practice servant leadership will run into their share of roadblocks and challenges. And at times, servant leadership may be difficult, if not impossible, to enact—some faculty attitudes are intractable, after all, and sometimes collaboration is impossible because of a lack of time or personnel. But servant leadership is beneficial for a number of reasons, both personal and institutional. Servant leadership not only brings satisfaction to the leader and those being served; it also inspires others to adopt a service attitude. Because it is future-oriented, servant leadership facilitates goal attainment for individuals and the entire organization. People working together and supporting each other are able to achieve goals more easily through their combined efforts, which increase productivity. Faculty retention is improved because servant leadership nurtures strong relationships and growth. Faculty members who feel good about helping each other and about others helping them are not likely to want to look for another job. Faculty members also know that their leader truly cares for them and is committed to removing barriers to their work.

To servant leaders, the true joy in leading comes from what is accomplished together, not in individual achievement. To that end, here are three keys to embracing servant leadership:

- The most important key to servant leadership is to commit to service. By making service the number one priority, a leader focuses on working through barriers to enable the success of those being led.
- Another important key is to promote collaboration by finding productive ways to engage employees in working with each other. Looking for ways to allow everyone to use their strengths or grow in a new experience is a priority for servant leaders. In creating an environment where everyone's ideas are valued, better problem solving can occur.
- The final key to servant leadership is to have humility. Giving others credit for their contributions and expressing appreciation are critical.

RESOURCES ABOUT SERVANT LEADERSHIP

Many resources are available to learn more about servant leadership. The original essay on the subject, *The Servant as Leader*, was written in 1970 by Robert Greenleaf. The Greenleaf Center for Servant Leadership website (https://www.greenleaf.org/) is an outstanding resource to read about the leadership philosophy and purchase essays, books, and audio and video materials on the subject. *Servant Leadership for Higher Education* is a book that applies servant leadership principles specifically to higher education (Wheeler, 2012). This outstanding book includes real-life examples of servant leadership in higher education, as well as common questions and myths about servant leadership. A leader interested in exploring how closely one's leadership orientation aligns with a servant leadership approach could benefit from completing an assessment. There are a number of tools to measure servant leadership, including the Servant Leadership Questionnaire (Barbuto & Wheeler, 2006), Servant Leadership Scale (Liden, Wayne, Zhao, & Henderson, 2008), the Servant Leadership Survey (Van Dierendonck & Nuijten, 2010), and the Executive Servant Leadership Scale (Reed, Vidaver-Cohen, & Colwell, 2011). However, the best resource to support an academic leader becoming a servant leader is to have a mentor who is a servant leader so that the individual's behavior can be observed and emulated.

References

Barbuto, J. E., & Wheeler, D. W. (2006). Scale development and construct clarification of servant leadership. *Group & Organization Management, 31*(3), 300–326. doi:10.1177/1059601106287091

Greenleaf, R. (1970). *The servant as leader*. Indianapolis: The Greenleaf Center for Servant Leadership.

Greenleaf Center for Servant Leadership. (2011). *What is servant leadership?* Retrieved from http://www.greenleaf.org/whatissl/

Liden, R. C., Wayne, S. J., Zhao, H., & Henderson, D. (2008). Servant leadership: Development of a multidimensional measure and multi-level assessment. *The Leadership Quarterly, 19*(2): 161–177. doi:10.1016/j.leaqua.2008.01.006

Reed, L. L., Vidaver-Cohen, D., & Colwell, S. R. (2011). A new scale to measure executive servant leadership: development, analysis, and implications for research. *Journal of Business Ethics, 101*(3), 415–434. doi:10.1007/s10551-010-0729-1

Spears, L. C. (1998). *Insights on leadership: Service, stewardship, spirit, and servant leadership*. New York: John Wiley & Sons.

Van Dierendonck, D., & Nuijten, I. (2010). The servant leadership survey: Development and validation of a multidimensional measure. *Journal of Business and Psychology, 26*(3), 249–267. doi:10.1007/s10869-010-9194-1

CHAPTER TWELVE

The Art and Science of Good Decision Making

Mark J. Braun
Gustavus Adolphus College

It is 5 p.m., and as you prepare to wrap things up for the day, you look back on what was accomplished. A curriculum committee meeting, two search candidates, lunch with a donor and the VP of advancement, a meeting with the president and a building committee on architect selection for a renovation, and an honor society induction ceremony in the late afternoon. But as you put your desk in order and look at tomorrow's full calendar, you are aware that you did not make headway on an important decision that needs to be made. A consultant's report has sat languishing for two weeks. It contains a recommendation to merge two academic programs and to combine the resources of the smaller program to strengthen the larger, growing program. True, the targeted small program is not exactly mission central, and enrollment has been dwindling for several years. But it is difficult to suggest merging a program that has been around for decades. You shudder at the thought of angry letters from program alumni. You fret about the impact on current students. You are not even sure how to broach the subject of a program merger. Where do you start? With the faculty in the programs? They may oppose the idea and launch a counterattack before the idea even gets off the ground. Do you take the consultant's report to the faculty curriculum committee? That will almost certainly politicize what you are hoping to be a data-driven discussion about small enrollment and escalating costs. When do you involve admissions and the president? Does the board need to be in the loop? At some point, you will have to get the process rolling. But how? You feel the weight of the decision is on your shoulders. But whose decision is this anyway? The administration's? The faculty's? The board's? Some combination of the above? With a sigh you slip the report back into the bottom of the in-box with the knowledge that you can't hide indefinitely from initiating the process.

Deans are constantly faced with making difficult decisions. Whether they involve personnel, budgets, or programs, every dean must make decisions that will affect how resources are allocated and how processes or procedures are carried out. A dean's decisions may at times be controversial and unpopular. But a dean who fails to engage in timely decision making can bring organizational processes to a standstill, resulting in confusion at best, and, taken to an extreme, can damage morale and negatively affect student learning.

FACTORS LEADING TO POOR DECISIONS

Many factors can lead to bad decision making. In the academic arena, an almost certain fatal flaw is forgetting about shared governance, failing to remember that academic decision making is rarely top-down, but is more often a consultative process.

When people get left out of decision-making processes, the necessary buy-in and required support for exploring a variety of creative solutions is eroded. Another pitfall is when participants in a decision-making process focus primarily on their own wants and forget about the larger picture, often characterized as a greater good. Hidden agendas and control issues can cause important underlying issues to be overlooked or ignored, or they can cause distracting side issues to take center stage. Deans often feel pressure to deal with what can seem like an endless and overwhelming array of problems and sometimes fall into the trap of just wanting to get an issue off of their desk so that they can make forward progress. Moving too quickly to a solution in order to avoid workload pileups or to avoid conflict often leads to insufficient consideration of a variety of possible solutions, as does taking shortcuts in the information-gathering stage. If a decision is seen as leading to "winners" and "losers," those who feel excluded or defeated often engage in behaviors to undermine or reverse the decision. The decision-making arena can indeed be fraught with mistrust and fear, especially when the decision involves the allocation of scarce resources. However, a dean must move forward without leaving important constituencies behind. Good decision making is both a science and an art that can be learned and practiced.

DECISION-MAKING BASICS

There are times when deans must make decisions in relative isolation. Often confidentiality issues constrain deans from consulting as widely as they would like. In addition, there are times when deans must take action in crisis-management mode, and hopefully good planning for such eventualities can reduce both the risk and burden for those involved. The decision making in such cases is always subject to clearer consideration in hindsight, but in the heat of the moment one must simply do one's best to act in a manner that serves both the institution and the individuals involved as well as possible. However, such situations are the exceptions, and most of the time a dean has the luxury of time and can bring multiple perspectives and sufficient data to bear on even the most difficult of situations. There are a number of basic steps in effective decision making. As a dean, you will be well served to be mindful of these tried-and-true process issues when faced with tough decisions:

1. **Engage in consultation**. Faculty and staff generally like to be, and should be, consulted about matters that will affect how they are able to perform their work. Inviting participation is not just good politics; it will help provide the multiple perspectives necessary to making sound decisions. College campuses tend to be especially democratic by nature, and remembering the principles of faculty governance in matters of curriculum and personnel can go a long way toward garnering the necessary buy-in for decisions to produce good results. This is true even where the decision involves matters beyond curricular or personnel issues normally in the purview of the faculty. Remembering the principles of *shared* governance and letting faculty and staff voices be heard normally pays dividends in the long run. Even an unpopular outcome generally gains greater acceptance if people understand how the decision was made and feel that their voices were heard in the process.
2. **Make sure the real issue is understood**. It is vital that participants in the decision-making process understand and agree on the actual matter at hand and don't become sidetracked by red herrings—or worse yet, bury the real issue under a mound of historical prejudices that obfuscate the real problem that must be solved. It is generally worth the extra time to carefully outline what issues are on the table and to seek agreement on the definition of the problem.
3. **Gather information**. Decide on where the needed data reside and how they will be collected, organized, and analyzed. Having a road map to data gathering is critical in order to avoid time-wasting sidetracks. Once the data are gathered, they should be organized and presented in a thorough and thoughtful manner so that all involved in the decision can sift through and analyze the data.
4. **Outline a variety of possible solutions**. This is where brainstorming can be very productive. Before getting too deeply involved in the details of any particular solution or outcome, it is a good idea to engage in some creative thinking about all the options at hand. Such an exercise may lead to surprising positive outcomes that may otherwise have not been adequately considered.
5. **Narrow the list**. Focus the most discussion on those choices or solutions that present the best alternatives for productive outcomes. Again,

make sure that both positives and negatives associated with possible outcomes are explored, but don't become so mired in the negative side effects of an outcome that you fail to take action.

6. **View solutions with a critical eye**. Encourage frank criticism of each possible solution. Let it all hang out. If people see potholes in the road, this is the time to acknowledge them. The freedom to speak frankly and critically can save you from headaches down the road. Almost no decision is without negative consequences, but having a firm handle on both the upsides and the downsides of a possible decision will enable the dean and other decision makers to go forward with confidence.
7. **Make the decision**. Once you have examined the necessary data and explored a variety of solutions, you must ultimately arrive at some decision. This should be done with the knowledge that despite the best of intentions in laying out a consultative process, few decisions are ever made on absolutely complete and full information. But we must act. As Oliver Wendell Holmes wisely said: "Every day we wager our salvation upon some prophesy based upon imperfect knowledge."
8. **Map out the sharing of the decision**. Plan out how the decision will be communicated. Look for ways to tweak or otherwise improve the proposed solution so that the decision has the greatest possible support both internally and externally. Anticipate challenges and sketch out counterarguments that may be necessary to support the outcome. Get the crystal ball out and try to look ahead to backup plans if the decision cannot be implemented as hoped.

Remember the bottom line: decisions that are hurried or made in isolation or without following appropriate consultation and information-gathering procedures can damage an institution's ability to carry out its mission, and they can create mistrust and suspicion. Conversely, decisions that are made in a thoughtful and thorough manner can move the institution forward toward more fully achieving its mission. Be sure to answer these three questions in a decision-making process:

- Who needs to be at the table to make a good decision?
- What decision-making process will we employ?
- How will the final decision be communicated?

CHAPTER THIRTEEN

The Art of Governance

The Dean's Role in Shaping Collective Decisions

Frank Boyd
Illinois Wesleyan University

Consider the "Allegory of the First-Year Seminar." A selective liberal arts campus—we'll call it Valhalla College—with 3,125 students established a required first-year seminar for entering students that replaced the existing composition and rhetoric course. For the first-year seminar, the curriculum committee proposed a revised set of learning goals that emphasized writing competency and critical thinking. The dean received regular updates on the committee's progress and offered full support for the effort, including the resources of an external grant to support faculty and curriculum development. The committee brought the new curriculum to the full faculty for discussion and a vote. During the faculty deliberations, there was debate about the learning goals and a near consensus that the first-year seminar represented an improvement that aligned the university curriculum with the ascendant trend of a writing-across-the-curriculum approach for first-year writing courses.

However, an important aspect of Valhalla's curricular initiative received little scrutiny: how it would be staffed. The seminar would be required for students but not for faculty, which is to say that faculty could choose to teach the seminar as guided by their teaching interests and not by the number of class sections needed for the incoming class. No predetermined staffing plan emerged from the extended discussions, nor did anyone (including the dean) see a contingent staffing plan was needed. Buoyed by grant-funded stipends for curriculum development and workshops, tenure-line faculty fully staffed the program for the first years of its existence.

The program reached its first turning point five years later, when assessment information indicated the need for more harmonized standards for the seminar and for the first time Valhalla's tenure-line faculty failed to provide enough seminars to serve the incoming class. The topic was discussed in the curriculum committee and in the general faculty meeting, where faculty cited a variety of reasons for not participating, among them the pressures of delivering their disciplinary curricula and the freedom of individual faculty members to move in and out of the first-year seminar program. The principle of academic freedom was often cited in these discussions. The dean acted quickly by working with selected departments to identify instructors, and she successfully convinced enough tenure-line faculty to join the effort for that academic year. This challenge became more formidable and the recruiting campaign more intense the following year and even more so in years seven and eight. Faculty began referencing the first-year seminar as an example of the "top-down approach" of the dean, occasionally at first, but soon cited the seminar as the best example of the "micromanagement impulse" of the dean and other academic administrators. Rather than be hoisted by her own petard, the dean abandoned the annual recruiting campaign for tenure-line faculty and began hiring adjuncts to teach the sections left unfilled by the faculty. This, of course, also torpedoed any significant effort to ensure consistent curricular approach in seminar sections across campus.

Colleges and universities face ever-increasing demands for accountability and an emphasis on the ability of academic leaders to make timely decisions. More than ever before, academic deans are expected to include faculty in crafting effective solutions to our institutional challenges and then to collaborate with faculty colleagues on the implementation of these reforms. Briefly stated, we are expected to govern ourselves. But rather than reflecting on our governance practices, our national discourse tends to provide *ostinato* appeals for leadership, calls for securing faculty buy-in, and the need for a campus climate that is "conducive to change." The emphasis on leadership is understandable, yet the success of our efforts ultimately will rest on the ability of academic leaders to enlist faculty in crafting shared governance solutions to our institution's challenges. A focus on governance retains the important role of leadership, emphasizes the behaviors in which effective deans actually engage, and suggests how a broader understanding of governance can be crucial in helping deans and faculty leaders make progress on their shared goals.

Who supports governance as important for our work at colleges and universities? Nearly everyone. The principle of shared governance receives almost universal approval among faculty, administrators, and boards of trustees, as reflected in the joint statement of principles by the American Association of University Professors (AAUP), the American Council on Education (ACE), and the Association of Governing Boards of Universities and Colleges (AGB).[1] The American Conference of Academic Deans (ACAD) also has focused attention on its importance, cosponsoring a governance conference with the AAUP. The formal statements on governance by the AGB, ACE, and AAUP (2006) provide some guidance on the areas for which faculty have primary responsibility (e.g., curriculum; faculty promotion and tenure standards) and the areas in which faculty, administrators, and board members have responsibility (e.g., fiduciary oversight, or strategic direction of the institution). Still, when examining how work proceeds on many of our campuses, these statements can seem oddly divorced from the decision-making processes (or lack thereof) that are actually used by faculty and administrators.

Part of this "governance gap" can be attributed to the overly broad and formalized notions of governance, on the one hand, and our ability to translate these principles into practice, on the other. Governance processes necessarily vary by institution and by issue area, sometimes widely. In Richard Morrill's words, "The notions of advice, consent, consultation, initiation, and decision are the variable forms of shared authority depending on the type of question under consideration" (2007, p. 25). What is needed, then, is a sense of how deans can transmute these general principles into an operational approach for work in the specific context of their campuses. Understanding governance in operational terms is crucial for academic deans whose work is positioned in a complex web of policies, procedures, and relationships that don't easily conform to our formal definitions. Simply stated, governance connotes all the mechanisms of cooperation and decision making for faculty, academic deans, and other constituencies.

Prior to beginning work on any significant campus issue, deans and faculty must have a shared understanding of the process by which they will reach a collective decision. What information is needed to make a decision? When will discussion end? Who decides when it is time to vote, if a vote is needed? Who votes? These are all very basic questions, yet it can be difficult and sometimes impossible for deans and faculty leaders to answer these basic governance questions while simultaneously debating the substantive issues that are under discussion. Also, deans are wise to consider the different venues for discussion and debate, the various constituencies that should be engaged in discussion, the means for ensuring that assessment data inform proposals, the resource implications for different options, and the processes for linking new initiatives or reforms to strategic goals and mission. Effective implementation requires agreement on how to measure the effectiveness of the effort, the means for gathering that information, and which faculty committees are accountable for this work. As stated earlier, leadership is important here, but it is essential that deans and faculty leaders have a shared sense of how they will make these collective choices.

When I have discussed the scenario I opened this chapter with—one that seems very familiar to colleagues from a variety of institutions—it is common for deans and faculty to quickly offer suggestions that would resolve the staffing issue. These reforms generally assume "strong leadership" and bold, unilateral action that would rarely be employed in reality. The more useful lessons from the vignette are found in a review of the governance issues at Valhalla that should have been part of the seminar's origin story. The "Allegory of the First-Year Seminar" rests on one of the most common failures of shared governance in higher education: a neglect of the need to reach a shared governance solution for resources, especially human resources, that will be required to sustain programmatic initiatives. Many programs begin with an enthusiastic and engaged cohort of faculty who are more than willing to forgo other professional opportunities, including teaching another course in their disciplinary specialty, to participate in a new initiative. This is especially true if there are externally funded stipends or other extrinsic rewards for engagement. These programs begin with a surfeit of enthusiasm and widespread agreement on the transformational potential of the work. Faculty engagement can be very high indeed, and sufficient faculty participation is less of a challenge. Inevitably, faculty have other professional opportunities, or they're engaged with artistic or scholarly projects that make it more difficult or costly to participate.[2]

These raise some of the governance questions that Valhalla might have addressed when initiating the seminar, questions that are fungible to many areas of our work. What might have been the responsibilities of the faculty for the staffing of the first-year seminar? And, by extension, what should be the obligations of faculty to cross-disciplinary or campus-wide initiatives? Under what circumstances do the campus-wide initiatives take precedence? The answers to these questions are institution-specific. Lacking a governance rule at Valhalla, the dean engaged in a post hoc, unsystematic negotiation process with department chairs to address the issue. As Gaff (2007) observes, chairs are usually chosen (with good reason) to advocate for department interests, not institution-wide initiatives. In fact, faculty often valorize the ability of a department chair to shield faculty from these types of obligations.

Thus, what was needed at Valhalla, and is needed on most of our campuses, are governance processes for adjudicating between these conflicting obligations. As stated in *Fitting Form to Function*, "In academic institutions the forces of nature are centrifugal; organizational art must be used to create propensities toward coherence" (Weingartner, 2011, p.16). One might modify Weingartner's claim slightly to state that "governance art" is required, which more accurately captures the creativity and imagination that deans must bring to bear in shaping collective decisions. To that end, one might consider the following questions to make the best use of our institutions' governance processes.

- What are the venues and processes for agenda setting? How might a specific issue be privileged in the governance system?
- How can assessment information be introduced into the deliberative process? By whom?
- What are the means by which a governance decision is made? If there is a vote, where does it take place (a committee, the entire faculty, faculty senate, etc.)?
- What are the consequences for inaction?

Notes

1. The joint statement is included along with other governance documents in the AAUP Redbook.
2. Some readers will recognize this as a classic collective action dilemma as described by Olson (1965) and many, many others.

References

American Association of University Professors. (2006). *AAUP policy documents and reports*. Washington, DC: American Association of University Professors.

Gaff, J. G. (2007). What if the faculty really do assume responsibility for the educational program? *Liberal Education, 93*(4), 7–13.

Morrill, R. L. (2007). *Strategic leadership: Integrating strategy and leadership in colleges and universities*. Westport, CT: Praeger.

Olson, M. (1965). *The logic of collective action: Public goods and the theory of groups*. Cambridge, MA: Harvard University Press.

Weingartner, R. (2011). *Fitting form to function: A primer on the organization of academic institutions*. Lanham, MD: Rowman and Littlefield.

CHAPTER FOURTEEN

Building a Shared Vision of Your Institution

Donald Tucker
Malone University

In an all-too-typical scenario that challenges the definitions and limits of shared governance, a member of the board of trustees asks a president to start a dual-enrollment program in his state at the high school where he is superintendent. The president agrees and promises that a program will be operational and established by the start of the next term. The president informs the faculty at the next faculty meeting that he is starting a new program in another state and has tasked the provost with working out the details. The faculty senate expresses concerns about who has authority and jurisdiction over the curriculum. The senate questions the president's authority to start a program without faculty input and oversight. The president says he has every right to start a new program and insists that it be implemented. Besides, the president promised the board member that the high school instructors could teach the same courses that the college faculty members teach on campus. For quality control, they would use the same syllabi, course material, and examinations already written by the home campus faculty. The curriculum committee insists that using high school instructors as adjunct faculty without appropriate terminal degrees to teach the various subjects is unacceptable. The committee balks at the idea of adding a new off-campus program when faculty loads are already high and department personnel are overworked. Furthermore, shared governance includes the principle that the curriculum is owned and managed by the faculty; it does not extend to allowing the president to arbitrarily give out course syllabi, subject content, and examinations to others. The provost expresses concerns about issues of accreditation and state approvals regarding off-campus sites. Academic departments are incensed and cry foul. Faculty members collectively bemoan, "I thought we operated under a principle of shared governance? This is our domain, not yours."

AN UNEASY DEFINITION

Shared governance is one of the dirty terms in higher education, even though everyone uses it and everyone has a different opinion of what it means. In a community that prides itself on evidence and empirical research, a common definition for shared governance does not exist. Who shares and who governs? When there are tensions over control of academic and institutional matters, the first response is often to invoke the concept of shared governance and to demand input and authority for decision making.

The difficulty lies primarily in who has the right to give input and who has the right to make the ultimate decision regarding the issue at hand. It is not always clear where the boundaries lie. Faculty members typically assume that any matter that affects their welfare or role as scholars and teachers, whether programmatic or curricular, and that includes issues such as instructional expenses, student learning, and facilities usage (or myriad other issues) demands their input and agreement. Administrators typically assume that because they are the ones held legally responsible for enforcement of regulatory requirements, budgetary expenditures, acquisition of resources, contracts, strategic planning and other matters, they have the right to make administrative and operational decisions for the best interest of the institution. Trustees are concerned about their role as fiduciaries, policy makers, and public stewards.

The rules have changed, and the current external environment strains against an old-fashioned understanding of patient deliberation, wide input, and incremental change. Because of numerous changes since the 1966 joint statement on governance was developed and offered as a guideline by the American Association of University Professors, the American Council on Education, and the Association of Governing Boards of Universities and Colleges, dozens of new federal regulations and compliance reports require institutions to hire specialized personnel to monitor and respond to constantly changing expectations. The rise of professional associations, labor unions and collective bargaining, increased public scrutiny, changing institutional types, and expanded program delivery methods further complicate the matter of timely input and broad-based control. Public systems, for example, are increasingly affected by legislative decisions, local governments, and diminishing resource pools. Reacting quickly to change limits opportunity for discussion, consensus-building, and buy-in. The party with authority and responsibility for each action is not always evident.

A healthy approach to shared governance requires that administrators have clear understanding of current trends, assumptions, historical practices, and potential emotional responses of different constituencies. Every decision deals not only with written policies but also with "gaps" in those written policies and varying interpretations of those policies. Views of the rights of individual professors may be different from views of the collective rights and responsibilities of departments and the faculty as a whole. Ideological preferences clash with practical realties and economic constraints. Different definitions of "the faculty" and "the administration," differing goals, institutional type, size and organizational complexity must be considered. Perceptions of institutional mission often conflict with changing demographic, legal, political, economic, technological, and cultural environments.

SOME QUESTIONS TO ASK REGARDING YOUR OWN INSTITUTION

It is often helpful to clarify what formal and written documents and guidelines exist. Once this takes place, you can brainstorm ways to respond to unwritten and informal practices. Here are some suggested questions to ask in order to determine how shared governance plays out at your own institution:

- What are the formal (written) policies and established procedures that identify which campus constituencies (students, faculty, dean, provost, president, board, or others) have oversight over various issues? How can we help to clarify these roles and expectations for the various constituencies?
- Who shares where and in what format? What items are open to consideration by which bodies? What assumptions are behind various perceptions of input, influence, control, and decision making? Are there identified limits to who shares and who governs? How much voice should be given to each party: faculty (which ones), administration, staff, students, and others?
- What histories, traditions, unwritten rules, and hidden agendas potentially conflict with written policies or create ambiguities that need to be clarified?
- What new policies, procedures, or venues for deliberation have risen as a result of governance changes, administrative expansion, external pressures, or other factors? Are there policies and procedures that need to be clarified, revised, or updated to reflect these new realities? Are there sacred cows to be considered or removed? How can you maneuver through various forces to effectively implement new strategies?

Finally, here are three concluding thoughts as you work within your own institution's shared governance system:

- *Consider multiple options for input and deliberation.* One of the most important things an administrator can provide is space and opportunity for discussion. Allowing opinions to be expressed, tensions to be released, and concerns to be vented is a first step to shared understanding and agreement. It is equally important to clarify the purpose for this input. What role will discussion serve besides just venting? Clarify how and when input will be used. Broad participation and compromise is important. Not everyone will concur with every final decision, but at least the opportunity to allow voices to be heard reduces the accusation of arbitrariness and the complaint of not considering alternative viewpoints.

- *Review current policies and practices for consistency and clarity*. Pay attention to written handbooks and policy manuals. As much as possible, clarify the criteria and boundaries for decisions that have to be made. Where there are gaps and silences, work with various campus bodies to correct these and to write new guidelines that reflect the institutional mission, goals, and values and that take into consideration limitations of resources (physical, personnel, and financial), important traditions and history, and individual perceptions of roles and responsibilities.
- *Reaffirm common goals and the larger institutional mission*. Think in terms of the whole and how members of the institution can move together into the future. As much as possible, responses to institutional decisions should be based on clear policies, clear structures of authority and control, and reasoned arguments. Practical matters such as the preservation of intellectual freedoms, economic constraints, and legal considerations obviously influence the discussion. But as much as possible, emotional responses have to be tempered when differing ideological preferences are expressed. Expect differences of opinion and reaffirm the value of the input received from others. Maintain an attitude of professionalism and respect. The best use of authority is to never have to use it to force compliance or to trump someone else. When a final decision has to be made, you can proceed confidently knowing that all who have views have been heard and considered. Celebrate victories together and give honor and gratitude where it is due. A healthy dose of humility and understanding can go a long way toward building a shared view of the institution.

CHAPTER FIFTEEN

Managing Change Successfully

Katie Conboy
Simmons College

A regional accrediting organization submits its ten-year report to Nochange College. The report includes both surprise and concern that the college's current self-study makes no mention of changes in general education, even though the college identified the need for general education reform ten years ago in its last self-study. The accreditors indicate that they will return in just two years, and that changes must be accomplished by then. A new dean faces the daunting challenge of leading this conversation and transformation.

The president of the faculty senate declares that there is no need for change in general education: "If we hadn't told them we intended to do this ten years ago, they would never have asked for reform. That was the bad idea of a previous dean. And we shouldn't now bow to external pressures." Several junior faculty members press for a more "global" program of study, noting that the current general education program focuses entirely on Western civilization. Another group suggests maximizing the Western focus with a writing-intensive "great books" program. Yet another faction protests that they "were never trained to teach subjects other than their areas of expertise, and that they certainly cannot teach writing." All faculty seem to agree that they are stretched to the limit under heavy teaching loads, demanding research projects, and extensive advising responsibilities; and they simply don't have time to think about change.

This scenario, at least in its broad outlines, must be familiar to provosts, deans, and other senior academic leaders who spend a good deal of time thinking about change. Although the question—to change or not to change anything in a college or a curriculum—might once have seemed to allow for a process-oriented exploration and an ultimate decision, the academic environment today faces myriad internal and external pressures to enact change. At almost any institution of higher learning, one will find leaders preoccupied with a range of common questions: Does our institution have a specific kind of identity, and are there programmatic or other pressures in maintaining that identity? Should we add or subtract programs to emphasize one aspect of our identity (the arts, business, communication, or science)?

How responsive should our offerings be to market demand? Do our academic programs require physical and technological resources to support them, and are we competitive with other colleges and universities that offer these programs? Even if we explore no changes in our programmatic offerings, should we consider new ways of doing our work? Can we gain efficiencies from technology? Should we explore additional modes of delivery for courses or programs of study? Will our faculty need support and assistance? And who gets to make such decisions, prioritize them, and lead the process of change that follows?

Indeed, today academic leaders do not so much ask *whether* they must change but *how* they can best manage the pace of change in their institutions. Institutions of higher learning tend to be self-preserving, filled with guardians of tradition, and one might argue that the resistance to change has created quality and value in higher education—and that the structure of the academy has changed little over centuries because it supports this quality. A leader—like the dean at Nochange College—may be willing to take on change but may find less appetite for transformation in groups he or she must work with to effect it. Using data or external pressures, matching changes and processes to a strategic plan, and communicating unambiguously and in thorough detail can help to build coalitions that understand the need for change and that make change successful.[1]

USING DATA OR EXTERNAL PRESSURES

Often, pressure for change comes from the external environment—from accrediting bodies or legislatures, or from deliberate comparisons to peer and aspirant institutions. But the structure of academic institutions may work against using such data effectively in an area such as the curriculum, which is at the heart of a university's mission and at the center of its financial investments. A long history of shared governance gives the faculty a rightful place in conversations about the curriculum. And yet, the faculty may be unprepared for such conversations. The dean's job is to facilitate such preparation with appropriate data and to set the tone for collaboration between faculty and administration.

The faculty is highly trained in a wide number of disciplines and is prepared to teach within them. Yet any faculty member also will agree that the body of knowledge in her field has become unmanageable. Organic chemists, for example, confess that although they know the general outlines of a physical chemist's work, they may understand very little about the specialized research undertaken by a departmental colleague. This gap is amplified when scientists talk across scientific disciplines, or humanists across humanities disciplines, and amplified again when faculty members in the humanities, arts, sciences, social sciences, business, and other disciplines seek a common understanding of what makes an educated person. This is the problem confronted by the new dean at Nochange College, who must engage the faculty in the construction of a new general education curriculum.

So, the dean's task is to bring a perspective that is broader than any disciplinary one to bear on the "change question" at hand—and to cultivate a broader perspective in others. The first step is to make clear the nature of the external pressure for change. Is accreditation actually in danger? What are the potential consequences of not acting? Is enrollment declining? Are peer institutions marketing their programs differently or offering more attractive courses or experiences? Are you in a proactive or a reactive position? Be clear about why you are asking people to invest time and energy in this change.

As a second step, share information with everyone who might be affected by an anticipated change. Make the accreditation report available; produce an account that helps nonexperts understand the enrollment concerns; create a website that shows comparisons of your marketing materials with those of other colleges and universities. Reproduce some research or other information related to the topic at hand. In the area of general education, for example, this might mean sharing publications or conference programs that are effective in establishing the national or international context. In addition, it might be helpful to create a library of materials that make available widely accepted standards—such as the studies of high-impact practices published by the Association of American Colleges and Universities.[2]

Simultaneously, a dean should identify a group of interested faculty members and administrators and begin assisting them as they gain expertise related to the desired change. Treat them as a kind of steering committee for the process. Offer to send a group or several groups to conferences related to the issue at hand. Suggest after the conference that the attendees identify a few of the speakers who might be appropriate experts to invite to campus to engage their colleagues. Have the faculty members act as hosts to these experts when they visit. Keep inching the conversation forward by presenting the options that have emerged, eliminating some that will not work at your institution, and zeroing in on the ideas that have gained momentum and support.

MATCHING CHANGES AND PROCESSES TO A STRATEGIC PLAN

Inching the conversation forward implies that you have a destination. And although you may not know exactly what the end result will look like, you do need a time line and a goal. The dean at Nochange College knows that the accrediting organization will return in two years, and he can "back into" a time line for exploration, assessment, review, sharing, and decision making. The changes he must effect go to the mission of the curriculum: in this hypothetical case, what the common requirements are for every student. Whether the changes you contemplate are mission-oriented, operational, structural, technological, or strategic, they should optimally be connected to a broader institutional plan. If your institution has not decided collectively that it intends to move in particular directions, your attempts to make change may seem arbitrary, and you will struggle to get buy-in. But a broader plan—especially one that has included input from all campus constituencies—is a license for change.

If the plan includes, for example, enrollment growth, you probably will have responsibility for recommending where that growth should happen, what curricular changes need to happen to effect it, and what resources the change will require. If the plan indicates that the institution will seek new modes of delivering a current program, or will develop a new program offered in a new modality, you will need to set a schedule and a deadline by which the team exploring and reviewing the options must make a recommendation. If the plan suggests the institution must alter policies and procedures related to faculty work, the faculty or its representatives must be engaged in the process of recommending, implementing, and evaluating such changes.

Of course, some changes are unexpected and will not derive specifically from institutional planning—and they may be urgent or important. But if a change can be linked to the shared values and aspirations of those who work within an institution and the time line can emerge from the specific goals of a strategic plan, the change leader is likely to find collaborators and the change is likely to be sustained.

COMMUNICATING

A dean is likely to determine the project time line and any parts of the exploration and implementation plan that can be ascertained from the outset. An important piece of this work is a communication plan that involves all interested parties. You should take some time at the start of the project to identify the individuals and groups that should be kept informed, and to build in some feedback sessions along the way. At some institutions, this is relatively straightforward: the faculty wants to be informed and general faculty channels can be used. At other institutions, specific governance groups will expect to be provided with information tailored to their needs.

One way to simplify communication even in a complex environment is to maintain an electronic site for the time line, the names of steering committee members or other participants in the process, all the most important reference documents, and a record of key decisions. Then the communications can reference specific elements of the project for a particular group, but can direct everyone toward the same electronic "reference room."

Communicate more than you need to. Remind people regularly of the importance of the project, and where you are in the time line. Celebrate milestones along the way if there are such highpoints. Include references to the strategic plan or other governing documents if this helps to lend credence to the project. And be sure to give credit to the faculty members or administrators who have brought leadership to the effort.

Change in organizations is inevitable, and deans must often lead, manage, or participate in accomplishing change efforts that involve educational mission, curriculum, faculty work, enrollment modifications, internationalization, and technology.

As you undertake the changes needed in your own college or university, keep these three important ideas in mind:

- Use external pressures like accreditation or enrollment trends to help build your team's expertise, and use published materials on change management to structure the process.
- Be mindful of your institution's strategic plan and find ways to match the change processes to time lines in the plan.
- Develop a system for communicating regularly about the changes and the anticipated time lines.

But remember that even excellent processes will not substitute for knowing the culture of your institution and for ensuring that you attend to what matters most to those in your particular milieu. In at least this way, the adage *plus ça change, plus c'est la même chose* turns out to be true: "the more things change, the more they stay the same."

Notes

1. Change expert John Kotter identifies eight steps to accomplishing change that work just as well in academic organizations as in others: (1) create a sense of urgency, (2) pull together the guiding team, (3) develop the change vision and strategy, (4) communicate for understanding and buy-in, (5) empower others to act, (6) produce short-term wins, (7) don't let up, (8) create a new culture. http://hbr.org/web/tools/2008/12/kotter-8-steps
2. George Kuh's publication, *High-Impact Educational Practices: What They Are, Who Has Access to Them, and Why They Matter*, is available as a download at http://www.neasc.org/downloads/aacu_high_impact_2008_final.pdf

CHAPTER SIXTEEN

Understanding the Game and Your Team

Succeeding at Working with Campus Constituencies

Kent A. Eaton
McPherson College

Imagine that with a strong commitment to building trust you move into a new position. Having been successful in fully integrating into a college or university before, you know the importance of networking with all internal and external constituents in your first weeks. Like a good coach, you have a realistic scouting report. You are committed to an all-out effort to show that you will be a good steward of institutional resources as you work to advance the mission of the college. This honeymoon period is productive. You know the importance of asking for the trust of others and then demonstrating tangible ways that you merit and plan to keep their trust. Yet as you talk with your new colleagues, it is becoming clear that the essential relational norm at your institution is to not trust anyone, especially between faculty and the administration.

To make matters worse, imagine that you are the first dean hired from outside the college faculty, and one of the few people in this small-town college who did not graduate from the college or have membership in the sponsoring denomination or local community organizations. Staff and faculty routinely represent the second or third generation who have labored selflessly to ensure the college's survival in an increasingly difficult market. You are on the outside looking in. In hiring you, the college recognized the need for outside energy and perspective and diverse experiences, but now the reality that you represent change, unwelcome change, has become apparent. Even though survival depends on immediate transformation, continual resistance persists, because positive change is really hard work. To complicate matters, the most intense and ongoing opposition comes through passive-aggressive behaviors; you are perplexed in dealing with detractors and obstructionists due to their stealth maneuvering.

The journey toward becoming a successful dean is comparable to coaching a high-level sports team, although winning or losing is more ambiguous as a dean. In both vocations, however, one manages resources, talent, egos, and even the future welfare and reputation of the institution. In both careers, coaches and deans work with people who have a much greater mastery of their specific disciplines than we ever will. Ours is a world of high performers and, as a result, presents significant challenges. So no matter how ideal our post, we acknowledge that managing challenging people always will be the case as we work with those who are hired to help us push limits. After all, have not most of us been labeled "challenging" at one time or another? There always will be those encounters resulting from personality differences or disagreements over resource distribution among departments. However, challenges become significant and grow into genuine critical situations when trust begins to erode. Mistrust in a system is like rust. If left unchecked, the corrosion eventually ruins everything.

The normal stages in the cycle that accompany change are not unlike the stages of grief. These consist of feelings of loss, doubt, and anxiety before arriving at the positive phases of discovery, understanding, and integration. Yet these stages do not correspond to what you, as the dean in the imaginary scenario, are experiencing. In moments of despair, you do not observe the staff and faculty ever advancing beyond doubt, bitterness, cynicism, and resistance. In meeting with individuals and small groups in this ongoing quest to build trust, you grasp that one of the principal problems is that in this closed system, the informal organizational chart, if one existed, would have shown that the genuine locus of power was determined by the relational web, not the formal job positions. You have a complicated roster; members of your team play positions that are different from those to which they had been assigned.

Furthermore, the informal network has been allowed to routinely trump the formal organizational structure, thereby determining the most important decisions in the life of the college. The exercise of power and how decisions were made seemed imperceptible until one knew the ancestry, familial relationships, and longevity at the college. How can you possibly achieve the needed change to move the college from survival mode into a season of vibrancy when you will always be external to the nexus of power?

One must first commit to take on the challenge—the game schedule does not change just because the coach finds it to be too demanding in midseason. It is too late to call in an intentional interim dean to set things right. In this situation, if we were to deny the problems or conform to the general dysfunctional patterns that seem normative inside this system, we would become a part of the problem and even begin to act and think like those whose passive-aggressive behavior is the source of the problem. This is crucial; we become a part of the solution or we become a part of the problem. Likewise, failing to address systemic dysfunction means that we will never be able to hire the high-performing diverse individuals who will ultimately lift the institutional perspective from the trenches to the horizon. Having made this commitment to engage and work toward the future health of the college, how can we turn the ship and get it on course?

The approach I suggest starts with the reality that as deans, we need an appropriate distance from the problem so that we are not burned out and consumed by those who seem to be our saboteurs. Still using the coaching metaphor, we need to learn to observe the game from the bench, never as player-coach, so that we can direct others with the proper perspective. How do we step back to gain perspective and some degree of objectivity? We acknowledge that if we are constantly labeled outsiders, we can use that to our advantage. This can be accomplished by making an intentional effort to step outside the relational web using the basic tools of an ethnographer. By asking questions regarding behaviors and customs, observing patterns of interaction, listening intently, and taking field notes or journaling about our initial theories on how things work, we gain perspective and a growing understanding of the formal and informal factors that define how insiders relate and work. These observations even help us know with whom to start a conversation when we find ourselves in a challenging situation. We ask for clarification about what is taking place and seek explanations for inappropriate behaviors, rather than returning hostility with hostility.

Second, we need to regularly and deliberately extricate ourselves from the group and the developing narrative of our institution and find a place of objectivity. Our identity becomes that of an observer so that these potential feelings of anger, judgment, and betrayal, which skew good decision making, are put aside. Thankfully, these same feelings relinquish control over us. As deans, we learn to see the world through the eyes of the other and locate their concerns and web of meaning. If we make no conscious and deliberate decision to put on the hat of the ethnographer, the alternative is to remain embedded in the unfolding drama. We allow others to have power over us as they loom larger than life. We find ourselves reduced to using moral categories to identify the others as wrong, bad, or even evil in their intentions. Just as deplorable, we so question our competence in the face of the opposition that we find ourselves frozen by fear and unable to make good decisions; our perspective has become twisted. It becomes hard not to retaliate with childish efforts to get even.

With a basic understanding of the cherished values as well as individual and corporate behavioral expectations, a dean begins to appropriately challenge the status quo even though, in many institutions, we perpetuate a version of the story of "The Emperor's New Clothes" through our fear of acknowledging reality. Yet, understanding our context more fully, along with a commitment to enact needed changes for which we were hired, we challenge any and all institutional myths so that our work might prosper. Astute deans are "myth busters."

Even as we become adept in the art of confrontation, there are those who never learn to abandon passive-aggressive behaviors. No matter our level of patience, in order for the work of the college to prosper, some people must be let go, even though as concerned deans we find it difficult to admit that some situations and relationships cannot be remedied. Perhaps with years of therapy we might get to the crux of the matter with individuals, but obviously that is a luxury beyond our reach.

When someone refuses to follow legitimate leadership for whatever reason and persists in activities that undermine authority, we must have honest and frank discussions about appropriate behavior. This is complicated by the long careers many faculty have at small colleges. For some people in a small college, their work and identity become so intertwined that they have little understanding of self apart from their role at the college. Yet all decisions must be based on what best serves the college, not those individuals who work there. Deans have to keep focus on institutional welfare above all else, even acknowledging that there will come a time when the college or university needs new academic leadership. Let us remember that if we believe unrealistically that change will happen and allow someone to continue to work at our institution, the longer we refuse to face reality the more difficult the removal of the person from the institution becomes, and the greater the damage in the meantime.

As change begins to take place, there will also be those who are not unrelenting obstructionists. However, they cannot seem to move from the discomfort of change to the discovery stage and possibly be energized by new perspectives and possibilities. The wise dean quickly engages these individuals with honesty and compassion. If early retirement is not possible, phased or otherwise, then discussions of where to relocate these faculty members so that they can contribute through a new, less demanding position are appropriate. Certainly, this kind of discussion is complicated because of tenure. Yet deans need to have the courage to insist that it may well be time for a faculty member to relinquish being department chair or serving on select committees.

Perhaps the most difficult group of people to manage consists of those who do not fully support our administration, yet who serve the school in such a way that they are not easily or immediately replaceable. They have a contribution to make, but it is clear that they are not entirely willing to trust our leadership. In their view, because too much change has taken place and they felt threatened, or because we bruised their ego or stepped on their toes, they view us with pause and a degree of skepticism. They see progress, they sense that the train is leaving the station, but they just cannot bring themselves to get on board. In cases such as these, we benefit from being as transparent and detailed as possible about behavioral and performance expectations. In our communication, we must state which behaviors will be tolerated moving forward and which ones will lead to discipline or termination. The point is to be as specific as possible so that inappropriate behavior is clearly defined.

Rather than allow the challenging people we manage to rob us of the energy and joy needed to stay in the game, let us step outside the dysfunction to remind ourselves that it really may not be about us, our lack of leadership experience or ability, or dispositions. Wisely understanding the game and our team, we can lead our squad toward better systemic well-being by focusing on three actions:

- Understand the unique features of our institutional culture; make no assumptions.
- Keep an objective distance from the unique micro culture as we progressively test our theories regarding behaviors and processes with insiders.
- Resolutely insist that programming and staffing decisions be based on expected contributions to greater student success.

CHAPTER SEVENTEEN

The Dean's Role in Mentoring

Adelia Williams
Pace University

Newly hired as an assistant professor at Western State University, Lisa Ross, a poetry scholar and poet herself, meets with her dean of arts and sciences, Sally Verdicchio, a biologist, for assistance in selecting an appropriate mentor. Professor Ross has published one peer-reviewed article on a contemporary American poet and several book review essays and has contributed poems to several collections of poetry as well as to two poetry journals. She has been accepted into a prestigious summer writing program, where she intends to complete her first collection of poetry. Ross has met with her department chair, who has agreed to serve as her departmental mentor. Although Western State does not have a formal mentoring program, both Professor Ross and her chair agree that a productive mentoring relationship with a colleague outside the department would be of great benefit because it will allow her to speak more candidly about concerns and problems, and to share issues that may be viewed unfavorably by those within her own department.

Dean Verdicchio recognizes the importance of mentoring as a result of her own experiences at Western. As a young scholar and new parent when she first arrived at Western twenty-five years earlier, her department chair assigned her a four-day-per-week teaching schedule. He also explained to her then that scholarly output had recently become a necessity at Western, although he himself had never published, because that had not been an expectation when he was hired. The young professor Verdicchio struggled to balance parenting with research; she was tenured but not initially promoted to associate professor.

Verdicchio's experience in administration was significantly better. The dean who preceded her recognized Verdicchio's promise. She took her under her wing when she became chair of biology, then promoted her to associate dean for the sciences. During this period, Verdicchio was funded to attend numerous conferences and workshops on academic leadership. Her dean provided her with increasingly demanding areas of responsibility and met with her frequently to discuss the challenges she was facing.

With these two distinctly different mentoring experiences from her own career, Dean Verdicchio deliberated on who might best help Professor Ross to maintain her scholarly pursuits and help her position her creative works to the university committee on tenure and promotion. The committee has not always recognized the scholarly import of the artistic output in a faculty member's dossier. After careful consideration, she proposes three individuals: the female chair of the visual arts department, an art historian; a senior male faculty member in the philosophy department who writes on esthetics; a recently tenured and promoted female faculty member in the music department who is a composer.

Each potential mentor offers a unique and useful set of benefits for Professor Ross. The chair of the visual arts department has successfully mentored two of her working artist faculty members through the promotion and tenure process. The philosopher is among the most esteemed and trusted members of the faculty and has served regularly on the tenure and promotion committee. The composer was recently promoted to associate professor and has two young children, as does Professor Ross. Each mentor, does, of course, also offer potential challenges, which senior academic leaders need to consider before pairing people up. For example, the chair of the visual arts department is already engaged in a position that requires a significant institutional time commitment, and her authority as a department chair complicates a mentor-mentee relationship

It appears that Dean Verdicchio has provided Lisa Ross with a thoughtfully considered array of mentor choices. She has selected experienced, respected, and knowledgeable members of the faculty who have demonstrated a commitment to institutional excellence. Each potential mentor brings a distinct and valuable set of experiences, including balancing personal and professional responsibilities, that will meaningfully help Professor Ross move successfully through the early years of her career at Western. She will clearly benefit from a mentoring relationship with any one of them.

The investment in a new faculty member, often following a lengthy and costly search, is significant for the institution. Mentoring is an essential component of a comprehensive approach to retaining junior faculty and assisting him or her in having a successful academic career as an active, valued, and engaged member of the community. It is highly beneficial for junior faculty to work with a mentor who will help guide his or her research, academic path, and career decisions, and deans play a crucial role in ensuring that these mentoring relationships get established.

Many institutions have formal mentoring programs with clearly spelled-out guidelines that typically include the purposes and goals of the program, strategies for establishing a strong mentor-mentee relationship, as well as the roles and responsibilities of the mentor and the mentee. Often a time frame is established for the mentoring relationship. Michigan State University's Resources on Faculty Mentoring is a comprehensive site that provides extensive information on faculty mentoring at MSU and elsewhere in the United States and Canada. In addition to a vast array of general resources, the site offers information on mentoring female and minority faculty. The USC Marshall School of Business website includes an exemplary faculty manual and guidelines for mentoring, and the Northern Illinois New Faculty Mentoring website includes The Ten Commandments of Mentoring.[1]

Deans should ensure that mentors receive training for this new responsibility, and at many institutions deans convene a conversation with mentors to help them become effective mentors. The mentor serves as an invaluable source of information and problem solving, as well as an advocate for the mentee, acting, if necessary, as a mediator in delicate situations or as a sounding board for ideas, concerns, and questions. Through e-mail, telephone, arranged and casual meetings, lunch or coffee, the mentor acts as a cheerleader, encouraging the new faculty member to explore the institution's resources and opportunities. The mentor recognizes the challenges faced by a new faculty member, including transitioning from graduate student to faculty member, working with undergraduates, teaching large sections, balancing professional and personal demands, adjusting to campus life, and acclimating to campus culture.

The mentor should provide information about services and resources on campus, familiarize the junior colleague with faculty governance, university and departmental structure, and most important the particulars and idiosyncrasies of the institution's promotion and tenure process. Contingency measures should be made clear in cases where the mentor-mentee relationship is not developing in a positive way.

Best practices include

- offering clear and constructive feedback in a supportive and professional manner;
- helping the mentee prioritize tasks, assignments, responsibilities, and time management;
- providing sensitive and thoughtful guidance rather than evaluation and assessment of performance;
- socializing and integrating new faculty into the institution's environment; and
- discussing short- and long-term professional goals.

"Worst practices" include

- "spying" on or competing with the mentee;
- viewing the mentee as a source of information useful to the mentor; and
- considering the mentoring assignment as a burden or added task.

Productive mentoring results in important benefits to the mentor as well, including having the satisfaction of contributing positively to the institution's and discipline's future and experiencing both personal and professional enrichment and satisfaction. Mentoring can be beneficial to senior faculty seeking new and worthy ways to engage with the university community and to share their deep knowledge and insights. It is important that deans articulate these multiple benefits to the campus, because some faculty may consider serving as a mentor just one more task, and fail to see the ways it can be beneficial to them.

Less common on university campuses are mentoring and leadership programs for new deans and assistant and associate deans. Baptism by fire is the customary approach at many institutions. If a formal program does not exist on campus, the new dean would do well to identify an appropriate mentor from the ranks above him or her, and to establish a relationship based on the best practices noted above. New deans should be encouraged to attend workshops and conferences sponsored by such higher education organizations as the American Conference of Academic Deans (ACAD), the Council of Academic Deans from Research Institutions (CADREI), the Council of Colleges of Arts and Sciences (CCAS), and the Association of American Colleges and Universities (AAC&U), as well as be given opportunities for professional development programs such as the Harvard Institutes for Higher Education and Higher Education Resources Services (HERS), which targets female leaders in higher education.[2]

In addition to establishing formal or informal mentoring programs, deans can greatly assist in facilitating positive experiences for faculty by offering opportunities for them to expand their university network by meeting one another socially and to share research and scholarly interests. The more opportunities junior faculty have to interact productively with their peers, and to meet regularly with their chairs and colleagues, the more likely it is that they will acculturate positively to the campus environment.

Deans must be sure to clarify and communicate expectations in teaching, scholarship, and service to junior faculty. They should be mindful of their faculty's strengths and weaknesses, serving, on the one hand, as talent scouts on the lookout for potential rising stars, chairs, and administrators, and, on the other hand, paying attention to those who might be falling through the cracks or struggling. They should enlist their chairs in these important activities.

When contemplating a mentoring strategy for a junior faculty member or a newly appointed administrator, the following steps are recommended:

- Provide opportunities, formal or informal, for identifying an appropriate mentor or mentors, and ensure regular means of communication.
- Make certain that expectations are clear and understood.
- Encourage and support professional development through academic and professional associations and organizations.

Notes

1. Michigan State's Resources on Faculty Mentoring: http://fod.msu.edu/resources-faculty-mentoring; USC Marshall School of Business: http://info.marshall.usc.edu/faculty/mentoring/Pages/default.aspx; Northern Illinois New Faculty Mentoring: http://www.niu.edu/facdev/services/newfacmentoring.shtml
2. American Conference of Academic Deans: www.acad-edu.org; Council of Academic Deans from Research Institutions: www.cadrei.org/; Council of Colleges of Arts and Sciences: www.ccas.net; Association of American Colleges and Universities: www.aacu.org; Harvard Institutes for Higher Education: http://www.gse.harvard.edu/ppe/programs/higher-education/index.html; Higher Education Resources Services: www.hersnet.org

CHAPTER EIGHTEEN

Academic Deans Balancing Professional and Personal Lives

Reframing Balance, Momentum, and Flow

Lisa Ijiri
Lesley University

> A new dean awakens at 4 a.m. with a start—she is anxious and uncertain but energized and alert. Was the e-mail sent or just drafted? Did the meeting with the attorney ever get scheduled? Did the permission form make it to the lunch bag? Is today the classroom visit? She showers while her mind races down a crowded narrow path that weaves through faculty, family, and a gauntlet of meetings and e-mails. If she squints, she can spot a moment of quiet and balance within an otherwise continuous flow of needs and activity.

Senior academic leaders are not the folks who spring to mind when we say "work-life balance." Quite the contrary, we weight the scale with unsustainable hours, late-night e-mails, departmental "immunity to change" (Kegan & Lahey, 2009), and blurry Aprils, and consider them as givens. As for the seemingly lighter *personal life* side, we might thumb the scale with reflections on mattering and bronzed quality family time or simply bracket the entire scale with our knowledge of the mercifully short 4.5 average years of service. Additional atmospheric pressure burdens both sides of the scale when we assume our deanships in midcareer, where we are especially vulnerable to the dense personal and professional weights that can sandwich us. Squeezed on all sides, we might care for aging parents while mothering disaffected teens, and mentor junior faculty while working to motivate tenured curmudgeons. Little wonder that the very word *balance* can itself trigger either anxious regret or resigned acceptance of a zero-sum defeat.

But three perspectives on professional and personal balance offer insights that can change the way we view balance and define work-life challenges:

(1) a developmental perspective from adult learning theory, (2) a momentum accounting and behavioral economics perspective, and (3) an organizational learning perspective featuring progress and presence as metrics for balance. These frameworks won't add hours to our days or remove e-mails from our in-boxes, but they can help us redefine balance and redesign work-life parts into more coherent wholes.

REFRAMING BALANCE FROM SUBJECT TO OBJECT

Dean pathways often naturally evoke a developmental framework, regardless of our academic disciplines. For many of us, our evolution from faculty to administrator brought forward visible, irreversible changes—keenly present and known to us even when or if we later return to our academic homes. We may even have felt guided on a seemingly inherent schedule that was both compelling and in retrospect, predictable. We communicated well, we facilitated forward progress, we chaired committees, we became deans. And now in these roles, we may feel our cognitive frames expanding, multiplying, and becoming more complex. Indeed, by navigating the structural, human resource, political, and symbolic frames that Bolman and Deal (2008) describe, we are able, over time, to become more distanced from that which previously was our "hidden curriculum" (Kegan, 1998) and recognize our movement toward a qualitatively different intellectual stage. In short, as chaotic, or frustrating, or challenging as our dean experiences might seem, they provide the raw experimentation necessary for pulling us forward to a higher developmental plateau.

Meanwhile, in our personal lives, Kegan might observe that we are simultaneously building our capacities as we navigate the increasing complexities of later adulthood. Where once it was sufficient to manage ourselves and perhaps a partner, mid- and later-career positions often mean concurrent mid- and later-life challenges. The emotional and pragmatic turmoil of aging relatives or our own health difficulties can create new tensions at the same time that our formerly little children (and their proverbial little problems) begin to more fully assert themselves. Contradictions abound in both home and work environments: a carpool can create both relief and chaos, or a department might require simultaneous nurturing and neglect. The boundaries are increasingly permeable as delayed memos or neglected family matters collide with college attorney's missives or cries for greater transparency. But from the perspective of adult developmental theory, such increased challenge is at the heart of the creative tension necessary to push and pull us into a new level of cognitive complexity—the critical experiences required for reframing balance.

In Kegan's language, such challenges help us become able to take as object that which previously held us subject—when, for example, we move away from a stage of merely fulfilling our roles and living our relationships to a stage when we are able to stand outside these roles, hold them as object, and recognize their influence within a larger system. In fact, the wonderful treasure of this enhanced perspective can be both an outcome *of* and a survival strategy *for* our deaning experiences. In this way, this developmental progress can serve to lighten both sides of the scale. By reframing the goal of balance as something different and distinctive (certainly beyond mere time distribution), such movement and distance is, in fact, remarkably liberating.

MOTIVATION AND MOMENTUM

A dean's work-life balance can also free itself from the more traditional accounting frame of debits and credits by considering a third entry. This proposed framework for viewing personal-professional balance integrates insights gained in the liminal space of my own personal-professional threshold. As a child of the academy, I grew up as a faculty brat of the Carnegie Mellon University's Tepper Business School (then GSIA, the Graduate School of Industrial Administration). My father's fields were accounting and economics, and his seminal works envisioned triple-entry bookkeeping—a means of recognizing the rate of change as equally significant to the traditional debits and credits on a balance sheet. He called it "momentum accounting" (Ijiri, 1986), and although he never applied the principle of triple-entry bookkeeping to academic administration, such concepts quite elegantly help us understand work-life balance by focusing on the frequently overlooked factor: rate of change.

Within the triple-entry bookkeeping framework, the rate of change in a dean's work-life balance would be expected to directly affect the perception and experience of balance—regardless of how the hours are distributed. Thus, if we have already been accustomed to a skewed distribution of professional time, our "frog in a pot" might not notice the temperature rising as e-mails continue into the evening hours and meetings creep onto the schedule earlier and later. On the other hand, if we have stepped into administration from a flexible schedule designed to sit neatly around school bus pickups or dedicated writing days, a shift in hours can trigger harsh growing pains. In either case, intentionally considering the rate of change tipping our scale can help to manage our current state, construct compensatory strategies, and notice the "pot" surrounding us.

A fourth factor beyond the debit, credit, and rate of change is equally important to note. Call it *motivation accounting*—this window through behavioral economics seeks to understand the *source* of the rate of change. Is the increase in hours due to the extrinsic demands of the job alone, or to the intrinsic motivation of a nagging internal push? The honest answer to this question can bring the goals of balance into clearer focus. Psychologists like Edward Deci (1996) or popular authors like Daniel Pink (2009) might argue that deans who are driven by intrinsic motivational factors can withstand higher rates of change in work-life balance.

Pink's three components of motivation—autonomy, mastery, and purpose—include two that are inherently connected to our roles either positively or negatively. Purpose, for example, is for many of us integrally linked with the mission of higher education and our institutions—offering built-in callings to serve our students and the public good. Autonomy, in contrast, is notoriously elusive, and in fact we deans are often mocked for our rather limited autonomy—think proverbial cats and curriculum reform or the limits imposed by typical budgetary constraints. Mastery remains the tie-breaker for assessing our motivation accounting. Certainly, experience influences "mastery," and we are grateful that lessons learned at least allow us to be more "masterful" deans over time.

Equally important influencers on mastery and motivation are our social networks and peers. Peer support through ACAD, regional think tanks, the American Association of Colleges and Universities, the Council of Independent Colleges, the Professional and Organizational Development Network, and other bodies give space and strategies for useful toolkit development. Notably, they also provide the raw camaraderie required to renew motivation in even the most skilled. Indeed, nothing is so restorative and motivating as the rejuvenation from a valued colleague. Such increased motivation not only lightens one's work but can also legitimately be credited as part of "life" accounting.

FLOW, PROGRESS, AND PRESENCE

A final perspective on balance takes insights from psychologist Csikszentmihalyi's (1990) work on optimal challenge, or "flow," and connects this with the plethora of airport management writings on progress and organizational learning. In his now classic description, flow, or maximally engaging in activities until we become lost in our actions, Csikszentmihalyi describes a series of points where our increasing capacities and abilities intersect with the rising challenges along an axis of perfect balance. In other words, we are most likely to be in a flow state when the work is Goldilocks's "just right"—not too easy, and not too hard, given our developing abilities. This reconceptualization of balance—not of work-life balance on a scale with discrete sides, but of work-life balance as optimization of both the work *and* life flow experiences—is a powerful reframing to consider.

Similarly, Senge, Scharmer, Jaworski, and Flowers (2004) write about achieving deeper levels of learning through mental models that reorient parts into whole systems thinking. *Presence* situates us in a temporarily suspended state where our keen awareness of our own "presence" can help bring clarity and depth to the ways in which our work-life systems fluidly shape each other. Rather than focusing on the parts of our separate and separable work-life components, we can learn to see the interrelated nature of the parts. Examples from typical dean moments of presence include responding to meeting dynamics with a willingness to step away from the meeting itself and to observe the often-ignored influences that affect a meeting, such as time on the academic term, the space in which the meeting occurs, and campus politics. Indeed, if we let go of desired specific outcomes and instead remain open to observing the outcome of an experimental question or a lightly tapped rudder, we can be served equally well whether in a chair's meetings or a family dinner. Through this increased depth and distance, and our movement back and forth, we can increase our time in these otherwise elusively balanced flow states.

If one were to visualize "balance," and especially the challenge of maintaining balance, one might imagine a young bicyclist. Tentative and jerky initially, the rider would eventually succeed after internalizing the need for forward movement as essential for maintaining balance. Teresa Amabile's *The Progress Principle* (2011) builds on Csikszentmihalyi's classic methodology and identifies visible small progress as critically important for momentum and job success, similar to our bicyclist. The researchers found job satisfaction highest when employees had experienced some form of progress in their immediate daily experience. Putting their findings together with the original studies on flow, one can envision an environment with visible forward progress (even small progress) and just-right optimally challenging experiences to provide the ideal movement necessary for our balancing deans.

Amabile (2011) also identified characteristics of individuals or events that contribute to, or impede, this progress. Labeling the former as catalysts/nurturers and the latter as inhibitors/toxins, the author advises that our ability to identify these influencers can affect our sense of progress. A colleague and I once took this notion one step further, wondering whether the visual image of our week would foreshadow balance if we were to color-code our Outlook calendars (catalyzing = pink; inhibiting = green). Better yet, would we be able to influence the balance with some strategic scheduling? A green week? Add a pink meeting to increase the opportunity for a small win → progress → balance.

Deans who find themselves in particularly unbalanced work-life cycles might benefit from several quick suggestions:

- Allow both sides of your scale to be lightened by embracing the impact of the difficulty of the work—let your scale become the object of your reflections rather than controlling you as the subject.
- If you must consider work and life as discrete categories to tally and debit, consider explicitly the rate of change you experienced in your distribution of time and the motivations that influence your perception of that rate.
- Remember that balance is best achieved in the context of forward progress—schedule your days intentionally to include meetings with nurturers and catalyzing forces that will likely contribute to progress, no matter how small.

A college president once advised that balance in academic administration requires the following minimum commitment to 100 percent nonwork time: one day a week, one weekend a month, one week a year. This seems like a useful concrete guide. But within the remaining work and pseudo-work time, the extent to which we experience and notice the above three perspectives—developmental growth, internally motivated and controlled rates of change, and forward progress, presence, and flow—can significantly affect how we perceive and evaluate our work-life balance. Wishing you well as you read this and wondering whether you considered the time spent to be part of your "work" or "life" time!

References

Amabile, T. (2011). *The progress principle: Using small wins to ignite joy, engagement, and creativity at work*. New York: Perseus Distribution Services.

Bolman, L. G., & Deal, T. E. (2008). *Reframing organizations: Artistry, choice, and leadership*, (4th ed.). San Francisco: Jossey-Bass.

Csikszentmihalyi, M. (1990). *Flow: The psychology of optimal experience*. New York: Harper and Row.

Deci, E. (1996). *Why we do what we do: Understanding self-motivation*. New York: Penguin Books.

Ijiri, Y. (1986). A framework for triple-entry bookkeeping. *The Accounting Review, 61*(4), 745–759.

Kegan, R. (1998). *In over our heads: The mental demands of modern life*. Cambridge, MA: Harvard University Press.

Kegan, R., & Lahey, L. (2009). *Immunity to change: How to overcome it and unlock the potential in yourself and your organization*. Boston: Harvard Business Review Press.

Pink, D. (2009). *Drive: The surprising truth about what motivates us*. New York: Riverhead.

Senge, P., Scharmer, C., Jaworski, J., & Flowers, B. (2004). *Presence: Human purpose and the field of the future*. New York: Currency Books.

CHAPTER NINETEEN

Modeling Active Engagement in Teaching and Research

James R. Valadez
University of Redlands

Ed Wilson approached the dean's office with some trepidation. Ed was concerned that he was not able to focus attention on his scholarship during his first year as a professor. He struggled establishing himself in the classroom, and he was feeling a great deal of anxiety about his upcoming second-year review. Ed felt confident about getting his teaching in order, but he was really looking toward the dean to provide guidance for helping him establish his research program. Ed believed in his research but was uncertain what his senior colleagues felt about his work, and he was unclear about how to articulate a research agenda. His first attempt to publish in a top-tier journal failed, so at this point he was in a quandary about where he should attempt to publish his work and which conferences he should attend. His senior colleagues were providing mixed messages, and he was hoping to get definitive information from the dean.

This scenario highlights a typical interaction a dean may have with an early-career tenure-track faculty member. Relatively inexperienced faculty members are often perplexed about establishing themselves in the department, and they periodically receive conflicting information about expectations for tenure. Taking time to advise and mentor early-career faculty is a critically important function of the dean and is crucial for effective faculty development and for helping faculty untangle the tenure process. This type of meeting typically occurs at the end of the academic year and provides an opportunity for the dean to give feedback to the faculty member and to help clarify expectations. These meetings can also be used as a time for the faculty to present concerns regarding impending probationary and tenure reviews.

Yet, expecting a dean to provide faculty with relevant feedback and guidance presumes that the dean has enough knowledge and experience in the teaching and research spheres to do so. Generally speaking, deans attain their positions because they have distinguished themselves in the academy with their well-established skills as teachers and strong bona fides as researchers. It is essential for the dean to speak from a position of experience or authority in a given field in order to provide credible advice to faculty members who are relying on the dean's wisdom to point them in the right direction.

There is, of course, a delicate balance here. Colleges and universities have expectations that a dean should be an academic leader, but the dean's attention and focus is diverted toward administrative functions, including budgeting, accreditation, and accountability concerns and personnel issues. As the leader of the school or college, the dean usually sits on the president's cabinet, where he is a contributor to the development of overall university policy, is called on to make clear and purposeful decisions, and, above all, is expected to be a strong advocate for the faculty in decisions that affect their futures. Because of these administrative demands, the dean may be tempted to lessen or even abandon his participation in scholarly pursuits. A complete shift toward administrative duties, however, lessens the effectiveness of the dean as an academic leader.

The wide variety of roles played by the dean limits her ability to accomplish what should be a primary task: modeling the life of an academic, being an academic leader. In particular, this means remaining active in the classroom and participating in some form of scholarly activity. Because deans must fulfill the responsibility as the unit's academic leader, it is incumbent on the dean to define and articulate expectations regarding teaching and scholarship. Part of the challenge for any scholar is to define the balance between teaching and research (very often seen as two competing forces). This, of course, varies depending on the particular classification of the institution. It is important for the dean to provide clear guidance to the faculty in this regard, and it may be necessary for the dean to help professors address subpar student evaluations of classroom performance or to question them about their lack of scholarly productivity. These suggestions from the dean, however, have more impact if the faculty recognizes that the dean speaks with authority on these issues. It is perhaps axiomatic that the dean should not expect the faculty to do what the dean would not expect of herself. If the dean does not teach or remain active in research, then how does the she justifiably exhort the professor to publish more articles or improve his or her teaching?

Because the dean's role is to support the work of the faculty, it is crucial for the dean to find the time to keep his hand in the research world, and when possible to take a turn in the classroom. The administrative demands may preclude the dean from spending the amount of time he once did in the lab or studio or in front of students teaching. A reasonable expectation is that participation in research will evolve into other forms of scholarship and teaching. Although the frequency of courses taught or articles published may decrease, active engagement will remain a priority to the dean. What is important here is not necessarily the form of the scholarly work but that the participation in scholarship and teaching remain consistent and rigorous.

Bowker (1980) explains that deans who keep up with their own disciplines are in a better position to understand and support research and teaching activity within their units. Deans who continue their involvement in research activities, teach an occasional course, devote time to professional reading, and remain engaged in scholarly activities engender the respect of faculty and maintain their recognition as a scholar. Deans who remain active in scholarly activity are in a much more favorable position to give knowledgeable feedback and career advice. Hough (1987) argues that overloading the dean with administrative duties distances her from the authentic activities of an academic, and serves to set up barriers between administrative and professorial life. Without the time devoted to pursuing scholarly activities, the dean assumes a persona that is barely recognizable as an academic.

To be sure, deans find it difficult to allocate time to teaching and writing. Sensing (2003) observes that deans, regardless of discipline, are finding it virtually impossible to perform their administrative duties while simultaneously teaching a class or attempting to participate in research endeavors. But unfortunately for the institution, deans who abandon their academic roles and devote themselves entirely to administrative functions are not as effective as academic leaders; they also may not be as effective in their work with faculty.

Deans can be particularly helpful to faculty as they provide guidance on how to juggle the various demands of an academic position. Sensing (2003) suggests that a primary responsibility of the dean is to guide faculty toward resolution of this dilemma. The dean's personal commitment to teaching and research is critical in professional development of faculty and is particularly crucial for the success of early-career professors. The primary responsibility of deans is to oversee the teaching and research functions of their institutions and to facilitate the attainment of that mission. To do this effectively necessitates the dean's ongoing participation in teaching and research.

Here are nine recommendations for providing academic leadership:

- Deans must not abandon their personal scholarly agendas. Finding dedicated time to write, at least weekly, should remain part of the dean's academic life.
- Deans can show their commitment to scholarly pursuits by promoting and encouraging faculty to participate in research through granting release time for research-active individuals.
- Recognize, publicize, and honor significant faculty research through publicity or awards; promote book signing events, departmental research symposia, or "brown bag" research presentations to help develop the intellectual climate of the unit.

- Deans should help faculty seek funding sources to assist individuals who need resources to pursue their research.
- Deans can remain active in research through their participation in student research, scholarship, and creative activity. At doctorate-granting institutions, this may mean joining dissertation committees or sponsoring student research projects.
- Deans show commitment to research by supporting student and faculty travel to professional conferences.
- It is important for the dean to maintain presence and participation at local, national, and international conferences. The dean should continue to present, organize symposia, or participate as a panel discussant or chair at conferences.
- It is important for deans to remain active in the classroom. This may mean teaching a seminar or course when feasible or accepting invitations to give guest lectures.
- Deans must promote and articulate the importance of teaching at the institution. Deans demonstrate this by encouraging teaching excellence, visiting classrooms and providing feedback to colleagues, and engaging in conversations about teaching methods.

References

Bowker, L. H. (1980). *Process and structures: The institutional context of teaching sociology*. Washington, DC: American Sociological Association.

Hough, J. C. (1987). The dean's responsibility for faculty research. *Theological Education, 24*, 102–114.

Sensing, T. (2003). The role of the academic dean. *Restoration Quarterly, 45* (First Quarter), 5–9.

CHAPTER TWENTY

Staying Alive in Teaching and Research

David W. Chapman
Samford University

Confronted with relentless administrative demands, from budget management to mediating faculty conflicts, many deans begin to lose touch with the classroom and with their academic disciplines. I remember hearing a senior administrator early in my career dismiss faculty concerns about workload with the statement, "They're only teaching three courses. What are they doing with all their time?" I thought to myself that this must be coming from a person who hadn't taught a course in a long time. All professors know that the demands of teaching far exceed the actual hours in the classroom. Preparing lectures, responding to the needs of individual students, and grading assignments have always made teaching a demanding profession. And the digital age seems to have increased those demands. Students wonder why the e-mail they sent at one o'clock in the morning didn't get an immediate response. Faculty who teach hybrid or "flipped" classrooms still have the same demands in regard to course content, but they must adapt to new means of delivery and create classroom environments that engage students in the learning process. The archetypal gray-bearded professor stumbling through yellowed notes is a relic of the past.

The expectations for teachers to be both academically prepared and pedagogically sound have never been higher. By continuing to teach on a regular basis, even if it's only one course a year, the dean not only maintains a symbolic connection to the faculty but has a "reality check" in regard to the actual demands of teaching. Staying in the classroom also means that the dean has a personal connection with the student body. No amount of reading or hearing conference presentations about "Millennials" can substitute for actual encounters with students in a learning environment. Deans who teach have a deep intuitive sense of the challenges presented by each new generation of college students. When faced with problems such as falling student retention, administrators who are out of touch with students are often tempted to hire a new staff person to focus on retention issues or invest in expensive software to track student progress. However, research on retention has shown that a student's relationship with the faculty is one of the most important factors in the decision to stay at the university. Deans who remain active in teaching are more likely to focus on this critical factor in hiring decisions and in encouraging faculty mentoring programs.

This is particularly important when dealing with vice presidents—who typically don't teach—on a variety of issues. I have heard CFOs proclaim that our goal should be 100 percent retention. Contact with actual students reminds the dean that not all students should be retained. Some are unprepared for the demands of college. Some are dealing with personal and emotional issues that make it impossible to function in the classroom. Some may have selected a school that just isn't right for their academic or social needs. Sometimes leaving the university, temporarily or permanently, is in the best interests of the student.

The CFO's concern is, and should be, for the financial health of the institution, but the deans must help shape those financial decisions. There is often pressure, for example, to increase class size, reduce or eliminate programs, or hire more contingent faculty. At the same time, the college or university may want to allot new resources to celebrity faculty, student amenities, or other programs that don't enhance the quality of the average student's educational experience. The teaching dean is the best advocate for the needs of the faculty and the students.

As these examples show, maintaining a presence in the classroom can help the dean be more effective as an administrator. Conversely, strong administrative skills can help the dean manage teaching responsibilities in the most efficient manner. Here are some tips for making teaching work even with a busy schedule.

GET HELP

As the dean, you have access to many resources, and you should take advantage of them. If you are at a university with graduate programs in your field, this might include having graduate students handle some of the routine grading associated with the course and placing course materials online. Use your administrative assistant to screen students who really need your assistance from those who just need to be told to go back and look at the syllabus to see when the assignment is due.

Getting help also may include inviting other faculty to guest lecture in the course. This has the dual benefit of exposing students to another point of view and building your relationship with that faculty member. Such lectures needn't always be replacements for when you must be gone, but opportunities for you to hear from your own faculty. And, by the way, I am using *lecture* here loosely to refer to any form of faculty-student interaction. It could be a class discussion or a problem-based learning activity. I regularly schedule a debate with another professor as a way of highlighting one of the crucial controversies in the field. Hearing from other faculty can not only expand your knowledge of the field but also suggest new pedagogical approaches.

HAVE A BACK-UP PLAN

Some last-minute conflicts will inevitably arise, when the president calls an emergency meeting or you have to deal with a faculty member meltdown. Some deans have a team teacher that can be called on at the last minute to cover for them. You may want to have an online assignment that can be substituted for a classroom meeting. Of course, students won't complain if you cancel classes, but you are setting a bad precedent for other teachers. I recall walking past a classroom a few years ago and hearing one of our professors tell the students, "I'm canceling class on Tuesday [the last class day before the Thanksgiving break], but don't let the dean know. He insists that we meet that day." By the time he returned to his office, he had an e-mail waiting from me, questioning both his undermining of school policy and the way he was setting up the dean as the "bad cop." If the dean is going to insist policies be followed, he or she must set the proper example.

DON'T OVERDO IT

It's really not as important how much the dean teaches as long as it's done on a regular basis. Many of us got our start in higher education because we love being in the classroom. The best part of my day is nearly always the time I spend with students, but teaching can be a way of hiding from other responsibilities. I've known a few deans who spent so much time with students that they weren't sufficiently available to the faculty.

Teaching

Soon after I became dean, I was begged to teach a course that was my area of special expertise and which I thoroughly enjoyed teaching. The person making the request was quite adamant that no one could teach the course the way I could. Despite the appeal to my vanity, I refused to take the course because I knew it would harm my effectiveness as an administrator. In some cases, *not* teaching is the best way you can serve your faculty.

In some colleges and universities, it may be impossible for the dean to teach on a regular basis. In those cases, the dean should look for other ways to maintain some contact with the students. Guest lecturing is a little bit like grandparenting—all of the fun and none of the responsibility—but it at least puts the dean into a classroom setting. Student advisory boards are another means of giving deans regular contact with students. However, nothing really replaces the actual experience of having full responsibility for preparing and delivering a course.

Research

Just as teaching regularly keeps the dean aware of changes in teaching methods and student expectations, the dean also needs to be aware of the changing nature of faculty research. The economics of publishing have made it significantly more difficult and time consuming for faculty to get their work into print. At the same time, the digital revolution has opened up new possibilities for online publication. Deans who are personally involved in research and publication are more likely to understand the changing dynamics of academic publication and to be advocates for faculty scholarship.

Having a dean who understands and values faculty research is increasingly important. It is perhaps understandable that the general public scoffs at academic research that seems obtuse or arcane, but it is inexcusable when academic administrators take the same tone. After all, despite the public's dismissiveness of much faculty research, they constantly turn to academic experts to explain Syrian politics, mental illness, or global warming. Admittedly, not every article or experiment will change the profession, but intellectual history—from Boolean algebra to the Doppler effect—is filled with examples of research that may have seemed trivial in its original manifestation but later proved to have far-reaching consequences.

Still, the demands of the dean's position inevitably change the amount and nature of the research being pursued. As a result, most deans engage in at least three kinds of scholarly activity:

- *Disciplinary Research.* Although most deans must scale back on their research agendas, they should continue to look for opportunities to engage in scholarly activity. This might include having a supervisory role in the laboratory, serving as a reviewer or a consultant on a project, writing invited chapters in edited collections, writing book reviews, serving on grant review teams, attending professional conferences, making conference presentations, or serving as a leader in disciplinary organizations. Many deans continue to publish articles or even books by taking advantage of downtime in the administrative cycle. Whatever form it takes, it is important for deans to lead by example through their participation in scholarly activities.

- *Professional Research.* Deans often find an outlet for their creative energies through publications intended for other academic administrators. Many times these articles grow out of the daily concerns faced by a dean. For example, when I observed that faculty often seemed greatly interested in inviting speakers to campus but were often disappointed in the attendance at these lectures, I wrote an article for *The Chronicle of Higher Education* on the essential requirements for successful academic lectures. Similarly, the selection of our university in the top twenty-five of a new ranking system led to an article, "Hitting the Rankings Jackpot," for *Change* magazine. The dean is often in a unique position, with both teaching and administrative experience, to speak to issues in higher education.
- *Public Relations.* Although public relations materials aren't, strictly speaking, academic research, they are based on an understanding of the academic foundations of the university. As more university presidents and other administrators are selected from outside the academic ranks, the dean plays an increasingly important role as the "voice" of the faculty. The dean has the opportunity through newsletters, alumni magazines, speeches and introductions, and even op-ed pieces in the local newspaper to challenge false assumptions about education and speak up for the important role the academy plays in creating a better society. At a time when the public is concerned about violence on campuses, the value of a liberal education, access to higher education, abuses in college athletics, and a host of other topics, the dean plays a vital role in providing informed commentary on subjects of intense public debate.

Of course, the other reason that a dean needs to maintain credibility as a teacher and researcher is that he or she may want to eventually return to the classroom. The former dean of my school spent ten years happily teaching and mentoring students after leaving the dean's office before he retired. Obviously, the dean who has continued to teach and publish regularly will have an easier transition back to faculty responsibilities. And there are times when having the alternative of returning to the faculty also provides a dean a measure of protection if he or she were ever asked to carry out illegal or unethical practices. This does happen on rare occasion, and the dean who is able join the faculty has some measure of professional security.

Finally, remaining active in teaching and research is a constant reminder of what is most important about the academic mission. Most deans were originally attracted to teaching because they had a deep love of their discipline and a desire to share what they knew with others. Being present as minds are opened to new ideas, as students discover their vocations, and as they grapple with life's enduring questions is one of the highest pursuits I can imagine. When facing the tedium of routine reports or the murkiness of university politics, it is my interactions with students and my scholarly activities that renew my energies and make all the administrative work seem worthwhile.

Here are four questions to consider as you work to remain connected to your teaching and research:

- What are ways that you can remain connected to and interact with students outside of teaching a class?
- Given the scope of your work, how could your administrative and public relations work be developed into an active scholarly agenda?
- How might the academic calendar allow you to be engaged in classes or research opportunities from the dean's office, and what resources would you need to stay engaged in teaching and research?
- What contribution does your institution need you to make to teaching? To research?

CHAPTER TWENTY-ONE

Self-Assessment, or How Do I Know If I Am Succeeding?

Kathleen Murray
Macalester College

> You're sitting in your office following a contentious meeting with faculty (doesn't matter whether it was a department, school, or college meeting). After having spent months working on a difficult issue, a faculty committee that you chair just presented its recommendation for action, with your full and publicly acknowledged support, only to have the larger body of faculty reject it. How do you try to understand your role as an academic leader in this situation? How do you assess your own work?

Being a successful academic leader requires a self-reflective personality, a willingness and, even better, a drive to reflect often and honestly about how things are going and the role you are playing in those successes, failures, and stalemates. Many of us, most naturally and immediately, focus on our shortcomings and blame ourselves whenever things seem to go awry. That compulsion will lead to a very lonely and unfulfilling (and probably short) period of service as dean. Most of us, at some point in time, are guided by a healthy sense of self-preservation and look for others with whom to share the blame. If carried too far and broadcast to a wider audience, that approach will alienate the people we need on our team in order to be successful in our work. There are still others for whom "full speed ahead" is the operative mantra. These people do not have (or take) the time for self-reflection and risk rushing into dangerous territory and needlessly repeating past missteps. There is ample room for all these approaches in the work that we do; finding the right balance among them is a critical element of our self-assessment efforts.

Perhaps the most important self-assessment we undertake happens before even moving into a leadership role. Do you want to take on this role? What are your motivations for doing this work? What do you anticipate will be your most helpful personal strengths and your most challenging personal weaknesses? Weaknesses do not necessarily disqualify you for the position; some you will need to address, whereas others you can simply acknowledge. What do you think you will find most rewarding about the work? Are you ready for your relationships with your colleagues to change? It's very difficult for any of us to anticipate all the changes that a move into administration will bring, but we need to allow ourselves (or push ourselves, depending on personal temperament) to reflect on what it might be like.

A lot of "what the job might be like" will depend on your relationships with others. The single most important relationship will be with the person to whom you report; without the support of that person, it is extremely difficult to do your work. Part of your self-assessment of your readiness to become a leader must be careful reflection on your relationship with that person. You don't need to be best friends; in fact, it is probably better if you are not. You don't need to agree on everything, but if you see the world through completely different lenses, it is going to be a rocky working relationship. Even if you are very skilled in your own self-assessments, you need someone with whom you can test your results; a skilled boss can be invaluable when it comes to reality checks.

Once you decide to accept a leadership assignment, it will be critical to make sure that there is a carefully developed position description for that role. Without that, you don't have a clear set of expectations against which to measure yourself. Particularly important are descriptors of the scope of responsibility, reporting relationships, and lines and limits of authority. Make sure the position description looks realistic; if it looks like too much before you even begin the job, it is certain to be completely unmanageable once you get into the trenches.

Now you're on board—you're a senior academic leader. How might you begin to figure out what others expect of you? What hopes and fears do they hold as they get to know you in this new role? What do they want or need that isn't in the position description?

There can be an overwhelming amount of work in these positions, so much that it seems advisable to hole up in one's office with the door shut, focused on getting the work done. No amount of self-assessment will be enough if that is your approach, because you will never really know if what you are doing is what those you are serving need you to be doing. Successful self-assessment requires you to be out talking to the people who rely on your leadership, figuring out how you can be most helpful to them.

That does not mean that your job limits you to responding to the goals of others. You do not get to set all the goals, but you do get to set some, especially if you are, or as you become, genuinely familiar with the culture of the institution or unit that you lead. Your self-assessment needs to include reflection on the balance you achieve between responding to goals set by others and developing and advocating for your own goals. Your goals need to be realistic, given the set of circumstances within which you must work. If the faculty with whom you are working are accustomed to trying out new ideas on a regular basis, you will be able to maneuver more quickly than with a faculty that is entrenched and satisfied with the status quo. The better you are at assessing the feasibility of your own goals, the more believable you will be as you talk with others about how realistic their goals might be. The process of assessing your success with one goal should include expectations for improvement within the next goal.

Most of the goals we set in our various leadership roles require weeks, if not months or years, to fulfill. How do you measure progress against these long-term goals? Some system of keeping daily notes can be very valuable as you look back over the various stages of your work. (Those same notes can be very valuable if you are challenged about your memory of a particular decision or, worse yet, if you find yourself in legal proceedings.) One possibility is to keep regular "day notes," brief notes about each entry in your official appointment calendar, that remind you about important decisions made, discussions held, and questions yet to be answered. Those notes can be archived by you and your assistant for quick searches either by meeting time, names of participants, or keywords related to projects. Pulling up the details of a particular project over time can allow you to see progress where you thought none had been made or remind you of next steps to be taken if things have stalled.

As we think about the role our assistants play, we should acknowledge how valuable they can be in our process of self-assessment. A good assistant knows what is going on in your daily schedule, both the routine meetings and the special events. A really good assistant can be a sounding board as you think about how things are going. He or she knows the characters involved, knows the other pressures on your time and energy, and may have a more realistic set of expectations for what can be accomplished. We have to be careful not to place too much pressure on the folks in this assistant role, but they will appreciate being included in the thinking about what is going well and what might benefit from additional attention.

Of course, these are people that you also need to evaluate in the context of your supervisory role, so they might be hesitant to offer any genuine critique of your work. You can learn a lot, however, if during the course of your regular evaluations of staff, you ask what they might need from you in order for their work to be more efficient and enjoyable. If this process works well over time, you will be able to develop a sense of the role you played in some of their successes and challenges.

At this point, we have added third parties into your process of self-assessment. Used thoughtfully, these critiques can provide valuable information. But, like the course evaluations with which so many of us are familiar, it is not enough just to read the praise, the criticisms, and the suggestions that the course would be better if you simply did not assign so much reading; we have to consider which views are valid and bring the issues full circle by considering what to do in response. Some of us focus exclusively on the negative comments. If that is you, it might help to tally negative versus positive comments to force yourself to look at the positive side as well. Some of us blame faulty evaluation methodology or misunderstanding for any negative comments. Those people need to consider carefully the context for any negative comments in order to determine when and how they originated. Third party comments are helpful only when combined with thoughtful self-assessment followed by responsive goal setting.

One of the major challenges to regular self-assessment is just finding the time to sit quietly and reflect on what has happened or even what you hope might happen next. Time to think feels like a luxury in our jobs, but it is critical to our success and to our ability to persevere in this very difficult work. Most likely, you will discover more successes than you had imagined, and you will find yourself energized for the next effort. If, on the other hand, there are more challenges than you previously thought, you will either make some significant changes, or you will decide this role is not an appropriate one for you. That is a perfectly valid response; you and those with whom you work will be better off if you are willing to make that decision.

Each time we engage in self-assessment, it is critical to bring the process full circle and use the self-assessment results to set goals for next steps. Those are the goals that you will continue to assess going forward. A good self-assessment of that process would include a review of the original goals set by you and the committee, the process used to try to reach those goals, the arguments for and against the committee's recommendation, and consideration of the final vote (was it close or a landslide?). At each step, a good leader weighs his or her contribution to the effort. For any of us, this requires three things:

- A reassessment of our overall goals for our leadership positions and the impact of our individual strengths and weaknesses on our work in this particular situation
- An assessment of the feasibility of the project undertaken that is informed by as many views as possible
- Using the first two steps to guide the development of new goals and next steps

CHAPTER TWENTY-TWO

Discerning When to Transition to New Opportunities

John T. Day
John Carroll University

Charlie was now in his fifth year as dean. A series of unexpected circumstances had brought him here. After tenure—because his colleagues came to trust his judgment and value his contributions—he had moved from being a faculty member to department chair. Before being chair and after, he had taken on a number of institutional commitments and assignments. Not always aware of where things might lead, he said yes to one request to head a task force, another to chair a campus-wide committee, a third to handle special projects as associate dean, and then to the big D itself! Others recognized in him the skills and aptitudes he was less clearly aware of himself. At some point, his own ambitions, the thrill of a challenge, and a sense of accomplishment kicked in, and by all accounts (including his own, he had to admit), he had been a successful dean.

But how long did he want to keep this job? The faculty had just approved a new curriculum that he (behind the scenes) had championed. That was very gratifying. But what next? Stay put? Unending administrivia and having to be "Professor No" when no else would take responsibility for the hard decisions? What other options were there? A return to teaching? A new challenge within his own institution? A higher position here or accepting one of the many nominations he had received for a higher position elsewhere? Should he even consider retirement from the academy and pursue the next stages of his personal life?

Whether determined by the academic rhythm of sabbaticals or some cosmic seven-year itch, the average term of a dean is six years. Shaping the faculty through successive hiring seasons; imagining, planning, and implementing a new curriculum; putting in place a comprehensive assessment plan—these are the work of years, not months. It typically takes three to five years to have a significant impact on an institution as dean: to complete the tasks for which you were primarily hired, clean up the messes you inherited, implement the agenda of a new president, catalyze the creative energies of the faculty to develop a new program or general education curriculum, or bring the faculty personnel practices in line with best practices.

Some deans are called upon to be "the fixer": to bulldoze the dilapidated tenement, develop the reconstruction plan, and perhaps lay the new foundations; often such a dean is not around for the ribbon-cutting when the gleaming new skyscraper opens. Such deans inevitably exhaust their political capital quickly and have no chance to replenish the supply; they move on when construction is well under way if not yet complete. Some may be told to go, but most deans determine for themselves when it is time to move on. As experienced deans will confess—even those who have been dean at one or two or more institutions—at some point the excitement of the new, the adrenaline that comes from responding to the steep learning curve of a new position or a new institution fades away to be replaced by the routine and predictable, the personalities and tedious politics. The chores of the annual academic calendar become monotonous. At this point the dean has a choice: more of the same or something new and different.

Experienced deans have lots of options. Assuming, on balance, you succeeded in your first deanship, you will be attractive to another school in search of an experienced hand. With the pool for prospective deans increasingly shallow, you become an attractive big fish in a pond populated by schools of aspiring smaller fry not yet ready for a deanship. You may feel that, despite your battle scars, you are attracted to a bigger challenge in academic administration—you make a reasonable candidate for a vice-president or provost position at your own institution or one similar to it. Still, having been able to teach little and publish less, you may yearn to return to the faculty, to the academic life that first attracted you decades earlier to the groves of academe as a bright, eager, talented young mind. Or perhaps you recognize that this deanship is the last stop in your career, and you look forward to a retirement that offers other fulfillment personally and professionally.

How do you know what to do? There are external factors to keep in mind. As noted, the average tenure of a dean is six years. Consider, too, the current state of affairs at your institution. Have things changed so that your portfolio of talents is no longer a good match for the institution's challenges in the foreseeable future? Has your boss (the academic vice president, provost, or president) changed and are further changes looming, especially in personnel? If you are a dean as well as chief academic officer, does a new president want to be the change agent that boards, pundits, and some academic communities frequently demand? There is no more visible change than to replace one or more of the vice presidents, regardless of their experience or talent. Although there are notable instances of chief academic officers serving more than one president at the same institution, these tend to be the exception that proves the rule. And this is not surprising, because one of the most important relationships for a successful CAO is that which he or she has with the president, the boss. With these questions in mind, use the critical and analytical skills that have made you a successful faculty member and administrator to examine rationally your current situation. A trusted friend or mentor often can be helpful in sorting out these issues as they apply to you.

As you move through this process, remember to look within yourself, as well; how do you feel about your current situation, and what do you want to accomplish in your life and career? Let me suggest one especially useful approach in decision making for one's life, the notion of "discernment" as developed in the *Spiritual Exercises* of Ignatius of Loyola, the sixteen-century founder of the Society of Jesus, the Jesuits. Ignatius's work is primarily about how a contemplative person should act in the world in accord with one's highest ideals and aspirations. His particular approach provides a psychological insight that has relevance for personal decision making concerning major life choices even in the modern world.

Ignatius foregrounds the affective dimension of decision making, or discernment, as he calls it. According to Ignatius, one should reflect on one's experiences and one's future options and consider how one feels about them during this examination. Does the reflection provide a sense of joy, satisfaction, accomplishment, or inspiration (*consolation* is Ignatius's term)? Or, does the reflection stimulate feelings of selfishness, failure, guilt, despair, or dread (*desolation* for Ignatius)? Ignatius was aware that the human psyche is complex: consolations can be false or true. Do not automatically or immediately follow the good feelings and avoid the path associated with bad feelings, although in many cases that can lead to an appropriate decision. But in the difficult or crucial decisions, paying attention to these feelings can lead to deeper and more searching considerations. Close attention to these affective responses—combined with conversations with one or more mentors or confidants and a rigorous, objective consideration of the reasons for and against various options, and of the advantages and disadvantages associated with each—can help clarify one's motives and objectives in choosing one course or another.

For Ignatius, and for deans, pivotal life decisions often involve two or more good things. If a decision is obvious, as sometimes occurs, one can move quickly. But more typically, the choice is between two actually or potentially good things: staying put or moving on; teaching or administration; continuing to work or retiring. Choosing the better path will mean considering your individual circumstances and evaluating them thoroughly. As you do, reflect on the affective dimensions associated with each. The conclusion you draw from this exercise may illuminate your path forward.

To get started, consider three areas of practical guidance:

- When trying to make important career decisions, assess your current situation thoroughly, rationally, and objectively.
- Seek the advice and counsel of a disinterested party who has your best interests in mind.
- Don't neglect your feelings—the affective responses you have as you consider your current situation and your future options.

CHAPTER TWENTY-THREE

When to Move On, Ready or Not

Eugenia Proctor Gerdes
Bucknell University, retired

A liberal arts dean found herself frequently challenged by the new president and provost about her college's policies and her associate deans' and faculty's handling of academic matters. In one meeting of the university's senior administrators, the provost and president actually shook their fingers at her over criticisms of their administration that had been voiced by her college's department chairs after the provost encouraged them to be brutally honest. The dean was told she needed to "keep [her] troops in line." This top-down view of her role clashed with the dean's own sense that she needed to serve as advocate for the liberal arts curriculum and for her students, faculty, department chairs, and administrative staff in addition to representing and supporting the president and provost. In spite of her popularity with her faculty and the sympathy of the other deans and vice presidents, she began to question whether she could continue to perform her duties effectively and with integrity. She believed she had found her true calling in academic administration, but she knew that continuing the long hours and high stress was not rational, and she could not imagine "starting over" by figuring out the conflicts and hidden pitfalls at another institution.

A deanship can be your dream job or serve as a planned stepping-stone to a higher position, or it may be intended as a limited phase in a faculty career—but you are badly mistaken if you believe you alone can control when your deanship ends. Despite "best-laid plans," mentoring, and expert advice, the average deanship lasts only five to six years due to built-in vulnerabilities.

Let's dispense first with the happy alternative of ending your deanship by receiving a higher position (most typically, academic vice president (VPAA), provost, or president). Much advice is available concerning preparing yourself for such a move. Briefly, you need to demonstrate success or potential for each of the qualifications relevant to the higher position, be well respected for the administrative work you have done, be generally well liked by both administrative and faculty colleagues, and you need to have been in your current position four years or more (to dispel concerns that you are flighty, only interested in stepping-stones, or are being "let go").

Furthermore, achieving reasonable longevity is a challenge for all deans, not just those who seek advancement. So, no matter how optimistically you begin, contract negotiation is crucial. Determine whether your initial term is a definite commitment or whether, as is often the case, you serve at the pleasure of the president or other superior. What will happen if your contract is not renewed? Make sure you'll have a paid leave, preferably at your administrative salary, to give you time to transition. Get tenure as a faculty member if possible, even if it means going through a review before signing the final contract. It is more likely than you might think that you will return to the faculty. In *College Deans: Leading from Within* (2002), Mimi Wolverton and Walter Gmelch describe a national survey of academic deans and report that a quarter of the sample intended to return to the faculty. Before Christopher Zappe's and my presentation at the January 2008 ACAD meeting, "The Ins and Outs of Deaning: Why We Become Deans, and Why We Quit," we surveyed our audience members. In our sample of fifty-four deans, 39 percent foresaw a time when they would return to the faculty; another 41 percent stated they were uncertain or it was possible that they would return. Even if you think it is unlikely you will want to return to a faculty position, you need this option as Plan B; so nail down some specifics in your initial contract or when you "re-up" after a review. Whether you ultimately move to another position or return to the faculty, or even retire, you need to be aware of four interrelated threats to your tenure as an academic dean.

The first threat is the dramatic *disconnect between the job requirements and disciplinary preparation*. The deans in Chris Zappe's and my ACAD audience generally described entering administration in terms of their own agency—the desire to make meaningful contributions to their institution and the desire to grow as leaders and administrators. Yet their move often was unplanned; over one-third of deans in our survey were prompted by unexpected circumstances or the urging of administrators or faculty members to pursue a deanship. Regardless of whether our moves into deanship were intentional or unplanned, how many of us were attracted to the image of deanships we developed from our service as committee chairs, department chairs, or part-time administrators rather than by considering a realistic depiction of the duties, such as outlined in Jeffrey Buller's (2007) *The Essential Academic Dean: A Practical Guide to College Leadership*? Buller illustrates the professionalized nature of the contemporary deanship, with heavy financial and quasi-legal responsibilities, as well as high-level conflict resolution and diplomacy.

Research demonstrates that the best hires are made when the fit between candidate and job can be determined based on objective evidence. In contrast, when deans are hired, the job often is poorly defined, and previous experience usually cannot demonstrate the candidate's ability to perform those job requirements. In their 2001 ASHE-ERIC volume, *The Changing Nature of the Academic Deanship*, Wolverton, Gmelch, Montiez, and Nies showed that actual job descriptions for dean positions typically are based more on the institution's experience with previous deans than on what the dean actually will do and the requisite skills. Indeed, many advertisements do not mention administrative experience as a requirement; an earned doctorate and the values desired are more likely to be mentioned. Truth be told, your disciplinary expertise and faculty experience prepare you only for a subset of the dean's responsibilities.

Lack of preparation is just one of the factors leading to the second threat, a *high level of stress*. On a five-point scale rating their stress level at their current job, from "Not at All" to "Extremely" stressful, the deans in our ACAD survey averaged between the midpoint of "Moderately" stressful and "Very" stressful, with those serving as chief academic officers scoring significantly higher than others. The most commonly cited sources of stress fell in these three broad categories: faculty relations, personnel problems, and conflict; relationships with superior or other senior administrators; and time pressure or workload issues. An earlier study in which I surveyed nineteen academic deans, provosts, and VPAAs who had stepped down from their positions from 2003 to 2007 yielded similar findings. Their average stress rating was just below "Very" stressful. The most common sources of stress were relationships with the president or other upper administrators, relationships with faculty or conflict involving the faculty, and workload. The 2002 Wolverton and Gmelch volume and the 2001 ASHE-ERIC report deal extensively with stress, using the extensive NSAD (National Study of Academic Deans) data. The most important stressor revealed was administrative tasks, which included deadlines and workload as well as the specific job responsibilities. The next most important stressors were relationships with the upper administration and relationships with faculty and chairs.

The prevalence of interpersonal stress is understandable given the third threat, the fact that deans *manage from the middle*. Deans both supervise and advocate for their faculty and others who report to them and, at the same time, are the representatives of and report to a higher official. The different expectations of those, figuratively, above and below them produce role conflict. Deans serve two masters and are representatives of two cultures: on the one hand, a self-regulated professoriate of teacher-scholars who must be led rather than supervised and, on the other hand, an administrative culture in which they are expected to be managerial change agents, including producing innovations in response to the external environment. And, deans often have to mediate between these two cultures.

If you wish to prevent a premature transition, you must never forget your position in the middle. You may be a newcomer compared to other upper administrators and may need to demonstrate your credibility as an administrator. But faculty members will see you as someone who has gone over to the "dark side"; they need to be comfortable that you still know and care about what they know and care about. If you are lucky, you can use your role to help each culture understand the other and to protect each culture from mistakes that could be made out of misunderstanding. But don't forget the bottom line: if you alienate or lose the trust of either culture, you cannot be effective as dean.

Fourth, managing from the middle makes deans prone to getting caught in *critical dilemmas,* situations that can make or break a deanship. In a 2003 *Liberal Education* article, James Pence discussed career-defining and career-ending dilemmas. Pence described the academic deanship as, ideally, a vocation in which one's principles help turn dilemmas into grounded decisions. But not every dilemma can be resolved in a principled way that also preserves one's ability to function as dean at the current institution. A mentor of mine once stated that he thought deans were not doing their jobs unless they risked them once a year. Sometimes you need to stick your neck out rather than keeping your head down. When you are considering that choice, you might appreciate Warren Bennis's chapter, "Quitting on Principle," from his 1997 book *Why Leaders Can't Lead.* Bennis's chapter is a good reminder to continually ask yourself what you would *not* do to keep your job. Although he advises that you "go out shouting" rather than accept a "soft" exit when matters of conscience rise above loyalty to the institution, you might want to forgo shouting if you hope to continue in academic administration.

When we asked our ACAD audience members what might cause them to quit their current position, the majority mentioned lack of support from their superiors and other administrators. A sizable minority mentioned each of the following factors: loss of effectiveness, failure to meet personal goals, and issues involving stress/burnout, workload, or balance with family needs. Only a handful mentioned the faculty. In my sample of nineteen deans, provosts, and VPAAs who had already stepped down, most mentioned wanting to do something else, generally retiring or getting back to teaching or research. But almost half mentioned at least one of these problems: stress/burnout or a problematic relationship with their superior. Issues with superiors were most frequently described as a change in leadership that either pushed them out or made them decide it was necessary to quit. As one put it, his own "style and priorities were not a good match for the leadership or direction of the university." Buller (2007) contends that problems in the relationship with your superior are more likely to be fatal to your deanship than are problems with the faculty.

Not sharing your superior's values or priorities constitutes a critical dilemma that may have no other solution than quitting. If you are unhappy in the relationship with your superior, your superior probably is also. That gives you a powerful bargaining position, as does support from loyal faculty or department chairs who would be upset if you were fired. If you think you are going to be asked to leave, take control; state the conditions under which you would be comfortable resigning first. Hopefully, some transitional issues, including a terminal leave, are covered by your contract; nevertheless, institutions' aversion to controversy makes possible additional requests that would make the move attractive. For example, you might need a start-up package to return to the faculty as well as a reduced load to prepare new courses or to give you time to answer questions you know will come from administrators. You might be able to negotiate what you will teach, how your faculty salary will be set, or how you will be reviewed for salary increases and other normal faculty resource decisions. Or you might need a temporary administrative position while you seek jobs elsewhere.

How do you know when you are ready to move on? Buller's final chapters contain good advice on three moves: returning to the faculty, moving to another institution, and moving up in administration. Moreover, he suggests specific questions (see feature) to assess your current situation. These questions showed me that it was time to step down as dean after seventeen years, a surprisingly long tenure for someone who is arguing here that a deanship should be considered transitory. However, I had learned my lesson early, as acting dean and a candidate in the national search when a nasty conflict arose between my superiors and the faculty's academic freedom committee. I didn't know about critical dilemmas then, but I saw that there was no practical solution for me, given that both "masters" would be powerful in the decision on the dean search. I had no choice but to stand on principle and was fortunate that that choice was respected. I knew the outcome could have been otherwise, and it became even more apparent as my experience broadened that dedicated deans expose themselves daily to the threats discussed above. Another dean gave me this wise advice early in my career: "Don't step in anything squishy—but remember everything can be squishy."

Buller (2007, p. 425) provides three important questions:

- Is remaining in my current position the best thing for my college and institution?
- Can I still be effective in this position?
- Can I still receive the satisfaction that I need from this position?

References

Bennis, W. (1997). Quitting on principle. In W. Bennis (Ed.), *Why leaders can't lead.* San Francisco: Jossey-Bass.

Buller, J. (2007). *The essential academic dean: A practical guide to college leadership.* San Francisco: Jossey-Bass.

Pence, J. (2003). Deans' dilemmas: Practicing academic leadership. *Liberal Education,* Fall 2003.

Wolverton, M., & Gmelch, W (2002) *College deans: Leading from within.* Lanham, MD: Rowman & Littlefield.

Wolverton, M., Gmelch, W., Montiez, J., & Nies, C. T. (2001). *The changing nature of the academic deanship.* In A. J. Kezar (Series Ed.), *ASHE-ERIC Higher Education Report:* Number 28, Vol. 1. San Francisco: Jossey-Bass.

PART THREE

WHAT A DEAN DOES

CHAPTER TWENTY-FOUR

The Administrative Dance

Managing Up, Down, and Across

Darla S. Hanley
Berklee College of Music

5, 6, 7, 8 . . . When a dancer hears these counts he knows it's time to start dancing. This universal system allows him to know the tempo of the dance, and gives him a moment to prepare his mind and body for what is about to happen. As a dancer, he uses his eyes and ears and relies on his inner monologue to guide decisions, recall dance steps, and anticipate. This inner monologue encompasses prior learning and personal experience, which influence his performance and contribute to his confidence level on the dance floor. Over time with dedication, hard work, and practice, a dancer's skill, ability, and artistry develop.

A dancer focuses on the elements required to execute a particular style, such as tap, jazz, hip-hop, ballroom, or ballet—or he embraces the opportunity to take risks and offer an original form of artistic expression. He moves in relation to the space and situation at hand, depending on whether he is, for example, in a studio dancing alone, in a practice session dancing with a partner, on stage performing with a dance troupe, or in a classroom teaching a young student and on whether he is responding to recorded music or performing with live musicians. In all settings, however, he must simultaneously focus on himself as well as the persons for and with whom he is dancing.

So what does dancing have to do with deans managing up, down, and across? Just as dancers work with master teachers, choreographers, partners, and students, so do deans regularly work with a variety of persons across institutions and beyond. We work behind closed doors and in public, alone and then with others; and we hone our administrative and leadership skills and abilities over time with dedicated practice. In addition, like dancers, deans develop inner monologues from personal experience and prior learning to guide our engagement in specific settings across all institutional levels.

Deans work with persons who possess a wealth of experience and expertise, persons with developing experience and expertise, and persons with similar experience and expertise to our own. We work with persons to whom we report and others "higher" than us on the administrative ladder (up), with persons who report to us (down), and with peers (across). Like dancers, deans routinely work in ways that require the ability to follow someone else's lead, create original steps, improvise from established practice, and make innovation and access possible.

Deans must learn how to effectively lead, manage, and interact with persons up, down, and across on a college campus and beyond. In addition, they must select management techniques that "fit" a particular situation—to frame topics and issues, achieve outcomes, and continuously strive to advance teaching and learning. Even though specific managerial roles and responsibilities for deans (up, down, and across) depend on many factors including the size of the institution, its administrative structure, and level of staffing, the following three questions are essential to guide this work:

- What does it mean to manage up, down, and across?
- How does the dean's role and approach change based on the persons with whom she is engaging?
- How do deans manage managing?

MANAGING UP

Managing up requires a dean to share information in ways that illustrate her strong leadership, commitment to the institution, fiscal and academic integrity, and dedication to faculty, staff, and students. Most directly, a dean manages up when she interacts with the person(s) to whom she reports. These interactions provide the opportunity for the dean to set the stage and shape the perceptions her supervisor has of her work. While managing up, she strives to

- inform, advocate, and promote;
- gain respect for her work; and
- deliver outcomes and tangible results.

Managing up also includes communications with the rest of the upper administration across an institution. In these interactions, the dean represents her unit *and* her supervisor as she works to foster relationships with campus leaders, stakeholders, and decision makers.

A dean manages up by sharing the work of her unit (illustrating contributions and accomplishments), and participating in college-wide committees, councils, or task forces. In this context she is able to shape how her entire unit or selected initiatives are positioned within the institution and perceived both internally and externally. In addition, a dean manages up by showing her ability to solve problems and conflicts, have difficult conversations, and make challenging decisions.

One of the most essential elements of managing up is a dean's ability to influence the allocation of resources (fiscal, human, physical, political) on a campus. In this area, she identifies needs and works to secure adequate support. Moreover, in this role, a dean strives to inform or translate requests that may be unrecognized, invisible, or disconnected from institutional priorities in the view of executive leadership. She manages up by offering her perspective (based on her knowledge, experience, and professional priorities) to guide and advance the work at hand.

Another essential component of managing up for a dean is the support she offers her supervisor. This support takes many forms including ensuring that the supervisor is informed and up-to-date with key information or the status of administrative issues in progress. The dean manages up when she speaks privately to her supervisor to raise concerns, offer perspective, or a way to reframe a situation, particularly if the supervisor is misinformed or operating with inaccurate information. The dean who manages up gracefully and deftly in this manner helps ensure the supervisor does not make a misstep that could be embarrassing or costly. Moreover, with these actions, the dean demonstrates loyalty and insight that the supervisor values.

MANAGING DOWN

Students are the primary focus of *managing down* for a dean; after all, they are central to the purpose of our work at all times. Accordingly, this form of managing down consumes a large amount of a dean's agenda. Before students enroll, a dean often manages these prospective students by monitoring recruitment initiatives and facilitating connections between the institution, high schools, community colleges, schools with articulation agreements to their institutions, or individuals. These connections, facilitated by the dean, often result in relationships between faculty and students and influence a student's decision to select a college. Once students have enrolled, a dean manages their academic progress (including the full spectrum of achievement—everything from placement screenings and dean's list recipients to those on academic probation) and ensures that all graduation requirements are fulfilled. In addition, the dean manages a variety of resources that support teaching and learning and the assistance offered to at-risk students, to mention a few categories.

Managing down requires a dean to know the "hearts and minds" of the persons on her team. By knowing individuals, she has the ability to personally relate to colleagues and foster strong professional relationships. With this approach, she works with clarity, honesty, integrity, and transparency to empower faculty, staff, and students to be successful by listening to their concerns, requests, and dreams. While managing down, the dean strives to

- advance her unit;
- provide resources and support;
- offer clear expectations;
- get out of the way to allow others to work; and
- acknowledge accomplishments and contributions.

Deans manage down by working closely with department chairs to position them as decision makers and leaders of their teams by offering support and "having their back" when difficult issues arise. They also manage down by providing chairs with resources, strategies, suggestions, guidance, and opportunities for professional development.

Another way deans manage down is by evaluating faculty and staff—assessing individual strengths and weaknesses and assigning roles and responsibilities accordingly. This means the dean is engaging her team by asking persons to complete tasks for which they are well-suited; taking advantage of talent, expertise, and ability; and positioning persons for professional challenges with successful outcomes—not frustration or failure.

MANAGING ACROSS

Managing across requires a dean to work with peers and colleagues who are in similar roles within an institution. Fellow deans are the most obvious persons in this category. They require particular consideration as they, for example, may compete for resources, attention, and (sometimes) students. Their relationships vary from sibling rivalry (with jealously and competition) to being in this together (where deans commiserate, assist each other, and celebrate together). While managing across, the dean strives to

- demonstrate respect and support for colleagues and their work;
- share, reach consensus, or compromise; and
- work together to achieve the institutional mission, vision, and goals.

There is built-in incentive for deans to "dance together," particularly given the frequency of their need to work together in small groups led by a provost, as part of task forces or committees, or on projects related to curriculum, program development, accreditation, or assessment. The dean relationship—as peers—is integral to advancing the work at hand; it is very common for deans to "vote" to approve each other's work (e.g., new curricula, policy, procedures, initiatives). Accordingly, the dynamic and professional relationships among deans must not be underemphasized; this sets a tone for academics at an institution and heavily influences educational opportunities and experiences.

THE COMMUNICATION OF MANAGING UP, DOWN, AND ACROSS

Communication (written, verbal, and nonverbal) is central to leadership and management for deans. Like the dancer who has a variety of cues to influence his movements, a dean relies on a range of communications to manage her complex interactions with persons across the spectrum of academia and in the professional world representing education in general, and her unit and institution in particular. This communication requires the dean to have a strong command of knowledge or information and awareness of current events and issues related to higher education, her institution, and her unit. In addition, the dean must have a keen ability to recognize her audience and tailor the communication and message accordingly.

The dean is the "bridge," ensuring that communication from *above* (up) is shared *below* (down) and that from *below* (down) is shared *above* (up). Moreover, she is simultaneously responsible for being the bridge that maintains strong and clear communication with peers (across). In this role a dean must remember that bridges take thought and vision to create and trust to cross. This means she needs to craft information that not only informs others but also engages them and secures their confidence and support. In addition, she needs to recognize that bridges can be approached from different directions and be open minded in accepting the ideas of others and offering her respect and support for their contributions.

As a manager, an effective dean frames topics to achieve successful outcomes and advance the work at hand. Her use of language is often pivotal and can diffuse a situation, persuade others toward a shared vision, advocate for her team, protect, motivate, or challenge others, and maintain a focus on quality education and the student experience. A dean's vocabulary and tone as well as body language and content convey the message being sent and how it is received. Accordingly, a dean's communication is essential to managing how she manages.

A dean regularly finds herself in a situation where she has a brief amount of time to share information about her work. As a result, she often crafts "elevator speeches" to summarize recent accomplishments, outline upcoming events, or share key challenges. These brief encounters with others (at all levels of the institution and beyond campus borders) require the dean to

- strategically select content for emphasis;
- illustrate the quality, range, and scope of the work; and
- demonstrate her command of a situation and leadership skills.

In these settings her approach should be as positive as possible, illustrating her commitment and enthusiasm to the institution and the topic.

Throughout her work, a dean must demonstrate clarity, confidence, and resolve. Like a dancer, she must know when to lead and when to follow, and in all settings, across all levels of a college or university, the dean must be purposeful in her words and actions as she engages in the administrative dance.

- Just as a dancer knows how to dance alone, with a partner, or share the stage with a large ensemble of other artists, a dean should always be aware of the persons with whom she is interacting, the specific situation and setting, and the goals being addressed. She needs to "listen to the music" (be aware), perform in the right style (engage as a manager interacting up, down, or across), and be willing and able to improvise (create steps and action plans or respond to others to advance efforts at all levels of an institution).
- Like a dancer, a dean is guided by her inner monologue (her prior learning and personal experience) as she assesses a situation and makes decisions and determinations as an administrator managing up, down, or across. Her administrative skills develop over time through her interactions with executive leadership (up); faculty, staff, and students (down); and peers including fellow deans (across).
- Like a dancer, an effective dean practices her craft and performs to the best of her ability. She is frequently asked to work in the spotlight (attracting attention and publicly sharing information about her work and unit), work backstage (creating, facilitating, and advancing efforts out of the public eye), and work in the wings (being prepared and ready to make something happen at the appropriate moment). Her efforts shape academics and the culture of an institution—and influence the educational and professional lives of others.

CHAPTER TWENTY-FIVE

Establishing and Implementing Your Vision

Strategic Planning in Academic Affairs

Katie Conboy
Simmons College

The first-term president of Strategy College holds a "State of the College" address and expresses pride in several accomplishments of her first year: the academic affairs division completed six new faculty searches; the faculty senate ratified two new majors proposed by the faculty; the student affairs division organized a new cocurricular calendar that supports the curriculum; and the campus community—led by the provost—collaborated to complete the stalled planning process. The president announces that, later in the month, she will present the new strategic plan to the board of trustees for their approval. She then opens the floor to questions from the assembly.

The first question to the president is polite: "While the new faculty growth is helpful, there is still need for further progress in other areas of the curriculum. What is your plan for growth?" The president points to the faculty size time line charted within the strategic plan. Another faculty member asks about the status of a long-discussed lab renovation. Again, the president refers to a capital project time line in the strategic plan. A third hand goes up, and the questioner demands: "Look, I know you are proud of your strategic plan, whatever that is, but what the faculty really wants is . . ."

Listening to the president as she tries to answer these questions, the provost and the deans suddenly recognize a pervasive problem that has never been named: Strategy College does not yet have a culture for planning. The faculty and other campus groups are accustomed to lobbying privately with the administration for their needs, hoping they can create a sense of urgency around the issues that matter most to them. They are not used to taking a global view of institutional needs, prioritizing those needs, and compromising on their own requests for the good of the overall institution. And although Strategy College had a plan to involve all campus constituencies in the planning process, a significant number of the faculty appear either not to have read the plan or not to have recognized how their needs and desires were represented in it.

A strategic plan lays out a series of goals and a time line for achieving them. It integrates the strategies and the tactics that are most likely to accomplish the goals and then stages them across a time line. It matches institutional resources to those strategies and tactics. But if the faculty at Strategy College really wants something that is not in the strategic plan, there is a problem. The provost at Strategy College realizes that she needs to help the new president in a different way: she needs to backtrack and build confidence in the current plan, and she also needs to think about how the planning process can be improved in its next iteration—because Strategy College will always be working from a plan in the future.

The academic leader of any college or university—or indeed any school within a college or university—has a certain level of autonomy in determining a vision for the academic program. However, in increasingly complex planning environments, a dean who is not the chief academic officer must work closely with a provost/vice president, and a provost/vice president must ensure that her or his academic vision aligns with a broader institutional vision, usually developed by the president. To this end, at many colleges the chief academic officer leads the institutional planning process, dovetailing the president's vision with the creative impulses of academic units and other college departments. And the chief academic officer is often a kind of translator: she must listen to the ideas of others and then work with a college-wide committee to create a plan in which others recognize both a leader and a democratic process.

This "translation" continues into the implementation process, when difficult decisions must be made and communicated: what will be done, in what order, and why. The plan is likely to be embraced if the entire campus community knows there have been opportunities to participate; if a robust cross section of employees have gained understanding about the environment in which the college is operating; if there is consensus about the vision, mission, and values of the institution; and if individuals and groups recognize the process by which the strategies and tactics in the plan were prioritized.

VISION, MISSION, AND VALUES

A planning process often begins with a review of an institution's mission and values. The president may articulate a broad vision for a future that retains or reshapes the mission and values. Of course, a college's mission does not usually change with five-year planning increments, but a review allows the opportunity for a confirmation of the mission and values and allows for the possibility of expanding or altering the mission in either minor or significant ways.

Such a process might begin with the planning leader asking what seem like obvious questions: "Why do we exist?" "Who is served by our mission?" and "What distinguishes us within our peer group?" The last question is the one that most institutions fail to answer. Indeed, an influential article by Michael Porter (1996) is titled "What Is Strategy?" And Porter insists, "Competitive strategy is about being different. It means deliberately choosing a different set of activities to deliver a unique mix of value" (p. 64). Given that many college faculty and other employees will not have been thinking about why a strategic plan is necessary and what a plan should do for the college (certainly, this is true in the hypothetical case of Strategy College), an academic leader has an opportunity to educate the community. She can demonstrate the ways that strategy will help forge a path to a greater distinctiveness within a competitive category—not simply by emulating the "best practices" of the "best colleges," but by capitalizing on *this* college's unique strengths and developing alignment across all college functions. The plan should

- assist the college in creating and executing strategies that generate a competitive advantage within the institution's competitive environment;
- facilitate important and timely decisions about new areas of focus the college wants to develop—*and* about areas of focus they might want to eliminate;
- help faculty and staff to maximize the ways that all college activities, infrastructures, and technologies can mutually support each other; and
- identify the resources (revenue generation, reallocation, and fundraising) available to support the strategies.

Usually, conversations about vision, mission, and values do not lead to a radical change in what a college does, but they may identify new ways of accomplishing the mission or recognize new programs that are consistent with the college's historic mission. Indeed, in many cases, a review of the history and of founding documents uncovers the original raison d'être for the institution and helps contemporary employees sharpen their understanding of an essential distinctiveness.

ENVIRONMENTAL SCANNING, OR THE SWOT ANALYSIS

One way a senior academic leader can gain consensus about a proposed vision is to undertake an environmental scan. Often called a "SWOT analysis" (**S**trengths, **W**eaknesses, **O**pportunities, and **T**hreats) or a "situational analysis," the environmental scan appraises the environments external and internal to the institution and attempts to identify both potential avenues of possibility and potential roadblocks. Looking externally, it should review demographic trends, choice trends among college-going students, enrollment projections, competitor institutions, technological changes, and economic factors to offer areas for campus discussion.

The internal focus should involve a survey instrument that measures levels of faculty and staff agreement with the presumptive vision, mission, and values; that apprehends subtleties in faculty and staff attitudes about governance, workload, and change; and that identifies the levels of sensitivity faculty and staff have to contemporary students and their needs.

The results of the survey can be widely shared and used as a starting point for gathering reactions to any proposed areas of focus for the strategic plan that may have emerged from the president's vision or the review of mission and values. It is important for faculty and staff to see themselves—their ideas, reactions, and concerns—throughout the planning process. So it is best to share both the positive attitudes and the negative ones with the whole community. Producing a "white paper" for the community can be a good intermediate step that summarizes the data from the environmental scan.

STRATEGY AND TACTICS

Once you have confirmed the mission and values of the institution and have gathered data about the strengths, weaknesses, opportunities, and threats facing it, you are in a position to begin the creative process of generating ideas for change and growth that are consistent with these findings. Start with community brainstorming sessions that invite "big" thinking. Make clear that there may be great ideas that simply cannot fit into the budget, but that you do not want to stifle creativity at the outset. From those sessions, cluster the ideas under themes, and after some evaluation, identify a maximum of five or six broad areas of strategic focus (e.g., creating global networks, building character, or enhancing diversity).

Then, use steering committees with broad institutional representation for each strategic focus area; these groups can flesh out the general idea and develop a limited number of objectives that can be accomplished in the time frame. Five years is generally a good horizon. For example, under "creating global networks," one might find objectives such as *develop faculty research on global issues* or *increase student participation in study abroad*.

The objectives, once identified, also will need to be supported by specific action steps that have measurable results. Again, using the example of "creating global networks," the strategy might cascade something like this:

- Strategic Direction 1: Expanding Global Networks
  - Develop faculty research on global issues.

  - Create designated international research seed funds and build by $10,000 per year over five years.
  - Designate five paid faculty-student summer research grants for international projects.
  - Offer $1,000 in enhanced faculty development funds to faculty presenting at international conferences.
  - Create a targeted hiring opportunity for two science faculty members with international research partnerships.
- Increase student participation in study abroad.
  - Target study abroad growth in countries in the developing world.
  - Create a cohort model for students in the business major, with destinations in China and India.
  - Phase in a 4 percent increase in international student enrollment.
  - Hire an additional staff member in the International Programs Office to develop an international internship program, beginning with three countries in which English, French, or Arabic is spoken

It is easy to see how these tactics can be prioritized across a five-year time line and can become the basis for an annual work plan that shows satisfying movement in a variety of areas of strategic focus. The final plan will have a limited number of strategic focus areas, several objectives under each focus area, and a sufficient number of tactics to demonstrate intentional movement in every area.

The language of strategic planning offers alternative vocabularies for *goals, strategic focus areas, objectives*, and *tactics*, but the overall concept is simple.

- A strategic plan should offer a vision of what a college can do over five years to position itself more competitively and to bolster its areas of unique strength. That vision should be divided into several areas of focus in which desired outcomes can be articulated—and it should be accompanied by methods for accomplishing and measuring them.
- The planning process should be participatory and should begin with an honest appraisal of both the institution's current position and the external pressures that may influence its future.
- The final document should contain both long-term strategic goals and shorter-term measureable tactics that fit into the annual goals for specific units and specific individuals.

More complex are the methods by which an academic leader involves her constituencies, summarizes and communicates the opportunities and threats that emerge from research, translates the ideas of others into strategies that inspire collaboration, and integrates—with creativity—the available or expected resources with the goals. These methods often prove to be more art than science, and they depend on sensitivity to the culture of the specific institution and openness to good ideas wherever they originate.

Reference

Porter, M. E. (1996, November-December). What is strategy? *Harvard Business Review*, pp. 61–78.

CHAPTER TWENTY-SIX

Working with Regional Accreditors

Karen Doyle Walton
DeSales University

The search committee for a new faculty member for the sociology department of Granston University forwarded to the dean of social sciences a short list of five candidates. The committee is requesting permission to begin the process of speaking with the candidates' references and Skyping the candidates. The dean is unfamiliar with Elliot University, where one candidate, Bradley Seymour, has just earned his PhD. When the dean searches for Elliot in the *2013 Higher Education Directory*,[1] she finds that Elliot is an online proprietary school that is not accredited by one of the six regional accrediting agencies. The dean asks the search committee to remove Bradley Seymour's name from consideration, but the committee responds that the Elliot University website lists five accrediting agencies. The dean responds that Granston University hires only faculty members who have earned degrees from institutions that are accredited by one of the six regional accrediting agencies. The search committee thanks the dean for informing them of the distinction between "accredited" and "regionally-accredited."

The chair of the search committee is also the chair of the sociology department. He recognizes the name of Elliot University because, coincidentally, he has on his desk a request from the admissions office to approve undergraduate courses from Elliot for transfer into Granston University. The dean informs the department chair that he should make sure that a prospective student's transcript is from a regionally-accredited college or university before he approves the transfer of credit.

Higher education in the United States is fortunate that our colleges and universities are not regulated by a highly-prescriptive federal ministry of education. Although institutions are not required to earn regional accreditation, most eligible institutions do so because of numerous benefits that are available to accredited colleges and universities (Western Association of Schools and Colleges Accrediting Commission for Senior Colleges and Universities, 2012). Another regional commission acknowledges that

> regional accreditation of postsecondary institutions is a voluntary, non-governmental, self-regulatory process of quality assurance and institutional improvement. It recognizes higher education institutions for performance,

> integrity, and quality to merit the confidence of the educational community and the public. Accreditation or pre-accreditation by a postsecondary regional accrediting agency qualifies institutions and enrolled students for access to federal funds to support teaching, research, and student financial aid. (Northwest Commission on Colleges and Universities, 2012, n.p.)

Since the early 1900s, institutions of higher education have joined one of the six geographic regional accrediting bodies (Middaugh, 2010). Member institutions of these accrediting bodies undergo self-study and document their adherence to the regional accreditation standards. Visiting teams of peers periodically evaluate the extent to which the host institution meets the standards. The diversity of the missions of colleges and universities in the United States and the strength of the higher education system are largely the result of this process of peer review and self-regulation.

In the 1980s, the United States government mandated that accrediting bodies require their members to provide evidence that their "outcomes" verify that they were achieving their institutional missions. Colleges and universities must clearly define the student learning outcomes that flow from their mission statements, and they must employ assessment methods to verify that they are accomplishing their educational goals. In 2006, US Secretary of Education Margaret Spellings appointed the Commission on the Future of Higher Education, which strongly endorsed the accountability movement. Following the Spellings Commission's report, boards of trustees, legislators, and other funders of higher education have requested or demanded substantive evidence that monetary investment in colleges and universities is yielding appropriate dividends (Suskie, 2009). Linda Suskie, formerly a vice president of the Middle States Commission on Higher Education, in her excellent book *Assessing Student Learning: A Common Sense Guide*, refers to Judith Eaton, the president of the Council for Higher Education Accreditation (CHEA):

> Judith Eaton . . . has noted that government, charities, religious institutions, and corporations are all being held increasingly accountable. She has argued that in this climate, it is "more and more difficult for colleges and universities, which spend hundreds of billions of public and private dollars annually, to argue persuasively that they should not be more accountable for what they produce with those dollars." (2009, p. 62)

CHEA's membership of approximately 3,000 colleges and universities makes it the largest higher education organization in the United States, and it is an advocate for self-regulation of academic quality through accreditation. Suskie poses the questions, "Will assessment ever go away? Is assessment another higher education fad that we can simply ride out?" She answers as follows:

> It's not likely. One obvious reason is that calls for greater accountability—and the U.S. regulations that have flowed from them—aren't likely to go away, and

> they may even accelerate. To be blunt, the American higher education community is now on borrowed time. If American colleges and universities assemble compelling evidence of student learning now, demonstrating through assessment that their students graduate with important skills such as writing, critical thinking, and analysis, they have a much better chance of warding off inappropriate mandates and are far more likely to receive the support they need. If they do not do so, the risk of an external mandate dictating what and how to assess—and in a useless, burdensome fashion—is very real. (2009, p. 62)

Alexander Astin and Anthony Antonio (2012) echo Suskie's warning:

> Sooner or later, in one form or another, most institutions in the United States will have to come to terms with the assessment issue. Simply continuing to ignore it or hoping that it will go away is becoming increasingly unrealistic, in light of mounting pressures from regional accrediting bodies and state governments, not to mention the growing number of internal initiatives being brought by a rapidly expanding pool of individual administrators and faculty members who see assessment as a powerful tool for self-study and reform. (p. 250)

KNOW THE ACCREDITATION STANDARDS OF YOUR REGIONAL ACCREDITING AGENCY

It is the responsibility of senior academic leaders to be knowledgeable about the academic standards of their regional accrediting agency, whether at a college or university. The content, quality, assessment, and outcomes of the academic programs of colleges and universities are the ultimate responsibility of the chief academic officers (CAOs), although deans at universities also often have their own accrediting processes for their colleges and must certainly be aware of the institution's accreditation cycle. Although each of the six regional accrediting bodies has its own evaluation standards, there is significant commonality in the standards across the regions. Schuh (2010) notes that the standards of the six regional accrediting bodies are alike in their emphasis on the importance of measuring student learning outcomes inside and outside the classroom.

In *Planning and Assessment in Higher Education: Demonstrating Institutional Effectiveness*, Michael F. Middaugh, former chair of the Middle States Commission on Higher Education, identifies "three critical functions" that are the foci of the regional bodies' standards for accreditation, namely "assessment of student learning outcomes, assessment of overall institutional effectiveness, and ongoing strategic planning activity that is informed by those assessments" (Middaugh, 2010, p. 16). Middaugh's table of the "Commonality of Assessment of Student Learning Standards Across the Six Regional Agencies" reports the position of each of the six regional accrediting agencies with respect to the three foci. Although Middaugh's book was published in 2010, a search of the website of each regional accrediting body revealed that their positions have changed very little or not at all in 2013.

Commonality of Assessment of Student Learning Standards Across the Six Regional Agencies

> *Middle States Association of Colleges and Schools Commission on Higher Education.* Assessment of student learning demonstrates that an institution's students have knowledge, skills and competencies consistent with the institutional goals, and that students at graduation have achieved appropriate higher education goals.
>
> *New England Association of Schools and Colleges Commission on Institutions of Higher Education.* The institution implements and supports a systematic and broad-based approach to the assessment of student learning focused on educational improvement through understanding what and how students are learning through their academic program and, as appropriate, through experiences outside the classroom.
>
> *North Central Association of Colleges and Schools Higher Learning Commission.* The organization provides evidence of student learning and teaching effectiveness that demonstrates it is fulfilling its educational mission.
>
> *Northwest Commission on Colleges and Universities.* The institution offers collegiate-level programs that culminate in identified student competencies and lead to degrees or certificates in recognized fields of study. The achievement and maintenance of high quality programs is the primary responsibility of an accredited institution; hence the evaluation of educational programs and their continuous improvement is an ongoing responsibility.
>
> *Southern Association of Colleges and Schools Commission on Colleges.* The institution identifies college-level general education competencies and the extent to which graduates have attained them.
>
> *Western Association of College and Schools Accrediting Commission for Senior Colleges and Universities.* The institution's student learning outcomes and expectations for student attainment are clearly stated at the course, program, and as appropriate, institutional level. These outcomes and expectations are reflected in academic programs and policies; curriculum; advisement; library and information resources; and the wider learning environment . . . The institution demonstrates that its graduates consistently achieve its stated levels of attainment and ensures that its expectations for student learning are embedded in the standards faculty use to evaluate student work. (Middaugh, 2010)

SERVE ON A VISITING TEAM OR A SUBSTANTIVE CHANGE COMMITTEE

An excellent way for senior academic leaders to engage in the "culture of evidence that requires institutions to qualitatively and quantitatively demonstrate that they are meeting student learning goals and effectively marshaling human and fiscal resources toward that end" (Middaugh, 2010) is to serve on a regional accrediting agency's visiting team of peer evaluators of a member institution. The website of the agency explains how one becomes an evaluator. Depending upon the accrediting agency, a visiting team can range from four to twelve members and might include a CAO, librarian, chief financial officer, student affairs administrator, faculty members, and other university administrators. The visiting team chair, who is usually a college or university president, assigns areas of responsibility to the team members. For example, the Middle States Commission on Higher Education's accreditation standards, *Characteristics of Excellence in Higher Education* (2006), include the following categories that align well with the background, experience, and expertise of a CAO: faculty, educational offerings, general education, and assessment of student learning. The team's on-campus visit normally lasts two or three days, and its final written report is submitted to the regional accrediting body's commission. The CAO undoubtedly has previously held a leadership role in his institution's self-study in preparation for hosting a visiting evaluation team. However, actually serving on a visiting team provides campus leaders greater knowledge and understanding of the accrediting body's standards and how the standards are measured and met by a sister institution.

Another way for senior academic leaders to become more knowledgeable about the regional body's accreditation standards, policies, and procedures and to acquaint herself with the accrediting body's professional and administrative staff is to serve on the substantive change committee. The Southern Association of Colleges and Schools Commission on Colleges (2011) states that

> when an accredited institution significantly modifies or expands its scope, changes in the nature of its affiliation or ownership, or merges with another institution, a substantive change review is required. The Commission is responsible for evaluating all substantive changes to assess the impact of the change on the institution's compliance with defined standards. If an institution fails to follow the Commission's procedure for notification or approval of substantive changes, its total accreditation may be placed in jeopardy. (n.p.)

Likewise, additional items that require substantive change approval from the New England Association of Schools and Colleges Higher Learning Commission (2011) are offering degrees at a higher or lower level, distance learning programs, off-campus programs, programs abroad, correspondence education programs, and contractual relations with other institutions involving courses and programs.

BECOME A LEADER IN YOUR INSTITUTION'S "CLIMATE OF ASSESSMENT"

Becoming a leader in this "climate of assessment" is professionally stimulating, elucidating, and engaging. Suskie (2009) wisely advises that "assessment is a critical tool to help ensure that teaching and learning in colleges and universities are the best that they can be" (p. 63). And, after all, isn't that the goal of every chief academic officer?

To help you get started in working successfully with regional accreditors, consider the following questions:

- What do you already know about the standards of your regional accreditor and how it conducts reviews?
- What are ways that you can be more involved with your regional accrediting agency, such as serving as a peer reviewer?
- Who else on your campus should be familiar with regional accreditation, and how can you best communicate the expectations to faculty, staff, and students?
- How is assessment talked about on your campus, and how might you contribute to and frame the conversation in positive ways?

Note

1. Mary Pat Rodenhouse, ed., *2013 Higher Education Directory*, Reston, VA: Higher Education Publications.

References

Astin, A. W., & Antonio, A. L. (2012). *Assessment for excellence: The philosophy and practice of assessment and evaluation in higher education* (2nd ed.). Lanham, MD: Rowman & Littlefield in partnership with the American Council on Education.

Middaugh, M. F. (2010). *Planning and assessment in higher education: Demonstrating institutional effectiveness*. San Francisco: Jossey-Bass.

Middle States Commission on Higher Education. (2006). *Characteristics of excellence in higher education*. Philadelphia: Middle States Commission on Higher Education.

New England Association of Schools and Colleges Commission on Institutions of Higher Education. (2011). *Standards for accreditation*. Bedford, MA: New England Association of Schools and Colleges.

Northwest Commission of Colleges and Universities. (2012). *Handbook for peer evaluators*. Redmond, WA: Northwest Commission on Colleges and Universities.

Schuh, J. H. (2010). Assessment in student services that foster student and program success. In G. C. Kramer & R. L. Swing (Eds.), *Higher education assessment: Leadership matters* (pp. 78–94). Lanham, MD: Rowman & Littlefield in partnership with the American Council on Education.

Southern Association of Colleges and Schools Commission on Colleges. (2011). *The principles of accreditation: Foundations for quality enhancement* (5th ed.). Decatur, GA: Southern Association of Colleges and Schools Commission on Colleges.

Suskie, L. (2009). *Assessing student learning: A common sense guide* (2nd ed.). San Francisco: Jossey-Bass.

Western Association of Schools and Colleges Accrediting Commission for Senior Colleges and Universities. (2012). *Handbook of accreditation*. Alameda, CA: Western Association of Schools and Colleges.

CHAPTER TWENTY-SEVEN

The Dean's Roles and Responsibilities in General Education Curriculum Development

Linda Cabe Halpern
James Madison University

Last summer, a parent attending my university's summer orientation program complained in an open forum about all the time and money his daughter would be wasting by taking courses in the arts and humanities to fulfill general education requirements. He was convinced that these courses were "fluff," unrelated to the real purpose of her education represented by her major in an applied health field. Fortunately, another parent spoke up immediately, defending the ideal of a broad liberal arts education as preparation for a wide variety of professional and life activities.

Episodes like this one have occurred on many of our campuses and are part of a larger national conversation about the role of the liberal arts in US higher education. The same divergence is played out in different ways as our institutions recruit growing numbers of international students, most of whom represent cultures that do not share our understanding of higher education and are mystified by our insistence on a broad liberal arts–based general education. Although a few high-profile non-Western institutions like the public universities in Hong Kong have adopted US-style four-year degrees with a broad-based general education component, this is still an unusual approach to postsecondary education in most of the world.

Frankly, general education is no less contested among the faculty on many of our own campuses. However, unlike this external dialogue, focused on whether general education matters, the internal "gen ed wars" are commonly fought over what is in the curriculum. Departments and faculties believe, rightly or wrongly, that inclusion of particular courses or disciplines in general education requirements both validates their importance and provides access to a large student audience. The battles over turf are therefore both pragmatic, when departments see the potential of addition or reduction of faculty resources based on general education commitments, and ideological, when departments believe so strongly in the centrality of their discipline that they are convinced that every educated person should study it in college. More recent curricular approaches may organize general education by student learning outcomes rather than by disciplines, but faculty can still clearly recognize the implied winners and losers among disciplines and departments.

Individual faculty members also seek to have courses they teach included among general education requirements, generally for similar reasons. Yet that attitude of "my course," as a faculty member might say, no matter how excellent, is always the enemy of an effective curriculum, for the obvious reason that curricular decisions should be based on articulating the content and skills students need and then developing a coherent and consistent plan for achieving them. Such a curriculum is necessarily independent of the personal enthusiasms of individual faculty. Added to these concerns is public suspicion that colleges and universities are not teaching the things we claim to teach, especially in core areas like written and oral communication and quantitative reasoning that are fundamental to our general education curricula.

In such an environment, it is small wonder that general education reform seems to be a constant on our campuses and that it demands the attention of most academic administrators at some point in their careers. A few institutions, like Columbia University, have long-established programs that are part of institutional identity, but most schools consider revisions and updates periodically. Some program features follow higher education philosophies or trajectories to some extent: first-year seminars, interdisciplinary capstone courses, service-learning or undergraduate research components, and requirements related to diversity, global perspectives, or environmental literacy, to name some recent examples.

One final issue that many institutions face is the extent to which program coherence is compromised by student attendance at multiple institutions and the wide variety of mechanisms by which students can earn college credit while still in high school, including Advanced Placement (AP), International Baccalaureate (IB), or dual enrollment credit. Many students earn the majority of their general education credits outside our institutions.

So, whether your institution is involved in seemingly endless cycles of general education reform or blessed with a stable and effective program, general education requires the regular attention of senior academic administrators and the engagement of faculty and students. Although deans and provosts should generally stay out of the curriculum battles, there are other crucial roles we can play—either in general education reform or in supporting an existing program.

Some of what follows is common sense, and would apply to any program on our campuses, but other issues really are specific to general education programs. Because no single academic unit owns the program, issues of authority, resources, and acculturation (program maintenance) are often a great deal thornier. They also manifest themselves differently at different stages of program maturity.

In general, encouraging agreement on authority—program administration and governance—in early stages of program development can be very helpful, and even long-standing programs may benefit from attention to oversight and support. There are no single models of best practice, because this depends very much on institutional size and governance traditions. However, there are some underlying principles that may be helpful:

- As much as possible, empower the faculty who teach the courses in the program with program governance. Many academics have strong feelings about what general education ought to be like, but those with direct experience in the program and ongoing commitments to it are in the best position to make good decisions.
- Make sure regular program governance is overseen by standing committees or other groups with well-understood roles. Large-scale general education reform projects are often undertaken by task forces and ad hoc groups, but unless these projects mesh with regular governance processes, program sustainability is in jeopardy.
- Invest the administrative structure with program authority. Make sure that program administrators have control of budgets, full engagement in institutional resource allocation decisions, and authority to speak for the program.

Lack of resources is as great a threat to program viability and sustainability as is uncertain authority. General education programs utilize the largest proportion of faculty time of any program on campus, and often also the largest proportion of contingent faculty. The largest major on your campus uses a much smaller percentage of faculty teaching power. Nevertheless, many institutions allocate faculty positions to majors and departments without fully taking into account general education teaching needs. Equally destabilizing is the expectation that program features, especially interdisciplinary components, can be shared across many departments without establishing firm commitments that assure enough space for all students over time. Again, the wide variety of programs and institutional cultures means that there is no one model for achieving this, but good practice includes the following:

- When there is institutional growth, allocate new faculty lines to accommodate general education as well as major and service course needs.
- Establish multiyear staffing plans that include firm expectations for individual units. We all know that faculty resignations, medical leaves, sudden growth in a particular major, and other circumstances will mean renegotiation of these commitments, sometimes at the last minute, but a realistic plan gives everyone a clear starting point for conversations.

Finally, program maintenance and acculturation are an important and ongoing need, whether for a new or a long-standing program. When a campus redesigns general education, widespread interest can lead to a shared understanding of program goals and expectations. A few years later, after some faculty have retired or moved on, and others have become involved in newer initiatives, engagement and understanding can lag. On our campus, we have had some success with faculty minigrants, teaching awards, extra travel support for attending a general education conference, celebration of student work within the general education program, general education components in faculty development initiatives, and periodic open conversations about aspects of the program. Regular and focused attention to communication and faculty development are key to program sustainability.

Another activity related to ongoing program maintenance is program assessment. There are many models for general education assessment, ranging from rubrics applied to senior-level work to ascertain the mastery of general education learning outcomes to e-portfolios maintained by students to the robust pretest and posttest model we use here at James Madison University. The best assessment practice for your campus is one that will give results that are meaningful and useful to program faculty and that is not so resource-intensive that it cannot be sustained over time. Attention to assessment findings and a willingness to seek good information and use it for program improvement are hard enough to sustain in academic majors, and the distributed and episodic nature of faculty involvement in general education makes it even more difficult there. Nevertheless, programs must seek a robust and sustainable assessment practice and program renewal based on assessment results.

General education programs, at their best, represent institutional commitments to shared student learning in the liberal arts and sciences and attention to the pedagogical practices most likely to engage students. They are both a celebration of individual institutional identity and a reinforcement of the highest ideals of US higher education. The investments of attention and resources that deans and provosts make to assure ongoing program strength and stability are essential.

Remember, senior academic leaders play a pivotal role in ensuring an effective general education program, and in working with the faculty during revision. Thus, it is important to keep a few points in mind:

- The curriculum is the *easy* part.
- Sustaining the program requires attention to resources, faculty development, governance, and administration, all areas where the senior academic administrator has influence and responsibility.

- Assessment is not only required by accreditors and other entities, it is the best mechanism for ongoing program renewal and can be used effectively by deans or provosts to ensure a general education curriculum that provides significant learning opportunities for students.

One final thought: you are not alone. Most campuses struggle with general education at one time or other. Fortunately, there are some very good resources available. In particular, there are two national organizations, very different from one another, that focus on general education. Both offer productive conferences and institutes as well as helpful publications: the Association of American Colleges and Universities (AAC&U) and the Association for General and Liberal Studies (AGLS).

CHAPTER TWENTY-EIGHT

The Role of the Dean in Department and Program Review

Joseph Favazza
Stonehill College

In a familiar story, a department chair comes to the dean with a proposal to undertake a thorough curriculum review. In this case, the chair has just come back from a professional meeting where she heard about other programs developing courses in a new field within the discipline, and now she wants to figure out how her department can do the same thing in order to stay competitive. She knows she could probably make the case to add a course or two as electives, perhaps taught by adjunct faculty, but she feels strongly that at least one course in the new field should be a requirement for the major. The least painful way to do this is to simply add a requirement, but the institution has a robust general education program to which her department needs to contribute, so she knows this will be a fight. Also, adding a major course could mean adding faculty resources, and she knows getting a new faculty line approved in these days of budget constraints is nearly impossible. So she makes a strategic decision: propose a curriculum review to see if she can build support for changes to the existing major curriculum to make room for the new course without adding a faculty position or to the overall size of the major. She brings her proposal to you, the dean, and is now awaiting your decision.

On the surface, a decision by the dean or provost to approve a departmental request for a curriculum review does not seem difficult. Senior academic administrators want departments to regularly review the major curriculum to stay current, competitive, and attractive to new students. Departments want these same things, and so in many cases, there is no problem especially in cases when the curriculum review is part of a regularly scheduled program review.

However, there are two particular topics that can cause conflict when a department seeks a program review: departmental expectations and, sometimes, unarticulated departmental agendas. Chairs and departments often make the assumption that the dean's support for the curriculum review also means that the dean will support all the recommendations resulting from a review, recommendations that often come with a price tag. So before approving a departmental request for a curriculum review, the dean would do well to manage departmental expectations by communicating clearly about not only the process of the review itself but also the process of how recommendations will be received, approved and, implemented. This should be spelled out in writing and with a time line, otherwise the chance of miscommunication is high.

Sometimes the chair may use a curriculum review to push a specific agenda, such as in the scenario above. This agenda may have the full support of the department, or it may be divisive. The dean may have to consult with department members to ensure that the curriculum review proposal has wide departmental support; if a sizable part of the department does not support it, even a sizable minority, the dean must move very carefully. A department at odds with itself is unlikely to produce actionable recommendations. Only when the expectations are clear and the department is on board is the proposal ready for approval.

Once approved, the decision about who will conduct the review is central. Is it going to be a purely internal affair, with the department itself conducting the review, or will it involve external reviewers, such as is more typical with full-blown program reviews? If the curriculum review is occurring as part of the program review, many campuses will require that external reviewers conduct the review. If the curriculum review is happening outside the regularly scheduled program review, the decision to involve external reviewers is negotiable; however, the dean should be aware that the stakes of the review rise dramatically if external reviewers are involved. Why? If the institution is providing the resources to bring in one or two external reviewers, the message to the department is that the review is a priority and, as such, the recommendations from the review also will be priorities. Given the institutional commitment, this message is understandable; in fact, the most important reasons to invite external reviewers is to involve those who are more likely to be objective and integrate other institutional perspectives. For these reasons, the decision about who will conduct the review is another point where the dean must manage departmental expectations. Although the institution is investing resources to bring in external reviewers, the decision to approve and implement the recommendations must remain with the dean's office and will be considered alongside other institutional priorities and available resources.

Besides external reviewers, others who might be asked to participate in the review include board of trustee members (yes, some institutions do this), faculty from other departments, and academic administrators who work closely with the department (such as the director of career services or international programs). There are pros and cons to each of these possible reviewers. A board member will have the opportunity to take a "deep dive" into the department's curriculum. The result could be a fierce advocate for the work of the department or a fierce critic of how the department deploys resources. Faculty from other departments, like external reviewers, bring a fresh perspective to the review, but their judgment may be clouded if they see themselves as competing with the department for scarce resources. An academic administrator may be valuable in helping the department gather useful outcome data about student success, but faculty members within the department may not respect the views of a reviewer perceived as a nonacademic. The dean must weigh all these factors in deciding who will conduct the review.

WHY

In the scenario above, the chair requested a curriculum review, but sometimes the dean is the one to request the review outside the program review cycle. The reasons for such a request are many: the retirement or resignation of a faculty member, a multiyear decline in the number of majors, or even a change in departmental leadership. Without such an invitation from the dean, departments will be tempted to hire new faculty or recommend a new chair based on the old curriculum rather than seeing a new hire or chair appointment as an opportunity to make curricular changes. If a department is losing majors, and possibly losing resources as a result, drawing a line in the sand to defend the "tradition" of the curriculum is honorable but not effective.

HOW

Ask departments to look specifically at a few bottlenecks that plague major curricula such as course sequencing, rigidity in how requirements are fulfilled, and static transfer policies. The dean must challenge departments to go beyond the "coverage" model when reviewing the curriculum. It is too easy for departments to say, "We simply cannot be a good department without a course in x." Although this may be true, the dean can at least raise questions about the desired course: Can it be taught using a different pedagogy beyond lecture? How might technology be useful? Must students take it at the institution or is it transferable? Are there other courses presently being offered that are less central? How might the course in "x" also contribute to the curricula of interdisciplinary programs? How might it contribute to advance a strategic direction of the institution?

THE DEAN'S RESPONSE

Departments or programs undertaking such curricular review ought to codify their findings in a written self-study. Once the review is completed and the recommendations have been submitted to the dean, what next? If the report is authored by external reviewers, some institutions insist that the department submit a follow-up letter that prioritizes the recommendations. If the report comes from the department, the dean might request a further clarification of priorities. In any event, once the priorities of the department are communicated to the dean, the dean must take action. Such action might take a variety of expressions, such as a follow-up meeting with the department or a letter indicating which of the priorities the dean will work on. But it is critical that the department see that the dean is responding to the recommendations of the review even if the dean decides to prioritize the recommendations differently; otherwise, the dean runs the risk of being judged ineffective by faculty or simply a bureaucrat who demands that departments complete reports only to fill up space on a shelf.

How might a dean prioritize the recommendations of a curriculum review? It all comes down to determining and weighing different levels of impact: fiscal, departmental, and institutional. Fiscally, recommendations without big price tags or with price tags that can be absorbed by either the departmental or the dean's budget should be implemented as soon as possible. Whether this is hiring one adjunct faculty to teach a course, purchasing a piece of equipment, or co-locating departmental faculty, the long-term appreciation of the department will outweigh the short-term expense. More expensive recommendations, such as a new faculty line or renovating space, must be negotiated with the department and placed in the queue with other priorities. If approved, these must be built into subsequent annual budgets. The critical point for departments is usually not *when* but *if*. As long as they perceive the dean as communicating a plan in response to these recommendations, even the most strident departments can be patient.

The dean also must look at the impact of the recommendations on the department. In the scenario above, the chair really wants to add a new course to the major requirements. If this is a recommendation of the review, the dean must weigh the impact of not approving this recommendation. Would an effective chair become disaffected, negative, or possibly resign her leadership position at a time when the dean needs her to advance other strategic priorities? Would the department be discouraged and view the dean as holding them back from making real and innovative changes to the curriculum? Each of these outcomes has a price, so the dean must determine the departmental stakes when prioritizing the recommendations of the review. It may be that the departmental cost outweighs the fiscal cost.

Finally, the dean must look at institutional priorities in prioritizing the review recommendations. A recommendation may have a big fiscal cost but may advance multiple departmental or institutional initiatives. For example, if a new course will not only strengthen the major curriculum but also add a needed course to an interdisciplinary program or the general education program, it may receive a higher priority. Likewise, if the dean can make the case that a recommendation addresses key institutional initiatives such as diversity, alcohol prevention, or globalization, the recommendation may move up on the priority list. All this is to say that fiscal cost is not the only determinant when considering priorities. The dean who thinks strategically, institutionally, and politically will recognize this.

On the surface, approving a curriculum review request appears simple for the dean. But it could be more complex than it first appears. In summary, here are three ideas for senior academic leaders to keep in mind:

- Manage the expectations of the department about the recommendations of the curriculum review whether the request for the review comes from the dean or from the department. Make sure the full department supports the review.
- Consider carefully who will be involved in the review. External reviewers bring value but also heightened expectations. Consider the full range of possible reviewers.
- Be clear about what topics and questions you expect the department and reviewers to consider in their written documents.
- Act on the recommendations of the review but prioritize carefully. Consider the fiscal, departmental, and institutional costs of each recommendation.

CHAPTER TWENTY-NINE

The Backward Design Process of Curriculum Development

Ross Peterson-Veatch
Goshen College

"[The educator] must constantly regard what is already won not as a fixed possession, but as an agency and instrumentality for opening new fields which make new demands upon existing powers of observation and of intelligent use of memory. Connectedness in growth must be [the educator's] constant watchword."

—John Dewey, *Experience and Education*

Years ago, when I was first starting out in a faculty development center, a young professor in a heavily quantitative discipline came into our offices and asked us to help him. He said that his students did not write well and he was tired of having to read such poorly written work—could we help him figure out a way to get them to brush up on their writing? I remember asking about what kind of writing he was having them do, what kinds of things he was trying to teach them by having them write, and why the writing was important to their learning. As a colleague of mine and I worked together with him over a few months, it became clear that he did not care as much as he had thought about their writing; what he really wanted was for them to demonstrate a healthy amount of critical thinking in a final project he had them do. From his perspective, they were hardly even answering the main yes-or-no question he posed to them in the project: would his imaginary company be better off buying a competitor company or not? As we clarified his purpose in the course and his intentions for the assignments, the whole semester plan began to change and he became focused on what students needed to know and be able to do in order to answer his yes-or-no question. Once we fixed our eye on that question, everything fell into place.

Curriculum development is one of the most exciting parts of being an academic leader. Engaged wisely, it can be one of the best opportunities to bring faculty and administrators together to reconnect with their deepest sense of moral purpose as educators. It can generate a strong sense of momentum in the institution and can support other changes that may be long overdue.

But without a clear set of process steps, it can also go astray and sometimes can devolve into bickering over content and delivery of our programs. In the worst cases, a failed process can even foster a sense of despair that, because we cannot agree, we cannot move forward.

This chapter will treat curriculum development first as an abstract process, and then will take up issues pertaining to curriculum at the department and program level, touching on online programs and, finally, the cocurriculum. In all these areas, the dean or other senior academic leader plays a vital role in ensuring that academic excellence is achieved and that the curricular processes run smoothly. In addition, it is imperative that deans and provosts understand best practices in curriculum design and can articulate them to their faculty. In short, the most important consideration in the process is to *begin with the end in mind*, and then stretch your planning *backward* to the beginning of the course, program, or degree, just as the young faculty member did years ago in working to advance his students' responses to the question of competitive companies.

This seems quite reasonable in the abstract, but it is not as easy as it sounds. For example, although issues around content and delivery are far from trivial, following a backward design process means that as much as possible they should be held until the last part of any curriculum development process. Keeping these considerations out of the early stages of development is often the biggest challenge.

CURRICULUM DEVELOPMENT AS A PROCESS

Any curriculum development—large scale or small—always benefits from elucidation of three important components before we put pen to paper drawing diagrams or other graphics that represent our ideas about the experiences we believe most likely to benefit students. Curriculum development at its best is an ongoing conversation about intentions, performances, and assessments that sharpens one's focus and shapes future intentions, performances, and assessments—it is the ultimate educative conversation. In fact, at the end of every course and curriculum development seminar, I pose these questions to help participants recall the most important factors in delivery and design:

- How will students be different when they are finished with this program? What will they know that they didn't know before, what will they be able to do that they couldn't do before, and how will their attitude toward the material be changed?
- How will I know they are different? What evidence will I have gathered to decide whether they have changed from the start to the finish?

- How will they know they are different? What will we do along the way that will help them reflect on and integrate their new knowledge, skills, and dispositions, so that they feel their own focus increase as a result of their work?

CONTEXT: PHILOSOPHY AND METAPHORS

Generally speaking, solid curriculum springs from a strong sense of shared understanding about what we are trying to accomplish in the world and why—what I will call an *educational philosophy*. Administrators and faculty have common interests as academic leaders in supporting students to develop themselves into competent contributors to whatever communities they enter after graduating from our programs. Strengthening those common interests can be as simple as appealing to the mission or vision statement of your institution, or as complex as hosting multidisciplinary symposia on philosophical themes. But early on in the process, as the leader, you need to find points of common interest and steer the conversation toward them. Developing an understanding together of what your group cares most about bears fruit later when votes must be cast and decisions must be made about planning and implementation. A sophisticated example of this is John Dewey's *Experience and Education* (1977; 1938). Whether you agree with his premises or not, his short treatise works through some basic questions about what makes an experience "educative," and it provides rich material for differentiating between activities that are aligned with your purpose and ones that are not.

One of the most useful results of focusing on what we all care most about is that it generally provides the source of the metaphors we use to describe what we do. Those metaphors influence our choices and our interpretations of experience. We have in the words ***curriculum*** and ***course***, for example, metaphors for what we are constructing—the Latin roots of both words connote a pathway on which students will run. Paying attention to the metaphors you and others are using helps with communicating the complex concepts built into curriculum and the inevitable trade-offs that come with bringing your plans to reality.

LEARNING OUTCOMES: KNOWLEDGE, SKILLS, AND DISPOSITIONS

Once you have a strong sense of your philosophy and a few good metaphors, you will be well equipped to translate your intentions into measurable outcomes. The increasing importance of assessment in higher education in a real sense demands that we have a clear notion of what "end" we have in mind for students who experience our academic programs. The clearer we can be about what we want students to know and be able to do, and the orientation with which we hope students view the world and their place in it, the better off we are when we enter discussions about how to deliver our programs. Because outcomes function best as guiding principles, they ought to be capacious enough to encompass big ideas and yet specific enough that you can gather evidence and make judgments about the extent to which students have made progress toward them.

There are many good examples of well-crafted learning outcomes. The Association of American Colleges and Universities (AAC&U) developed a set of "essential learning outcomes" (ELOs) for undergraduate education during the course of their project Liberal Education and America's Promise (LEAP). Their website has many of these materials available for free (http://www.aacu.org/). Paired with their ELOs, AAC&U also fostered development of rubrics to accompany them in a project called the Valid Assessment of Learning in Undergraduate Education (VALUE). The VALUE rubrics capture a great deal of conversation among academics regarding the ELOs. The rubrics help expand the utility of the ELOs through including descriptions of expectations at different milestones along the trajectory toward mastery.

But the most important thing about specified learning outcomes is that they should represent an agreement among faculty about what knowledge, skills, and dispositions students should acquire by the time they complete your program or graduate from your institution.

RESOURCES: FACULTY, FACILITIES, AND TIME

Most of the time, when we deal in curriculum plans, we are not starting entirely from scratch. We generally have resource constraints that are important to remember. When we engage in curriculum design we are often developing something that feels precious to us. This emotional connection to the curriculum is most certainly a necessary resource to sustain it in the long term.

Early in the process, however, we can compromise the connection's long-term utility if we focus too sharply on questions about more concrete resources such as staff, facilities, and time. Reminding ourselves about them can be either freeing and can support the process or can bring a heavy sense of dread that we will not be "allowed" to be creative; deans need to carefully articulate the parameters of the curriculum design so as to ensure both creativity and responsibility. In chapter 10 of *Why We Do What We Do* (1995), Edward Deci writes about setting the context of "autonomy support" and how the way leaders communicate about resources can either support creative action by a group or can actually constrain it. He suggests that when we set limits—even on ourselves—we need to be clear about the reasons for them. "Understanding the usefulness and importance of the tasks people are doing and of the organization's policies allows people to feel more a part of the organization, less alienated from it" (1995, p. 150).

CURRICULUM MAPS AND MATRICES FOR PROGRAMS AND DEPARTMENTS

One important tool senior academic leaders can employ in larger scale curriculum development is a curriculum map or curriculum matrix (see figure 29.1). Once you determine learning outcomes and program experiences, it is useful to create a grid that allows you to see the points in the program where you plan to introduce, reinforce, and evaluate the outcomes. Not only useful for planning, it is also a good tool for assessment, and for supporting conversation about what we are trying to accomplish across a series of courses.

Online Programs

Perhaps because communication with students is heavily mediated in online programs, taking the time to engage the contextual factors and to complete the four steps outlined at the end of this chapter as you develop the curriculum is particularly important. Developing programs with distance learning components is often an excellent opportunity to embed a backward design curriculum development process because faculty are already open to and excited about bringing their courses to new audiences.

Cocurricular Programs

Like other educational programming, cocurricular programs are most productively engaged as exercises in developing students in certain ways. Although these developmental trajectories may seem obvious to those who are delivering or overseeing a program, having clear learning outcomes is essential to good delivery of any program. And as assessment continues to take on a larger role in our institutions, being able to assess cocurricular programs is critical. The dean's leadership is needed to carry through such assessment.

Often cocurricular offerings support the larger institutional learning outcomes and help students connect their perspectives to the institution's identity, so having a well-structured cocurricular program—one that also uses the context, as mentioned earlier, and that follows the four steps listed at the end

Goshen College Core Curriculum Summer 2011	delivery/ outcome			First Year Experience and Foundations - Total hours 15							Perspectives - Total hours 15					"SST" -12-13	"Post SST"
Curriculum Map of the Student Learning Outcomes				3	1	3	1	3	1	3	3	3	3	3	3	12-13 hrs	3
Learning Outcome	I	R	E	Intercultural Seminar	Learning Community	Academic Voice	Wellness	Goshen Seminar	Learning Community (2)	Engaging the Bible	Physical World	Social World	Religious World	Artistic World	Peace-making	Intercultural Semester	Global Issues Seminar
Knowledge																	
The Christian Story	3	10	10	R	I/R	R		R/E	E	I/R/E	R/E	R/E	I/R/E	R/E	E	R/E	E
Identity	2	10	13	I/R/E	I/R/E	R/E	R/E	R/E	E	R	R/E	R/E	R/E	R/E	E	E	E
The Social World	2	12	5	R	I/R	R		R/E	R/E	R	R	I/R/E	R	R	R	E	R/E
The Physical World	2	13	6	R	R	R	I/R/E	R/E	R/E	R	I/R/E	R	R	R	R	E	R/E
Creative Expression	2	11	5	R		R		R/E	I/R/E	R	R	R	R	I/R/E	R	E	R/E
Peacemaking	2	12	8	I/R/E	R/E	R		R/E	R/E	R/E	R	R	R	R	I/R/E	R/E	E
Skills																	
Communication	3	13	11	I/R/E	R	I/R/E	R	I/R/E	R	R/E	R/E	R/E	R/E	R/E	R/E	R/E	E
Quantitative literacy	3	13	6	R	R	R	I/R/E	I/R/E	R		I/R/E	R/E	R	R	R	R/E	R/E
Inquiry	2	14	12	R/E	R	I/R/E	R/E	I/R/E	R	R/E	R/E	R/E	R/E	R/E	R/E	R/E	R/E
Critical and reflective thinking	3	12	13	I/R/E	R/E	I/R/E	R/E	I/R/E	R	R/E	R/E	R/E	R/E	R/E	R/E	E	E
Problem solving	6	11	8	R	R	R	R	I/R/E	R		I/R/E	I/R/E	I/R/E	I/R/E	I/R/E	E	E
Intercultural competence	3	9	7	I/R/E	I/R	R	R	R/E	R			I/R/E	R/E		E	R/E	E
Responsibilities																	
Faith in action	3	12	10	R	I/R	R	R	R/E	I/R/E	E	R/E	R/E	R/E	R/E	R/E	I/R/E	E
Ethical reasoning	2	12	14	I/R/E	I/R/E	R/E	R/E	R/E	R/E	E	R/E	R/E	R/E	R/E	R/E	R/E	E
Intercultural openness	3	8	9	I/R/E	I/R/E	R	R	R/E	R/E			E	E	R	E	I/R/E	E
Local and global community engagement	3	10	10	R	I/R/E		R	R/E	I/R/E		R/E	R/E	R/E	R/E	R/E	I/R/E	E
Lifelong learning	3	12	11	R	R		I/R/E	I/R/E	I/R/E	R/E	R/E	R/E	R/E	R/E	R/E	R/E	E
Living sustainably	2	11	8	R	I/R		I/R/E	R/E	R/E		R/E	R/E	R	R	R/E	R/E	E
Integration																	
Make connections, synthesize and transfer learning	4	12	11	I/R/E	I/R	I/R/E	R	I/R/E	R/E	R	R/E	R/E	R/E	R/E	R/E	E	E

In this summative portfolio, students will incorporate artifacts from a collection they have been building from FYE, SST, Perspectives Courses and other curricular and co-curricular experiences. The Post SST Sem does not need to generate lots of new artifacts, but should provide the platform and support for students to begin to assemble their showcase from collected works, then connect pieces together with new artifacts or reflection components.

I = Introduce or Introduced
R = Reinforce or Reinforced
E = Evaluate or Evaluated

These Foundations courses are intended to build and cement a student's capacity for rigorous academic work in the 2nd, 3rd and 4th years. As shown in dark gray, students will generate artifacts that demonstrate where they are in their first year with regard to the Student Learning Outcomes. This approach uses the basic curricular principle of reinforcement across courses in order to support students in achieving our goals for them.

In these distribution areas, students must generate and collect e-portfolio artifacts—as they put together a collection, they can then choose from that set which ones they would like to include in the final showcase as part of the Global Issues course.

(dark gray) = Program component should generate a portfolio artifact as part of an assignment
(light gray) = Program component could generate a possible portfolio artifact

This graphic accompanies the Narrative version of the Goshen Core Curriculum Summary document. It is intended to help clarify and align our conversations about how to ensure that students have a coherent experience in the Goshen Core and how they will demonstrate that they can indeed integrate what they are learning here into their lives. This map is primarily descriptive.

Figure 29.1 Sample Curriculum Matrix

of this chapter—is one of the best ways to help students see the larger purpose of education for their lives. Absent focused attention to learning outcomes, students can find these programs disconnected from their academic course work and either not relevant to their education or, perhaps worse, the only reason they are in college. Either way, a strong bridge between the curricular and cocurricular is best built on the foundation of shared learning outcomes that can be assessed in both areas.

Backward Design: Four Important Steps

In the most abstract sense, curriculum design is most productively accomplished in four steps, once you have worked with your faculty to determine what your institution's guiding philosophy of the course or curriculum is.

Step 1. Determine learning outcomes. Ideally, learning outcomes are broad enough to give the people teaching a course or set of courses ample room to determine appropriate content and delivery methods but specific enough to guide gathering evidence of learning and making a judgment about it.

Step 2. Create an assessment of the learning outcomes. In a program this could be a capstone project, a certification exam, or even a particular set of required courses students must pass with a certain grade; in a course it could be an exam, a project, a paper, or any task or set of tasks that helps you gather evidence of learning.

Step 3. Develop a set of experiences and performance tasks that gives students appropriate preparation to do well on the outcomes assessment. In a program this might be best conceived of as courses, specific projects in courses, or final exams; in a course this might be smaller assignments, daily readings, course discussions and other activities that support students in performing well on a final exam or a final project.

Step 4. Determine, articulate, and communicate expectations for the assessments (both large and small). The AAC&U VALUE rubrics are excellent models for how you can do this step efficiently. Rubrics are convenient ways to communicate a great deal of information about how you will make the judgments you will make. Other tools include study sheets, checklists, and assignment descriptions that include information about what is most important in a given assignment or project. Be careful that you also communicate, though, that rubrics, checklists, and other tools you use to communicate expectations are not contracts, because judgments about quality are not always easy to describe in precise terms.

Completing these four steps does not signal that your curriculum is complete, nor should it—a message that the dean will need to carry to the faculty. Once the four pieces above are in place, however, decisions about content, delivery, and the use of resources become better directed by your overarching purpose. You can also, then, shape the educational experiences you choose for students to fit well in the context of courses, departments, programs, or your institution.

References

Deci, E. L. (with Flaste, R.). (1995). *Why we do what we do: Understanding self-motivation*. New York: Penguin Books.

Dewey, J. (1977; 1938). *Experience and education*. New York: Touchstone.

CHAPTER THIRTY

Curricular Development in an International Setting

The Arts and Sciences

Mark Rush
The American University of Sharjah

It is early in your career as dean of arts and sciences at a university in the Middle East. You have just left a meeting at which faculty and administrators discussed strategies for promoting the liberal arts disciplines as majors unto themselves and also through the university's general education requirements. But, as the meeting went on, it became clear that constraints on hiring, major requirements, and a deeply embedded student preference for professional study offered precious few—or new—resources for promoting the liberal arts. The liberal arts and sciences are fighting the same fight here as they are in the West—without the benefit of decades and centuries of tradition. Now what? Can lessons learned overseas provide practical help in the West?

The crisis in US higher education, in general, and the challenges facing the liberal arts and sciences, in particular, were already well established when I accepted an overseas posting as a dean of arts and sciences. The impact of the economic downturn was being felt across colleges and universities as scrutiny came to focus on the rising cost of higher education and students and parents became correspondingly more concerned about tying university education to employment prospects. As a result, the arts and sciences were under particular scrutiny because they did not seem to bear the close relationship to particular employment opportunities that the more professionally-oriented disciplines did.

In the United States, it was not difficult for advocates of the arts and sciences to mobilize in response to the challenges that the economic downturn presented. Initiatives like the AAC&U's LEAP program arose in order to celebrate and promote the well-established liberal traditions that form the foundations of Western education. Drawing upon those traditions, the AAC&U and similar organizations have formulated effective responses to the challenges confronting liberal education in the West.

In other parts of the world, however, no such tradition or foundation exists. As a result, serving as dean (and therefore promoter in chief) of arts and sciences in a university that seeks to combine the Western liberal tradition with the values of the Middle East embodies a host of challenges that did not exist half a world away. How do you promote the arts and sciences in a setting where they do not have the benefit of decades- and perhaps centuries-old traditions? In the West, where the economic downturn has rendered resources increasingly scarce, the arts and sciences could, at least, draw upon their most powerful resource—tradition. Absent that tradition, however, the concept of resource scarcity took on a different character and magnitude. But, the lessons one learns on foreign shores should prove useful and encouraging to liberal arts and sciences in the USA.

Despite the speed with which the economy of the Middle East and North Africa (MENA) region has grown over the last four decades, the global economic downturn had a clear, pervasive impact across these societies. It was manifested most obviously in the stirrings of the Arab Spring and, more subtly (but not surprisingly), in the aspirations of university students. Like their Western counterparts, they too are preoccupied with securing jobs after education.

In such a setting, however, there is no refuge to be found in assertions to the effect of "the value of a liberal arts education is self-evident." Absent long-standing educational traditions, the value of the liberal arts is anything but self-evident to young people (and their parents) who are confronted with expensive educational choices.

Within such a context, promoting the liberal arts required a two-pronged strategy. On the one hand, it was necessary to remind students of the role that the arts and sciences already play in their lives, their history and culture. On the other, it was necessary to "market" the liberal arts in a nontraditional manner. Instead of seeking to convey their value, which Western proponents consider to be self-evident, it was necessary to connect them to the more pragmatic or professional programs of study to which students were flocking in droves. Instead of maintaining the dichotomy between the arts and sciences and the professional disciplines, it was necessary to pursue a strategy in which that dichotomy is dismissed as false and in which the arts and sciences are cast as key complements to the more professional disciplines.

From a Western perspective, the strategy my colleagues and I pursued at the American University of Sharjah might be described as "the road not taken." We sought to promote the liberal arts in the same spirit as that of Benjamin Rush, whose legacy was to "offer to a scrappy [young United States], born directly out of a revolution, an ultimately practical vision of the liberal arts" (Durden, 2003, para. 8). Some forty years after its founding, we sought to offer the United Arab Emirates a similar vision.

Although the College of Arts and Sciences at the American University of Sharjah houses two of the larger majors (international studies and mass communication), the vast majority of students major in the College of Engineering or the School of Business and Management. Accordingly, to some, the College of Arts and Sciences seemed relegated to a mere "service" position insofar as it shouldered the burden of supporting the broad general education program's many course offerings. Aspiring engineers, accountants, and architects pass through our classrooms (many times grudgingly) but seldom wish to continue. How could we convince them to stick around?

A first step was to make our courses more accessible and attractive. In some cases, we sought to shave a course or two from the major requirements. In this respect, we made our majors more accessible by decreasing the cost (in terms of total courses) of taking them. In other cases, we encouraged students to add an arts and sciences minor as a complement to their major field of study. We seized upon the regional desire to promote culture and language by creating a new interdisciplinary minor in Middle Eastern Studies. Drawing upon faculty from the colleges of Arts and Sciences and schools of Business and Management and Architecture and Design, we coordinated the creation of a new minor that allowed students to design their own course of study (drawing where possible from their own majors) while ensuring that they made attainments in Arabic language and heritage.

Internally, we promoted one another's minors. Through our registration procedures, faculty promoted majors in other arts and sciences departments and encouraged students to enroll in them. We became our best public relations agents.

We took advantage of a natural strength of the arts and sciences: interdisciplinarity. In cooperation with the vice provost, we implemented a collaborative teaching grant program. Our faculty took advantage of mutual interests across departments and dominated the first rounds of collaborative, interdisciplinary teaching.

As well, it quickly became obvious that fine colleagues in the professional schools were eager to join forces and teach a collaborative course in the humanities or sciences. Many of our colleagues in the professional disciplines relished the opportunity to teach outside the rigid disciplinary constraints imposed by the professional accrediting agencies. In this respect, arts and sciences faculty provided an opportunity for pedagogical freedom to their colleagues in other schools.

One final strategy was to take a page from our fellow colleges and trumpet the preprofessional aspects of our curriculum. We made minor adjustments to our premedical curriculum and then established relationships with the three medical schools in the region (American University of Beirut, University of Balamand, and Lebanese American University) that also share our institutional commitment to the Western model of undergraduate education. The result was the first ever premedical information session with some ninety students in attendance.

These efforts had almost immediate results on enrollments and interest in the arts and sciences. The collaborative courses were all oversubscribed. The Middle Eastern Studies minor flourished. The premedical initiative created a buzz across the campus.

The early success of these efforts was accompanied by challenges to which any colleague at a US university could relate. The curricular approval process can and will sometimes require a tremendous amount of effort just to run the many potential and real traps required for changes. Interdisciplinary courses and new interdisciplinary minors require more than the routine amount of cross-checking and review. Furthermore, existing curricular requirements may make it difficult for departments to allocate faculty to a collaborative course. On the margin, the deans and department heads need to make it possible for faculty to do so.

As well, accreditation requirements for professional majors (such as engineering) may leave students precious few degrees of freedom in their schedules to take electives. In an international setting, this can be particularly onerous if a university holds national and international (particularly American) accreditations.

Despite the hurdles and the pressures we face, the challenges faced by the arts and sciences overseas offer lessons for domestic strategies.

- It is clear that the arts and sciences can benefit from a detour onto Benjamin Rush's "road not taken." So, arts and sciences faculty should not refrain from emphasizing the professional, practical importance of what we teach.
- Of course, in these times, morale is an issue. If the arts and sciences are shrouded by the stigma associated with service courses, it takes a lot of energy and persuasion to convince the faculty that their perceived position of inferiority is more akin to that of the slave Hegel describes in *The Phenomenology of the Spirit* than it is to any position of true bondage. Hegel's slave found power in the position of perceived inferiority. Arts and sciences faculty shouldered with service teaching responsibilities can look upon this position as one of empowerment. We have access to many students early in their careers. We are easily able to offer attractive interdisciplinary courses. Thus, by stooping, we can conquer. (Apologies to Hegel and Goldsmith.) If our majors are decreasing, it gives us the freedom to pursue more interdisciplinary work and to recast what we teach in a slightly more practical or professional light.

- **Finally, insofar as we highlight and emphasize the critical thinking, creativity, and flexibility that inhere in the arts and sciences, meeting the challenges of the current economic and environmental milieu certainly gives us an opportunity to demonstrate the importance and impact of the skills that we teach. Reach out to your colleagues in the professional or technical schools. You will find that more than a few will be happy to join forces in interdisciplinary teaching. This in turn will amplify the attractiveness and the practicality of the arts and sciences to our students.**

Reference

Durden, W. G. (2003, July 18). The liberal arts as a bulwark of business education. *The Chronicle Review*. Retrieved from http://chronicle.com/article/The-Liberal-Arts-as-a-Bulwark/3677

CHAPTER THIRTY-ONE

Online Curriculum Development

Pamela Monaco
Southwestern College of Professional Studies

Since the recession, your college enrollments have not been as robust as the president wants. Concerns about access and affordability seem to be a part of most conversations. The decision to limit growth at the undergraduate level reflects the concern that tuition and state appropriations are the only sources of support, and neither will increase. Strategically, more emphasis will be placed on expanding existing graduate programs and developing new ones, and leveraging technology to greater effectiveness. Technology can stimulate innovative teaching, increase the exchange possible between faculty and students as well as peer collaboration, and leverage the resources to increase access to more students. You have been charged with developing distance education programs in high-demand disciplines, particularly at the graduate level, that correlate with the strengths of your university. Market research and analysis have suggested what these curricular programs might be. Where do you start putting these new programs into operation?

Unlike market analyses undertaken at colleges without online programs, colleges that develop online courses and curricula must consider the national demands for a particular degree as well as the competition nationally to fulfill these demands. Just as the employment outlook is not just for the regional area, so too the other educational providers range from for-profit colleges to private colleges to state schools, some located on the other side of the country. Thus, when considering the resources necessary to develop and offer a program, it is important to consider the resources of the entire college or university and how these compare to what competitors offer to support a program.

Deans need to understand that it is imperative that the development and support of any online course or program extend far beyond the teaching faculty; online programs require myriad resources, from exploring the new databases that must be added to the online library resources to the audio visual and technology support required to develop a robust experience for faculty and students. Conversations within an academic department to explore research and teaching interests in a new program must occur simultaneously with the student support office, the center for teaching and learning, the instructional technology office, the marketing department, the admissions and recruitment department, and alumni affairs. For example, if the program under consideration will be most marketable if it includes an internship experience, alumni may be vital in helping establish these opportunities in markets across the country from which students will be enrolled. Or many online programs, particularly at the graduate level, include a low-residency component. This might require coordination with the events office to determine the best timing from a campus or community perspective to bring the students to campus, or it might mean working with residential life to use dorms during the summer. Careful consideration of all these details and close consultation with stakeholder groups throughout the college and community will provide the information to determine if a new online program will actually be a good fit for the college's resources. At all times it is essential to weigh the necessary but ancillary support in comparison to what the best competing educational providers can offer. The online market is too competitive to offer courses or programs that pale in comparison to others.

Once the decision has been made either to develop new courses or programs for online delivery or to migrate existing courses or programs to this model, the course development process must be implemented. Some of us may remember the days when developing a new course meant research in the library, developing the lectures and thinking of assignments, and then turning in the syllabus and book list to the department. Online course development requires a team of specialists and a detailed project management plan. The course development team includes a content expert, a course designer, a technologist, often a programmer, often a peer reviewer, and a project manager. These people may be housed in different departments, and if working with a course development office or team, often others will actually manage the process.

All roles are important, but it will be essential to rely on a content expert who is open to suggestions and interested in how technology can inform the teaching and learning process. The course designer will work closely with the content expert to provide guidance on how best to deliver content and engage students in the online environment. The course designer suggests how to frame discussion questions in order to invite good discussion among students in the online class. She or he might also suggest working with a programmer to develop a simulation or add graphic or visual elements to avoid a completely text-based course. With the growing popularity of MOOCs (massive open online courses), more and more students have experienced rich course design and will be less satisfied with the static, textual course that is the most common online design.

The course designer also will share pedagogical and design theory that content experts might not know. The art historian knows what principles must be included in a basic art history course and will know the artists and periods to cover, but the professor may not be as aware of the reasons not to use publisher-provided PowerPoint presentations or not to include a lecture of the professor from her standard art history class taught on the ground three times a week. Most course designers are familiar with standards of excellence for online courses, such as Quality Matters, which has become a widely accepted rubric to assess quality. Often someone responsible for assessment also will consult with the course designer and content expert to discuss how best to capture evidence of students' meeting the learning outcomes.

The project manager will coordinate the schedule and make sure everyone keeps on track for an on-time delivery of the course. The project manager may also be the person working with the Dean's Office and the other offices to track expenses. Unlike traditional course development with little or no upfront expense, the online development process may be expensive upfront, but the return on investment, if managed correctly, also can be high. Many colleges have a centralized course development office that is responsible for the design and management of all courses across the campus. Without a careful plan, any course can become a very expensive course. Art courses may require purchasing the rights to use many images; a music course may require not just access to audio files but the creation of videos demonstrating certain techniques or of audio reproducing certain sounds. Establishing a budget for securing rights or designing video, filming lectures, creating simulations, and so forth should be done during preliminary discussions. Usually, either the course designer or instructional technologist will do the actual work in the learning management system; thus, it is important that the content expert keep on schedule so the other members of the team can do the actual building of the course.

The editor ensures there are no errors before the course is put into development. If a peer reviewer is used, which is recommended, the peer reviewer functions as a sounding board for ideas and as a detached observer who can give advice as one who might teach a class someone else designed. Once an investment is made in the development of a course for online delivery, most institutions use this course as the template or master course from which individual course sections are copied. It is very likely in most institutions, that eventually instructors other than the original content expert will teach the course too. It is important that the design, principles, and strategies for good online instruction be understood by others.

A high-quality online course needs a maintenance schedule. Online courses rely on technology, from the learning management system to the links to articles, video clips, demonstrations, or outside learning and teaching tools.

Learning management systems experience upgrades and have a variety of enhancements that can be purchased and added to an existing system. Often these upgrades mean the courses in existence need to be upgraded. Links get broken, and materials become outdated. Although instructional technologists can fix many problems and carry out upgrades, a content expert needs to provide the guidance for the actual content changes. Part of the contract written with the content expert must include expectations about course maintenance responsibilities. The contract also should make clear who owns the course material and design and who can teach the course.

At least one other crucial component of online curriculum development is faculty support and training. Many learning management systems exist, and there are also different versions within one company's system. Anyone who is going to develop an online course or teach one should go through a training program. Ideally, the training program includes information about how to use the system—how to add announcements, how to respond to discussions, how to post grades, and so forth—as well as best practices for teaching online at your college. How often does the college expect the instructor to be in the online classroom? What does engagement mean? Is there an expectation for direct instruction? Before a content expert develops an online course, he or she needs to know how to use the system and how to design a course that encourages the best practices the college expects. If the college will use a course as a template from which others will teach, it will be important to offer support in how one teaches a course already designed by another.

Not every college develops all the online offerings in-house. Several publishing companies and learning management systems offer services and expertise to develop the content and courses for a college, and there are a number of companies that offer online course development expertise, for a fee. Usually this means the course is a "packaged" course, meaning it is fairly generic and may be offered by other colleges. This does not mean the college cannot customize the course. Usually the company will have the course available on a "cartridge" that can be added to the LMS (learning management system). A content expert and designer could then make adjustments to the course. The advantages in terms of time and expense savings are obvious. If there is not a lot of in-house talent, this can be one way to offer online courses that usually include metrics to help assessment of student learning objectives and use a variety of assignments and technology tools. This is often an option with lower-level general education courses. More specified course developments also can be contracted with a professional company, but the costs can increase fairly quickly. It is important to weigh where one wants to make the investment of time and resources. Remember, too, that if the entire course development process is outsourced, some of the revenue return will also be shared with another company.

As more options become available to enrich the online experience, conversations and planning with the IT department become more important. Students appreciate welcoming announcements that include a video of the professor. PowerPoint presentations with audio add a customized touch. Providing the YouTube video in the course shell rather than as a link to the web can create greater immediacy for the student. All of these require considerably more server space too. Discussions across campus on a regular basis about how to improve the teaching and learning experience need to include those responsible for the hardware.

Gone are the days when offering online courses or programs brought easy access to new markets. The competitive market requires careful thought and planning before adding this offering. Three questions should be considered carefully, and their answers should be used wisely in the decision-making process:

- Is there a niche in your curriculum design that will mark your offering as different from others?
- Do you have the technological support for faculty and students to offer a first-rate course?
- Do you have the resources to develop and maintain an online program in-house, or is it more advisable to outsource the curriculum design work?

CHAPTER THIRTY-TWO

Representing Your Institution Well

Engaging with the Media

Larry J. Frazier
LeTourneau University

As I opened the door to enter the media briefing room, I had no idea what to expect other than I thought I might have some chance to catch my breath. I was wrong. As soon as I stepped into the room, a reporter jammed a camera in my face. Immediately, he began firing questions at me.

"What can you tell us about the situation?" he asked.

"Not much really. We have only just begun gathering information."

"Our sources are reporting that the individual involved is a disgruntled student and that he has barricaded himself in the area of the building that houses the Office of the Dean. Is this true?"

"I had not heard that, yet," I admitted.

"As this tragedy emerges, can you give us some idea of the individuals who may be at risk?"

"Well, I guess that would mean my secretary, perhaps students. No, I really don't know."

"If students are currently being held hostage, what is your opinion of the university's approach to student safety and crisis communication?" he asked.

"Well, I really don't know."

"You do not know the university's approach to student safety?"

"No. I mean . . . no comment."

This nightmare likely would have gone on for another thirty minutes, or until the reporter got tired, but mercifully he ended the interview and instructed me to leave the room. The reporter was not an actual reporter, but rather a media consultant and trainer who had been brought to our university to engage in media training with our university's leadership. Even though the scenario above was only a drill, I can confirm that it felt very real. As the reporter drilled deeper with his questions, I had a general idea of where he was going, but I had no idea of how to stop him. As my mouth moved and words came out, I knew that I was only compounding the problem and creating potential problems for my university and for first responders, hypothetically. Yet I felt compelled to stand my ground with the reporter, to take whatever he might fire at me, and just weather the storm as best I could.

In that experience, I learned the most valuable lesson of working with media: never allow the media representative to control the interview. Information is the commodity that draws the university representative and the reporter together. And although these two parties need not engage in an adversarial relationship, we would be wise to recognize that the media representatives have a different perspective regarding information than the typical university spokesperson. Often, the typical spokesperson is someone in a communications office who has been designated to be the prime media contact; deans will do well to know who that person is and to rely on him or her.

In other situations, however, deans and other senior academic leaders do represent the college or university, and we want to enlighten, to inform, and to promote. Perhaps we see ourselves as providing a public service. Maybe we even see the media as a source of free advertising for the important work faculty and students do in their classes, or in their scholarship. The media, on the other hand, are in the business of generating sales, increasing viewership, or elevating web traffic, in addition to their primary purpose of serving as a source of information to the general public. This is not to say that they are bad people or that they even have ulterior motives. It is only to recognize that ultimately this is a business and our motivations differ from theirs, and thus, the story may then take a form that runs contrary to the spokesperson's original intent.

The solution to this potential problem is to enter into any contact with the media with the knowledge that the university representative has the commodity that the reporter needs. Without this commodity, the reporter has no story to tell. We can control the transmission of this commodity in several ways. First, engage the university's public relations staff. Make it a policy that you will not speak with any media member who has not first been vetted by a member of your university's public relations staff. Then before the interview, speak with that PR representative. Gain some idea of the angle and bias of the reporter. What is the story he or she wants to tell? Talk over your message points with your PR representative and perhaps even practice the interview with your PR representative.

Second, do not respond to comments or information that originate from a "blind" source. In the example above, the reporter affirms that his "sources" know something that the university representative does not. The reporter is not especially concerned if this source is accurate, but if he can get you to respond to the source, he then has a university representative making a comment on the record. Rather than responding to information from a blind source, say only what you know to be factually true.

Third, do not take the bait and respond to the "What if" question. Do not speculate. No one has the ability to look into the future. The right answer to this sort of question is always "I do not know."

Fourth, do not allow a reporter to frame a question negatively. In the example above, the reporter refers to a tragedy. Tragedies sell newspapers. At this point no tragedy has occurred—at least not to your knowledge. Do not follow the reporter down this negative path. In response to a question like this, replace "tragedy" with "incident," until you can confirm whether there has been a tragedy.

On the other hand, there is no need to be overly optimistic and make promises that you cannot fulfill. State only what you know to be true.

Fifth, do not get drawn in to talking about personal opinion. You are speaking for your institution. Your opinion is neither important nor relevant.

Sixth, never say the words "No comment." Saying "No comment" is, in itself, a comment. Instead, state why you cannot comment: "I do not have enough information at the moment to address that question." These guidelines should be followed regardless of the context, and deans should know that media can be utilized effectively to promote events and significant accomplishments at the institution.

But crisis communication warrants a few additional comments. In a crisis situation, the stakes are higher. In the scenario above, people's lives may actually be in danger. In other types of crises—scandal, personnel issues—the reputation of the institution may be at stake. Any situation that has the potential to harm the university's reputation or weaken the university's brand should be approached as a crisis situation.

In times of crisis, someone must address the media. If a reputable source of information is not on hand, the media will find other sources of information. The story will be told. Better that you do what you can to shape that story. Keep in mind that the final shape of the story is in the hands of the reporter. Despite your best efforts, the story may be told in a way that runs contrary to your wishes. In the end, the best we can do is to represent the university professionally and mitigate potential damage to the university's reputation.

If the institution has an official spokesperson who is not yet on site, the first task is to establish the location for official media briefings and then confirm that the spokesperson will be available as soon as possible. Deliver this message quickly and briefly, and then walk away. Update the media on the status of the spokesperson. If you are the spokesperson, start by identifying yourself. Remember that for individuals affected by this crisis, your words may be the only information they receive, so it is important, even in the lack of factual information, to communicate a sense of calm and concern. Beyond that, stick to what you know factually to be true. Unless you are a law enforcement official, never comment on security procedures. And most important, once you have said what you need to say, walk away. The longer you stand there, the more difficult it will get.

Thankfully, for most institutions, the crisis communication scenario is rare. Most times we are interacting with the media in the normal course of communicating what is happening on our campuses to the broader community. In these situations, the guidelines above still apply, but the institutional representative should still be involved in guiding the story. What is your agenda behind the story? A skillful interviewee finds ways to turn the conversation back to what he or she really wants to say. Answers to every question should circle back to the core message. We have seen politicians who have honed this skill to an art; some politicians practice this approach to the point that the reporter's question is irrelevant and never answered. Somewhere short of this extreme is an approach that gives the reporter his or her story, while also emphasizing the bigger message. So if a core message at the institution is enrollment growth, almost any question can provide a point of access to emphasize that message. In response to a report about the visit to campus of a famous musician, for example: "We are very proud to welcome Professor Parker to perform here at our university. With our record enrollment of freshmen, we will have an exciting opportunity to enrich the lives of our students."

As you contemplate working with the media, keep these five rules in mind:

- Take control of the interview. You have control over the essential commodity—information.
- In a crisis situation, always communicate that student safety is of paramount importance to the university.
- State only what you know to be true. Once you have said all that you can or want to say, end the interview.
- By speaking in short sound bites and circling back to your messages, embed your agenda into the interview. Be graceful in doing it, but guide each answer to the reporter's question back to the central message you want to communicate.
- Get media training and practice crisis communication scenarios with your PR staff.

CHAPTER THIRTY-THREE

The Entrepreneurial Dean

Kent A. Eaton
McPherson College

"When will things ever change?" you wonder as the twentieth-day census approaches. Fall-to-spring retention has taken a nosedive once again as students time out or "swirl" from college to college. The state has reduced its grant to in-state students, and the advancement office is not reaching its targets. That tough cabinet meeting looms tomorrow. After an initial 3 percent budget cut in the fall when enrollment tanked, you can only hope that this round of cuts is not greater. When *bare bones* already describes your budget, where do you turn?

Your gut tightens as you despair that current positions may be on the line; budget lines for travel, faculty development, and plans to hire for positions still vacant certainly will be. You remind yourself of the need to remain positive in all your communications, but the lyrics of Jackson Brown's "Running on Empty" haunt your consciousness. Do you dare check the job postings in the *Chronicle*?

Your day begins with a proposal by the chair of the math department for new faculty lines; next you attend a senior staff meeting focused on the state of campus facilities; midmorning finds you meeting with your staff to discuss how to trim the office budget, again; over lunch student government leaders advocate for a broader range of internship opportunities. Four meetings in one morning and each boils down to the same topic: how to get the essential work of the university accomplished in an era of limited resources. Sometimes, it feels as if all you ever do is talk about money and how to use less of it. When you started your administrative career, it was with the aim of helping creative people—students, faculty, and staff—bring their innovative ideas to fruition in ways that would enhance student learning, advance important scholarship, and allow your institution to be a vital member of the larger community.

Most of us reading this scenario could have written it. It is central to our work as deans and chief academic officers. In the current chaotic state of higher education, where previous road maps seem inadequate, how we respond to fiscal challenges will likely determine the success or failure of our careers and the future of our colleges. Although the current administrative hiring tendency is to respond by recruiting for academic leadership from the ranks of development professionals (under the rationale that more donations will solve all the problems), a more sustainable solution may well be to rethink and restructure the university as essentially a community organized for innovation and creativity. Certainly there are no silver bullets, but the combination of attitudes, knowledge, and abilities that are essential to the entrepreneur comprise an important part of the tool kit of any dean called to navigate the current crisis in higher education.

Leading our institutions in embracing entrepreneurship is an immense undertaking because it normally requires a significant cultural shift. Embracing entrepreneurial practices and ideals on a micro level in one's office as a dean is essential; but it is not enough. We have to assist in righting the ship as well. To start, establish a common definition, and understand some common or predictable challenges to this exercise. A common hurdle encountered with academics is the assumption that entrepreneurship is just about capitalism and increased profits. The tendency is to confine the term to the fields of business and economics. Therefore, attention must be given to explaining the principles of entrepreneurship as a means of enacting positive social change. In order for the definition to be accepted by all, crafting the meaning needs to involve the entire community, perhaps a specially formed task force, and needs to be supported by the president of the institution. To ensure successful completion, consensus building in an interdisciplinary and system-wide approach must not be underestimated.

Essential components of *entrepreneurship* include innovation, creativity, and sustainability. Your definition must instill a level of self-confidence that is a constant reminder that ideas are the engine of innovation leading to positive social change, and that this conviction is a fundamental competency available to all. Such a definition will serve to *sow seeds of entrepreneurship* across all dimensions of the student experience, not just the academic curriculum. Our college spent much of one afternoon hammering out a definition on which we could agree: "Entrepreneurship is the creative process of developing sustainable, innovative ventures that solve problems or meet the needs of the greater community. Balancing opportunity and risk, the entrepreneur manages resources and constructs solutions that benefit both self and society."[1] In hindsight, the definition should have included some element of "learning to be comfortable operating in a resource-poor environment."

However, our broad definition did serve as a catalyst for a new minor in entrepreneurship studies that is interdisciplinary and able to be combined with any other major field of study on our campus. The definition also served as a welcome mat for all units and departments on campus to embrace and implement entrepreneurial principles. Soon after defining entrepreneurship, students began thinking about beginning commercial and social enterprises. The administration saw the wisdom in supporting this movement by offering microgrants to those students who were willing to pitch their ideas to a group of staff and faculty, venture capitalists, assembled for the purpose of helping students through this period of gestation. Additionally, students and faculty began to envision new forms of project-based learning, which led to the creation of enterprises to serve the needs of our community, especially in cooperation with existing not-for-profit organizations. One example of a partnership occurred when our business and graphic design students opened an off-campus full-service graphic design company dedicated to working with local charitable organizations. Even implementing principles of a continuous improvement process became easier as many at the college lost their fear of, and resistance to, change.

A significant outcome of this experiment to redefine the college and student experiences around the principles of entrepreneurship logically steered the college toward finding ways to narrow the usual town-gown rift. As new project-based learning started becoming commonplace, invitations to form innovative strategic partnerships with school districts, businesses, ministries, and a variety of nonprofits steadily increased. Project-based learning by nature promotes clear learning outcomes as well as accountability and metrics for measuring student success. Our partners came to expect success when working with the college. By invoking the common phrase "we are a teaching institution, not a research institution," we offered those intent on preserving the status quo a way to participate in the entrepreneurial approach.

Many faculty began applying to the Opportunity Fund, established for entrepreneurial endeavors for faculty and staff. Our offer to establish joint ventures allowed our institution and our community partners to take appropriate risks while exercising critical reasoning and creativity in the search for solutions. An increased number of individuals and organizations began finding new reasons for being excited about the college and supporting its mission. As just one example, a public relations class worked throughout the term to develop a comprehensive PR campaign to promote a newly formed mobile medical outreach in Haiti. As they worked to craft messages, target volunteers and donors, and design websites and brochures, the student experience took on special meaning. Students understood that their work could lead to tremendous difference in the world. Not only did the plan exceed the expectations of the mission's founders, the participants grew in their capacity to relate to others compassionately.

In addition to these partnerships we also experienced the increasingly cultivated and expressed "soft skills," in and by our community. As educators perhaps the greatest joy of our vocation comes when we see the light go on in our students as they grasp the fact that true meaning and significance in life come through serving others, and being fully present with those living at the margins. The entrepreneurial mind-set increases the likelihood of our students moving beyond self into an understanding of self-in-community; they develop a greater sense of social responsibility. Entrepreneurship propels the student into active engagement of real-time in situ issues facing others. These experiences that invite students to think with their hearts as well as their heads thereby become the incubator as well as the accelerator of maturation.

In leading this kind of institutional change, the dean or chief academic officer must recognize two principal obstacles that stand in the way. One is structural; most forms of faculty governance exist, in part, to make change, even innovation, slow and challenging. Preservation of present process and form is a primary raison d'être for many faculty governance structures. Conservation—even inertia—has a higher value than change. As one faculty member is prone to remind us, "There are good reasons why faculty outlast administrators." Faculty handbooks make permanent those processes to ensure that cogs move slowly so that due diligence is done. A culture develops that is more comfortable with items still in committee than with expedient decision making. Redundancy is tolerated and then codified.

To make matters even more difficult, the dean has so many committee appointments that setting aside time for creativity is only a fantastic notion. Therefore, an essential parallel activity to organizing for entrepreneurship is to remodel, if not deconstruct, and put into place a structure in which efficiency is valued so that opportunities do not appear and then disappear before we can take advantage of and seize the moment. This does not mean that faculty abandon established principles of governance, but it does insist that we be realistic with the exponential rate of change and organize ourselves in light of this new reality.

Perhaps more difficult to address than structural resistance is that less tangible resistance, a more generalized fear of change itself. This is due in part to the fact that most of us do not acknowledge that we fear change. We fail to recognize it in operation around us because it hides, even embeds itself, into more acceptable or virtuous forms of resistance to change: those *universally* accepted principles of the college and institutional memory. Resistance to change and fear of change are antithetical to the heart and soul of entrepreneurship. The patient yet shrewd dean will experience a degree of success in coaching some faculty and staff through the cycle of change. For others, the noise will never get loud enough that they see the value of joining the journey. Therefore, nothing that the dean does becomes more important than leading search committees in the selection of candidates whose lives show a commitment to weaving entrepreneurial values and practices into the student experience.

The work of the dean is not for the fainthearted. Entrepreneurship cannot be forced upon the community.

- An academic leader must be both humble and patient, qualities not normally considered important for entrepreneurs.
- Consequently, nothing becomes more important than care of one's self and soul in the process. A few of us might be so gifted that creativity comes naturally and does not have to be cultivated. Yet for most, the challenge will be finding the time and place to nurture our own creative selves so that we can move beyond the immediate context, often defined by limited resources, and begin to imagine new possibilities and alternative future narratives.
- Thankfully, as we experiment with new hobbies, journal, meditate, listen to our inner self, or begin learning a new language, the connections that bring meaning and solutions to our personal and institutional dilemmas often emerge. How we find space for unbridled creative thought is fundamental. The question of how each of us will find meaningful ways to foster our own imagination as well as the collective imagination of the university is not a secondary issue but central to the work of the entrepreneurial dean.

Note

1. As your school works to create its own definition, excellent common reading for the community is *Entrepreneurship in Higher Education: Especially in Non-business Studies*, which defines the concept as "an individual's ability to turn ideas into action. It includes creativity, innovation and risk taking, as well as the ability to plan and manage projects in order to achieve objectives. This supports everyone in day-to-day life at home and in society, makes employees more aware of the context of their work and better able to seize opportunities, and provides a foundation for entrepreneurs establishing a social or commercial activity." European Commission's Directorate-General for Enterprise and Industry (2008), http://ec.europa.eu/enterprise/policies/sme/files/support_measures/training_education/entr_highed_en.pdf

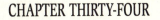

CHAPTER THIRTY-FOUR

Creating Powerful Collaborations between the Academic and Development Divisions

Michael K. Wanous and Susan S. Hasseler
Augustana College, South Dakota

Olivia is the new dean at Quadrivium College. Over the years, several attempts have been made to start the planning process for a new science building. But with changes in presidents and chief development officers, and downturns in the financial markets, the fitful starts have never materialized into a sustained effort. After discussing the situation with the president, faculty, and students across campus, Olivia recognizes the college's urgent need for new space for the sciences. The current building was built in 1965 and is showing its age, both functionally and aesthetically, and enrollment growth in the sciences at Quadrivium continues to put pressure on the existing facilities. There is a sense among the faculty that the condition of the building is affecting not only the delivery of a quality education but also the ability to recruit prospective students and faculty. Olivia has decided that working with the development office to raise funds for a new science building must be one of her highest priorities and so she embarks on an adventure to understand the inner workings of fundraising for an important capital project.

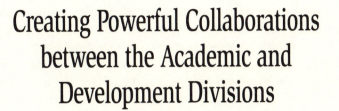

The development office provides leadership for the complex task of gathering resources and soliciting estate and deferred gifts for the endowment, major capital projects, smaller programmatic initiatives, and the general operating budget through an annual fund. Even though Olivia is embarking on a major capital project, it is important to understand that all these areas will play a significant role in making this project successful. Not only will Quadrivium need funds for the new building itself, but it will need to equip the building and the faculty with the materials needed to teach well. The school also will need a strong annual fund to ensure that an appropriate cohort of students will be there to enjoy the new facilities. These funds will come from individual donors, foundations and granting agencies, and the campus community. Academic administrators can play an important role in working with the development office to develop resources in all these areas.

One important task of the development office is to cultivate relationships with potential donors, whether individuals, foundations, or granting organizations. The cultivation process is cyclical in that development officers must first assess the potential for support from these varied funding sources, find a match between the interests or mission of the funder and institutional needs, and finally solicit the resources. In a perfect world, the institution would engage students while enrolled and then engage alumni from the time they graduate. The development office also would maintain relationships with relevant foundations and potential granting organizations over time. Given the mobility of the American population, staff turnover in development offices and in granting organizations, and limited time and energy, the institution is often reconnecting with potential donors, discovering new or emergent donors, and developing new supporters. No matter whether these are new connections or old ones, increasing the number and cultivating existing champions for the cause is ultimately all about relationships.

Because alumni (and their parents or other family members) have had a personal experience with the institution, they are a primary potential source of funds. The Converge Consulting national study on college donor motivation identified three alumni personas: "champions," "friends," and "acquaintances" (Vineburgh, 2012). These three categories were found to be in roughly equal proportions among alumni. Champions were characterized as individuals who are the strongest advocates for the institution and are most likely to donate and give major gifts. Friends are proud graduates who regularly donate but at a lower level than champions, and are often more interested in other philanthropic initiatives in their communities. Acquaintances are the least engaged and least likely to contribute to their alma mater. Champions and friends donated to the institution at the same frequency in the last twelve months, but the champion donors' average size of gift was about 80 percent more than friends' donations. The total donations to all charities were similar for champions and friends. Champions gave the most to education, and friends gave at a higher rate than champions to causes such as fighting poverty, environmental issues, and medical research. These trends suggest that friends have more capacity to give to higher education and that an important strategy for fundraising is making compelling connections between donors' areas of passion and the priorities of the institution. For example, if a donor is most passionate about environmental issues or medical research, these interests could align with aspects of a science building; if a donor is interested in social justice issues, an endowed program or chair in the social sciences or scholarships that target underrepresented students might be of more interest.

Development officers have a number of resources available to determine the approximate size of gift that an individual donor is capable of making, including software packages and information available in the public domain. Research is also conducted to discover the type of projects an individual has contributed to in the past. Having done this homework and after making an initial personal connection with the donor, the development office moves the conversation to another level.

Those on the academic side may be involved in the process of identifying potential donors and making initial contacts, but academic leaders and faculty members can also make valuable contributions to sharing the vision regarding the academic programs that the resources will be supporting. A particularly effective communication strategy includes making sure the donor understands why the current reality is unacceptable, what the ultimate goal is, and the specific ways the team envisions getting from the present situation to the new reality. This will likely involve helping the development team create promotional materials that communicate the vision and sharing these materials with potential donors. Compelling stories from students and faculty can be very effective when combined with specific plans for reaching new goals. Senior faculty members or emeriti can be especially powerful partners in sharing the vision, because many alumni have positive memories of their interactions with certain faculty members. Sharing the vision is much like teaching—it involves a strong understanding of the content, as well as passion for the subject. If teachers are well informed and passionate, their audience is much more likely to catch the vision for themselves.

Also like teaching, donor cultivation can occur in one-to-one, small-group, or large-group settings. Some academics express discomfort about asking for money, but the task is not that different from the primary mission of higher education: engaging students in transformational learning that connects their "deep gladness and the world's deep hunger" (Buechner, 1973). Assisting someone in investing their resources in a project that connects their passions with a program that can meet one of the world's deep needs is an extension of faculty and academic leaders' daily work with students. Through hard work and careful planning, donors have been blessed with the resources to be able to be generous, and they want to give back. Educators can be a part of making their joy complete by helping them find the right place to make their investment.

In addition to gathering resources from individual donors, the academic and development divisions can work together very effectively to develop relationships with foundations and granting organizations. In addition to federal granting agencies, there are myriad foundations looking for partners to join them in pursuing their varied missions. The webpage www.grants.gov can be used as a starting point for finding federal grants. With the aid of proprietary databases (e.g., Foundation Directory Online and GrantStation) and professionals with grant-writing experience, local, regional, and national foundation funding sources that match key funding priorities for the institution can be identified and pursued. Collaborating with other institutions can be an effective way to prepare a winning proposal and secure outcomes that meet mutual goals. With both granting agencies and foundations, once funding has been secured, it is important for the institution to be intentional about sustaining the relationship with the funding organization. Specific individuals should be assigned as liaisons to maintain contact with the appropriate funding agencies to develop a long-lasting relationship between the institution and the granting organization.

In addition to assisting in telling the institutional story, faculty, staff, and students play an integral role in developing innovative projects that could potentially appeal to external funders. Some faculty and staff members also have significant experience with grant writing and can be recruited to pursue foundation and grant funding for institutional projects that connect with their passions and expertise. It is important for deans to provide appropriate support and release time for faculty and staff involved in fundraising activities. Making sure that this work is recognized as valuable institutional service in the tenure and promotion process is especially important for faculty.

Although faculty, staff, and students often have innovative project ideas for which they would like assistance in soliciting external support, development office efforts are appropriately focused on specific initiatives identified in fundraising campaigns and on cultivation of the annual fund. The academic dean plays an important role in prioritizing faculty-led initiatives and requests for support from the development office and in facilitating appropriate communication among faculty, development staff, and potential donors. A formal communication process can help ensure that institution-wide priorities are followed and that everyone's time and resources are used most appropriately. Procedures that guide the submission of grant proposals, the direct solicitation of funds from donors, and the provision of fundraising support from the development office for specific projects can be very helpful. Some campuses have a committee that includes members of the academic and development divisions that determines whether a project will receive direct institutional fundraising support, will receive guidance for the project leaders in engaging in the fundraising process themselves, or should not be pursued at this time. Such a committee can promote positive communication among faculty, staff, students, and the development office. As a result, the institution can ensure that resources are used efficiently and in accordance with the institutional mission and goals.

One of the challenges faced by many development offices is developing effective strategies to solicit financial support for the institution from current faculty, staff, and students. As with engaging faculty and staff in grant writing activities, it is important to develop campus giving opportunities that align with on-campus personnel's interests and expertise. It is essential for faculty and staff to know that support from internal constituencies can be a critical variable in successfully attracting external funding. A high percentage of giving from board members, faculty, and staff communicates that there is broad-based support for the mission among those associated with the institution. The dean can support this effort by leading by example through personally supporting areas of passion, and by working with faculty leaders to find ways to appropriately encourage the faculty to financially support the institution.

Involvement of students in fundraising activities is critical in order to plant seeds for future successful alumni engagement. Students should be involved in activities that increase their awareness of the importance of philanthropy in the funding of their own educations, encourage their gratitude for generosity shown to them by donors, and give them opportunities to participate in giving back even as students. Class gifts for particular programs or capital projects based on student interests can be an effective way to engage students in fundraising. The dean can be supportive by encouraging sensitive approaches to involve students in giving back to the institution even while they are students.

At Quadrivium College, Olivia is eager to be part of a leadership team as she prepares to collaborate with the development office in leading fundraising efforts for the new science building—and there are a number of important lessons she has learned in the process:

- Fundraising for a new facility is a complex process that includes making connections among development staff, external funders, and faculty, staff, and students.
- A strategic capital campaign and a robust annual fund are both essential for the support of this particular project, and donor cultivation includes both external and internal constituencies.
- Developing procedures to prioritize fundraising efforts will minimize misunderstanding and use everyone's time and energy most effectively in reaching their shared goal of providing an excellent new science facility at Quadrivium. She is eager to be part of a leadership team that works together to make this dream a reality.

References

Buechner, F. (1973). *Wishful thinking: A theological ABC.* New York: Harper & Row.

Council for Advancement and Support of Education (CASE). www.case.org. Includes a section titled The Faculty & Staff Role in Fundraising.

Lilly Family School of Philanthropy, Indiana University-Purdue University, Indianapolis. www.philanthropy.iupui.edu

Vineburgh, J. (2012). *Findings from the field: The donor motivation study in practice.* Retrieved from Converge Consulting, www.convergeconsulting.org

CHAPTER THIRTY-FIVE

Productively Working with Advancement and Development

David Timmerman
Monmouth College

"If we cannot come to an agreement about how my gift will be used, I'll be happy to give the money to the local shelter. I will understand and I hope you will understand as well." So said the generous, gracious elderly alumna to me at the end of a two-hour donor call for which I had spent a day traveling and would spend another day traveling back. The potential donor had very specific designs for the gift, and I believed that with some shaping the gift could be extremely helpful to the institution. As it was then framed, it would not be. And yet even after I explained this to the donor, she was not willing to budge. And so I learned firsthand that donors, particularly those willing to give significant funds to an institution, can have fixed ideas about how they wish their gifts to be employed.

Deans involved in fundraising must learn to work productively with donors, but they are just the first of the three constituencies in fundraising. Deans must also learn to work productively with faculty members, the president, and the rest of the president's cabinet. Deans stand in the middle of these three constituencies, and these constituencies often have competing and difficult-to-reconcile perspectives on the institution and, in particular, the manner in which funds are raised and dispersed.

The president and the vice president for development also are key players. Even though the chief academic officer for the institution has significant and ongoing ability to shape the focus of the institution's fundraising strategy, it is the president who ultimately makes these strategic decisions. For the dean, it is important to consider two questions: where is the president in terms of his or her tenure with the institution? What has been the fundraising strategy to this point, and what lies ahead?

A standard faculty perspective on fundraising might start with the contention: "If only our development staff would pitch academic projects instead of athletic facilities and dormitories, this school would be a lot better off!" I had harbored and stated this same sentiment as a faculty member many times myself. Perhaps it is only in taking up the administrative duties of dean that one is able to see things differently.

Immediately after finishing my college degree I began a five-year stint as a "preloader," working for United Parcel Service (UPS). Working on a conveyor belt with packages is quite like what I do working with the three named constituencies on fundraising for my institution. At UPS, I took packages as they came down a conveyor belt and loaded them onto one of three or four brown "package cars" that were behind me. If we imagine that each of the packages coming down the belt is a message to the dean from one of the constituencies, then what the dean does is to pick up that communication and take it to the proper other constituencies. The process, like the boxes coming down the belt, never ends; there are always more messages to share. But, like the package cars, there is a limit as to how much each can hold. Our task as deans is to be selective in what we share so as not to overload or overwhelm donors, faculty, or the president and the development staff.

The dean can best shape and influence fundraising for the best interests of the institution by listening, reflecting, and communicating with these three constituencies. The dean must listen to the members of the development staff, to donors, and to faculty. Deans must reflect on what they hear from these constituencies and see how what they hear connects with the best interests of the institution. Deans also must converse, sharing what they learn from one constituency with the others even as they seek to shape understandings and commitments toward institutional ends.

It would be understandable for deans, having typically achieved a good deal in academe and having been selected by a president and faculty to serve in the role, to imagine that the various college constituencies would be quite interested in hearing their opinion on matters related to the academic program. This would be understandable, but not realistic. Although the dean's views are indeed extremely important and have a significant impact, donor constituents, such as faculty members, staff, and alumni clearly value a dean who listens. What they desire from their dean is a listening ear that takes their ideas, vision for the institution, and concerns seriously and respectfully. The ability to fully and completely listen may in fact be the single most important skill for a successful dean.

The two most important constituents for deans to listen to regarding fundraising are the donors themselves and the faculty and staff on campus. Giving donors a full hearing of their visions of and for the institution is critical. The commitment and passion they feel for our institutions is not generic and homogenous but rather quite particular to them as individuals. Their commitments are completely intertwined in their history with the institution, including their experiences with faculty members, classmates, and staff. These commitments are dramatically shaped by their particular history both before and after attending our institutions. All of these elements are the storehouses from which they derive and formulate their current and future commitments. A fundraising call, a conversation at a homecoming event or reunion, or a chance meeting of any type are all opportunities for a dean to learn what is in these storehouses of experiences, vision, and emotion.

The dean also must listen to faculty and staff on campus; they are the ones who will make use of donated funds. Faculty and staff members know the institution best, including all its potential, weaknesses, and idiosyncrasies. Deans need to continually monitor where faculty momentum is headed and where there is and is not capacity for the use of donations and external funding. One of the most significant disappointments I have had as dean was a case in which the institution received a grant from an external organization but then was unable to use the funds in a timely manner and so had to send the funds back. This is not good for anyone and, in addition to the loss of opportunity to advance the institution, leaves everyone deflated from the development office to the faculty members themselves.

Listening passively, however, is not enough. Deans need to develop and perfect the question. As in good teaching, so too in good academic fundraising: ask good initial questions and good follow-up questions. Good initial questions will be open-ended and not subject to yes-or-no answers. Good follow-up questions demonstrate true interest in what has been said and a desire to understand the person, their experiences, and ideas more fully; to connect the answer from one question to another; to connect the answer from a donor back to the institution, its strategic plan, and its current moment. Good questions are asked with a measure of enthusiasm, good eye contact, and body language that communicates the message "I really want to hear your answer to this question."

The best way to test our understanding of others is to reflect back to them what we have heard them say, both the gist of the content and the emotion or passion accompanying it. In addition, we give the person help in clarifying his thoughts for himself. It is more likely than not that in answering our question the person is articulating his thoughts fully to himself for the first time, even as he is doing so for us. Of course, this may not always be the case—it could be that he has expressed his thoughts on a particular topic many times—but often it is a first opportunity. When he then hears another person reflect back what he or she has heard, he can clarify, alter, extend, or even change what he has said based on this step.

Another step in this stage is to reflect on what we have heard. Prior to communicating what they have heard from donors to the president, development staff, or faculty members, it is important for deans to consider what they have heard in light of everything else they know—in light of faculty interest, the strategic plan, and the current state of the institution. It is easy for any of us to err on the side of communicating too quickly, thus skipping or short-circuiting this step of consideration. The time pressures of our job and the tyranny of the urgent seem to force such behavior, but we must push back against this tendency with several questions:

- What are the current needs within the academic program?
- What new initiatives have faculty members begun that would benefit from additional funding support?
- Where are new opportunities just emerging over the horizon?
- Where is the institution in the formation or execution of its strategic plan?
- Where is the institution in terms of its business model and in particular its funding cycle and cash flow?

Once deans have considered what they have heard, they then must take the next step of communicating with each constituency or, when appropriate and possible, of bringing those constituencies together. Deans function as translators, and their communication should be clear, iterative, and prompt. This is so even when communicating information that others may not wish to hear. Even a president who has come from the faculty may find that after a goodly number of years in the role, she has lost some of her ability to grasp and appreciate the faculty perspective. Donors also vary in their understanding of and appreciation for the faculty, as well as the constraints of the educational environment, the actual rather than perceived needs of an institution, and abilities and desires of our students. The dean plays the vital roles of listener, communicator, and translator so that all constituencies are best prepared to advance the educational goals of the institution.

In your fundraising function as academic dean—receiving, translating, and sending messages—remember four essential tasks:

- Listen carefully and fully to all constituencies in the process.
- Reflect back what you have heard, and reflect on what you have heard.
- Communicate continuously with donors, faculty members, and the president and the rest of the president's cabinet.
- Prepare to let go. Despite our own passion and vision for our institutions and the incredible investment of time and energy demanded from a dean, we often will find ourselves with personal expectations that cannot be fulfilled. Never anticipate that a fundraising initiative or gift or the use of a gift will come together precisely as you would like.

PART FOUR

FOSTERING TEAMWORK ACROSS THE INSTITUTION

CHAPTER THIRTY-SIX

Using Conflict-Handling Modes to Solve Problems and Create New Collaborations

Peggy Rosario
Pennsylvania College of Health Sciences

Budgets for new faculty positions at Middleground State University were limited in the current economic climate. But two deans at the university developed a plan: Dean Smith had funding for one full-time position, and there were a number of different areas where the position could be well utilized. Dean Jones also had one full-time faculty position to fill and had two outstanding candidates, both contingent faculty. To meet the needs of the two deans and the faculty, Dean Smith suggested that both faculty members be hired to work full-time, splitting their work equally between the two divisions. This collaborative solution enabled everyone to assert their needs and accommodate the needs of the others. The university was able to use the talents of both faculty members in teaching different courses in their areas of expertise. The deans were able to keep two outstanding faculty members and expand their contingent workloads into part-time ones. The faculty members were able to transition from part-time to full-time positions. Such a collaborative solution to what was potentially a conflict-laden moment built a bond among those involved, strengthened their relationships, and created a positive work environment.

Granting a department's or division's request for a new tenure-line faculty position was once a decision that could incite enormous conflict among competing units. During times of economic crisis, however, simply renewing a temporary position or allowing an academic unit to retain a tenure line left vacant by retirement or resignation can infuriate any faculty who feel that their program is understaffed—and which programs on your campus does that not describe? So, when Provost Sidestep walked into his meeting with the deans to discuss staffing for the coming year, he did so with dread. He knew that Dean Terminator from health sciences had courses in a variety of related areas that needed coverage but not one focused position request. In addition, it had proven difficult and costly in the past to hire in her area, given the competing opportunities in industry. But those facts were unlikely to stop her from demanding two tenure-line positions. In arts and sciences, Dean Surrender's natural science faculty were deluged with students needing required courses for other majors (particularly in the health sciences) and with majors of their own. In addition, their contingent faculty included two recent PhDs with multidisciplinary training who were well regarded by both peers and students. But in two years as dean she had rarely spoken at these meetings and her faculty were beginning to wonder if she had the ability to advocate on their behalf.

When faced with a problem or conflict, a dean or academic leader has choices about how to respond, and frequently these choices are intertwined with the needs and decisions of others. Making a decision based only on personal needs can have a negative impact on others and hinder working relationships. Giving in to others' demands can mean that personal needs are not met and job effectiveness and satisfaction can suffer. Various modes to handle conflict, most particularly collaboration, can be used to solve problems and resolve conflicts that deans and other academic leaders may encounter.

THE CONFLICT-HANDLING MODES

According to Thomas (1976), handling conflict can be understood in the context of the degree to which one's own needs are satisfied, which he labeled *assertiveness*, and the degree to which another person's needs are satisfied, which he called *cooperativeness*. *Avoiding* is the mode in which an individual neither asserts personal needs nor acts to meet others' needs (Kilmann & Thomas, 1977). Some people find that ignoring problems is the most comfortable approach to take because they despise conflict. They think that if they pretend everything is fine, perhaps it will become a self-fulfilling prophecy and everything will be fine. Sometimes problems do go away without addressing them, but it takes keen insight to distinguish those types of problems from those that should not be ignored.

Accommodating is the mode in which an individual meets another's needs while ignoring personal needs (Kilmann & Thomas, 1977). Individuals who desire to please others like this approach the best because it fulfills their need to avoid saying no to others. But being stuck in the "yes" trap can lead to frustration when personal needs are being sacrificed for others.

Competing is the mode in which an individual's personal needs are met but this is at the expense of others not getting personal needs met (Kilmann & Thomas, 1977). An appropriate slogan for the competing mode is "my way or the highway." Insecure and inexperienced leaders sometimes use this mode to assert authority as a way of demanding obedience because they don't recognize they have alternatives. Some circumstances warrant enforcing a decision that meets personal needs at the expense of others', but individuals who repeatedly use this mode can be viewed by others as bullies. The higher-education environment embraces faculty involvement in decision making, and using the competing mode runs counter to having a collegial relationship with faculty. Trying to repair relationships with faculty after developing a reputation as someone who uses the competing mode can be very challenging.

Compromising falls in the middle of the other modes because it involves getting some personal needs met while also meeting some of others' needs (Kilmann & Thomas, 1977). The flip side to compromising is that the individual must give up some personal needs, and others must do the same. Compromising is a partial solution that brings some satisfaction and some dissatisfaction to each party involved. Although it is not a completely satisfying solution, it has fewer negative ramifications than the previously described modes because at least some of everyone's needs are met.

Collaborating is the mode in which the needs of all parties are met, so it moves beyond the partial satisfaction of compromising. Collaborating requires communication so everyone's needs are understood, as well as trust and creativity in working together to find a solution that satisfies everyone's needs. The vignette example of collaborating is much-simplified compared to the amount of time that is usually needed to satisfy all needs in a given situation, but it does illustrate the benefit of identifying one solution that meets the needs of all involved.

WHEN IS THE BEST TIME TO USE EACH CONFLICT-HANDLING MODE?

Each of the conflict-handling modes has advantages and disadvantages that are important to consider when choosing an approach to implement. No one mode is appropriate or inappropriate for all circumstances, and in some cases using several strategies can be the best approach. Recognizing the benefits and drawbacks of each mode can help a dean choose the best mode for the situation.

Avoiding

In avoidance strategy, conflict will still exist and the dean will not be addressing it. Using the avoidance strategy can hurt a dean emotionally; the energy it takes to continually avoid conflicts can lead to significant mental anxiety. It can also damage relationships with others because the dean is perceived as uncaring. In addition, it harms a dean's professional reputation for being effective in working with others and resolving problems.

However, the avoiding mode can enable a dean to continue the appearance of productive work relationships by treating others as if no conflict exists. The approach could be seen as "rising above the conflict" in situations where a conflict is minor or temporary. In some cases, acting as if everything is fine can result in everyone putting the conflict behind them. In other situations, the avoiding mode can be helpful to buy time. Stepping away from the conflict to manage emotions, assess options to address it, and gather more information about the circumstances can create the opportunity to use another mode more effectively. For these reasons, the avoiding mode is best utilized as a temporary measure before choosing another mode or in circumstances where the conflict is minor or temporary.

Accommodating

In the accommodating mode, needs may not get met, which is frustrating and can lead to negative feelings about those who are making the decisions or allowing decisions to stand. If a dean is not advocating for the faculty's needs and others' decisions hurt the faculty, the dean could be viewed negatively by those faculty members. A dean who is particularly accommodating could develop a reputation as a pushover because others know they can get what they want from this person.

The accommodating mode is helpful to use when building relationships because it ingratiates the accommodator to those being accommodated. Accommodating could also be used as a negotiation strategy by which giving in to another person's needs one time creates an opportunity to call in a favor to get the other person to give in the next time. Giving in also can bring a quick resolution to a minor or temporary conflict. Another reason a dean might choose to use the accommodating strategy with faculty is to enable the faculty member to learn from mistakes. Conversely, in circumstances where a dean realizes that his or her own position was wrong, accommodating others shows character by admitting a mistake.

Competing

Competing hurts relationships because it results in another person losing. A dean who makes decisions based on personal interests, rather than considering those of others, risks being alienated from others due to a lack of trust. A lack of respect is also likely to be associated with a dean who frequently uses the competing mode.

The competing mode does allow a dean to assert power to reinforce who has the ultimate decision-making authority, especially when unpopular decisions need to be made. For a dean who is frequently accommodating, this mode can be used effectively in situations where a compromise cannot be found and a decision is too important to compromise. Competing should be used in circumstances where there is no alternative course of action except to enforce a rule, especially in emergencies.

Compromising

In compromising the parties involved are left with a solution that is only partially satisfying. Because some needs are not being met, a future conflict might arise around those needs. Another challenge of this conflict-handling mode is that it limits the opportunity for relationship building by reaching an agreement before all needs are fully understood and satisfied. Deans who always seek a compromise could be viewed as giving up on a better solution.

One significant advantage to using compromise is that it allows everyone to have some of their needs met, which helps build goodwill among those involved. A compromise can usually be reached more quickly than a collaborative solution, so it can be the best option for decisions that are important and time-sensitive. Compromising can also be a good backup strategy when a collaborative solution cannot be achieved.

Collaborating

Collaborating requires time to understand all perspectives. Another drawback is that it takes creativity to integrate everyone's needs into a solution that satisfies them; sometimes that solution cannot be found. Finally, a dean cannot choose the collaborative strategy alone because it requires buy-in from everyone involved in the problem to work together on the solution.

Nevertheless, collaborating has many advantages. Identifying a solution that satisfies everyone's needs creates a long-term resolution to the conflict. It also creates the opportunity for those involved to better understand each other's needs which can aid in avoiding problems in the future. Collaboration requires creativity and can result in exciting innovation and improved practice. Deans who are able to implement collaborative solutions are viewed as being successful leaders who can address conflict in a positive manner by honoring their own needs and those of others.

When faced with a conflict, a dean has choices about how to respond and should keep the following points in mind:

- Although most people are more comfortable using some approaches as opposed to others, the benefit of being able to suit the style to the situation can be significant.
- Asking how the advantages and disadvantages of the five conflict-handling modes apply to the situation can help a dean choose the most appropriate approach.
- If a dean can find the time and buy-in to facilitate a collaborative approach, it can provide the most complete and satisfying solution.

References

Kilmann, R. H. & Thomas, K. W. (1977, July). Developing a forced-choice measure of conflict-handling behavior: The "MODE" instrument. *Educational and Psychological Measurement, 37*(2), 309–325. doi: 10.1177/001316447703700204

Thomas, K. W. (1976). Conflict and conflict management. In M. D. Dunnette (Ed.), *Handbook of industrial and organizational psychology* (pp. 889–935). Chicago: Rand McNally.

CHAPTER THIRTY-SEVEN

What Teams Are You On Now?

John T. Day
John Carroll University

This morning Terri entered the president's expansive office for the first cabinet meeting at her new institution. Hired because of her experience in a series of administrative positions of increasing responsibility at a sister institution, Terri is about to encounter her new vice presidential colleagues as a group for the first time since the cordial meeting with them during the interview process. Each of the other vice presidents is experienced in his or her role; in contrast, this is Terri's first deanship. Several of her new colleagues have been at this institution for their whole professional careers. One is an alum and former captain of the basketball team, one of the college's storied championship teams in its most high profile sport. How would they treat this new colleague, with her impressive academic pedigree?

Terri was now at a small college in a different part of the country from where she grew up, from where she had been educated, and from where she had most recently worked. None of her new colleagues had the educational credentials or prior experience to suggest deep understanding of the academic enterprise. Only the president, a young star as an art history professor early in his career, had an academic background, but that was at a major research university many years ago. Since then, he had devoted his career to this well-regarded, regional college with many good qualities, though neither a stellar faculty reputation nor a Phi Beta Kappa chapter was among them.

What would Terri face here? Would she be all alone fighting for academic standards—and resources—in constant budget battles at a spartan institution whose financial practices were dictated by a former banking executive, now vice president for finance? A vice president who had the ear of the president and the backing of the board, particularly its chair, the blue-collar entrepreneur who had turned a family business into a Fortune 500 company and successfully fought unionization in the court? Was Terri alone to champion the liberal arts and sciences against the tyranny of the bottom line—after all, the budget had been in the black for the last twenty-five years—could she expect any allies in the room? Were there any common goals around which they could collaborate? Was she joining a team?

Whether it's the solitary scholar in the isolation of the ivory tower of yesterday, or the entrepreneurial independent contractor of today, the stereotype of faculty life is one smart person working alone. As has often been said, the scholarly career is usually about learning more and more about less and less. Moving to a deanship from the faculty presents many new challenges. You need to learn—fast—about a lot of different things you haven't encountered before, and you need to learn to work effectively with others: the person to whom you report, people who are your peers, people with whom you work on a day-to-day basis, and people who report to you. For many deans or other senior academic leaders, some of the most satisfying work (and work with the greatest long-term impact) comes not through working alone as the sole agent of change but rather as a member of a team.

Depending upon the administrative structure of your institution, you will likely be on several "teams," the most important of which may include your boss in a president's or provost's cabinet or council. I've witnessed president's cabinets that are purely pro forma, with all of the action happening elsewhere, often in the one-on-one meetings between the president and each of the vice presidents (or at least those VPs the president regards as important). Other cabinets are the primary locus of the president's work, where real issues are addressed and debated, where decisions are made, plans developed, actions put in motion. One such group at its best functioned in accord with the motto of one of my former colleagues: "All of us are smarter than any one of us."

To be successful in such an environment, the dean not only needs to have a good interpersonal relationship with the boss, but the dean also has to interact effectively with other vice presidents or deans. Where the dean is also the chief academic officer, it is important to work well with others who also deal with students—enrollment and student affairs, for example—and with those who ultimately make your work possible, finance and development. In most healthy institutions, the chief academic officer is truly the "first among equals" but when you are new to your position, you must earn the respect of and learn to work effectively with your vice-presidential colleagues. In these arrangements, you almost always have the moral high ground as it were—we are all about educating students, and that requires faculty, and that requires resources. This should indicate priority and clarity with respect to the institution's mission.

A council of deans will have different dynamics. A group made up entirely or almost entirely of deans is likely to lead to jockeying for position, resources, or preeminence. One feels compelled to look out for one's own—you are the advocate for your school or college—but this understandable self-interest needs to be balanced by a sense of the greater good. Especially as institutions think about new programs and as disciplines become inherently more interdisciplinary, it is not only necessary but also desirable to bridge the gaps between schools and colleges in order to move the institution forward. The leader of the group needs to set the tone and the expectation for cooperation and collaboration.

At one institution I know, the president's cabinet was widely regarded as dysfunctional, but the dean's council—consisting of five associate deans and several others—was the incubator of significant administrative and programmatic change. That group, working together and empowered by the deans to be creative, put structures in place that are still evident more than ten years later. Working effectively in such a group requires respect for the integrity of others and the ability to see the problem at hand from others' points of view.

As my own experience illustrates, in the president's or provost's cabinet or council as dean you are a member of a team led by someone else. You need to be a good colleague and team player, respectful of the areas of responsibility of your peers. Develop relationships with these colleagues outside the context of meetings and official responsibilities—over coffee or lunch—so you can better understand each other's perspectives and values. This advice is especially true if you are new to an institution, as is Terri in the opening scenario of this chapter. You are the new kid on the block; you can build relationships with others by seeking guidance and advice as you adjust to your new institution.

In the two institutions where I have been the chief academic officer, I have depended heavily on a subset of my direct reports. I typically meet weekly with this group in a problem-solving mode—the agenda is set by what any one of us is dealing with at the moment.

In both institutions, I also have less frequent meetings (once or twice a month) with larger groups of those with administrative responsibilities in the academic area: when I was a dean, the department chairs and program directors; now as provost, with the academic administrators who report directly or indirectly to me (directors of the library, service learning, global education, sponsored research, career services—such units will vary from institution to institution). These sessions tend to be more informational in focus, but they have the benefit of fostering informal communication among those present and nurturing a sense of community within academic affairs, which is typically a larger and more complex division of the institution than those devoted to enrollment or fundraising, for example. Less often I also meet with the lower-level administrators and office support staff in small and larger groups, for information, professional development, and sense of community.

In the opening scenario, the new dean quickly learned that all the members of the president's cabinet were committed to the mission of the institution, which was explicitly about undergraduate liberal arts education. They had the support of the president and the board to work together to do all they could to enhance the educational experience of their students.

Teams that you lead can require a variety of leadership skills. You must help set the vision and direction and inspire your team members in pursuit of shared goals. You must delegate, empower, support, and hold accountable those with particular responsibilities. Few teams succeed for long without their leader's explicit recognition and expressions of appreciation.

There are many ways to help build teams, but you will find most teams want to experience the same sense of trust and cooperation that you seek as a team member yourself. Despite difficult issues and persistent challenges, teams want to enjoy the experience of working with others in pursuit of the common good. Your role is to facilitate that work and celebrate its accomplishment; to that end:

- Assume the professionalism and best intentions of your teammates and take the initiative to engage the other members of the teams you join.
- Treat others on teams that you lead as you would like to be treated on teams where you are a member.
- As a team leader, hold high expectations and recognize (and reward if possible) the contributions of the members of your team.

CHAPTER THIRTY-EIGHT

Deans in the (Academic) Game

Darla S. Hanley
Berklee College of Music

As a Bostonian, and a proud member of Red Sox Nation, I anticipate "Truck Day" every February. Truck Day is literally the day that the Red Sox truck, full of team equipment, leaves Fenway Park to go to Florida for the start of spring training. Each time this occurs, there is an excitement in the air about a new season, a fresh start, a distinct team, and the possibilities of great accomplishments obtained when all players perform at their best and work together to reach shared goals. As I think of Truck Day, I also cannot help but think about the work that I do as a dean, orchestrating colleagues to come together for the greater good of educating students, gathering our respective areas of expertise to create a diverse and accomplished team, and realizing that just as there are many persons who are responsible for the Red Sox organization, so too, are there many faculty and staff responsible for the team that is my college.

So, what does Truck Day have to do with being a dean or with serving on academic teams? Like the Red Sox, colleges and universities are complex organizations that require leadership, vision, management, inspiration, assessment, and resources. Our institutions also require hard work and peak performance to achieve shared goals. Each school year offers a new season, a fresh start, a strong and newly configured team of faculty, staff, and students—and is ripe with possibilities for academic and creative accomplishments. Our first day of classes are our colleges' and universities' versions of Truck Day, if you will. Moreover, each school year requires deans to serve on a variety of teams (both on- and off-campus) to drive the institution and maintain a healthy organization where teaching and learning occur at the highest levels.

Deans often serve on many kinds of academic teams, and so it is vital to recognize the role and responsibilities of the dean within these bodies, and the essential skills and qualities portrayed by successful and effective deans within the contexts of academic teams. These elements are guided by the following three essential questions:

- What are common academic teams on which deans serve?
- What is the role of the dean on the team?
- What skills and qualities are required by deans to advance teamwork, their unit, and their institution?

TEAMS FOR DEANS

Although every college is unique, all college deans regularly work with others—in teams. These teams are frequently labeled committees, councils, cabinets, task forces, and work groups, based on the culture of an institution or the specific task to be completed. (For the purpose of this article, all these groups will be generally referred to as *teams* or *academic teams*.)

Academic teams are designed to engage combinations of administrators, chairs, faculty, staff, students, alumni, members of professional organizations, potential donors, friends of the institution, or the community to work together to form or facilitate a shared vision to accomplish a goal. They range from small and intimate groups to very large and unwieldy bodies—depending on the organizational structure of the institution, nature of the work, vision for the project, or resources, to name several categories.

Deans serve on many teams over the course of an academic year. Some teams are ongoing, related to the administrative structure of the institution, such as regularly scheduled meetings with all college administrators, with provosts and other deans, with department chairs within the unit, or with faculty. Some teams are ongoing, related to topics or projects, such as regularly scheduled curriculum committees, budget planning committees, or groups that plan and implement annual events and initiatives. And some committees are singular in nature, such as search committees for open positions and committees to organize visits by artists, scholars, and lecturers, or to organize new facility planning and opening.

Academic teams focus on just about all areas of the institution, and deans are often asked to engage with and lead groups that explore and advance much of this work. Academics are at the heart of deans' work and address the what, where, when, why, and how of student learning. Deans focus on educational effectiveness and strive to improve teaching and learning for students across all disciplines, core requirements, competencies, and professional standards. Examples of these kinds of teams include committees and ad hoc working groups, or regional consortia and national organizations.

Teams related to students, faculty, and staff—the human element—also fill a large part of a dean's agenda. These teams focus on identifying the persons who study and work at an institution (the student affairs and human resources for the school). They also are commonly responsible for policies and procedures that ensure effective engagement, and professional and academic progress. Deans engage with student affairs and student support professionals, admission and financial aid staff, and others on campus who deal directly with student services, as well as with human resources and union representatives.

In addition, deans serve on teams that address campus planning and utilization—the physical and structural elements of an institution that create effective educational and work environments, enhancing professional and creative opportunities. These teams often focus on building construction or renovation projects, building maintenance, equipment, safety, and space configuration as related to academic program development, technology needs, and accessibility. They also consider the health and safety of persons in the college community and strive to make their campus a great place to work, teach, and learn.

Real-world connections, professional collaborations, and opportunities for students, faculty, and staff in a global society are topics frequently addressed by deans. These topics require deans to think and engage beyond the borders of a campus to interact with alumni, other institutions, community members, professional organizations, and artists/scholars, to mention a few. Selected examples of teams on which deans serve that reach outside their institutions may include community partnerships and regional institutions, local and state governments, and international consortial institutions.

Budgets and finance are among the most significant topics deans address—funding fuels the work completed within an academic unit and across an institution. Accordingly, deans often serve on multiple teams related to securing funds, preparing requests for budgets, determining budget allocations, and managing operating and capital budgets. These teams require deans to employ strong communication skills and attention to detail, and to have a vision for the unit and a dedication to students. Common teams on which deans serve related to finances include budget work groups, strategic planning committees, advancement collaborations, and union leadership.

The last category of teams on which deans frequently serve includes those addressing campus culture, public presence, and stature. These teams enhance a campus community, raise visibility, and call on deans to reflect on achievements, milestones, signature events, celebrations, and various faculty, staff, student, and institutional accomplishments. They often focus on academic and artistic excellence or the history of an institution, and they help shape a campus culture and form institutional legacy. There are many teams on which deans serve related to campus culture and events, such as orientation or commencement committees, presidential inauguration planning work groups, or new facilities planning groups.

Regardless of the name, focus, or frequency of scheduling, a dean's calendar is regularly full of team meetings. We are key players in assuring the life and vibrancy of our institution—and through these collaborations we provide insights, experience, and vision to help shape every topic or situation that presents.

THE ROLE OF THE DEAN WITHIN ACADEMIC TEAMS

Effective deans serve their academic teams much as their counterparts in sports do, by being general managers, coaches, trainers, scouts, and players—depending on the team. Deans wear different hats and perform different roles based on the goals, objectives, and contexts of the work at hand. In all team settings, however, deans strive to advance the student experience and the educational process. A dean's role within academic teams is analogous to positions found in professional sports in terms of decision making, budget management, personnel evaluation, program development, problem solving, and community engagement.

Dean as General Manager

Deans oversee a unit of faculty, staff, and students on a college campus. In this context, we serve as the *general manager*—the person who needs to see the big picture and who sets the tone and direction for the unit. The dean offers a vision for her area of the institution that flows from the mission, strategic plan, master plan, and institutional history and that advances teaching and learning. As GM, the dean is responsible for assembling and evaluating the team, making decisions regarding the implementation of programs and curriculum, ensuring the unit has adequate resources and facilities, and inspiring and motivating the team, to mention a few examples. In this role, the dean is engaged in high-level work that requires the ability to

- see the forest (as well as the trees);
- communicate clearly;
- guide others to reach consensus;
- make sometimes unpopular and difficult decisions; and
- advocate for the unit.

The visionary GM leads teams with a sense of thoughtful purpose and direction. She creates agendas and facilitates meetings to engage persons in the work at hand while recognizing that she must always lead by example. Moreover, the dean as GM is uniquely positioned to contribute to the institution at large and simultaneously shape how her work and unit fit into the organization.

Dean as Coach

Deans serve as *coaches* of faculty, staff, and students within teams on a college or university campus—grouped by schools, departments, disciplines, majors, or assignments. In this role, the dean is responsible for knowing his players, providing clear directions and expectations, and working to ensure that all team members feel motivated and supported. In team settings, the dean often coaches his colleagues to see a viewpoint, reach consensus, or advocate for a particular position. The dean as coach requires the ability to

- use language to guide and motivate others;
- evaluate team members and offer support to prepare them so they are able to contribute to the group;
- offer constructive feedback; and
- demonstrate a record of success and encourage trust and buy-in from the team.

Dean as Trainer

Deans serve as *trainers* of faculty, staff, and students within teams on a college campus. In this role the dean strives to nourish her teams to allow them to work effectively by providing resources and other support—to keep them healthy, happy, and in the game. Faculty and staff development (on- and off-campus) are essential components of successful work, ensuring that the persons being asked to complete a task are able, prepared, and empowered. As the trainer, a dean needs to

- nourish the team;
- identify appropriate development opportunities for team members (classes, learning communities, mentors, suggested readings, etc.); and
- secure resources.

Dean as Scout

Deans serve as *scouts* of faculty, staff, and students within teams on a college campus. In this role the dean strives to identify the best team members from existing personnel, make requests for additional positions, and engage beyond campus boundaries to make connections with persons who will enhance teamwork, the institution, and the student experience. Moreover, the dean as scout recruits students that *fit* his institution and does what he can to position them for success. The deans as a scout needs to

- recognize talent, ability, and accomplishments of team members (and potential team members);
- seek new opportunities for his academic unit, academic team, or strategic initiative; and
- be engaged in the campus community and beyond.

Dean as Player

Finally, deans must be *players*. In this role they lead by example and balance being the person in charge of a team with being a contributing member of a team. This balance requires deans to know when to share and when to allow others to take the lead. The dean, as player, is able to advance the work at hand because she is at the top of her professional game. Deans, as players, need to

- be engaged in personal creative scholarship and professional activity;
- listen and observe;
- be well-read and informed; and
- offer *best thinking* and *best practices* framed by experience, logic, intellect, and compassion.

Deans shape the educational lives of students and the professional lives of faculty and staff, and they influence a campus culture and community. Our work is challenging, rewarding, and always involves working with others—in teams.

As deans we navigate numerous topics and issues that require our attention on a daily basis. Much like sports, our work in academia requires us to be flexible, nimble, strong, clear, thoughtful, creative, attentive, and motivated. We are a source of inspiration and knowledge for those around us, especially in team settings, and would do well to keep several questions in mind:

- What role should I play in each situation?
- What are the roles I am strongest and feel most comfortable in, and what roles are challenging for me to play?
- What new ways can I celebrate the accomplishments on the campus?
- How can I best share my knowledge and experiences, cognizant of the cultural expectations and concerns of my institution?

CHAPTER THIRTY-NINE

Working with Other Deans

Bonnie D. Irwin
Eastern Illinois University

The student body president stood up and greeted the graduating class. He reflected on the good times they all had had at the local bars, and he gave a special shout-out to his fraternity brothers, listing several by name, to the discomfort of the rest of the platform party. The continuing education dean looked out over his candidates, many of whom had completed most of their degree off campus or online and had never set foot in the local watering holes, but for whom this commencement ceremony was every bit as important as it was to the graduates sitting among them who were young enough to be their children. The student at the podium was not speaking for them, nor was he speaking for the masters and doctoral candidates, sitting quietly, their long-sought-after hoods neatly folded over their arms, awaiting the moment when the dean would place this symbolic garment over their heads and onto their shoulders. The graduate dean frowned as the next speaker, an invited alumnus, trod the same ground as the student body president, recalling the parties and the football games, seemingly not realizing that the graduates were a far more diverse group than the class with whom he had graduated many years ago.

At the next deans' council, the graduate and continuing education deans presented an issue to their colleagues: Did their colleagues feel that adult learners and graduate students were disenfranchised by the typical commencement remarks? Was commencement an event over which deans should have more say? Did the academic deans have the time and will to take on this issue?

COLLABORATION AND COMMUNICATION

On a campus where there are several deans, working together has its advantages. If one dean has an issue, chances are that all do, and by working together, representing the faculty and departments, they often can have a greater influence than any one dean will have lobbying for a change alone. Open communication sets the standard for sharing both ideas and the responsibility for advocacy. A single dean lobbying for the interests of a relatively small group of students will not have nearly the same pull as a whole team of deans lobbying on behalf of the students as a whole.

Collaboration can flourish in all manner of contexts. When a new strategic plan is put in place, deans can work together, sharing ideas about how to implement the plan in the academic units. Although each unit will do so in a different way, there are some shared values, such as academic excellence or resource support for faculty that all share. Similarly, if there is an institutional mandate that must be implemented that may be unpopular with faculty, deans can work together so that all faculty members receive the same message. If one dean implements a policy in a wildly different way from her peers, and faculty members begin to compare notes, an environment of second-guessing and resistance may arise. If all deans are transparent with each other and to the same degree with their faculties, the information will be better received by the entire community. A conversation among deans might start with something as simple as "What concerns have your faculty raised about x?" Chances are the same concerns will come up elsewhere and can be anticipated by one's colleagues.

No amount of communication will lead to collaboration, however, without deans making the effort to understand the culture of the other colleges or schools on campus. Typically, as one rises through the ranks from faculty member to department head to dean, one sees the world through a broadening but still limited perspective. Taking some time to learn the pressures and needs of one's colleagues makes for a better working relationship: What kind of regulations is the college of education subject to? Which departments on campus need to seek external accreditation? How expensive is the equipment needed by the bench sciences? What kind of class size is appropriate for a writing-centered or studio-based class? Understanding the answers to these and myriad other cultural questions will make collaboration among deans easier. In addition, if a dean wishes to apply later for a vice presidential position, being able to demonstrate that one has a basic understanding of the needs of academic affairs as a whole is essential.

RESOURCE SHARING

One might think that in an era of scarce resources, deans would find their relationships strained, but the opposite is often true. With the growing interest in interdisciplinary programs, there is more and more need for flexibility regarding faculty lines and operational budgets. If the business school, for example, is providing support for a public health or arts administration program that is growing, then the business school may need a new faculty line. If the philosophy department wishes to invite a prominent yet expensive speaker to campus to address issues of medical ethics, perhaps the nursing program also may provide funds and invite their students. Although these collaborations can happen at the departmental level, the deans are better positioned to initiate these arrangements on behalf of their departments. Rather than each college acting independently and on a smaller scale, they may work together combining resources for a greater impact on an institution and its students.

Under financial duress, a senior administrator may be making cuts that are equitable but not equal. If deans have clearly communicated with one another and with their vice president or chancellor, they will better understand differences in resource allocations and be able to better explain them to their faculties. Understanding does not necessarily mean agreement; however, if an open and cordial relationship exists among deans, you will feel much more comfortable raising an objection or questioning a difference in funding that does not appear to be equitable. Indeed, genuine disagreements are most likely to arise around resource issues, and it is useful to enter into any negotiations or discussions with that in mind.

In good times, deans also may collaborate in resource areas such as alumni relations or development. A single alumnus might have a relationship with more than one college: perhaps the student was a management major and an English minor but had a work-study appointment in the department of psychology. When the business dean meets with the alumnus as a donor, she may hear that the truly transformative experience took place in a writing course, to which the former student now wants to donate funds. In this situation, one can either try to talk the donor into another course of action or pass the information on to a colleague dean under the theory that a rising tide lifts all boats. Our development professionals will tell us that a happy donor is a generous donor. Recognizing the helpfulness of all concerned, that donor may very well come back with a donation to the business school on another occasion. Collaborating on campus-wide development projects is an increasingly common activity. If all deans collaborate, they often can garner enough donations to fund the faculty research grant program that none can fund individually.

SETTING THE STAGE FOR COLLABORATION

Often the vice president for academic affairs or the president sets the tone for the deans' relationships. If the VPAA encourages collaboration, consensus, and a cordial working environment, the team of deans will find that their common interests outweigh their competing ones. Under the guidance of a good leader, the deans' council becomes a site of collaborative problem solving, safe and open discourse, and budget planning. Just as faculty expect, or even demand, transparency on the part of their deans and department heads, so, too, should deans expect it on the part of their president and vice president for academic affairs. In such an environment, the deans together become allies for the senior administration, bringing their combined intellect and creative energy to bear on new initiatives, old problems, and day-to-day challenges.

If, however, you are unlucky enough to have a leader who relishes the competition and pits one dean against another—yes, this can and does happen—the deans can resist the temptation to play into this strategy and hold their ground as a united body, working together for the betterment of the university. A united or at least collegial group of deans can also succeed in converting their supervisor over to their way of thinking. There is indeed safety in numbers; deans generally persist longer in their positions than do senior administrators. This longevity, a firm grounding in institutional culture, and a collaborative working relationship with other deans enables deans to lead from the middle.

In our opening scenario, the deans proposed a competition to select who would be commencement speaker, a plan that, using a diverse selection committee, would both raise the stature of the student address and give the deans a bit more control over the content of commencement remarks. They also pooled their resources to offer the winning students small cash awards. As a group, they petitioned the vice presidents and the commencement committee, and future ceremonies became occasions of both celebration and academic achievement. By communicating openly, working together to find a solution, and by sharing monetary resources, what began as the concern of one dean became a solution to a problem that the others did not know they had until one of their colleagues raised the issue. An institution and its students will always benefit from effective collaboration among deans, so here are five keys to working with other deans:

- Take the time to learn about the unique challenges and opportunities each of the other colleges or schools on your campus face.
- Keep lines of communication among you open and share concerns. If you have an issue, chances are one of your colleague deans does, as well.
- Build collaborative relationships around common interests.
- Be willing to share resources and ideas.
- Resist being drawn into competition.

CHAPTER FORTY

The Role of the Dean in Decision Making at the University Level

Laura Niesen de Abruna
Sacred Heart University

Midwest University is a 3,000 FTE comprehensive university that is fifty years old and serves a public state system. Well-respected Midwest University has four colleges, but that organizational structure is recent, as are the deans of the individual colleges and the general understanding of their roles. The university is tuition-driven and has faced yearly budget deficits since 2008, as well as continual erosion of state support. The new president is from a large company in the state capital and knows a number of influential people in the state government. The governor's and the president's vision is that there will be more graduate programs to drive enrollments and, they hope, increase revenue. The president is also drawing his communication style from the corporate world.

Everyone is enthusiastic about the new leadership team that will be fiscally disciplined and entrepreneurial, but there is some concern among the liberal arts faculty that there will be too much focus on professional preparation to the detriment of quality education. No one is talking about these conflicting opinions, because the new officers of the institution are busy with new initiatives and feel that they do not have the time to talk to everyone about their plans. Lately, no one above the level of department chair feels the need to share his or her academic plans with anyone else. As a dean at Midwest University, you are committed to helping students and faculty succeed, but you find that the poor communication is making your job even more challenging and is impeding your ability to make good decisions.

One of the most salient issues in decision making is effective communication to broad constituencies. Balancing the budget and maintaining bond covenants while building expected athletic facilities and dormitories are foremost on the minds of the trustees, president, and other vice presidents. They believe it is unnecessary and less efficient to make sure that everyone who might benefit from hearing about a decision is apprised of that decision before it is implemented. The president, who sets the leadership tone in the university, has not changed his management style since joining Midwest. He likes to work as quickly as possible and informs subordinates of his plans on a need-to-know basis. He knows that balancing the budget while getting financing for a new dormitory is his main concern.

The provost and the deans share these concerns but think that there are other issues that are equally important. Their leadership style is not corporate but is based on peer-to-peer persuasion because they consider the faculty to be equals and not employees. This flattened model of organization is commonplace among deans who come from the faculty and who have themselves been involved in shared governance models of communication and decision making. Most deans gain their experience through work with colleagues as department chairs or through work with college-wide colleagues in curriculum development.

Many of the lessons deans have learned as they have moved through faculty and administrative ranks can be implemented as a dean. In the case of Midwest University, the deans and the provost should work together to share as much information as possible, particularly around matters that require faculty input. In the case of curriculum, deans should make a point of leading by example, irrespective of the leadership style espoused on a campus, to let the provost know what curriculum is being explored in the college or school. Likewise, there should be some general meeting time each week for the deans and the provost to share their plans with one another. Problems should be ironed out at the lowest possible level of decision making. Doing this is not only more efficient in the long run but also avoids the drama that comes from conflict imported to a higher level.

Although communication is the sine qua non of the academic affairs team, the practical reason for the team's existence is to move the operational business of the university forward. Ideally, the deans and the provost meet one-on-one to share information from both positions, but also in a separate deans' council or provosts' council whose purpose is to advance the operational and strategic agenda of academic affairs. To one degree or another, the academic team must process the development of the academic budget, gain permission to hire new faculty lines, make sabbatical decisions, create academic policies and procedures, generate curriculum, evaluate tenure and promotion packages, promote faculty development, process graduation and commencement activities, and resolve conflicts in shared governance. In a tuition-driven environment, the team should be consulted for enrollment planning on a regular basis. The most important element in this list is the determination of the share of the university budget that will go to academic affairs.

It is a commonplace that the more the overall business decisions are delegated to the finance department, the less authority the academics have for the development of the budget. Remember the corporate rule of "need to know."

The more we ignore the numbers, the more often other officers decide that academics do not need to know what the exact financial information is that is being shared with the president and the trustees. Deans and the provost must work with the staff in accounting and financial analysis to develop business plans for their departments. These are absolutely necessary for launching new programs in the current environment. An attractive plan will need a net growth over a three-to-four-year time period and will have at least a regional market potential to be persuasive. In the ideal scenario, the trustees will allow the department to borrow the money necessary to launch a program, including funding for faculty positions, with the responsibility for paying back all costs by the end of a three-to-four-year period. It is impractical to expect departments to create new programs if there is no opportunity to hire instructors to teach these courses. On the other side of the equation will be a reasonable expectation from the trustees to evaluate programs that are draining resources and to shut them down.

Essential to the process of becoming an active part of budget decisions is having access to accurate data. Ideally, the Office of Institutional Research, which is responsible for reporting IPEDS information to the federal government on behalf of the university, should report to the provost and should be seamlessly available to the deans to provide accurate and timely information about enrollment numbers, profit and loss statements, academic costs, and similar information about other units. The finance office also needs to provide the deans with accurate and timely information on budget actuals. Deans need to have information to make good decisions, but it is not always communicated to them.

Finally, we come to the vision thing. Granted this is a term that has been overused since at least the Bush administration. But there is a need for the academic leadership to think of new initiatives and to reconceive the mission of the university in ways that respond to the current economic environment. At every institution there is chatter about online initiatives, three-year degrees, accountability, debt loads, and so forth. These issues are real and will not go away. However, there are also real-time initiatives that are choice-worthy and that can be accomplished during the span of a dean. Shaping and sharing new curricular directions in the university is one such area. Deans have tremendous opportunities to enrich the overall learning environments of their students and to measure success in those environments. They have opportunities to engage in what AAC&U calls the high-impact practices of common intellectual experiences, first-year seminars, service learning, living-learning communities, global opportunities, capstone experiences, writing-intensive courses, internships, and other forms of experiential learning. At universities with graduate programs, the deans can chart the path for graduate programs in new markets and thereby change the overall direction of the university.

There are many opportunities for the academic team to work with the president, other officers of the college or university, and the board of trustees to accomplish the overall goals of the university. There are major questions to address, and deans should be part of those discussions, whether it is what the mix of liberal arts and professional studies should be, or how much tuition discounting should be extended, and to whom. The academic team has the responsibility to communicate their sense that the academic enterprise and the life of the mind are the most important values in higher education. They have an important role in helping trustees to understand the role of academic affairs as the core business of the college and to educate them in that direction.

Communication is arguably the most important element in the working relationship among faculty, deans, provosts, and other senior administrators. Second is taking charge of academic decision making by taking ownership of the appropriate institutional data. Third is the ability to share the goals of the university so that they support the core values of higher education. If all these elements are in place, then you have one of the most rewarding jobs in higher education. Be sure to keep the following points in mind:

- Communicate with your colleagues about matters involving the curriculum.
- Take ownership of financial decision making by accessing accurate and timely data.
- Work with the provost, president, and board of trustees to keep education as the major goal in the business of higher education.

CHAPTER FORTY-ONE

Productive Relationships with Department Chairs and Program Directors

Virginia Coombs
Council of Independent Colleges, retired

The dean wants to strengthen the effectiveness of departmental and division chairs and program directors, and would like to find ways to create opportunities to further develop the chairs' leadership skills and help them develop a broad perspective on campus issues. A broader vision of campus priorities as they relate to mission and strategic initiatives will improve the chairs' ability to participate effectively in decision making that may affect not only their own department or division but the entire campus. Finding the extra time for professional development is a challenge to overly busy schedules. The dates and times for the regular department chairs' meetings are already set in the campus calendar and may provide a solution. Most chairs' meetings are made up of announcements related to due dates for reports and requests, information that could be communicated in a different form. By refocusing part of the meeting time for professional development activities, the dean can provide chairs with the opportunities to develop their leadership skills without scheduling extra meetings and also tie the topics directly to the work of the chairs.[1]

The discussion of topics in this chapter—the budget process, using data effectively, and managing personnel challenges within the department—includes suggested activities for deans and chairs or directors to pursue jointly. Moreover, deans should strongly consider that such training includes not only current but also incoming or prospective chairs and directors.

BUDGET

Normally, faculty members do not have extensive experience with budgets and how the department's resources fit into the larger campus-wide budget situation.[2] Chairs should recognize how the campus budget functions as a planning document that coordinates campus priorities with available resources. They can participate in the development of the budget for the academic affairs unit if they are part of the planning process and are familiar with the time line and deadlines for making budget requests. In order to make convincing arguments for the departmental requests, chairs need to understand the financial resources available in the department budget that may support new requests. The dean, the budget officer, or the chief financial officer can provide guidance on how a request is constructed, what types of data are needed, and how the accompanying narrative effectively uses data to tell a convincing story.

The chair also must communicate the budgeting process and decision-making process to departmental colleagues. If deans use meetings of department chairs to discuss the institutional budget process and its relationship to department budgets, chairs can present drafts of their budget requests to each other and receive feedback. Discussion among the chairs about the details of their colleagues' requests will inform chairs about priorities beyond their own unit. Participating in an open, transparent process helps chairs assess requests from other departments and can greatly assist in the prioritization of all requests. Transparency in the process equips chairs to communicate budget decisions to their departmental colleagues with greater specificity, especially when the outcome does not result in a positive decision for the department's plans.

If an institution has not used a transparent process at the chair level, discussing short budget scenarios first will help chairs sharpen their problem-solving and negotiating skills and learn new approaches from colleagues. The following scenarios involving some common budget dilemmas at the departmental level provide opportunities for practice.

- The budget for department copying has been depleted by March 1. How does the chair prepare for the discussion at the next department meeting? What budget information does the chair provide to colleagues about the overspending? What lines in the department budget might support this expense for the remainder of the semesters?
- Department budgets have been frozen for three years. The request for budget information for the next year indicates that there is not much available for new initiatives. Department colleagues want to propose an initiative that will cost between $2,000 and $2,500. The new initiative might be shared with other departments. What amount for the total cost might come from existing budget lines? How does the chair lead colleagues in constructing the proposal?
- A colleague has secured an invitation to a regional meeting where students who have worked collaboratively with your colleagues will copresent on the results of their research. There has been no prior planning for funding

to cover the students' expenses. Is it possible to provide this opportunity for the students? If so, where might the funds come from? What discussion should take place in advance of the budget cycle in future years?

DATA

In the past decade department chairs have become more aware of the ways in which institutional priorities and the criteria used to make resource allocation decisions are dependent on a variety of accurate data.[3] Departments are the primary source for data about academic program content, including course enrollment patterns in general education, as well as in major and minor programs; student credit hours generated in the department; and student course evaluation data. Student data frequently include assessment of student learning, retention and graduation rates for students in majors and minor programs, the number of transfer students in department programs, and the number of student advisees. Data on faculty members usually include faculty teaching loads, statistics on tenured versus nontenured faculty members, the number of adjuncts teaching in department programs, and faculty participation in institutional governance.

Data come in many forms, and the amount and variety of data that chairs collect can be overwhelming. Even though the data originate in the department, it is not only the chair who is responsible for collection. Data are also collected by the registrar's office and institutional research offices. Deans must communicate to chairs the importance of data collection and the variety of situations in which data are needed. Deans should provide chairs with direct and regular access to the individual or office that manages institutional data resources.

A hands-on activity that can be scheduled for a portion of department chair meetings might involve a series of data problem exercises. Some topics might include knowing what data are needed to support additional course section requests and where to find them; what data sources support a new faculty line request; or the acquisition of new instructional equipment for classroom use. Brief scenarios can be used quite effectively to problem solve for missing or incomplete data. Combining a data exercise with a budget exercise reinforces the importance of having good data with an effective, supportive narrative.

Knowing which data to use to support an argument is just the beginning. Numbers alone do not make the case; not all data that chairs collect have numerical values. Numerical and qualitative data require the addition of a well-constructed narrative that makes the argument for adopting or rejecting a course of action. Chairs need to practice constructing effective narratives that interpret the data. Deans may choose to invite the campus institutional research professionals to lead these exercises. This opportunity not only helps chairs learn to use effective methods for presenting arguments supported by data but also establishes a relationship with staff members with whom chairs can regularly consult.

The following scenarios combine both data collection and budget considerations.

- Junior faculty members in several departments have been successful pursuing undergraduate research projects with their students. Currently no campus-wide budget support for an undergraduate research program exists. What data would support the inclusion of this pedagogy in departmental budgets? How much of the existing individual budgets might be reallocated for this purpose? What would a proposal look like?
- The modern languages department at a nationally ranked liberal arts college is facing the retirement of a longtime faculty member in German. This faculty member is the only German teacher on campus and is essentially the German program. The program offers a BA in German in a very traditional format. Enrollments in the German major have been dropping for several years to the point that in the upper division courses there are rarely more than three students. As a result the German teacher has been doing a number of independent study or tutorials with individual students to help them complete their degree. The administration has questioned the feasibility of the German program for some time based on low enrollments and would like the languages department to drop German and develop a program in Asian languages and culture, transferring the tenure-track line from German to this Asian studies area. The administration also notes that prospective student interest in Asian languages is growing while interest in German is declining. The department is opposed to this change. The chair has appointed a subcommittee within the department to study the situation and draft a recommendation for future action. What data should they consider? What sources beyond the campus might be consulted?

PERSONNEL CHALLENGES

Speaking with individual department colleagues about personnel matters are among the least favorite responsibilities that chairs are asked to assume, but the chair's intervention at the department level can prevent many issues from escalating into crisis situations that find their way into the dean's office.[4] Chairs are frequently called on to resolve conflicts between students and faculty members or disputes among their faculty peers. However, chairs may hesitate to initiate action, such as speaking directly with a colleague, because they lack the skills to address the problem, to encourage change, or to deliver bad news.

Chairs should develop the skill of framing the problem or issue, which includes considering the issue from multiple perspectives, articulating a specific goal, and stating the desired outcome.

Deans can assist chairs in developing the skills for facilitating difficult conversations by providing opportunities to practice and prepare for these conversations using a structure that includes the following steps. *The key to a successful conversation lies in the preparation and practice for the actual conversation.*

Preparation

Preparing for the conversation includes gathering the information and determining who else might be consulted. A written script containing the key points to be covered helps the chair stay on track. Because these conversations can be stressful for both the chair and the faculty colleague, the script also should include "reminders" about employing active listening during the conversation. The chair should request the meeting and location. Depending on campus culture and department politics, the meeting might be in the faculty member's office, the chair's office, or some other location that offers privacy.

The Conversation

A calm demeanor on the part of the chair can offset a defensive posture on the part of the faculty member. The opening should acknowledge that the issue is a difficult one for the chair, state clearly that the conversation is the first step to seeking resolution, that no decision has been reached in advance of the conversation, and that the faculty member will be asked to take an active role in framing the issue from his or her perspective and participate in crafting a satisfactory solution. The conversation ends by defining clear next steps with target dates for completion of actions that have been mutually agreed to and by setting a follow-up date to assess progress.

Follow-Up

The information from the conversation is useful in preparing written documentation of the conversation that identifies the key issues, possible solutions, and the action plan. Share the document with the faculty member and ask for a signature to acknowledge that the document reflects the faculty member's understanding of what occurred. The chair should follow up on any commitments made during the conversation.

Role-playing exercises are useful tools for chairs to practice their newly acquired skills. The following scenarios offer opportunities for discussion and role playing.

- Professor Baker does all work assigned and expected of tenured faculty members, but all at the minimum level. Since a pay cut on the campus two years ago, Baker has disengaged. Complicating matters, Baker is a former chair who is a know-it-all, refusing to cooperate on any new requirement or initiative. How can the chair help Baker to improve?
- Jones is a faculty member who has just been denied tenure. Jones is angry about the decision and holds you, the department chair, responsible because you addressed her failure to meet the tenure standards in your written evaluation as chair. She shares her anger with colleagues, some of whom become concerned when her commentary includes threatening statements about her desire to show up in your office and "have it out with you." Should the chair initiate the conversation or wait for Jones to call for an appointment?

Departmental and division chairs and program directors occupy a pivotal role in the administrative structure of a college or university. Most chairs come into their positions with little training for leadership responsibilities or experience cultivating a wider view of campus challenges. As the role of the department chair expands to include more administrative responsibilities, chairs need opportunities to learn about the administrative aspects of their jobs in order to be effective in their administrative roles, whether they report to the chief academic officer or to a school dean. Deans can enhance the effectiveness of chairs and program directors by providing hands-on opportunities for developing administrative skills, thereby creating a stronger cohort of midlevel administrators who will be empowered to lead their departments more effectively.

Here are some questions to consider:

- Regularly ask department chairs and program directors what training they would like to receive.
- Establish regular meetings of chairs and devote part of each meeting to development. Chairs are important academic leaders and their vision and practices are valuable resources to the campus.
- Be sure to compliment and thank department chairs for their service; serving as a chair can often be a thankless job, and support and encouragement will be appreciated.

Notes

1. These topics have formed the nucleus of the Council of Independent College's annual Workshops for Department and Division Chairs since 2010.
2. My thanks to Mark Braun (Gustavus Adolphus College), Mary Ann Gawelek (Seton Hill University), Rita Knuesel (The College of Saint Benedict/Saint John's University), and Liz Rudenga (Trinity Christian College) for materials in the budget section.
3. Thanks to Bill Deeds (Morningside College) for the wealth of data sources he has collected and skillfully uses in presenting this topic at CIC's Workshops for Department and Division Chairs.
4. Thanks to Jeanine Stewart (Hollins University) for sample scenarios and for the protocol for difficult conversations.

CHAPTER FORTY-TWO

Developing Productive Relationships with Assistant and Associate Deans

What They Might Want You to Know

James M. Sloat
Colby College

You are looking forward to your first day as dean of faculty at a new institution. During the interview process, you were impressed by the president's vision, by the quality of the faculty and students, and by the good fit between the institution's needs and your skills and experiences. You are excited to begin your work. As you enter the office, you are greeted by your administrative assistant, who informs you about several meetings that are already on your calendar. Two of these meetings are with the assistant and associate deans in your office. You met these colleagues during the interview process, but your conversations since being hired have been with the president, and your thoughts have been occupied with the strategic initiatives that you are being expected to launch in your first year. Quite frankly, you have not given much thought to the assistant and associate dean positions. As you plan for the conversation, you have some things you would like to share, but you really would like to know what the associate deans (a) really want to know from you, and (b) really want to say to you.

The following is a version of what an associate dean[1] might want to say to a dean—if it were safe to do so.[2] There are, of course, numerous appropriate responses to offer to any of these concerns raised, and they depend on a variety of factors. The intention of this chapter is to provide the perspective of associate deans, and in so doing, provide deans, provosts, and

This article is informed by a series of associate dean workshops over the past few years held in conjunction with the ACAD annual meeting. These workshops have been facilitated by a number of different associate deans (with particular thanks to Kathleen Harring) and attended by many associate deans and the occasional dean. Many of the observations from this article come from advice that associate deans offered at the workshops.

others who work directly with associate deans, important points to consider when developing these crucial interpersonal relationships.

Please be clear about the nature of my position—I want to be able to focus on my work without having to constantly wonder what my responsibilities and authority are.

When I initially accepted the associate dean position, I was never given a clear job description; instead, there was the understanding that we would "work the details out" over time. I was (and am) willing to be flexible, but we have never gotten around to clarifying those details. First, it would help me out to know specifically what my term of service is. Although it seemed initially reasonable to sign on for a "two-to-four-year term," this uncertainty has proven difficult for me and my department. My department chair wants to know when (or if) I am returning, in order to plan staffing. I understand that you may not be certain about how long you would like me in the role, but it would be better to preserve flexibility by means of a renewable, fixed term (e.g., two years) rather than an uncertain term length. The fixed term will "force" a conversation with me and my department and will allow for better planning.

With respect to my job responsibilities, I understand that the duties will evolve over time; however, it would help me and my colleagues to know which particular responsibilities are "mine." In the absence of such knowledge, all of us in the office end up fielding the same questions from different parties. After I have worked hard to find information for a faculty colleague, I then discover that my fellow associate dean worked equally hard last week to answer the same question for a different faculty colleague. This is inefficient and frustrating. If I know where my boundary lines are, I can accept and refer requests more appropriately. Once we have defined these responsibilities, please communicate them clearly and consistently to both faculty and staff. This will allow all of us to work more efficiently.

While we are defining responsibilities, it is important for me to understand my authority in these different areas. In which areas am I free to negotiate solutions with others? In which areas do you want me to carry forward a recommendation for your decision? With a different dean, I worked hard to craft a difficult compromise with colleagues. I was discouraged when the dean overruled the decision—because I had thought that I had authority to negotiate the deal. My faculty colleagues noticed what happened, and they are now avoiding me and bringing everything to the dean since "Clearly no decision matters until it comes from the dean directly." I absolutely respect your right to make ultimate decisions (and even to overrule me if necessary), but I suspect that you would prefer to save your energies for bigger questions than

"When can students have access to empty classrooms for study space?" If you let faculty (and me) know where my legitimate authority lies, I will be better able to serve your interests.

Let me know what you're thinking—I want to support your vision.

I can do my work more effectively if I know what you are thinking. What are you working on? What are you passionate about? What is your vision? What is your plan? What are you concerned about? The answers to these questions help develop my peripheral vision that allows me more effectively (and faithfully) to carry out your interests as I work with colleagues. For example, if I know that the budget is unusually tight, I can employ the language of prudence to help colleagues understand that "this might not be the best time" to request new equipment. Alternately, if you are being asked to "spend down" an endowed fund, I can be listening for likely projects as I meet with departments on other issues.

I have worked with different deans, and I recognize that each has had different preferences with respect to communication. Some prefer regular, scheduled meetings; others prefer e-mail or phone interaction; others welcome the "drop-in" question or conversation. Let me know what you prefer. If you need to see data, ask me for data; if you only want the bottom line, ask for the bottom line; if you want written project updates, say so. Having said that, I would ask that we find time for a regular, scheduled meeting. Some of the issues we should discuss are too "heavy" for a drop-in and too sensitive for written communication; a regular meeting is a good time to discuss these issues. This is also a good time to share nonpressing updates on projects.

Deploy me effectively—I want to make your life easier.

I know that you are busy—really busy. I see the hours that you put in, and I note the time stamp on many of your e-mails. I have some small sense of how stressful your life must be. Let me help you. What can I take off your to-do list? Which of your current responsibilities might I be able to assist with? Is there preparation work that I can do to minimize the time it takes you to do your part of a project? Please delegate; I am ready to work.

As you delegate, do so strategically. As it turns out, I have particular skills and talents that can be especially useful to you. Perhaps I am really good at running public meetings, or organizing data for a presentation, or speaking to a group of prospective parents; take advantage of my best talents—recognizing that they may be different from those of my predecessors or peers. Further, I am glad to be deployed strategically in ways that exploit (in positive ways) the difference in our roles. For example, we can plan together to have me reach out to departments with some trial balloons to see if the ideas fly. By using me for this role, we preserve your ability to intervene (either to endorse, modify, or reject). (Note: Please make sure that I know that this is the plan before I stake my credibility to a course of action that we might ultimately abandon.)

Support and protect me—I am particularly vulnerable.

Because my role is an in-between role, I can find myself under attack from multiple sides. Disgruntled faculty may seek to undermine my authority because they are upset about a decision that I have made. Administrative colleagues (both in and out of academic affairs) may resist initiatives. Senior leaders from other divisions may seek to co-opt my labor in support of their projects. Perhaps even the president might ask me for elaborate defenses of the work our office is doing. In all these cases, I need your clear support and protection. This support may come in several forms: a call to a department chair with a clear affirmation of my authority to act, an overture to another vice president urging cooperation from their staff, or a request that the president talk with you about the operations of Academic Affairs (with the understanding that you will talk to me as necessary). I am glad to do the "connective" work of the associate dean, but I need to know that you will have my back as I venture across the institution. I also need "operational space" as I work in support of your vision. This sort of support will allow me most effectively to identify and address problems before they explode publicly.

Be a mentor—I want to keep growing professionally.

I entered the position of associate dean in part to explore administrative work as a possible career. Although there is much that I can offer by virtue of my experience as a faculty member (or previous administrator), there is still much for me to learn about high-level administrative work. I would benefit from your wisdom and experience. As you mentor me, you need to know my professional goals—and how this position fits into those goals. I may see this position as a temporary diversion from my life as a faculty member. In such a case, I would appreciate insights about how to be a more effective faculty member when I return. Alternately, I might be quite interested in pursuing advanced administrative positions. In such cases, I may need a safe sounding board as I explore the question of whether administrative work or faculty work is my best option. I would welcome guidance about how to build my CV, cultivate the necessary skills, and form the appropriate networks that will help me secure a position. It would also help me if we could talk frankly about questions of timing and options. Are there likely to be options at this institution? When would I be ready to go on the market? Is a vice presidency a viable aspiration for me?

As part of my mentoring, I would benefit from the more formal conversation that comes with an annual performance review. Although I certainly appreciate regular feedback and affirmation, such as "You're doing well," I need the more substantial and precise review of my work as associate dean. What have I done particularly well this past year? Which things have not gone as well—and why? What skills or aptitudes should I look to develop going forward? (Incidentally, I would particularly appreciate having a written review that I can refer to throughout the year.) This annual conversation is also a good time for us to discuss my evolving professional aspirations.

I appreciate the personal touch—we are in a human enterprise.

I am very serious about my work, and I am very glad to work hard in support of your vision. My work, though, is not my full life. I appreciate it when you ask about my family or my hobbies or my weekend. I am glad for the validation that these other parts of my identity matter. I know that you may not always (or often) have the luxury of evening time or free weekends, but I am glad when you recognize that my role is different from yours—and that the obligations of the associate dean are not as extensive (nor as invasive) as those of the dean. I notice (and smile) when you extend a Happy Birthday wish or congratulate me when my team wins a big game. I am grateful when you extend condolences and understanding when a loved one passes away. The quick thank-you for a job well done helps restore my energy for the next big task. These thoughtful gestures add meaning to my life and my work.

Ultimately, I love this work that I have chosen, and I appreciate that you were thoughtful enough to ask about (and listen to) what I would like you to know. I look forward to our work together.

Here are three pieces of concluding advice to assist you in effectively and enjoyably working with associate deans:

- Be clear about what you want—with clear expectations and regular communication pathways.
- Be strategic in deploying your associate deans to achieve your goals.
- Understand what your associate dean wants—and work intentionally to help meet those needs and interests.

Notes

1. For the reader's convenience, I use *associate deans* as a proxy for the full range of titles that report to a dean or to a provost. Some examples include assistant deans, associate deans, assistant provosts, associate provosts, or associate vice presidents of academic affairs.
2. The following narrative is crafted in the first person, to preserve the conversational feel of an associate dean speaking. The content of the narrative is drawn from the feedback provided by many associate deans at the ACAD workshops.

CHAPTER FORTY-THREE

Effective Hiring and Evaluation of Staff

Alison Benders
Ohio Dominican University

> Enrollment in the graduate business and education programs in your institution has been stagnant in the past couple of years. The graduate program directors have been principally responsible for securing enrollment in the graduate programs, with some assistance from other areas. (The director of admissions has handled only undergraduate enrollment.) The graduate programs are key to the financial health of the university, so as academic vice president, you have been charged with creating a new position for director of graduate admissions, reporting to you. The challenge is to define the new role of director of graduate admissions and expected outcomes, hire an appropriate person, and develop the director through regular evaluations.

Hiring staff is often new territory for chief academic officers (CAO), who are frequently promoted from faculty ranks without direct business and management experience. A CAO will increase the chances of hiring excellent staff members by approaching the process with methodical planning, attention to outcomes, and concern for the human dimension of the workplace. Hiring personnel is a time-consuming process, but the time spent initially to ensure a good strong employee avoids the expense and headache of terminating a poor choice when the situation does not work as expected.

IDENTIFY THE NEED

As with any position, one of the most important initial steps is to clarify the need for the position, including a financial analysis. To do this, the CAO must determine what the new employee will do and what outcomes are expected. At the outset, it is essential to review the university's strategic plan and make sure that the highest priorities are in fact driving the decision to hire new staff. Next, the CAO must create a budget projection of the expected revenue that a position will generate (or potential savings) measured against the full costs, such as salary, benefits, training, and search expenses, if any. The CAO should meet with senior administrators in the finance office and human resources office to draw on their more formal knowledge of prevailing wages, hiring costs, and employee value. A review of the employee handbook and other relevant policies is warranted at this stage. This is also the time to consider how to attract candidates who may diversify the workforce at the university and to consult with HR or the multicultural affairs department for specific support. In short, the objective at the initial stage is to justify the need for the position with substantial detail, to identify the contribution that the new hire will make to the institution over the long term, and to clarify your understanding of staff hiring practices at your institution.

DEFINE THE RESPONSIBILITIES AND OUTCOMES

At this stage, the CAO should fill in the details of the position, including the anticipated percentage of time for each task; outcomes and general metrics for success; the minimum and preferred education, experience, and skills; the resources in terms of staff and budgets available to the position; training provided; and the surrounding organizational structure. Some of these items will be included in the job description as advertised, while others will be part of the profile to be shared with candidates or the new hire when appropriate. To assure consistency and clarity, the CAO might consider creating a record for performance evaluation, which incorporates the specific outcomes and metrics that are identified in the position description. Before proceeding, the CAO should consult the HR manager to ensure that policies and expectations are consistent with other staff positions.

CONSIDER THE "FIT"

Most searches go forward after the desired professional knowledge and skills have been defined. However, a growing body of research on business performance demonstrates that employees' emotional intelligence can be a decisive factor in institutional success. Emotional intelligence means the ability, first, to recognize, control, and utilize one's own emotions productively and, second, to recognize others' emotions and address them effectively, as Daniel Goleman (2011) has argued. Most often, interviewers simply seek a candidate with a professional demeanor and, as such, fail to appreciate expressly the interpersonal dynamics within the academic affairs office or across the institution. Therefore, in the process of developing a position profile, the CAO should identify the institutional culture, the personality types of the employees who will principally be working with the new staff member, and the personality traits and qualities that will enable the new hire to be successful in the near and long term. Again, the human resources office may be able to provide input on the desired soft skills in potential staff members.

SCREEN AND INTERVIEW EFFECTIVELY

When job applications are submitted, the CAO must supervise the screening process diligently, and work closely with the search committee that has been assembled. This means both staying in close communication with the HR manager who is screening the applicants to ensure that the screener can read between the lines of past experience, and guiding search committee members to a clear understanding of the requirements of the position as they interview, interact with, and ultimately recommend a candidate for the position. When looking for a particular fit, the candidate with the "best" academic and professional experience is not necessarily the right person to hire. After ensuring that a candidate has the requisite level of education and experience, then the decision becomes one of determining how the person will function within the institutional culture, values, and temperament. Questions will reveal emotional intelligence and allow the CAO to evaluate whether the candidate is the best match for the institution, and include the following:

- *Personal self-awareness*. How do you recognize when you are stressed at work (about either personal or professional issues), and what do you do about it?
- *Personal self-management*. Describe how you might handle a situation where you found that a person reporting to you is insubordinate. Who has directly challenged your authority?
- *Awareness of others' social interactions or emotions*. How will you learn the culture of our university over the first few months of work here?
- *Managing others' social interactions or emotions*. Relate a time when you felt you needed to confront a colleague regarding different values on a significant issue. Speak about your preparation for the conversation, your communication style, and follow-up.

EVALUATE TO NURTURE PERFORMANCE

Once the appropriate candidate is identified and hired, it is imperative that the CAO play an active role in orientation, formation, and supervision. In addition to any formal orientation handled by the HR office, the CAO should meet with the new employee to discuss expectations. This meeting should cover the job description, communication style, values, and the evaluation process. The well-crafted job description that started the hiring process becomes the tool to shape the employee's job performance. Clear communication is absolutely necessary here, including the activities and dispositions that the employee is expected to demonstrate. The CAO, as a supervisor, must help the new employee develop a good sense of the university culture and values. Along the way, the CAO can observe, and correct if necessary, the new employee's performance to ensure that the new employee is developing to meet the university's need.

Although informal feedback on a regular basis is important for a new employee, a formal evaluation within ninety days of hire is vital for a long-term employment relationship. As mentioned previously, the job description will include specific performance outcomes as well as dispositions and emotional management. All evaluations should begin with the employee's self-evaluation, input from direct reports, and the CAO's evaluation. These should be discussed in a timely, frank conversation followed by a written summary and goals for the next period.

One of the most common mistakes is the failure of the CAO or other administrators to give negative feedback to staff in an accurate and direct way. Staff members who are not performing well are entitled to know whether or not they are meeting expectations as soon as possible; they should be given specific guidance to improve their performance. Not infrequently, employees will realize then that they are not meeting the institutional expectations and resign on their own when they find a situation better suited to their talents and interests. In the event that employees need to be let go, there

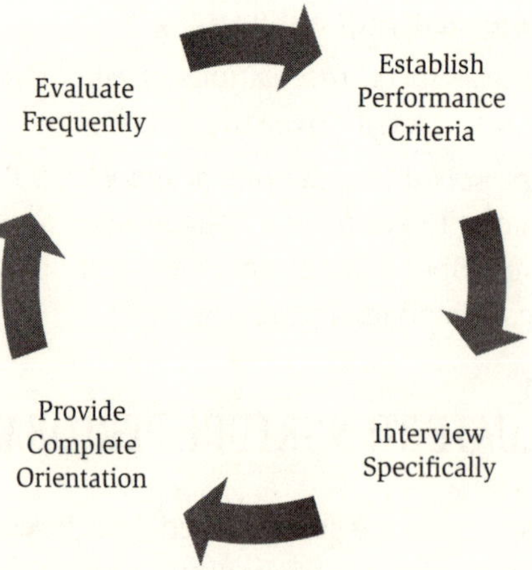

Figure 43.1 The Hiring and Development Process

will be no surprises and a clear record will be available to support the decision to dismiss. The HR office can provide input before, during, and after employee evaluations.

The hiring and development process for staff is best viewed as a cycle to be planned and managed with care.

The CAO's efforts to hire and train staff who are personally and professionally trained is well worth the time invested, and five guidelines, in particular, are important:

- Job descriptions for staff should be clear with defined outcomes.
- Outcomes must include responsibilities, dispositions, and metrics for achievement.
- Interview for cultural fit as well as for skills.
- Provide full orientation for new hires.
- Evaluate regularly, forthrightly, and fully.

Reference

Goleman, D. (2011). *Leadership: The power of emotional intelligence*. Northampton, MA: More Than Sound.

PART FIVE

DEVELOPING FACULTY EXCELLENCE AND ACHIEVING STUDENT SUCCESS

CHAPTER FORTY-FOUR

Setting Expectations, Intentionality, and Clarity in Faculty Hiring

Stephanie Fabritius
Centre College

John was a candidate in numerous faculty searches in a wide range of institution types. When he read the advertisement for the faculty position in art history at Perfect College, he saw a good fit with the advertised characteristics of the "successful candidate." He felt very confident, that is, until he set foot on campus. Once on campus, there wasn't anyone to greet him. He had received a map of the campus in his hotel room and a note telling him to grab breakfast and take time to walk around and familiarize himself with the place. When he finally did get to the department, the search chair was in a rush, but met with him quickly to review the schedule and to introduce him to other faculty. He met briefly with the academic dean, but the conversation revolved around the dean's hope for changing both the nature of the institution and the faculty culture. They did discuss salary ranges and teaching load but had time for little else. John was surprised that he didn't have the opportunity to meet with students, and he was disappointed that he didn't meet with faculty in other disciplines with whom he might be able to collaborate or socialize. As he was setting up for his talk, the search chair apologized for the fact that although the candidate had been requested to speak about his fairly complicated research project, the only students available were first-year introductory art history students. The chair hoped he would be able to make the work understandable to students with little background in the discipline. The meeting with the committee went fine, but during the dinner, several committee members got into a discussion of college politics. By the time the evening was over, John no longer felt like he was the perfect fit. All that he knew was that he couldn't imagine his future involving Perfect College.

Making the right hire is not merely a happy accident. It requires care and intentionality, clarity in communicating the goals and mission of the institution, and concern to ensure that the candidate's experience in the hiring process mirrors what she can expect during the long term. Careful work during the hiring process will lead to an outstanding faculty with staying power. Given the demographics of higher education, most of us in chief academic officer positions will hire a significant number of faculty over the next five to ten years. For example, after seven years in my current position, I have hired 42 percent of the tenured and tenure-track faculty beginning the 2013–2014 academic year. At most institutions, academic departments take primary responsibility during a search process; however, it is the dean's responsibility to set expectations for how those processes will unfold.

Although work happens before the actual interview process, I will begin this discussion with the first meeting of the search committee and then move to the narrowing of the pool, the phone or meeting interview, the campus interview, the offer, and finally, the closing of the deal. I will focus on four important issues: (1) telling an accurate story about the institution and its mission; (2) making certain that the committee and administration are clear and aligned about the characteristics of the ideal candidate; (3) clearly communicating the mission, expectations of faculty members, and the allocation of faculty resources; and (4) informing the candidate early in the process as to the expectations during the visit.

Prior to the hiring process, but after search committees are formed, I hold a required informational meeting with all search committee members for all upcoming searches. I review our process and strategies for attracting a diverse candidate pool and remind them of the importance of consistency in sharing the formal and informal college mission and culture. Perhaps as important as my words are the stories from faculty members who served on search committees in the past, sharing practices that did or didn't work. At our institution, search committees are appointed by the dean following consultation with the appropriate division chair and the search committee chair. They include five members—three from the searching academic program, the division chair, and a faculty member from outside the discipline who represents the broader institutional perspective.

FIRST MEETING OF THE SEARCH COMMITTEE

Before posting a job, it is important for the search committee to meet and to discuss the desired area of the search. At our institution, this includes the desired subdiscipline(s), the expectations of the candidate beyond the expectations of all faculty candidates (e.g., engagement in collaborative undergraduate research or participation in an interdisciplinary program), the courses the candidate will teach, and what evidence the candidate will need to provide in order to address the expectations of the institution and the particular academic program. Details such as whether the position is tenure-track or not, and the rank at hire, will have been determined through the position approval process. The purpose of this meeting is not only to develop the advertisement but also to be sure that all members of the search committee are of one mind. It also ensures that the candidates will be getting a very consistent message in terms of expectations.

NARROWING THE POOL AND INITIAL INTERVIEW

All members of the committee read applicant files, and narrow the candidate pool to a group of eight to twelve candidates who are interviewed either by telephone, through videoconferencing, or at a professional meeting. The choice of whether to interview at a professional meeting or by phone or video is largely a disciplinary one. Some disciplines have a tradition of interviewing at professional meetings, and to do otherwise is rarely considered. One disadvantage of interviewing at a conference is that only a subset of the committee participates in the actual interviews. During our phone interviews, the entire committee participates, asking questions and reflecting on the answers. Another potential disadvantage of conference interviews is timing. For example, both the American Economic Association and the Modern Language Association hold their annual conferences in January, a month when other disciplines have already completed their tenure-track searches. A strong advantage of interviewing at national conferences however is, of course, the face-to-face time.

Following this round of interviews, committees generate a list of top candidates. The list includes a brief summary of each candidate interviewed, where each candidate ranks, and a brief explanation of that ranking. Once committees receive approval for bringing in their top three candidates, they conduct a reference check. This small step has proven to be crucial for detecting previously unrealized issues of concern.

CAMPUS INTERVIEW

We pick a time where activity on campus is very comparable to our normal long-term schedule. Our search secretary, working with the search chair, arranges the logistics of each visit. We send out information in advance to each candidate about our campus and community, as well as a detailed interview agenda. Candidates typically arrive the night before the interview and are housed in one of our campus guest cottages. A member of the search committee will pick up candidates arriving by plane. This extra time is invaluable because it gives us time to get to know the candidate better and gives the candidate a chance to ask questions before the hectic interview schedule begins. In summary, we try to present the campus as it typically is; we provide information about the campus and surrounding community; and we try to use routine tasks (airport transport) to get a fuller picture of the candidate.

On campus, the candidate meets with the college president, the academic dean, the division chair, members of the search committee, faculty and students in the department, potential faculty collaborators, and our human resources director. We also schedule a tour of campus and the local community, and a more detailed tour of appropriate campus buildings. Our goal during the visit is twofold: to get to know the candidate and his or her talents, and to enable the candidate to get an accurate picture of who we are. We intentionally send consistent messages about things such as the mission of the college, the campus culture, and the expectations of faculty with respect to teaching, scholarship, and service. We don't present the college as something we're not, or even something we aspire to be. This is a key point: even if such portrayals bring in candidates that wouldn't otherwise come, it is unlikely that they will be happy or stay for the long term. We are very careful to be sure that students, faculty, and administration all send consistent messages.

On campus, candidates typically give a demonstration of teaching, and often a research talk. Sometimes the demonstration of teaching involves an exploration into the candidate's scholarship. We provide expectations for talks, including student level, topic, and the importance of student-faculty interaction, when first scheduling the interview. Faculty and students both evaluate this classroom experience. Students take candidates to lunch and have an opportunity to ask questions. Their feedback is always solicited.

In order to get a fuller picture of the candidate, I start my meeting with her by asking how she found her academic passion. Even the way in which she goes about the explanation can be revealing. I ask her to talk with me about her dissertation topic, providing enough context so that a nonspecialist can understand. This has been useful in determining how well a candidate will be able to untangle complex ideas for our students. And then I spend time telling the candidate about three very important general expectations of faculty at our institution: engagement in the life of the college, embracing the teacher-scholar model, and maintaining a collegial environment. I talk about our role as a liberal arts college and about resources that are available to faculty members and how these align with the expectation of our faculty as teaching-scholars. We then talk about annual reviews, the tenure/promotion process, and the support available as one moves through these processes. Often candidates will ask about my vision for the institution; we talk about that, as well, frequently tying ideas back to the college's mission. I end our interview by sharing more information about the search process—where we are, what will happen next, and our expected timetable. I invite the candidate to contact me with questions as the process continues. My job in this process is to describe the institution, campus culture, resources and expectations. Our president, during his meeting, spends much of his time getting to know each candidate, and selling the institution and the surrounding community.

NEXT STEPS

After all candidates have been on campus, the committee meets and provides me with a written report that assesses each visitor and indicates his or her acceptability and overall ranking. Committee and student feedback about candidate strengths and weaknesses is always part of the report. I may follow up with further questions and prodding, or I may make an immediate job offer to the candidate. It is my job, as dean, to make the offer because I have the ability to negotiate (or not) on salary, start-up, and other details of the offer. All offers of employment are contingent on a successful background check. Following a verbal agreement to take the job, we prepare a contract that the candidate signs and returns. After a successful hire, the search committee chair calls the candidates who came to campus but were not offered a job. We intentionally made the choice to call those who spent time with us, rather than just sending them a form letter. Although it is a difficult call to make, we feel that we owe them this courtesy. The use of wikis and blogs by candidates have made this even more difficult, as the news of a hiring may reach social media venues before we have a chance to make a call; deans could request of successful candidates to delay announcing their good news via social media until unsuccessful candidates have been notified by the college or university. Candidates who did not come to campus are notified by e-mail or mail.

Hiring faculty is one of the most significant and enjoyable tasks of chief academic officers—and it also is one of the most time- and labor-intensive. As you might imagine, substantive disagreements between the dean and the department or chair can happen throughout the process and are usually tricky to tackle. Resolving these conflicts requires that the dean has clear expectations, consistently abide by these expectations, and be constantly and clearly communicating these expectations along the way.

To ensure best outcomes for your institution in the hiring process, keep these four ideas in mind:

- Best practices in the hiring process all involve the consistency and accuracy of message not only from the various constituencies the candidate will meet while on campus, but also about what we expect the candidate to do and demonstrate while on campus, and about our institution's expectations, evaluations, and resources.

- Candidates should be confident that what they see while on campus is what they will experience in the long term.
- Because candidates are interviewing us, just as we are interviewing them, we should ensure that candidates are comfortable and well treated during their visits.
- Finally, I would also recommend reviewing the search process annually and making adjustments, as needed. Reviews should include feedback from all or most constituencies—search committees, student advisory groups, administration, and recently hired faculty members. These can be conducted anonymously through online surveys or by having a neutral party, such as an assistant or associate dean, collect the information. The important thing is to constantly adjust your process in order to make it even stronger.

CHAPTER FORTY-FIVE

Diversifying the Campus

Some Steps for Deans to Take

Laura L. Behling
Knox College

The comments and questions from faculty and students at Greenfield College had always been present and consistent about diversity. "We need to recruit more students of color," many faculty would say, or "Why don't we have more women faculty, particularly in certain disciplines?" Students pushed for programs that addressed issues related to sexuality, race, and disabilities, and some faculty, but not all, regularly advocated for curricular requirements focused explicitly on diversity. Students and faculty both were quick to seek greater support for student services that addressed the needs of students of color, GLBTQ students, and non-Christians. As the chief academic officer your influence is limited when it comes to admission decisions and staffing in student affairs. However, you do have the opportunity to have significant influence over both faculty hiring and curriculum development. Your first step may be to change the conversation from "Diversity is the right thing to do" to "Diversity is essential in order to achieve excellence." The first view tends to reinforce the notion that somehow majority white institutions are doing people of color, non-Christian religious traditions, and non-Western countries a favor by including them on the faculty or teaching their languages and cultures in the classroom. That feeling about diversity has a tenacious grip on the worldview of many on campus, but it is quietly and steadily being replaced by the view that no campus can make a legitimate claim to excellence if it does not include a wide range of perspectives within its curriculum and embodied by its faculty. But after this shift in narrative frame, what else can a dean do?

Enhancing diversity on a campus is no easy task, and even though campus constituencies may publicly express commitment to diversity's essential role in excellence, putting rhetoric into action requires a clear, multipoint plan enacted by the dean. In particular, there are two areas on which a dean exerts significant influence and that thus provide two crucial points for a dean's leadership: faculty hiring and curriculum development.

HIRING

With few exceptions, colleges and universities are always seeking to diversify their faculty, either in terms of sex and gender, race or ethnicity, or in some cases, international faculty. Yet despite this expressed desire, many colleges and universities struggle to recruit or retain faculty candidates who offer such diversity to their campuses. There are, of course, many reasons institutions struggle in this area in faculty hiring—the limited number of candidates who are women or of color in certain disciplines, geographic location of campuses, and, to be frank, attitudes on campuses regarding diversity. As dean, you realize that the philosophies and practices governing faculty searches are established and implemented by your office, and that you, personally, are involved in conversations with search chairs and candidates as faculty hiring progresses through an academic year. Chief academic officers must provide leadership, ideas, a clear philosophical stance, and at times, difficult conversations with their campus colleagues in order lead their campus to a commitment to diversity, and success at faculty hiring.

Begin conversations about hiring for diversity before searches begin to provide enough time to have more thoughtful institutional conversations. What does diversity mean on this campus? What are ways we can work together to diversify the faculty through hiring? What support can the dean's office provide to ensure hiring departments and programs make effective efforts at diversity hiring? How does the curriculum offered by the individual department or program, or the college or university as whole, reflect the institution's commitment to diversity and invite underrepresented candidates into the department?

Also be sure that language you use to talk about diversity is consistent among all faculty searches, as well as staff searches in your office. Understand what role the human resources office on your campus has in hiring, and support them in their work. Be sure to know what policies and expectations are already in place, particularly if you are new to the institution. Many colleges and universities have developed faculty hiring handbooks, or administrative guidelines to faculty hiring as one way to ensure consistency—both procedural and philosophical—in hiring. In many of these guidelines, there are special sections devoted to diversity in faculty hiring.

Search committees should create position descriptions that are aligned with visions of the future held at the department or program, college, university, and institutional levels. Search committees must guard against writing a position description that could automatically exclude or "define out" candidates who have a diversity of experiences, including experiences that may not be traditional routes into academia. Instead, the goal is to write a position description that attracts a diverse group of applicants—defined broadly, including but not limited to race and ethnicity, gender, sexual orientation, age, religion, disability, economic or social class, national origin, or other legally-protected categories, and multi- or cross-disciplinary expertise—and then develop and execute a plan to recruit such applicants. Boilerplate equal-opportunity language does not signal to potential candidates that your institution has a commitment to diversity. Examples of wording used in position descriptions to signal a substantive interest in diverse perspectives include the following:

- Conducts scholarship in areas related to diversity
- Experience with a variety of teaching methods and/or curricular perspectives
- Previous experience interacting with diverse communities
- Experience in cultures other than their own
- Academic experiences and interests in culturally diverse groups
- Interest in developing and implementing curricula that address multicultural issues
- Demonstrated success in working with diverse populations of students

During the interview process, ask about each candidate's commitment to diversity and how each might manifest that through work at your institution (e.g., teaching, advising/mentoring, recruiting). For instance, it would be appropriate to ask: "Please describe your commitment to diversity, and give us specific examples how you have manifested that in your professional life." Or, "How would you encourage more underrepresented students to consider a career in the fields related to your discipline?" Or, "Please discuss advising tactics for differing subsets of students." Or, "How would you promote and model acceptance and inclusivity on campus outside the classroom?" Or, "Why is diversity important in higher education?" Each successful candidate must demonstrate an understanding of and commitment to the vital importance of a diverse learning environment. Make no assumptions about a candidate's commitment to diversity simply on the basis of her or his race or ethnicity, gender, sexual orientation, age, religion, disability, economic or social class, or national origin. Everyone needs to be able to answer these kinds of questions.

Make all best efforts to bring diverse candidates to an on-campus interview. Document the search committee's efforts to recruit a qualified and diverse candidate pool. Prior to issuing on-campus interview invitations, the chair of the search committee, the chair of the relevant department/program, the chief diversity officer, the associate dean, or the dean should meet to decide if the steps cited above to recruit diverse candidates were followed.

In all recruiting, placing advertisements is merely a beginning step. Advertising is necessary but is *not* sufficient to ensure that there will be applicants of the desired caliber and diversity in the final candidate pool. It should be incumbent upon the search committee and its chair to do more to identify and attract the most highly qualified applicants.

- All search committees should indicate specific steps that will be taken during the search to maximize the number of minority applicants and to ensure their being given careful attention.
- The search committee chair should contact selected university graduate departments/programs to seek information about potential minority applicants. For example, the publication *Diverse* lists universities producing significant numbers of minority PhDs. National lists of minority faculty and recent doctorates are usually available and should be used as part of the search strategy. Telephone calls are preferred to mailed announcements because they have been demonstrated to be far more effective than written alternatives in generating applicants.
- Personal contact by letter or telephone with leaders in the field to solicit nominations of potential applicants is a crucial adjunct to the above efforts. Direct contact with those who train graduate students and those who are well established in the field, especially those who themselves are minorities or women, often leads to the most promising applicants. Such calls should describe the position and its relation to the overall program; ask about possible applicants, especially minorities and women; and ask about others who might know about such potential applicants.
- Use e-mail lists to send position announcements directly to appropriate professional organizations and associates, and relevant departments at universities that are members of historically black colleges and universities (HBCUs), Hispanic-serving institutions (HSIs), and tribal colleges and universities. Also mail to institutions that are leaders in granting PhDs to minorities.
- Order mailing labels from the Minority and Women Doctoral Directory (www.mwdd.com), which will supply labels for a wide array of disciplines for a nominal fee.
- Make numerous word-of-mouth contacts, especially with potential applicants from underrepresented populations.
- Incorporate issues related to cultural pluralism and diversity into the curriculum and pedagogy where possible.

- Provide encouragement to colleagues from underrepresented populations to apply, and encourage faculty to contribute to a welcoming and affirming on-campus experience for them.

CURRICULUM

In addition to challenging departments to address diversity by examining how their field has changed over time and is now addressing such questions, it is also possible to hire for curricular diversity by carefully identifying subspecialties that will be preferred in the hiring process. For instance, if the religion department needs to hire a New Testament scholar, suggest they advertise for someone with one of the following subspecialties: feminist theology, liberation theology in South America, or interfaith dialogue. If Spanish needs to hire someone to teach language and culture, suggest they prioritize those whose research agenda includes Central or South America or Borderlands perspectives. These suggestions may be met with resistance because you may have religion faculty who don't value feminist theology, or Spanish faculty who strongly resist the Central/South American background. But it is important to remember that this is a win-win strategy. The department is granted permission to make a tenure-line hire in the primary area of specialization that they requested, and you are simply advising them to contribute to the campus diversity initiative through that hire's subspecialty.

On small campuses, in particular, developing interdisciplinary majors and minors is feasible, and even desirable. Many campuses have found ways to develop gender and sexuality programs, Latin American studies, or Asian studies by bringing together interested faculty with relevant expertise (often a subspecialty developed midcareer) to identify appropriate courses, tweak existing courses, advise students, and promote the program.

You can promote diversity through interdisciplinary programs in the hiring process. When departments with small enrollments seek to replace a tenure-line faculty member, advise them to create a position description that addresses their primary departmental needs and that also supports one of the campuses diversity-related interdisciplinary programs. Ideally, the hire would be a joint appointment in the department and the program.

Another way to promote diversity in the curriculum is through faculty development programs, now commonplace on college and university campuses. Such programs allow for a natural structure in which to embed such development. Workshops on teaching multiculturally, curriculum development on incorporating diversity and diverse perspectives, and pedagogical discussions about working with diverse students are only a few examples of ways a faculty development program can support the diversity initiatives of the dean and the institution. Some initial low stakes and important ways to initiate faculty development programming on diversity are to share institutional data collected by the National Survey of Student Engagement (NSSE), Community College Survey of Student Engagement (CCSSE), Cooperative Institutional Research Program (CIRP), or alumni surveys, as well as demographic data of faculty, staff, and students.

There are many ways faculty members can demonstrate a commitment to diversity. For some, it may seem easy and obvious, given their training, research agenda, and courses. For others is comes from expertise developed along the way that allows them to bring a broader range of perspectives into their courses. Faculty also demonstrate their commitment through engagement with the campus diversity center, advising student groups with a multicultural agenda, or taking students abroad to someplace other than Europe or other Western-influenced cosmopolitan cities.

Recognizing and valuing the myriad ways faculty can contribute to a campus atmosphere that promotes and supports diverse perspectives is critical and must be done at those decision points that result in tangible benefits to faculty members. Deans, with their faculty personnel committees, examine their tenure and promotion expectations to ensure that faculty commitment to diversity is one of the criteria. Post-tenure reviews also should incorporate such expectations, as should merit pay decisions. Working with faculty to craft language that best expresses the institutional commitment to diversity is key, as is the dean providing leadership on this by engaging appropriate faculty governing committees in the development of such expectations.

Each institution must provide a clear sense of the role and importance of diversity—messaging that needs to be clear at and from all levels of the organization. The academic dean's office, because the academic enterprise is central to the college or university, has to provide prominent leadership in all these areas and provide much-needed coordination among them. Because the faculty teach students as they progress through a curriculum, the call to increase diversity on a campus requires more than the desire to do so; it requires specific actions by the chief academic officer, including the following:

- Understand your and your institution's commitment to diversity, and be willing to publicly state this philosophy to faculty, staff, and students in areas such as hiring, curriculum, and retention.
- Scrutinize your office's practices for ways they do and do not support efforts to diversify your campus, and if absent, develop and implement clear policies and practices to ensure efforts toward diversity.

- Hold people accountable. It is not enough to simply ask search chairs and committees to provide their best efforts toward hiring diverse faculty; it is too easy to simply fall back into old, often counterproductive, habits. Ask for the department's plan to advertise faculty positions, for example, to candidates of color, or challenge departments to embrace diverse issues as part of curricular scrutiny and revision. And hold yourself accountable—keep track of exemplary efforts, practices, and successes on your campus; and use these stories publicly to show the ways academic affairs addresses increased calls for diversity.
- Keep working toward enhancing diversity. Even for those colleges and universities that succeed in changing practices and attitudes, enhancing diversity in institutions is difficult, and often may not have immediate success. Your role is to change culture and attitudes—and to ensure that your institution's and your own commitments to diversity are clear.

CHAPTER FORTY-SIX

Enhancing Faculty Relationships through Transparent and Consistent Evaluation

Stephanie Fabritius
Centre College

Sandy, a fifth-year tenure-track faculty member, reflects on her past annual evaluations and considers her progress as she moves toward her tenure review. Sandy feels a bit lost and wonders how she is really doing. Her other colleagues in the process have started talking and speculating about the things necessary to do if one wants to be successful in the tenure process. Is it really true that she needs to serve on the curriculum committee? Does she really have to direct a college study abroad program or engage in collaborative research with students? The more she speaks with untenured colleagues, the more she hears that is disconcerting. She also wonders whether her annual reviews are consistent with the kind of scrutiny she will ultimately receive from the tenure committee. She begins to question her interpretation of the criteria for successful evaluations (both annual evaluations and tenure and promotion evaluations). Does she really understand what is expected of her?

This chapter will address some of the things deans should do to assess their institution's faculty evaluations for clarity, accuracy, transparency, and consistency and to ensure that processes provide formative (as well as summative) feedback along the way. At most of our institutions, we evaluate faculty through at least two separate processes: the annual evaluation and the tenure and promotion process. I will discuss both of these and focus on some common expectations and best practices that apply across the board. I also will discuss how the results of these evaluations are revealed to the faculty member and how they may be used by the institution.

ANNUAL EVALUATIONS

At my institution, all full-time continuing faculty members are subject to an annual review. Faculty members submit activity summaries each January that cover the previous calendar year. In these summaries, faculty provide straightforward data about their teaching, scholarship, and service and also have the opportunity to address the impact they have made in each of these areas. Although the specific process we use to evaluate the year's work is interesting, I won't go into that here. But we do use the activity summaries, course evaluations (submitted by students in the course), class visit forms that have been completed by colleagues visiting a class, CVs, samples of syllabi, unique assignments, and evidence of scholarly work to assess all three areas evaluated (teaching, scholarship, and service). We then use a set of adjectives (excellent, low excellent, high good, good, low good, adequate, and unsatisfactory) to assess the faculty member's performance in each area of evaluation.

To be successful, a faculty member needs to establish the ability to hit "excellent," and rarely be below "good" in all three categories. Excellence in teaching involves high marks for organization, effectiveness, level of challenge, and evidence of student transformation. For scholarship, peer review is required to reach the level of "low excellent" or "excellent." Regular, sustainable progress on projects, along with regular attendance (or presentation) at conferences—even without peer review—would land at "high good." Service is evaluated based on the committees and activities in which the faculty member engages, along with the impact they make through this engagement. All continuing full-time faculty members are evaluated annually, but only untenured faculty members receive an annual letter. Faculty members at the rank of associate professor receive a letter every other year, and faculty members at the rank of full professor receive a letter every third year. The letters share the results of the evaluation, offer the evidence used by the evaluators to arrive at these adjectives, and offer some suggestions for further improvement, including expectations or benchmarks for the next and succeeding years so that faculty have a clear sense of expectations.

TENURE AND PROMOTION EVALUATIONS

At my institution, the tenure and reappointment committee is an elected group of six faculty members who are charged to review material regarding teaching, scholarship, and service for faculty at the start of their third year (midprobationary review) and sixth year (tenure and promotion to associate professor). Some institutions have a slightly different schedule, reviewing the materials in years 2, 4, and 6, allowing for an additional review. Because of our robust annual review process, we do not feel the need for an additional review by the tenure and reappointment committee.

After eight years at the associate professor level, faculty members are eligible for a review by the Special Committee on Promotion in order to be considered for promotion to full professor. These elected committees are looking for similar progress and achievement in teaching, scholarship, and service as in the annual review process. I liken the difference (other than the structure of who is doing the review and the amount of evidence that is examined) to a comparison of a snapshot and a movie. The annual review is a snapshot, whereas the tenure and promotion reviews are like a movie; the tenure and promotion reviews look at the trajectory of progress over time.

COMMON EXPECTATIONS AND BEST PRACTICES

No matter how well you do in terms of transparency and communicating expectations for a successful review, the faculty members undergoing review will still have concerns. But our job is to make the process as clear, thorough, and well-communicated as possible. Probably more important than the rigor of the expectations is the clear communication of what is required. Although the criteria for evaluation can never (and should never) be watered down to a simple checklist, faculty members should have an understanding of what the committee or the evaluator(s) are looking for in terms of teaching, scholarship, and service. These criteria are often laid out in the faculty handbook. At our institution, I also talk about these expectations during the hiring process, during new faculty orientation, and during open question-and-answer sessions held for those faculty members within a year or two of review. It is important that my message be consistent with that of the tenure and reappointment committee, the other annual evaluators, the criteria articulated in the faculty handbook, and other official institutional messages. It also is critically important that the resources available for faculty development, the mission of the institution, and the messages given are all consistent with the criteria by which we evaluate faculty. When I follow up on evaluations, whether the tenure and reappointment process or through the annual evaluation process, I am intentional about using the same language in the evaluation letter or meeting. The faculty member undergoing review needs to feel confident that the stated expectations are, indeed, what he or she will be measured against. And, in our case, the faculty members need to see consistency among the various annual reviews and the more formal reviews involving tenure, reappointment, and promotion. If we use, or appear to use, different criteria, the faculty member will not have an opportunity to make appropriate adjustments. It should be exceedingly rare for the annual reviews to indicate good progress and the tenure decision to be negative (or vice versa). If such a thing does happen, it is important to go back and review where things became inconsistent.

The most common trouble spot I have encountered is when a course exhibits several characteristics of excellence that automatically lead to a high course evaluation. For example, if evidence of transformative teaching is the key characteristic leading to an outstanding rating for a course, then transformative teaching can sometimes override undesirable actions in the classroom, such as late grading or the telling of inappropriate stories. In that case, an annual review may result in high teaching evaluations, but the more thorough tenure reviews may reveal student discontent from slow return of work, lack of student-professor boundaries, and inappropriate jokes. In addition to being consistent among your evaluations, among your messages, and through your language, it also is important to give careful feedback to the faculty member undergoing review. At my institution, this includes detailed letters following annual reviews, as well as conferences and letters following reviews conducted through the tenure, reappointment, and promotion process. (The tenure and reappointment committee actually reads the annual review letters as part of their review in years 3 and 6 and at promotion to full professor.)

Virtually all colleges and universities have a tenure, reappointment, and promotion process that involves numerous layers of evaluation, but I also recommend having multiple evaluators in the annual review process. Although this is very time consuming and resource-heavy, I believe that our process is a strength of our college. Our president, the appropriate division chair, and the associate dean join me in the evaluation process. (The president is less involved and is mainly there to listen, ask questions, and help shape consensus.) The advantage of multiple reviewers is that the final "adjective" assigned to each area (teaching, scholarship, and service) is the result of a consensus among three individuals who have independently reviewed the evidence. This is helpful in coming up with a fair and accurate evaluation and is also helpful in putting the individual being reviewed at ease. One person's bias won't be able to drive the process. The various reviewers (VPAA, associate dean, president, and division chair) all review the criteria before starting to evaluate specific faculty members. Having the president present in reviews is very helpful in terms of having him aware of the work of the faculty. It would be problematic to have the president involved if he or she took on a more active role. Fortunately, the time of the president rarely allows this to happen!

Some institutions rely solely on one measure of evaluation for each of the criteria examined. For example, student course evaluations are commonly used as "the" measure in annual reviews at a number of institutions. Although I am often struck by the careful reflections of our students on these forms, I feel more confident in our evaluation process because we use multiple pieces of evidence when trying to evaluate a faculty member's teaching. In our case, for annual reviews, we use class visit reports that are generated by peers, student course evaluations, and the faculty member's own reflections in their Faculty Activity Summary. During the tenure, reappointment, and promotion process, we also use letters from current and former students who were selected by the faculty member under review plus letters from students randomly pulled from current and past course rosters, as well as reflections from the appropriate division chair. In the vast majority of cases, the evidence from these various sources tell a common story and is helpful in filling in a more complete picture.

There are three significant takeaways from this chapter to ensure that faculty evaluations are clear and consistent and that they benefit both the faculty member and the institution:

- Set and overcommunicate clear expectations that reflect the messages (direct and indirect) of the institution and its mission.
- Postevaluation follow-up, whether through letters or conversations, should always use language consistent with the evaluation itself. Indeed, consistency is imperative both in terms of what is important and in terms of what is specifically laid out as expectations for faculty members as they conduct their work.
- Consider relying on a strong annual evaluation, using multiple reviewers and multiple sources of evidence for each area of teaching, scholarship, and service.

CHAPTER FORTY-SEVEN

Contingent Faculty

Strategies for Developing an Essential Resource

Maria Maisto

New Faculty Majority (NFM), NFM Foundation, and Cuyahoga Community College

Adrianna Kezar

University of Southern California

Carol Kochhar-Bryant

The George Washington University

Close to winter break, a dean is contacted by two new department chairs expressing frustration because their predecessors had no systematic way of making contingent faculty assignments, leaving it mostly to the department administrative staff. Now the chairs are being bombarded with requests from part-time faculty for the chance to teach more or different classes or sections than they have taught in the past. The dean also is in charge of faculty hiring for the next academic year, and pressure is coming from tenure-line faculty to hire tenure lines, while upper administration is pressuring for more contingent faculty to keep costs down. Meanwhile, some students have complained about not being able to plan to take courses with contingent faculty members they like, and others are registering complaints about not being able to meet (or to meet privately) with part-time adjunct instructors. Finally, contingent faculty across campus have formed an association and have approached the dean with a desire to talk about their concerns, which include access to orientation, professional development including evaluation, and representation on faculty council. However, some tenure-line faculty are objecting to giving contingent faculty representation and voting rights in departments, committees, or campus-wide governance bodies, arguing that many part-time faculty are not sufficiently familiar with or invested in campus issues.

LEADING FROM THE MIDDLE

Perhaps no issue better exemplifies the challenge of "leading from the middle" than the need to confront the national trend toward a mostly temporary faculty, historically referred to as *adjunct* and now increasingly termed *contingent.* On the one hand, deans must manage institutional priorities set by boards and senior leadership to cut budgets, raise enrollments, and increase prestige, which leads to increasing use of temporary, low-wage faculty. On the other hand, they must engage with faculty concerns about classroom quality, scheduling, and student success, which, research demonstrates, contraindicates the use of an overwhelmingly non-tenure-track faculty (NTTF). These pressures play out in the context of highly specific institutional cultures in which most campus policies dealing with faculty were constructed long before the percentage of faculty working off the tenure track in both full- and part-time positions reached its current rate of 75 percent. Even private liberal arts college figures, according to the Delphi Project on the Changing Faculty and Student Success (Besosa, 2011), range from 62.9 percent (40.2 percent PT and 22.7 percent FT, all NTTF) at private nonprofit research institutions to 70.5 percent (53 percent PT and 17.5 percent FT, all NTTF) at private nonprofit comprehensives.

In a recent national survey, deans reported that they do not often consult broadly to address the problems of the shifting faculty—they do not enlist faculty leaders below them or administrative leaders above them, but tend to go it alone. This isolation may be due to seeing the competing interests at play: they understand the long-standing value of hiring field experts who are employed full-time in their fields, but they also know that the pressure to reduce costs contributes to the attractiveness of hiring temporary, short-term faculty, even though low salaries and lack of optimal working conditions jeopardize academic quality. As a result, deans often find themselves unable to do more than react to NTTF-related problems as they arise. Alternatively, the fact that many institutions view themselves as "transitioning" to adding more tenure-track faculty seems to justify paying little attention to the NTTF needs.

Research (see the website of the Delphi Project on the Changing Faculty and Student Success, thechangingfaculty.org) demonstrates that such reactive approaches, even as part of a "transition," seldom ensure that all faculty work in conditions most conducive to excellent teaching. We suggest, therefore, that academic leaders who are charged with leading from the middle on this issue examine and confront campus culture, invite honest, inclusive conversation across faculty ranks and administrative roles, and collectively devise a long-term plan that defines desired outcomes, identifies achievable goals, and lays out benchmarks to measure progress and assign clear roles and accountability.

At the root of this multilayered approach is the conviction that the urgent national issues of access, cost, and quality in higher education come together in the arena of faculty working conditions. Former ACAD board chair Jim Pence articulated the ethos of this approach when, writing in *Liberal Education* in 2003, he noted that

> over the years, I have come to recognize the need for a compelling academic vision by having to deal with the consequences of not having one . . . Definitive frameworks of thinking provide a kind of cognitive discipline as an anchor in the midst of ambiguity, dissonance, and equally compelling arguments. The paradigm is a simple one; I ask myself: "How will this decision affect student and faculty learning?" (para. 9)

The question is important because unless systematic changes in campus processes concerning contingent faculty occur, the scenario in the opening vignette will continue to replay on college campuses and to erode the quality and community of academic and campus life.

EFFECTING CHANGE IN CONTEXT

Ideally, deans should take a leadership role in proactively advocating for and implementing a campus-specific strategic plan to address NTTF issues, even as they are dealing with individual NTTF-related crises and problems. Resources to help initiate the process are offered at the Delphi Project website. Based on research into successful change efforts on a diversity of campuses, the Project suggests the following principles, which complement efforts that NTTF nationwide are already undertaking themselves to initiate and effect change (see Kezar, 2012).

Make Faculty a Priority and Open Dialogue

In recent years, faculty have been underused as a resource for meeting institutional mission. Other external priorities—assessment, technology, and revenue generation—have taken precedence, even though, ironically, faculty are key to most of the external challenges that confront campuses. Deans having trouble making a discussion of NTTF working conditions a priority on campus can use the guide "The Imperative for Change" (on the Delphi website) to build a case with administrators and tenure-track faculty. This document outlines the way that lack of appropriate policies and practices for NTTF negatively shapes student learning, campus equity, and risk management. It can help to get differing groups, such as NTTF, tenure-line faculty, and administrators all on the same page about the importance of addressing this issue as a campus community.

Assess Conditions on Campus

It is important not to be lulled into thinking that a few isolated actions to improve NTTF working conditions will suffice, like simply offering professional development or inviting adjuncts to meetings. Instead, integrate those actions into a comprehensive assessment of existing conditions. Listen to NTTF about their concerns through focus groups and anonymous surveys that can be announced at professional development events and meetings. Make space available for adjunct-only meetings in which faculty can discuss their experience and perceptions with each other—and ensure that there will be no reprisals against faculty who participate, as such assurances will do much to foster a sense of trust (Rooney, 2012). Such meetings may also provide for a more coherent articulation of these faculty members' needs and concerns.

Because campuses typically have little data or information about NTTF that can help with ongoing planning, leaders should encourage data collection about numbers of NTTF, policies and practices in place, and campus climate. Among other things, these data will typically reveal that there are many more NTTF than originally assumed. Some campuses will find that hiring is occurring at the very last minute and that faculty are being placed in courses with days to prepare—a national trend that has been documented by the New Faculty Majority as well as the Higher Education Research Institute (Street, Maisto, Merves, & Rhoades, 2012).

Other campuses will find that there is no orientation, leading to significant NTTF turnover and an inability to make the most appropriate teaching assignments. Still other campuses will find that NTTF are barred from governance in many of their departments and that a negative climate has resulted and is seeping into departmental life and even the student experience. Only through ongoing data collection can these problems be assessed and addressed. (For detailed case studies about campuses that have undergone change by collecting data on campus policies to better support NTTF, please see Kezar, 2012.) Deans will usually delegate this process of assessment and data collection, but they need to be involved in the formulation of the plan.

Invite Dialogue

Once you have armed yourself with data about policies, practices, and issues, it is important to have a broad dialogue about what the data mean, to discuss possible strategies to address the findings, and to develop a way forward that involves multiple constituents. Such discussions might result in a campus-wide or school-wide task force to develop a plan to ameliorate problems that emerged in the assessment. The guide noted above on the Delphi website can help provide the framework for such a discussion.

It is important that such dialogues begin by acknowledging the difficult working conditions for NTTF and the assets they bring to campus in terms of expertise and skill so that they are not unintentionally demonized as a problem in discussions.

Formulate and Execute a Long-Term Plan

As a task force or ongoing advisory group assesses progress, helps correct problems in new policies, and begins to formulate a long-term plan, it is critical to involve NTTF in the process. It is also imperative that core big-picture principles and goals based on institutional mission and context govern decision making and that the institution hold itself accountable to the campus community for its progress.

EFFECTING CHANGE IN CONTEXT II: THE HIRING AND REAPPOINTMENT PROCESS

Issues that come up around specific topics like those in the opening vignette provide an opportunity to reflect on the systemic and mission-critical nature of the problems, and therefore, to work at a micro and macro level simultaneously. One such issue is the hiring/appointment process. Tenure-line faculty bias against contingent faculty—seen in the resistance to giving them representation in governance, for example—often stems from the difference between rigorous, formal hiring practices for tenure lines and informal, arbitrary ones for non-tenure-track lines. Informal and inconsistent NTTF hiring practices stand in stark contrast to formal, intensive practices that are expected in tenure-line hiring processes. Thus, formalizing the NTTF hiring process can be an important step in changing campus-wide faculty culture, which in turn promotes collaboration on the activities necessary to effect long-term change.

Additionally, NTTF, and the students they serve, have a fundamental need for *stability*, both for learning and for professional engagement. Research on NTTF, consistently reveals a high level of concern about job security (Valadez & Antony, 2001) and the professionalism of their work environment. Lack of orientation can lead to NTTF, through no fault of their own, providing wrong information to students. Overreliance on student evaluations rather than on formative and summative evaluations by mentors, colleagues, and supervisors can reinforce poor pedagogy and deprive NTTF and their students of the opportunity to improve teaching and learning.

Lack of knowledge and ineffective communication—about teaching assignments, rehire procedures (including access to grievance processes), class cancellations, contingent faculty rights to unemployment insurance between terms and to programs like public student loan forgiveness—can instill cynicism toward the institution among NTTF and cause real economic harm to these faculty. Even such faculty who do not depend on their teaching income tend to feel that assignments should be timely and commitments kept as a matter of professional courtesy. And although most NTTF members recognize that institutions need to be able to handle fluctuating enrollments, it is important for academic administrators not to overstate the need for flexibility. Surveys show that significant numbers of NTTF serve at a single institution in so-called temporary positions for many years (Street et al., 2012).

By working to initiate a campus-wide strategic plan to integrate NTTF, deans can approach individual crises and problems with the big picture in mind and use the experience as a useful form of data collection. For example, if a NTTF association is forming, then provide it with the charge—and the resources—to collect some of the data that are necessary for a long-term, campus-wide project to improve faculty working conditions. Not only will this encourage faculty self-representation, but it will also jumpstart the data collection process. Such efforts are imperative because the stability and development of NTTF are crucial to the intellectual life of higher education, to the quality of academic programs, and to the professional and ethical reputation of the institution as a whole.

In sum, there are three key points to keep in mind:

- Approach all situations or problems involving NTTF with an awareness of the structural and systemic nature of the problem and its relationship to student learning, and consider how the particular issue you are dealing with fits into that larger context and the institution's overall goals for addressing this issue.
- Don't wait for problems to arise. Begin working collaboratively with tenure-track and NTTF to assess campus conditions for NTTF and to develop a long-term institutional plan for addressing contingent faculty employment practices.
- Prioritize providing stability for contingent faculty that will allow them to both teach more effectively and participate in collaborative reform efforts by providing them with clear hiring, evaluation, reappointment, and grievance policies and longer-term contracts.

References

Besosa, M. (2011). *Faculty forum: Ways to organize non-tenure-track faculty*. The Delphi Project on the Changing Faculty and Student Success. http://www.thechangingfaculty.org/

Kezar, A. (Ed.). (2012). *Embracing non-tenure track faculty: Changing campuses for the new faculty majority*. New York: Routledge.

Pence, J. L. (2003). Deans' dilemmas: Practicing academic leadership. *Liberal Education, 89*(4), 38–45.

Rooney, J. (2012, December 4). 5 Ways deans can help adjuncts. Inside Online Colleges. http://www.onlinecolleges.net/2012/12/04/5-ways-deans-can-help-adjuncts/

Street, S., Maisto, M., Merves, E., & Rhoades, G. (2012, August). *Who is "professor staff" and how can this person teach so many classes?* Center for the Future of Higher Education. http://www.nfmfoundation.org/ProfStaffFinal.pdf

Valdez, J. R., & Antony, J. S. (2001). Job satisfaction and commitment of two-year college part-time faculty. *Community College Journal of Research and Practice, 25*(2), 97–108.

CHAPTER FORTY-EIGHT

Working with People in Conflict

Conversational Strategies for Deans

Thomas W. Meyer
Broward College

As a dean, you have had plenty of experiences in working with colleagues on the faculty. But you also have always known that though you may be the leader of the faculty, faculty members are autonomous and don't always feel the need or desire to be led. At times, you've been accused of making decisions without taking into account the opinions or attitudes of the faculty. Sometimes the faculty have liked the idea, and so there has not been an issue. At other times, one dissatisfied or "difficult" faculty member expressed a concern and brought an initiative to a halt, especially because the faculty senate or union was involved. Students, also, have challenged your leadership because of their desire for instant gratification. You've heard faculty complain about the sense of entitlement that students have, or the lack of effort they expend to earn a decent grade. As dean, you often have found yourself mediating conflicts that have arisen between faculty and students due to such perceived characteristics of the student population. And, finally, as an upper-level administrator, you have sometimes encountered difficult coworkers or colleagues who can be surprisingly territorial or uncollegial. Such persons pose a challenge to accomplishing goals, especially because you needed something from them in order to complete a task.

Conflicts in the workplace are nothing new, but in an academic setting, they often surprise us. After all, colleges and universities are places where free thought and freedom of expression prosper; this would lead one to believe that conflict would be less likely to arise. Maybe it is precisely because of academic freedom, diversity, and well-informed constituencies that conflict occurs just as often as in any other workplace. All deans have encountered colleagues or clients in conflict at some point in their career, and in a collegiate setting these difficult people can broadly be categorized into faculty, students, and coworkers.

A CONVERSATIONAL ANALYSIS

A traditional approach to describing personalities or people in conflict has been to categorize them into groups based on characteristic stereotypes such as bullies, backstabbers, passive-aggressives, vipers, gossipers, and even so-called psychos. Although this might be a convenient model for describing employees in workplace settings, in this chapter, I have outlined a sociolinguistic approach to the topic of dealing with a "difficult person." In the field of conversation analysis, scholars approach discourse as embedded in context. Sociolinguists consider various elements: the participants or interlocutors, the language they use, their role in the conversation, their backgrounds, and the setting in which the conversation is taking place. As illustrated in figure 48.1, there are numerous factors affecting a conversation, including the context such as the seriousness and timing, the personal characteristics of the participants, expectations or desired outcomes, and the history behind the topic.

In short, what goes into the conversation affects or informs what comes out (Meyer, 1996).

Every situation is unique and should be approached as such. Approaching a conversation with a difficult person using this cerebral approach may help you understand why the person is behaving the way he or she is and what you may be able to say to defuse the situation. The disgruntled faculty member often has a good reason for his or her dissatisfaction, the unreasonable student may simply have a different view of the world, and the negative coworker may be upset for just cause. Build on previous experience and knowledge using what you know about the person

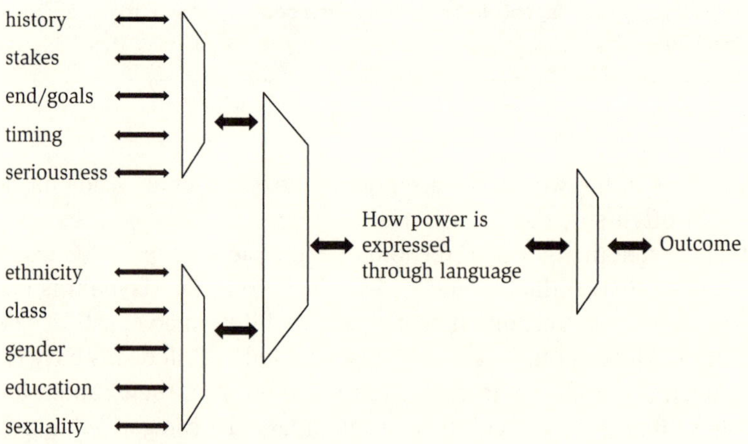

Figure 48.1 Factors Affecting Conversation

with whom you are interacting, but know that each difficult conversation you enter into is uniquely defined according to the context, participants, and power dynamics.

Crucial to this model is your position as dean and the notions and stereotypes surrounding such a position. It is important for you to be aware of the dean's position of power—or the perception of it—because this affects the context of the conversation, the way people approach the conversation, and the expectations regarding your behavior. People often believe deans have more power than we do, and it is easy for them to forget that deans face restrictions and make mistakes as well. When dealing with difficult people, I often find myself reminding others that I don't have a special computer that can make concerns go away and that my powers are limited to the policies and procedures of the college, but I assure them that I will assist them in every way possible within the confines of my abilities with respect to my position as dean.

USEFUL LANGUAGE

Language is key to resolving difficult conversations with challenging faculty, students, and coworkers. When confronting a difficult person, certain "deanly" phrases of reassurance and insight can help keep the conversation focused and grounded. I've included a few that have proven useful over the years.

"If I can help you, I will."

When a difficult student or faculty member enters my office, he or she often feels that no one is willing to help, or that no one is making an effort to understand or appreciate his or her situation. I find that this one phrase of reassurance is very powerful and often calms the situation—after all, why wouldn't I, as dean, help someone when I can? There is nothing to be gained by not assisting someone.

"Please call me when you have a minute so we can talk."

When handling difficult situations, be cautious about communicating via e-mail. E-mails are void of tone, inflection, and facial expressions and should not be used as a substitute for a meaningful conversation. When an angry student or faculty member e-mails you a complaint, think carefully about the best way to proceed with communication. As a dean, you have a variety of options for communication, so choose wisely according to the context. Some can be handled via e-mail, but some can go back and forth, quickly developing into a tit-for-tat e-mail exchange. In such cases, pick up the phone or schedule a face-to-face meeting.

"Can we please start over?" or "I'm treating you respectfully, I'd like the same."

Oftentimes it is helpful to try to start a difficult conversation anew or request a more courteous discourse. I have found this phrase especially useful when I feel that someone is not treating me respectfully, especially a coworker or fellow administrator. This may also prove a useful phrase when the tone of the conversation turns negative or escalates.

"May I please finish what I was saying?"

With more talkative coworkers and faculty, it may be difficult to finish thoughts or sentences, especially when you are trying to choose your words carefully. Requesting that you be allowed to finish what you were trying to say is a very diplomatic way of remaining assertive and making your point.

"That's important too, but that's not what we're here to discuss."

Many difficult conversations lack focus, and issues often surface that are secondary to the presenting matter at hand. Students are especially prone to raising many extraneous issues in one conversation. By acknowledging that the other issue has merit (even when it may not) and can be revisited at a later point in time, you will be able to keep the conversation on track toward resolution.

"We're all on the same team." or "We're all in this together."

This is a helpful phrase with a coworker or faculty member who may feel you are working toward different goals. Sometimes a simple reminder that you both share the same goal (such as student success, curricular approval, or efficient operations) can bring the conversation back to a level of civility.

IMPORTANT REMINDERS

In addition to useful phrases, there are many other factors to consider when working through a difficult situation with a coworker, student, or faculty member. Keeping these things in mind as the conversation takes place will help you reach a solution or resolution more quickly and effectively.

Listen

Active listening skills are crucial when working with a difficult person. As mentioned previously, a difficult person may not even be sure what he or she is unhappy about. Listen to the person and try to get to the core of the issue. Help the student, administrator, or professor whittle away at the issue by listening. Ask the person to clarify things you don't understand by saying something like, "Please explain what you mean when you say . . ." and use confirmation checks like, "So if I understand you correctly, you would like . . . Is that correct?" Think of the topic as a dartboard, with the real issue at hand being the bull's-eye, and the rest of the board representing other concerns surrounding the real issue. The complaint at hand is often far from the bull's-eye and only through active listening will you get to the core problem that brought the person to your office.

Don't Take It Personally

When you perceive that someone is being difficult, it is important that you as dean not personalize the matter. Most often, a person is being difficult because of something that happened to him, or the way she feels she has been treated. If you can keep this in mind, it will help you approach the matter from a more objective viewpoint. The student who is challenging a grade is concerned about his or her future. The adjunct faculty member who didn't receive a paycheck has bills to pay. Such stressors often lead to anxiety, which in turn affects people's behavior. And you can't control their behavior. You can only listen, try to understand, and remain in control of your reactions.

Make Time

Deans are busy, and if you are working on a project with a tight deadline, the last thing you want in your office or e-mail queue is a complaint. It may be difficult to remain understanding when you are having a bad day yourself and have a lot on your calendar. Timing is critical to the way one responds or feels about a situation or difficult visitor.

The fact is, you have no control over when complaints arise, but as dean, you do have control over how you will handle the situation. Many complaints do not need to be handled immediately. As dean, you should discern between immediate needs versus those that can wait. Scheduling an appointment will remove stress from you so that you can approach the situation with a fresh mind. It also serves as a cooling-off period for the individual making the complaint and gives you more time to gather some information prior to the meeting. All of this helps calm the situation, and may eliminate the disruptive or difficult demeanor of the person making the complaint.

Admit Mistakes

If someone comes to you upset or angry about a mistake that you made, admit it and move on. Trying to hide the mistake, or trying to explain it away will only serve to exacerbate the situation. Similarly, if one of your subordinates has made a mistake or there is a flaw in the system, take ownership of it. In cases where a difficult person is pointing out that there is a real problem, this difficult person is actually helping you make improvements. Thank the individual for bringing it to your attention, implement changes to rectify the wrong, and follow up with the person to let him or her know that you appreciate that it was brought to your attention. Without such difficult conversations or complaints, you might never have known the problem existed.

Move On

There is no room in the workplace for grudges. If you have been involved in a situation with a difficult employee, coworker, or student, you as dean must move on afterward. You don't have to like the person, but you do have to be able to work together—a message the dean must consistently convey. In my years of experience, I have often been surprised by the difficult student who surpassed my expectations, or the difficult employee who was able to turn things around and learn from the experience. As dean, you must promote civility and tolerance—moving on after an altercation is essential to maintaining an atmosphere of collegiality.

NO ONE WANTS TO BE DIFFICULT

I have found that very few people are purposely or intentionally difficult. I concede that some people truly *are* "difficult," and as dean, your skills will be tested repeatedly. However, most often, it's the problem, not the person (Coleman, 2013). By analyzing the conversation and taking into account the multitude of factors affecting the conversation and the issue at hand, you will often find that a so-called difficult person is really just another individual with a concern he or she is having difficulty expressing.

It helps to understand the following:

- The dean plays a critical role in working with difficult people to raise awareness of how their behavior is perceived, to resolve issues, and to create learning experiences for students, faculty, and fellow administrators alike.
- Conversation analysis can help one determine if it's the problem or the person, and can help a dean steer the dialog to an effective resolution.
- The dean needs to promote civility among faculty and staff for the betterment of the institution.

References

Coleman, D. (2013, January 3). It's the problem, not the person. [Web log post]. Retrieved from http://www.linkedin.com/today/post/article/20130103173853-117825785-it-s-the-problem-not-the-person

Meyer, T. (1996). *Language and power in disagreements*. Ann Arbor, MI: Bell & Howell.

CHAPTER FORTY-NINE

The Responsibility of Leadership in Dealing with Difficult People

Donald Tucker
Malone University

> Maybe you've heard this or something like this: "I've had it with Professor Green. He's unreasonable, uncooperative, belligerent, abusive, and close-minded! He thinks he knows it all and that nobody else's viewpoint matters. He has no appreciation for rational thinking, doesn't contribute anything meaningful in our committee meetings, and complains that everyone else's ideas are stupid. That's what we get for hiring those 'artsy' types. He's such a prima donna!"

THE HUMAN CONTEXT IN HIGHER EDUCATION

Every institution has its eccentric people. Those like the absented-minded professor who forgets to comb his hair or the one who insists on always wearing the same tweed jacket with worn-out leather elbow patches or the one who constantly blurts out in unexpected venues, "Kill those damn Yankees!" Odd behaviors, eccentricities, and incompetence are easily identified, but these are not the most difficult scenarios for administrators to handle. Personality quirks can be tolerated, and although sometimes complicated, incompetence can be documented and dealt with in direct ways.

The more difficult scenarios in higher education involve issues of incivility, dishonesty, disruptive behavior, and outright rebellion. Consider the faculty website that touts one's experience and background as a program director. Reading the vitae suggest that this person was solely responsible for the vibrancy and success of the program, but it fails to mention that the individual was removed from that position due to incompetence, wasteful spending, and irresponsible conduct. Consider the faculty bully who constantly demeans others with abrasive comments and by sheer force of will makes demands that are unreasonable, coercing colleagues to do his bidding, or the Jekyll-Hyde passive-aggressive personality who is pleasant in public but privately is a nightmare. Consider the subtle behind-the-scenes harasser who sends irritating and accusatory e-mails, refuses to answer the phone, and locks herself in her office with loud rock music blaring into the hallways.

THE RESPONSIBILITY OF LEADERSHIP

A good leader recognizes that the values held in highest regard—academic freedom, exploration, argument, analysis, and dialogue—create a stimulating and exciting but stressful, competitive, and volatile organizational setting. Key elements in redirecting tensions include creating organizational structures for process and exploration, understanding personalities and individual motivations, diffusing tensions, minimizing conflict, and learning basic principles of mediation and ways of interaction.

Complex organizations like colleges and universities operate with multiple grids—grids of communities, influence, authority, policy, people, and expectations. These grids do not always coincide equally. Each grid assumes certain protections and "rights" of individuals, departments, and the institution. It is inevitable that priorities, processes, assumptions, and goals will conflict.

Understanding the thought process, emotions, and work habits of analytical, entrepreneurial, and creative individuals is complicated. As a concentrated center of scientific, intellectual, and creative capital, the college is filled with highly trained, passionate, and competitive individuals. We have been trained to be argumentative, persuasive, and questioning. We explore unknown territories and create new knowledge, products, and artistic expressions. And we try to convince others that we are right. Crossing the line into our turf and suggesting we are mistaken does not sit well with our academic personality. John Bennett (2003), provost emeritus at Quinnipiac University in Connecticut, calls this direction of energy to self-protection and self-promotion *academic insistent individualism*.

Even the dean or provost has emotions, stresses, passions, and needs that affect how we communicate and interact with and react to those around us. Maintaining a calm demeanor and an attitude of professionalism and objectivity, especially in times of opposition and conflict, can be difficult. Every human interaction uses energy. For some, these interactions paralyze the spirit and drain emotional and physical strength, but for others they are stimulating. In either case, human capital is not limitless. The stresses we bring from home; the visceral reaction to a policy decision; the trivial and mundane interactions with colleagues, superiors, or subordinates; the glorious and ecstatic celebrations; and the tragedies and sorrows of life press against the human capital that has been developed (or destroyed) through daily interactions with others.

SOME PRACTICAL IDEAS FOR EVERYDAY SURVIVAL

Keep in mind the framework in which you operate. It is not about the individual versus the institution, but the individual versus the institutional mission, values, and purpose. How do the mission, vision, and values of the institution supersede the individual persons in it? Individual rights and freedoms are not limitless. When individual emotional expressions or behaviors negatively affect safety, security, or flourishing of the group, they must be addressed in a direct and positive way.

Individual faculty sometimes need to be reminded that being a part of the university means you are not a faculty member in isolation, you are a part of *the* faculty body. This means there are collective as well as individual responsibilities associated with the privilege of joining this great academic community. The interests of the whole have to be protected from the domination and self-interest of one.

Every institution has a set of expectations for its members. Remind the renegade about the requirements—teaching loads, expectations for service, advising and mentoring students, service on committees, scholarly output, conformity to behavioral policies, and expectations for collegiality. Clarify expectations for performance and how one is to be evaluated. Don't just let things slide; hold people accountable for following established guidelines. Any time you can be proactive in preventing a crisis, you minimize unnecessary overreactions and having to clean up a bigger mess later.

It may be helpful to remind others that as the dean or provost, you also are accountable. There are other people that expect you to perform and respond according to certain expectations. There are external pressures that demand your attention and there is the ultimate oversight of presidents or board members. A disruptive colleague needs to know when his or her behavior is detracting from the larger goals of the institution. As much as possible, make expectations a community endeavor.

And be careful to understand how individual personalities express themselves and how individuals process data and situations. A typical stereotype assumes that creative individuals are arrogant, self-centered, insensitive, and unwilling to compromise. Analytical persons are often viewed as intellectually arrogant, uncaring about feelings, and so serious about analysis that they can't ever commit to a final conclusion. But these stereotypes are not entirely true.

Be cautious about jumping to conclusions and prejudging a person without knowing the context behind emotions and behaviors. What is the issue behind the issue? Perhaps there is a family crisis, financial emergency, illness, or some unexpected issue causing duress. Check things out thoroughly and do not rush to judgment. Is there a difference in culture or philosophical perspective? Is there a difference in opinion, strategy, or priority? Is the issue personal (ad hominem attacks, threats, bruised ego, selfishness)? Personal attacks are often defense mechanisms. If someone is trapped in a corner, don't push. Step away and provide some distance for diffusion, process, and clarity.

At the same time, don't ignore inappropriate behaviors and comments. Bullies need to know that they are offensive and that their aggressive tactics will not be tolerated. Explain why the behavior violates others and insist that it stop. But unless there is an immediate threat of physical or psychological harm, give some time for volatility to settle before further corrective measures are implemented.

This may seem like a balancing act, and it is. Leadership requires wisdom and intuition to know when restraint is necessary. The danger for a leader is to take short cuts and determine "I'm going to fix this right now." You cannot let things simmer until they boil over, but at the same time you need to be as certain as possible about the context and root cause behind behaviors. Listening actively is the most difficult step in this discernment. Take time to listen and determine the underlying cause. Keep things in perspective and don't blow things out of proportion.

Once you know with reasonable certainty how and why the inappropriate behavior occurred, address it promptly. Allowing things to linger or to remain the same will only cause further damage. Ignorance is *not* bliss; avoidance is *not* a strategy. Avoiding conflict or confrontation often has unintended consequences—tensions increase, disruptive behavior accelerates, the circle of those affected enlarges.

You can reasonably predict that there will be conflict in higher education over resources, office or laboratory space, department or institutional assignments, or positions of influence. But any number of seemingly insignificant things can set someone off. Conflict can occur spontaneously and without warning. When these things occur, address issues with civility. Calm yourself to avoid overreaction or tit-for-tat comments. It is okay to say to someone that you disagree, and this may be a necessary starting place for achieving resolution. But an emotionally laden response typically comes back to bite you.

In times of disciplinary action, reinforce and preserve the self-respect of the individual. Attacking character and personhood erodes the worth of an individual. Addressing an issue of behavior or competence is necessary, but destroying the person is never acceptable. People are not *things*. Avoid alienation, insults, and depersonalization. These responses erode trust and produce a litigious environment.

Every person has certain individuals or a group of others who support them and look to them for guidance, encouragement, and wisdom. If you destroy the individual person, you remove the moorings, foundation, and hopes from other people as well. Behavior, not the value or role of the person, is the issue. Try to be constructive in comments and interactions rather than accusatory. Affirm and accept the person but not the inappropriate behavior or attitude. Clarify expectations for performance and how resolution of this incident helps to move us forward past this unfortunate situation.

Maintain professionalism in demeanor and actions. Remember your manners in a meeting, on the telephone, when sending e-mail, or when meeting face-to-face. When possible, keep things informal and private. Airing dirty laundry in public rarely helps to resolve disputes. However, if the situation is volatile, it may be necessary to widen the circle and avoid one-on-one confrontation. Individual confrontations are too often subject to misunderstandings, distortions, inaccuracies, and accusations. Neutralize the location and get outside help if needed (mediation, multiple voices, or a respected colleague).

Perhaps the offender has a friend whom they trust and to whom they listen; maybe there is a veteran dean who can help, or a human resources director, even an outside mediator. Look into employee assistance programs and counseling services. If necessary, consult legal counsel about appropriate sanctions that can be imposed along the way in order to avoid the need for more troubling consequences or ultimate dismissal.

Behaviors of colleagues are unpredictable, and we can't control them. What we can do as administrators is make sure that irrational and inappropriate behaviors are not tolerated or given free rein. We are human, and even though we have great potential for good, we are also fallible. We are subject to emotional volatility, misunderstanding, miscommunication, and the occasional bout of jealousy, pettiness, or anger. How we deal with these things is one measure of our strength and character.

We are all part of a shared community with a common vision of intellectual and personal growth and only as we work in harmony toward these larger institutional goals can we be truly effective in assisting our students in their own individual development. Whether someone likes the metaphor of the "family" or doesn't like this, it is a fitting picture. We are in truth a family—which means we need to learn to respect one another, call each other to task when we are out of line, and sometimes check our own egos and desires for the good of the whole.

The job of the leader is to keep the larger picture in mind and to look toward the future. Do I really want someone after me to have to clean up messes that I was too timid to address? Every institution has enough unexpected trouble and unfortunate incidents that you don't need to contribute to this by refusing to deal with something that disrupts the present. Pave the way for a better future for your successor. Remember the sage advice of Robert Fulghum (2004; 1988) in *All I Really Need to Know I Learned in Kindergarten*: "Play fair, don't hit people, clean up your own mess, say you're sorry when you hurt somebody, and when you go out in the world, watch out for traffic, hold hands and stick together."

Here are some important questions to keep in mind when working with people on your campus:

- What exactly is going on? How and why did this happen?
- Do I feel comfortable dealing with this, or do I need to solicit assistance in order to deal with the behavior?
- Am I calm, adequately prepared, and willing to follow through?
- Is there a plan in place to prevent a reoccurrence of this?

References

Bennett, John. (2003). *Academic life: Hospitality, ethics, and spirituality*. Bolton, MA: Anker.

Fulghum, R. (2004; 1988). *All I really need to know I learned in kindergarten* (15th ed.). New York: Ballantine.

CHAPTER FIFTY

The Bully on Campus

Productively Working with These Difficult People

Elizabeth A. Throop
University of Wisconsin-Platteville

"Sam" was known all over campus for his ideological rigidity, loudly and frequently provided, and his unwillingness to take no for an answer. He was convinced that he knew best how to run everything, and he criticized everyone in academic leadership ceaselessly, both publicly and privately. When the committee that a junior faculty member chaired announced a decision with which Sam disagreed, he confronted the junior faculty member and threatened to make sure that the junior faculty member's tenure bid was unsuccessful unless the decision was reversed. After consultation with senior leadership and college attorneys, my supervisor and I confronted Sam and imposed consequences for his bullying behavior. In the meeting, Sam expressed shock and disbelief that his behaviors would be characterized so negatively given that he had nothing but the best intentions; as we pressed him, he began to shake and was close to tears. It seemed that, throughout his career, Sam had never been confronted effectively. After this event, Sam seemed to completely alter his behavior—so much so that students remarked on how nice he was, an unusual interpretation of his demeanor!

A recurring issue for deans on many college and university campuses is how to work with difficult and unpleasant faculty members, a small but engulfing and enervating subset of our faculties. We often gloss the varieties of behaviors we encounter as "bullying." We come across people who demand more resources than their colleagues, hectoring committees, chairs, and coworkers until everyone is exhausted and just gives in; we meet people who insist there is but one process, theirs, that must be followed (whether factually or legally correct or not) and again they insist, sometimes loudly, until the others give in. There are the hierarchy-jumpers (going to the dean or the president and bypassing department committees or chairs entirely). And then there are the faculty members who "mentor" junior faculty so poorly that either the junior faculty members make huge and irreversible mistakes causing a *no* vote for tenure, the junior faculty members leave due to a poisonous atmosphere, or the junior faculty members try to fight the bully through building alliances (sometimes successfully).

We have the job-threatener: "If you don't understand that I am entitled to teach whatever I want whenever I want, regardless of enrollments, you're in trouble; I'll make sure you lose your job if you get in my way." There is the emotion manipulator: "Oh, you're going to upset lots of people if you do that!" There is the territory marker: "I know Suzy Junior Faculty Member came up with the idea, but she's too inexperienced to do it well, so I'll just take the credit but let her do the work." We come across the spokesperson allegedly speaking on behalf of the entire faculty: "Many faculty members think that you must do *x* or there will be trouble." There is the misunderstood hero: "My motives are pure and you people are all simply misunderstanding my nobility even though I'm yelling, screaming, and threatening to withhold tenure approvals for those who disagree with me."

One of the most important things to remember about campus bullies is that they are significantly unhappy people. It is easy to develop contemptuous and dismissive attitudes given the often vituperative behaviors that we observe, but it is our role as campus leaders not to indulge in the "there she goes again" response. All of these people do considerable damage to our campuses (and I've encountered each one of these types in my academic career). The question is, how do we productively manage these difficult persons?

The most important stance is, I think, one of compassion partnered with courage. Although we have to stand up to bullies on behalf of our colleagues, our students, and our campus, we need to find ways to view the bullies with kindness. Most often, bullies on campus have pushed limits. Many of us are uncomfortable with confrontation, so bullies get what (they think) they want over and over again. It is a shock to the bully when someone says "no more." Without being able to push people around, the bully isn't quite sure what to do. When imagining the bully's interiority, even in the midst of a frank discussion of what is and is not allowable behavior with that person, I often envision Edward Munch's painting *The Scream*. There is, for many bullies, a gaping emptiness inside, one that they attempt to fill with self-importance and bossiness. Terror accelerates when a difficult person is limited in her ability to harm others. I am always mindful of that terror of emptiness when dealing with a campus bully.

This does not mean, of course, that we allow troublesome behavior to go unremarked or unaddressed. A laissez-faire management style is often how bullies flourish. A responsible dean will document a pattern of troublesome behaviors, consulting with provosts or VPAAs, a faculty ombudsperson or other relevant parts of the governance structure if salient, human resources, and, perhaps, the college attorneys, as consequences are devised. The dean then will sit down with the bully (preferably with a strong associate as a witness), outlining specific incidents in which the bully has participated that will not be tolerated if repeated, along with clear consequences. We have to be ready to initiate peer-led assessments, such as posttenure review if applicable; more important, we need to be able to begin dismissal proceedings should the problem be severe enough.

The key to managing bullying behavior really is creating a strong support network. Without the backing of senior administration, decanal colleagues, and department chairs, a dean will be ineffective when trying to halt bullying behaviors. As is true for almost any campus initiative, gaining the allegiance of the key opinion makers on campus, and those with both formal power and informal influence, will be crucial. Many faculty members (and not a few staff members as well) likely will be cheering you on from the sidelines, grateful that someone is finally putting a halt to destructive behavior. It can be a delicate juggling act, however—there are limits to what personnel issues you can disclose. Staying focused on the issue publicly rather than the person is one strategy that is effective.

Indeed, maintaining that focus for yourself is important. Some bullies are exquisite observers of behavior and have an uncanny ability to offer remarks about things that are sensitive spots personally. It is absolutely vital that the dean not react to jabs, insults, and innuendo offered by the bully (or anyone else, actually!). I know that I am in the presence of a bully when I begin to feel defensive, angry, or trapped. An effective dean will be able to monitor her own emotional state well enough to separate out responses appropriate to a particular situation (a campus tragedy, for instance, or a truly angering situation) from those automatic reactions to emotional manipulation.

Most of us would agree as well that many (not all, but many) of the difficult people who take up so much of our time exhibit bullying behaviors. Though it varies by campus, the adage that 5 percent of the faculty take up 95 percent of the dean's time is an accurate reflection of both emotional energy and managerial effort expended on bullies. A reality of the job, the bully can take enormous amounts of time and emotion if the problem is not faced. If much of our effort is focused on coping with the aftermath of a bully's work, it means that we cannot attend as much as we would like to those faculty members who are doing well—the grant getters, the outstanding teachers, the terrific scholars, and the individuals contributing positively to the mission and the goals of the institution.

Finally, it becomes a matter of justice. Those who are constantly looking for a fight, arguing with leadership for the sake of argument, or pushing junior faculty or staff members around, often do so with a veneer of social awareness, emotional double-talk, or overt political stances. Sometimes, for instance, they try to argue (against the clear facts) that administration continues to expand and enrich itself although instruction is starved, while insisting on reduced teaching loads and small class sizes for themselves. Or they try to engage in a discussion of feelings inappropriate for the workplace and for the supervisory relationship. Or, as alluded to above, they paint themselves as Faculty Heroes, attempting to assist junior faculty when they "err," sporting nothing but the purest of motives. None of these stances are legitimate, and we as leaders must remember that. We don't necessarily have to point out the inconsistencies or hypocrisies. Our job does not have to be about changing minds but it *is* about encouraging behavior change. Indeed, it is far beyond the scope of our authority to try to insist that bullies change their interiority. All we can do is insist on reasonable, rational behavior.

This can be the hardest part—separating the emotional mess that many bullies create (and experience!) from the behavioral morass we encounter. Although it is tempting to try to create psychological profiles (and cures) exploring the bully's emotional state, that is a strategy destined to fail. Of course compassion calls for us to understand that bullies are emotionally damaged, but it is not the job of the dean to fix that damage and in fact such an attempt is a serious overreach. Instead, the best we can do is insist on the exhibition of collegial, productive behavior, or we must work on separation of the bully from the institution.

Ultimately, a dean who is trying to manage bullying behavior requires the following:

- Compassionate courage in order to confront, with understanding, bullying behavior
- A strong network of allies who can provide necessary support and positive reinforcement
- An ability to self-assess to ensure that one's own response to bullying behavior is collegial and productive
- A focus on behavioral outcomes for the bully rather than his emotional state

CHAPTER FIFTY-ONE

Difficult Disciplinary Decisions

Dismissing Faculty

Alison Benders
Ohio Dominican University

> Imagine that a department chair comes to you, just after the fall semester starts, to report that a tenured faculty member appears to be employed full-time with another academic institution. You are only mildly surprised because you have been hearing rumors that the faculty member had not been pulling his weight in the department. He has been absent from key curriculum and assessment meetings and students have reported an unusually large number of class cancellations and his failure to be available for advising appointments. You are generally aware that the faculty handbook requires all outside employment to receive your approval. Therefore, if the rumors are true, the faculty member may be violating this handbook section and perhaps others. Additionally, the fact that both students and colleagues have been grumbling about this faculty member suggests that you need to take swift action to secure the quality of the students' experience and to protect faculty confidence in the integrity and effectiveness of your administration.

The chief academic officer (CAO) bears the primary responsibility for the quality of the faculty. Generally, faculty members are likely to respond positively when everyone knows that strong performance is rewarded and that inadequate or improper performance will be reproved. When the full faculty has confidence in the senior academic leader's integrity, fairness, and commitment to quality, an atmosphere of trust will develop. Unfortunately, it may be necessary to dismiss faculty members—either during the probationary pretenure period and on rare occasions, the posttenure period—who are not meeting expectations in order to ensure the overall quality of the faculty. Grounds for separation can include inadequate performance as measured against review criteria or, less frequently, specific violations of faculty or employment standards, such as dishonesty or insubordination. Although disciplinary actions are difficult and avoided by many supervisors, there are some specific steps that can be taken to assure that the outcome is defensible and just.

STRATEGIC AND PROACTIVE FACULTY DEVELOPMENT

A proactive CAO can avoid problems and strengthen performance by ensuring that the faculty performance standards and expectations are clear and integrally designed to develop the characteristics most valued by the institution. A commitment to clearly defined standards begins with a review of the faculty handbook sections on tenure and promotion. In this review, the CAO should evaluate the criteria, first, to ensure that they actually identify the qualities valued at the institution. Then, the criteria should be examined for clarity, consistency, and progression. Thus, the teaching-scholarship-service expectations for faculty members should build in a principled manner as faculty progress through their careers.

The review also should investigate the time line for the faculty review processes, that is, when information is submitted, when and how it is reviewed, and when outcomes are communicated. The events should coincide with other administrative time lines at the institution, such as the issuing of contracts, board meetings, disbursement of funds, or faculty awards. Carefully planned time lines will reduce the time faculty and administrators spend on evaluation and ensure consistency of results. It's clearly problematic for the administration, for example, when a faculty member who has just been chosen Best Instructor does not receive tenure. Senior faculty members, committee chairs, and faculty administrators will be excellent resources to help a CAO know how the handbook is interpreted and applied. Any necessary changes should be taken through the appropriate committee structure, including faculty senate approval if necessary. Again, intentional planning of which provisions to revise, who must be included in the conversations, and when to implement changes will help the CAO achieve a better process for all involved.

With good practices in place, the most important obligation of the CAO is to ensure that they are followed fully. One of the most common mistakes is the failure of the CAO or other administrators to give negative feedback to faculty members. Faculty members who are not performing well should receive feedback as soon as possible and should be given specific guidance to improve their performance. Course evaluations at the end of a term and annual reviews are important opportunities that should be capitalized on by the institution. Clear and thorough record keeping of these evaluations is crucial if a faculty member needs to be dismissed. In some cases, faculty members will realize that their performance in teaching, scholarship, or service is not meeting the expectations of their college or university, and will actively seek employment elsewhere.

DISMISSAL FOR POOR PERFORMANCE OR FOR CAUSE

The decision to dismiss should be based on substantiated facts and follow the procedures in the faculty handbook and any other applicable employment manual. Generally, the steps to dismiss a faculty member must include ascertaining the facts and procedures, communicating with appropriate personnel, and following all processes designed to safeguard the faculty employee and documenting behaviors, conversations, and actions.

Investigating the Facts

The first step in considering whether to dismiss a faculty member is to investigate the situation as thoroughly and quickly as possible. Any delays create the impression that the questionable conduct or poor performance is not really a problem. The CAO should review the following documents and piece together an understanding of the faculty member's performance or behavior:

- Annual evaluations by department chairs, deans, or the CAO
- Promotion and tenure documents, such as departmental reviews or committee minutes and statements, where available
- Student course evaluations for all semesters available
- All communications in personnel files in the CAO's office and in Human Resources, including any complaints filed

With respect to faculty performance issues, the CAO should have direct conversations with faculty administrators (such as the department chairs or deans). With respect to improper conduct, the investigation may include interviewing students, faculty, and staff who have complained or who have relevant information, including the target faculty member. Public sources of information, such as sites on the Internet, should not be overlooked.

Communicating with Those Who Need to Know

The president of the institution should be kept fully informed of the issue, the investigation, and the course of action. The dismissal of a faculty member is always a significant event in an academic community and, even when warranted, will bring scrutiny. Although there may be no specific action necessary by the president, that executive must be prepared to respond to questions from any quarter. The president will decide whether board members need to be informed. Additionally, the HR manager should be informed, principally for the CAO to get advice and assistance from a seasoned personnel manager. Involving HR also may invite the chief operating officer into the conversation as the person who oversees all financial obligations and manages risk. Depending on the situation, internal or external counsel may be asked for advice, especially when litigation is a possibility. Finally, the academic administrator (dean or chair) with responsibility over the faculty member should be informed. This person may be able to provide a context or relevant facts and will certainly be able to describe the steps needed to ameliorate the impact of the dismissal.

Implementing the Decision to Dismiss

If the evidence points to the need to dismiss, then this must be implemented according to the proper procedures. An important step is to document succinctly the reason for the decision. All evidence should be gathered, including copies of relevant evaluations, copies of letters in the personnel files, e-mail communications, summaries of conversations, and any other files that bear on the situation. In following the procedures for dismissal in the faculty handbook, or another employee manual, the CAO must be meticulous about following the time line and the notice provisions. As a matter of due process, a faculty member must be given an opportunity to respond to the CAO's declaration of intent to dismiss, including an option to resign in lieu of dismissal. All of these steps take time, and the CAO is responsible for efficiently shepherding the process toward a resolution.

The opening scenario presents a specific instance of a faculty member who has violated at least one common faculty handbook provision. Generally, handbooks require that full-time faculty commit without reserve to the institution, meaning that they should not have another job or obligation that interferes with their teaching, scholarship, and service obligations. In a related vein, handbooks also may require that faculty members receive administrative approval annually for obligations that exceed certain minimal parameters. In this instance, a factual investigation should involve a direct interview with the faculty member and contact with the institution where he was alleged to be employed. Assuming there has been a violation of the conditions of faculty employment, essentially a breach of contract, the procedural investigation must determine what rights a tenured faculty member has during a termination proceeding. Depending on the faculty handbook, these rights might include notice, opportunity to respond or correct, review by a faculty committee, and review by any other body, such as the president or the board.

The CAO should then write a letter notifying the faculty member of the intention to dismiss and the factual basis of the action. The letter should cite the relevant handbook provisions: the provision violated, the provision giving the CAO authority to dismiss, the procedure that applies, and any others that pertain. The letter also should allow the faculty member to resign voluntarily by signing and returning the letter to avoid procedural actions. It is advisable to invite the HR manager and possibly institutional counsel to review the letter. The letter should be presented to the faculty member in a face-to-face meeting with the HR manager present. If the faculty member does not resign, the procedures in the handbook must be followed to their fair resolution. If the CAO has investigated fully and evaluated the situation fairly, it is likely that the faculty member will be dismissed and the decision supported upon subsequent review.

There are three guidelines to follow as you consider dismissing a faculty member:

- *Research the situation and the rules.* The CAO must clarify as fully as possible the facts of the situation and the relevant provisions of the faculty handbook and the employee handbook. Researching facts may include conversations with people who have information (including the faculty member whose conduct is in issue), reviewing personnel and performance files, and studying the relevant provisions of the applicable employment documents (contracts and handbooks), as well as discerning how the provisions have been interpreted and applied in the past. The CAO must develop the facts and run the process in a way that protects both the institution's and the faculty member's interests.
- *Keep the president informed.* Throughout the process of the investigation and remedial action, the CAO must keep the president informed because of the possibility of liability (a lawsuit by the aggrieved faculty member). The HR manager should be consulted. Other people who also might need to be included are the institution's attorney, the dean or chair of the department, and the chair of the rank, tenure, and promotions committee, depending on the structure of the institution and the nature of the issue. In every instance, it is important to guard the confidentiality of the information and the events.
- *Document, document, document.* The CAO must keep a complete record of his or her actions throughout the process of dismissing a faculty member. Documentation should include, at least, the facts of the situation, including written records; the relevant provisions that provide the grounds and the process for dismissal; actions taken by the relevant faculty committee and supporting documentation, if any; the communications made with the faculty member, including all letters sent; and communications made with the president, HR, or other people with authority in the institution, including any approvals received. It is a good practice to have a third party (such as the HR manager) present whenever the CAO meets with the faculty member, as part of the record-keeping and documentation process. Documentation demonstrates that the process has been followed and that there are grounds for the action in the event that it is challenged subsequently through internal or external reviews, including in some cases litigation.

CHAPTER FIFTY-TWO

Legal Issues in Faculty Evaluation

Jon K. Dalager
Wayne State College

Jane Smith applied for tenure in the sixth year of her tenure-track position at your university. Over those six years she has received poor student evaluations of teaching, she has one publication from her second year but has no subsequent publications or conference presentations. She has not served on any faculty committees at the department or college level. The letter written by her department chair, on behalf of the entire department, suggests she be denied tenure because department colleagues consider her a difficult person. The faculty personnel committee has split in their decision providing the dean with little direction. Some on the committee have expressed qualms about denying tenure to a forty-five-year-old bisexual Hispanic woman with cerebral palsy, who is a practicing Buddhist and who frequently criticizes you and university policy in her classes.

Although this scenario is extreme in its facts, it does reflect real issues that deans face when considering faculty evaluation, especially tenure and promotion decisions, and other personnel decisions. For deans who do not have training in the law, these decisions can often feel overwhelming—and the stakes high. There are, however, particular procedures and approaches deans can and must take to ensure a fair process, help departments understand the appropriate and limited role collegiality may play in a tenure decision, educate the faculty personnel committee on employment discrimination, and avoid costly litigation for the college.

PROCEDURES AND CRITERIA FOR EVALUATION

Before conducting his or her first evaluation, a dean must know the institution's procedures and criteria for evaluation. Failure to follow the correct procedures is not always fatal to evaluation decisions in the case of tenure-track faculty, although courts do frown on universities not following their own procedures. From a practical standpoint, however, if the faculty member believes that his case was handled fairly, even though he does not like the result, then he is less likely to seek a remedy in the courts. On the other hand, if the decision appears to have been made without adequate input from the candidate and his supporters, then those hard feelings are likely to lead to litigation.

The criteria applicable in most cases are *teaching, scholarship, and service*. Because of the differing nature of institutions, the dean must know how much weight will be given to each category at his or her university. At a research institution, publications and grant production are essential, whereas at a small liberal arts college, teaching is the priority. Some institutions already have determined the weight given to each criterion, and the dean must be aware of that scale.

In our vignette, the department chair has raised the issue of *collegiality,* as well. As an evaluation criterion, collegiality has caused controversy. On the one hand, many institutions have incorporated it as a factor to be considered both in promotion and tenure decisions and in recruiting and hiring new faculty. On the other hand, collegiality may be used as a subjective means to discriminate. The American Association of University Professors (1999) notes in "On Collegiality as a Criterion for Faculty Evaluation" that a collegiality standard may encourage homogeneity among faculty at the expense of diversity may threaten academic freedom, and have a chilling effect on faculty debate of important issues. Despite this word of caution, the courts have generally supported the institution's use of collegiality as a criterion, but the facts of the cases have exhibited extreme behavior. I would suggest that if lack of collegiality is the only reason for termination or denial of tenure, it may be closely examined by the court to determine if it is only a pretext for what may have been illegal considerations (i.e., discrimination) as discussed in the next section.

DISCRIMINATION

Higher education in the US is a highly regulated industry. Many employment decisions that are routine for private employers are scrutinized at both public and private colleges and universities. The public schools' decisions represent state action and are regulated by the state and federal constitutions, and many private institutions subject themselves to regulation because they are recipients of state or federal money. If Professor Smith is denied tenure, there is a chance that she may claim illegal discrimination in violation of the following laws.

Race, Color, or National Origin

Professor Smith may argue that she was denied tenure because of discrimination on the basis of race. Her claim would be based on the US Constitution's

Fourteenth Amendment, which prohibits a denial of equal protection under the law. If a state college or university discriminates in its promotion, tenure, and dismissal decisions, those constitute "state action" and are unconstitutional. In the case of private institutions, there is no state action, but they still are prohibited from engaging in discriminatory hiring practices. What the Constitution failed to do has been done by Congress. Title VII of the Civil Rights Act of 1964 provides that it is unlawful for any employer "to fail or refuse to hire or to discharge any individual, or otherwise to discriminate against any individual with respect to his compensation, terms, conditions, or privileges of employment, because of such individual's race, color, religion, sex, or national origin" (Sec. 2000e-2 (a)(1)). If the institution receives federal funds, which most do, then Title VI of the Civil Rights Act of 1964 also applies. That section prohibits discrimination on the basis of race, color, or national origin.

Finally, members of the faculty may find protection under state law. Most states have a specific provision in their constitution or in their statutes that prohibits discrimination by employers based on race, color, or national origin.

Sex

There is limited protection under the US Constitution when discrimination is on the basis of sex, but federal laws close this gap. Public and private institutions are expected to comply with Title VII of the Civil Rights Act of 1964, which outlaws discrimination in employment on the basis of sex as well as race and national origin. For recipients of federal money, Title IX of the Education Amendments of 1972 prohibits any discrimination on the basis of sex, including recruitment, hiring, firing, and tenure decisions, as well as the more publicized treatment for women's athletic programs. And beyond the federal laws, most states prohibit discrimination on the basis of sex as a classification that cannot be used to discriminate in employment.

Religion

If Jane Smith claims she was denied tenure because she is a Buddhist, she may rely on the First Amendment, which prohibits the federal and state governments from making any law prohibiting the free exercise of religion. The Supreme Court's interpretations of these clauses have evolved over time, but the effect of their decisions in the employment arena is that *public* institutions cannot discriminate based on an employee's religious beliefs. The Constitution does not prohibit private institutions from considering a candidate's religious beliefs.

However, Title VII of the Civil Rights Act of 1964 prohibits employment discrimination based on religion and applies to all employers, private or public. Therefore, even a private college or university may not discriminate in its employment practices on the basis of religion, with one exception. A religiously affiliated college or university may use religion as a factor in hiring employees who do work connected with the institution's mission. In essence, faculty personnel who teach, write, and advise students are carrying out the educational mission of the private institution, and a religion requirement may be imposed on them. State laws may include religion as a category in their civil rights statutes and may be more comprehensive than federal statutes.

Age

The dean may agree that it is time to dump the older, higher paid Professor Smith and replace her with a cheap adjunct or assistant professor, but he or she had better have a valid reason other than her age. In 1967 Congress enacted the Age Discrimination in Employment Act (ADEA), which applies to public and private employers and prohibits age discrimination. The one limitation is that the claimant must be forty years old or older. Persons who have not yet turned forty are not covered and may not claim age discrimination in employment. Once again, state legislatures have mirrored the federal legislature and have, in many cases, enacted prohibitions against age discrimination in employment.

Disability Status

Federal law prohibits discrimination in the employment situation if the person is able to perform the essential functions of the job. If Professor Smith claims she was denied tenure because of her medical condition, the Americans with Disabilities Act of 1990 (ADA) and its predecessor, Section 504 of the Rehabilitation Act of 1973, may offer her protections. The ADA prohibits discrimination against persons with disabilities and requires the employer to provide "reasonable accommodations" for the disability. For example, a wheelchair-bound employee may have his or her office located on the first floor rather than being required to climb stairs to the third floor in an elevator-less building. However, the statute allows consideration of the disability if it prevents the candidate/employee from completing the essential functions of employment or if the "necessary accommodation presents an 'undue hardship'" for the institution. The ADA applies to both private and public institutions that have fifteen or more employees. State laws provide varying protections for persons with disabilities—some include a line in their civil rights provision, others have enacted laws similar to the Americans with Disabilities Act, and some are more expansive than the ADA.

Sexual Orientation

Despite the efforts of gay rights groups, a person's sexual orientation still has no special status under the Constitution. In addition, neither Title VI nor Title VII of the Civil Rights Act of 1964, nor Title IX of the Education Amendments of 1972 covers discrimination on the basis of sexual orientation. State discrimination laws often fail to cover sexual orientation discrimination as well, but there is a trend to expand those laws to include some protection. As of April 2007, nineteen states and the District of Columbia had enacted laws prohibiting discrimination on the basis of sexual orientation (Robinson, 2009). But that leaves thirty-one states that do not prohibit discrimination against lesbian, gay, bisexual, transgender, and queer (LGBTQ) employees. Professor Smith's only hope for this claim is that her state offers protection.

HOW TO ADDRESS DISCRIMINATION CLAIMS

The courts have established a special procedure to follow in the case of discrimination claims, and this is extremely important for deans to understand. The plaintiff, the person claiming to be the victim of illegal discrimination, must first establish a prima facie case of discrimination. This can be done by comments, e-mail, witnesses, or circumstances that support the claim of discrimination. The burden then shifts to the employer, who must establish that there was a legitimate basis for the negative decision. In our vignette, the dean can point to the low teaching scores, and lack of scholarship and service. Then the plaintiff has an opportunity to show that those proffered reasons are mere pretext—excuses to cover the true, illegal rationale.

ACADEMIC FREEDOM

Finally, Professor Smith may claim that she was denied tenure because of her classroom remarks that are protected by academic freedom. The dictionary definition of *academic freedom* is quite simple: it is the "freedom to teach or to learn without interference (as by government officials)" (Merriam-Webster). But it is seldom interpreted that broadly. In the "1940 Statement of Principles on Academic Freedom and Tenure" (American Association of University Professors, 2006) academic freedom is limited to research: "subject to the adequate performance of their other academic duties" and although teachers have freedom in the classroom to discuss their subject, the document warns "but they should be careful not to introduce into their teaching controversial matter which has *no relation to the subject*" (p. 3; emphasis added).

Academic freedom does not protect poor teaching or inadequate research—members of the faculty must still perform their duties and meet their responsibilities as set forth in their employment contracts, the faculty handbook, or the collective bargaining agreement. The question of whether the dean could deny tenure on the basis of classroom statements alone depends on the nature of the class and the protections in place in the university's policies. In our vignette, the dean can find better reasons for his or her decision without breaching that topic.

Recommendations for Deans

Faculty evaluation decisions are perhaps the most significant and most stressful decisions for a dean. People's careers are at stake, but so is the quality of the institution and its students' education. If the dean is too careless, then the negative decision may result in litigation. And as anyone involved in a lawsuit can tell you, that process is time consuming, stressful, and best to be avoided. In order to avoid litigation, here are four recommendations:

- Follow university *procedures* to the letter, giving the candidate plenty of notice regarding each step of the process. Remember, if a candidate is treated fairly, he or she will be less likely to seek other remedies, so be fair above all.
- Apply the *criteria* to the candidate's record in the manner dictated by the university policy, faculty handbook, or collective bargaining agreement. Arbitrary and subjective decisions are litigation fodder, so be reasonable and use objective reasoning in applying the criteria.
- *Document,* document, document. It is important to document the basis for your decision so that if a claim of illegal discrimination is made, it will be easy to put forth a legitimate basis for the denial of tenure and promotion that is nondiscriminatory. In truth, a candidate who has been denied tenure will not be very happy with the decision and may be willing to challenge that outcome by all means available to him or her. But in that case, the dean's best defense is good preparation. As an attorney, I advise my clients to document everything and to retain all relevant items. I also suggest that they write down the basis for the decisions at the time the decision is made by either a letter to the employee or as a dated note to the file. For example, if the reason is poor teaching, keep a record of the student evaluations, missed classes, or faulty syllabi, and make a note on how you considered it in your recommendation. If the main reason for recommending denial of tenure is a lack of research productivity, list the expectations for faculty, note the quantity and quality of the research, discuss the significance of the journals in which the candidate published (if any), and so on. I believe that documentation of the evidence supporting the decision, made at the time of the decision, is far more valuable and persuasive than trying to recollect reasons for the recommendation several years later.

- Keep the faculty member *informed* as to his or her status at all times. It is relatively easy to be supportive of a tenure-track faculty member during his or her annual evaluations or third-year review, but there have been many, many cases where an applicant has been denied tenure after years of positive evaluations. For the failed candidate, logic would dictate that the denial of tenure must have been based on something other than legitimate reasons, given the positive nature of the previous evaluations. Such questions lead to litigation, and the headaches that such a process entails.

References

Age Discrimination in Employment Act of 1967, 29 U.S.C. § 621 *et seq*.

American Association of University Professors. (1999). *On collegiality as a criterion for faculty evaluation*. Retrieved from http://www.aaup.org/file/collegiality-evaluation.pdf

American Association of University Professors. (2006; 1940). 1940 Statement of principles on academic freedom and tenure. In *AAUP Policy* (10th ed.). Retrieved from http://www.aaup.org/file/principles-academic-freedom-tenure.pdf

Americans with Disabilities Act of 1990, 42 U.S.C.A. § 12101 *et seq*.

Merriam-Webster Online Dictionary, s.v. "academic freedom."

Rehabilitation Act of 1973, Section 504, 29 U.S.C. § 701.

Robinson, B. A. (2009). *Employment discrimination on the basis of sexual orientation*. Ontario Consultants on Religious Tolerance, http://www.religioustolerance.org/hom_empl1.htm

Title VI, Civil Rights Act of 1964 42 U.S.C. § 2000d.

Title VII, Civil Rights Act of 1964, 42 U.S.C. § 2000e–2.

Title IX, Education Amendments of 1972, 20 U.S.C. §§ 1681–1688.

CHAPTER FIFTY-THREE

Addressing Concerns about Harassment, Grievances, and Discrimination

Charlotte G. Borst
Whittier College

This is your first year as dean at Medium-Sized University. So far, you feel like you are getting to know the faculty and staff, and you find the atmosphere very congenial. But late in the fall semester, a junior faculty member makes an appointment, and then comes, very tentatively, to talk to you. She tells you that the atmosphere in her department is "toxic," and that a senior member of the department has been making off-handed comments and jokes at the faculty meeting about her looks, her teaching style, and her private life (she reveals to you that she is gay, but that the rest of the faculty do not know this—or so she believes). She tells you that another faculty member revealed to her that the senior faculty member "always jokes like this with pretty young women," and that he has a reputation among the students for hitting on upper-level undergraduates. However, Professor Senior Faculty is a highly regarded faculty member, known for his public scholarship, and the advancement office and the president have lauded him for his ability to get the university good publicity. Professor Junior Faculty tells you she is fed up with this kind of atmosphere, but she is "too scared about tenure" to file a formal complaint.

This scenario incorporates a number of points of potential harassment—gender, sexual, and possibly nationality. But the first point any new administrator needs to understand is that you should *never* handle these types of cases by yourself. Harassment and discrimination charges involve a number of important legal issues for which you should seek counsel. Indeed, your institution's ability to receive federal (and state) dollars depends on adequate enforcement of antidiscrimination laws that are prescribed in state and federal statutes, and thus you should familiarize yourself with your institution's policies long before a real case arrives at your office.

HARASSMENT

Every college or university should have a statement in both the faculty handbook and in the staff handbook noting that the institution does not tolerate unlawful harassment. The statement will usually go on to note that their policy against harassment applies to all persons involved in the operation of the college and prohibits unlawful harassment by any employee of the college, including supervisors and managers, as well as vendors, students, independent contractors, suppliers, and any other persons. Institutional policies also will define harassment types—these generally include the categories of race, color, national origin, ancestry, sex, gender, religion, creed, age, mental or physical disability, veteran status, medical condition (including pregnancy, childbirth, and related medical conditions), and marital status. Depending on the state, further categories can include registered domestic partner status, citizenship, sexual orientation, gender orientation, gender identification, gender expression, or genetic characteristics.

For these purposes the term *harassment* includes slurs and any other offensive remarks, jokes, and other verbal, graphic, or physical conduct. In addition to the above-listed conduct, *sexual harassment* also can include the following federal or state examples of unacceptable behavior:

- Visual conduct, such as leering, making sexual gestures, displaying of sexually suggestive objects or pictures, cartoons or posters
- Verbal sexual advances, propositions or requests to include unwanted verbal abuse of a sexual nature, graphic verbal commentaries about an individual's body, sexually degrading words used to describe an individual, suggestive or obscene letters, notes or invitations
- Physical conduct including assault, unwanted touching, intentionally blocking normal movement or interfering with work because of sex, race, or any other protected basis
- Hostile work environment, which includes conduct of a sexual nature that has the purpose or effect of unreasonably interfering with or altering the individual's work performance or creating an intimidating, hostile, or offensive working environment.
- Quid pro quo—offering or demanding an employment benefit (such as a raise or promotion or assistance with one's career) in exchange for sexual favors, or threatening an employment detriment (such as termination, demotion, or disciplinary action) for an employee's failure to engage in sexual activity.

The important issue for you is to remember that as a dean (as is the case with assistant and associate deans, and department chairs), you are considered an "officer of the institution" and a supervisor. Thus, if a faculty member, staff member, or student comes into your office to talk to you, you cannot treat the conversation as one that will remain a secret. Federal and state laws mandate that you, as a supervisor, *must* act to investigate the matter. The employee or student will be asked to provide details of the incident or incidents, names of individuals involved, and names of any witnesses. It would be best to communicate the complaint in writing, but this is not mandatory. Depending on the nature of the complaint, your institution may have different investigative procedures for staff or students than for faculty, but in all cases, to protect victims and accused alike, your responsibility is to use the utmost discretion in investigating complaints. Likewise, know that employees or others who are involved in any aspect of the investigation must avoid discussing the case with any other person.

NEW FOCUS ON TITLE IX

In April 2011, the Department of Education's Office for Civil Rights sent a nineteen-page "Dear Colleague" letter, as it is now known, to elementary, secondary, undergraduate, and graduate schools across the country. The letter said that if a school doesn't have systems in place to deal with sexual violence, then they're violating Title IX, the gender discrimination law passed by Congress in 1972 that has been famously exercised to enforce equal access to sports participation. But Title IX has a much broader application. The law prohibits gender discrimination in all educational activities, covering everything from sexual harassment to opportunities in math and science. Under Title IX, discrimination on the basis of sex can include sexual harassment or sexual violence, such as rape, sexual assault, sexual battery, and sexual coercion.

The Office for Civil Rights (OCR) in the US Department of Education is responsible for enforcing Title IX. OCR uses compliance enforcement to fulfill its responsibility to ensure that institutions that receive federal funds comply with Title IX. The principal enforcement activity is the investigation and resolution of complaints filed by those alleging sex discrimination. In addition, through a compliance review program of selected recipients, OCR is able to identify and remedy sex discrimination that may not be addressed through complaint investigation. OCR has discretion to select an institution for review in order to assess its compliance with Title IX, even absent the filing of a complaint.

The directive came about because many schools were not conducting very thorough investigations of sexual assaults. Thus, the letter sent schools scrambling to tighten their sexual harassment procedures or risk losing federal funding. Though the letter included clear orders that colleges should change the way they prosecute sexual harassment crimes, develop brochures explaining procedures, and choose one employee to be the permanent "Title IX coordinator," other parts of the letter were less clear. In particular, there is a substantial lack of clarity about who is supposed to be the "responsible employee" charged with reporting sexual harassment to the designated Title IX coordinator. The Office for Civil Rights wanted deans, directors, assistant directors, vice presidents, and provosts to be the "responsible employees," because these generally are the people who can find solutions to a sexual harassment problem. But a real problem has arisen because the Title IX coordinator, according to the federal government's newly articulated policy, must decide whether the school can respect the victim's wishes for confidentiality. For example, if the Title IX coordinator has information indicating that the alleged perpetrator has previously sexually assaulted other students on campus, it may be necessary to override this student's request for confidentiality in order to pursue disciplinary action against the alleged perpetrator.

As a dean, you are clearly designated as a mandated reporter. You may find, however, that your institution has broadened this function to include all staff and faculty on a campus. You may be charged, in fact, with cajoling or even coercing faculty and staff to attend the training sessions. In some institutions, in fact, you may be named as a Title IX coordinator, in part to deal with the special issues of faculty and their rights of academic freedom. If this is the case, your HR director should provide you with the special training necessary for this task. Moreover, because the wider application of this law is new and mandates separate investigative and deliberative bodies, you should plan to work with your faculty governance body to develop appropriate processes for handling Title IX cases.

The scenario that began this chapter includes a number of categories that are covered by antiharassment statutes. Thankfully, these sorts of issues are rare, but the scenario also notes complaints that are far more commonly brought to the Office of the Dean. They come under the rubric of "grievances" that are not legal ones but that can be even more difficult to resolve. In general, your faculty handbook should spell out a grievance process for faculty. The most common ones, of course, relate to tenure cases, but many grievances relate to issues of general faculty civility. The advice offered above—to be as discreet as possible and not to talk about these cases with other faculty—holds true. Because grievances often involve student-faculty relationships, it is a very good idea to have a good working relationship with the Office of Student Life, and to understand the extent of its jurisdiction with regard to student grievances.

The life of a dean is generally a really wonderful job. But grievances, including harassment cases, can be daunting. They can be enormously time consuming and emotionally exhausting. Your best defense is to be educated long before someone walks into your office, and then, when the concern comes your way keep the following points in mind:

- Remember you are an officer of the college/university. No conversation that involves charges of illegal harassment can remain a secret. You must act!
- Know your institution's policies about handling harassment of any sort. Pay particular attention to your faculty handbook's language. If the handbook language is vague or nonexistent, then you have a duty as dean to help the faculty develop policies.
- Issues related to Title IX in higher education are now frequently in the news. Keep up to date on the latest interpretations of how your institution will handle these issues.
- Review your institution's policies for grievance procedures—many of the issues that will land in your office involve process as much as actual fact.

Reference

US Department of Education, Office for Civil Rights. (2011). *Know your rights: Title IX prohibits sexual harassment and sexual violence where you go to school.* Available online at http://www2.ed.gov/about/offices/list/ocr/letters/colleague-201104.html

CHAPTER FIFTY-FOUR

Fostering Excellent Teaching

Kerry Pannell
Agnes Scott College

A student has come to your office with a grievance to air about a faculty member's teaching. The student has already taken her concerns to the department chair but was dissatisfied with the outcome of that meeting. College policy dictates that your office is her next stop. First, you ask the student for details about the course and classroom environment, gradually probing to ensure that the student is providing a fair representation of what is happening in the course. This student is not complaining about the faculty member being a tough grader or having students work "too hard," in which case you could have taken advantage of the teachable moment to explain the value of taking on the intellectual challenge to gain enormous benefits from pushing beyond what the student perceives as possible. Instead, this student paints a picture of a faculty member who seems bored by the subject and unresponsive to students' academic needs. At this point, you may recognize an echo of similar comments from last semester's student surveys for the same course (but would never confide as much to the student sitting in your office). The student wants her complaint to remain anonymous until after the term is complete, and perhaps until she graduates, to avoid any awkwardness with the faculty member in future classes. You take notes on the details of the conversation and wrap up by thanking the student for her feedback.

Students may not be the best judge of the quality of their college educations, particularly while they are in the midst of them, but this complaint may point toward a genuine concern. This scenario has no quick or easy solution, but there are steps you can take to help faculty members broaden their viewpoints and appreciate students' perspectives, while providing a boost to the teaching culture in your department or school and on your campus as a whole.

Faculty are at the heart of any college or university, providing students a learning agenda and the means to achieve academic goals. Given the cacophonous admixture of demands from various stakeholders in the student learning process, it's no wonder that some faculty members become inflexible, ardently attached to a single approach to teaching. Occasionally it will be the inexperienced or overconfident new faculty member that generates complaints about teaching like those portrayed in the scenario above, but at least as often the grievance will be about a senior faculty member who has failed to renew her pedagogy or has lost touch with students' learning needs and academic habits. The faculty member in this situation is typically stuck in a rut and needs inspiration, information, and motivation. In my experience as a department chair and as a dean of faculty, fostering excellent teaching is the most rewarding aspect of the job, but also the most time consuming. It requires major investments of energy into building a network of faculty relationships, research on a variety of pedagogical approaches, and attention to the teaching strengths and weaknesses of faculty members in your department, school, or college.

One of the first items on the agenda when you begin a new administrative role supporting faculty in their teaching is to figure out the styles and strengths of the faculty's pedagogical approaches. If you have been in a department for several years before becoming department chair, you may already know the teaching fortes of members of the department. But if you're taking on a director- or dean-level role, discovering and cataloging the best of what your faculty do will take time and research. One approach is to meet with department chairs individually to discuss teaching in their respective areas. Another would be to gather information from related administrative and support staff, and your predecessor may already have notes that will help you understand the landscape of good teaching at your institution. Once you have this information, you'll be able to productively connect faculty in ways that take advantage of the breadth and diversity of teaching expertise at your institution.

If you are someone who hasn't spent much time with the academic literature on teaching and learning, your next step is to both read foundational works on excellent college pedagogy (such as Bain's 2004 *What the Best College Teachers Do*) and discover themes in the current discourse about pedagogy in higher education. If you have a teaching center on campus, these resources will be easily accessible there. If not, then you can quickly find web resources available at teaching center websites from a variety of institutions. To help you get started, I've included references to teaching center websites for Loyola Marymount, Oberlin, Penn State, and Stanford in the note.[1] *The Chronicle of Higher Education* and *Inside Higher Ed* both have regular contributions on pedagogy that will keep you up to date on what people are talking about on campuses across the country, and the Association of American Colleges and Universities maintains a set of valuable resources available on its website.

All these resources can be especially helpful in generating discussions about teaching on campus. Reading groups, roundtable conversations, and learning communities are mechanisms to bring people together to talk about what it means to be an excellent teacher in higher education. Stimulating a lively discussion is essential to fostering a supportive environment for new instructors and more senior faculty members alike, and the recognition that there are diverse pedagogical methods and teaching styles that produce good student learning ensures an inclusive and supportive teaching community.

Equipped with information about the teaching landscape on your campus and what instructors nationwide are doing in a variety of fields, you are now ready to build an intentional local network that will support excellent teaching on campus. Much of this infrastructure may already be in place at your institution, through a teaching center, a faculty committee on teaching, or via instructional designers and technologists. Your campus already may celebrate outstanding teaching, which is all for the good. What the existing teaching development network may be lacking is a good coordination mechanism and the information about where the most support may be needed. If students have serious complaints about the quality of teaching, that faculty member is probably not actively participating in the network of support that is available. Use your knowledge of strong teaching practices on campus to connect faculty to one another in productive and creative ways. Faculty members do not need to be in the same disciplinary area to mentor each other and develop new ways to reach students and improve their learning. In fact, it is preferable to cut across disciplinary boundaries when connecting faculty for the purpose of talking about teaching because someone outside the field is more likely to leave disciplinary baggage behind, bringing the fresh perspective that students have when entering a course.

For the case of the individual in the opening scenario, the resources you put into the network discussions of teaching will be beneficial, but only if faculty avail themselves of the opportunities. Specific invitations to campus events that would be most interesting for that faculty member are helpful, particularly when close colleagues will also be attending. If possible, ask the faculty member whom they would like to invite to campus to talk about pedagogical issues, and then create a reading group of that person's work to meet a few times prior to the visit. (This works particularly well if the speaker has both disciplinary and pedagogical expertise to share, but such speakers may be hard to find for the faculty member's disciplinary interest.) Create a dyad or triad of instructors working on similar issues, grouping new faculty with those who are more senior in order to capitalize on differences in pedagogy, experience, and perspective. Connect these groups back to the larger teaching community by inviting members of the group to lead a discussion or give a presentation demonstrating what they have been working on. As noted above, such public recognition of good work on pedagogy not only spreads new ideas through the community but is also good for morale.

If the faculty member is reluctant to become part of the teaching development community described above, then, if you are a department chair, it is time to invite the faculty member to have lunch or coffee to discuss teaching issues. If you are the dean, it is time to encourage the department chair to do so. The student making the complaint didn't want to be mentioned, so you'll need to have other evidence of what is happening in the classroom, perhaps from student surveys, peer observations, annual reports, or enrollment data. Keep the conversation general, if possible, encouraging the faculty member to reflect on pedagogical practice, allowing her to raise the teaching issues she would like to work on. If the faculty member does not provide a productive way into the concerns you have, then raise them directly based on your evidence. Pare your concerns down to essentials of teaching that the faculty member is failing to meet—like not providing timely feedback or not meeting students "where they are"—and offer whatever support and assistance you can make available, ranging from books to funding for off-campus workshops.

Thus far, the kinds of actions discussed have all been based on positive incentives designed to create a supportive teaching culture. In your administrative role, you may have access to negative incentives like limiting merit pay or using other levers based on budgets or scheduling. I advise not to use these measures except in extreme cases. Once you go down the negative path, positive incentives become less effective in general, unless there is a pervasive perception among the faculty that fairness required the negative tack.

Teaching is at the core of any institution of higher education, and the framework for learning is embedded in faculty-student interaction, both in the classroom setting and contained in course assignments and activities outside of class sessions. Fostering excellent teaching through a supportive network of practitioners can address all aspects of the relationships between students and faculty, and it provides the best opportunity to improve student learning.

Consider three key steps to take in building teaching infrastructure on your campus:

- Assess the teaching landscape at your institution. Where are needs the greatest, and who on campus has expertise to share?
- Develop your own expertise in the theory and practice of pedagogy so that you can provide advice and see new directions that are possible.
- Build the network by coordinating pieces that already exist and connecting faculty via discussions, mentor relationships, and learning communities.

With any luck, the difficult scenario that opened this chapter will not present itself, and you will be able to focus your energies on building a strong, supportive teaching culture at your institution.

Note

1. The Center for Teaching Excellence at Loyola Marymount University http://www.lmu.edu/libraries_research/cte.htm; Oberlin College's Center for Teaching Innovation and Excellence (CTIE) http://www.oberlin.edu/ctie/; Schreyer Institute for Teaching Excellence at Penn State University http://www.schreyerinstitute.psu.edu/resources; Stanford University's Center for Teaching and Learning http://www.stanford.edu/dept/CTL/Tomprof/index.shtml

Reference

Bain, K. (2004). *What the best college teachers do*. Cambridge, MA: Harvard University Press.

CHAPTER FIFTY-FIVE

Creating and Maintaining a Supportive Environment for Research, Scholarship, and Creative Activity

Kerry Pannell
Agnes Scott College

An unhappy faculty member walks into your office, slumps down in the chair across from you and proceeds to tell you a long story about the trials and tribulations of a scholarly project she has been working on for some time. Ostensibly, she is asking you for money or time away from teaching (which you have some authority, but limited ability, to grant in your role as dean). But it appears that her concerns go beyond the details of this project. After a few more minutes of discussion, it is clear that something else is worrying this faculty member—a deadline looms and frustrations are mounting. The faculty member's concern might be an upcoming promotion review or worries about merit pay, or the desire to receive an endowed chair or some other award for which the faculty member is eligible. You need to help her get out of her rut and back on track to a fulfilling and productive intellectual life. But how?

Over the course of an academic career, a faculty member's scholarly and creative productivity naturally waxes and wanes, peaking in anticipation of rewards or milestones like hiring and tenure, and falling at other times to focus on teaching, service obligations, or personal obligations. Untenured researchers, scholars, and artists typically find incentives embedded in institutions' personnel processes complex and confusing, but the knife-edge nature of the tenure decision produces strong extrinsic motivation for completing and disseminating scholarly work early in a faculty member's career. The stakes are high around tenure time but trail off thereafter. Contingent faculty members face varying levels of pressure to produce scholarship over time and can also get stuck in an extrinsic motivational rut like the one described in the scenario above. The challenge for you as an administrator is to provide a supportive research environment in which faculty members' intrinsic motivation—the joy of doing good work in their field—supersedes the kind of nervous, negative energy that results from the typical personnel process in higher education.

The best strategies for fostering engaged research depend to some extent on institutional culture, boundaries delineated by digital scholarship, and an institution's position within the ecosystem of higher education. The best strategies also depend on how an institution defines and measures research within its personnel process and on how these definitions necessarily change as academic disciplines evolve, which in turn affects faculty choices regarding their research. And, it matters whether your institution endorses Ernest Boyer's (1990) definition of scholarship, and how closely merit, tenure, and promotion standards follow Boyer's model. Leaving aside these differences between institutions, in this chapter I highlight three categories of administrative action designed to provide the basis for a supportive research environment, one where intrinsic motivation prevails: connecting and coordinating; empowering and supporting; recognizing and celebrating.

CONNECTING AND COORDINATING

The stereotype of the lone researcher, slavishly scribbling notes in a dark corner of the library, has gone by the wayside. In many fields, teams of coauthors are the norm, with some disciplines even accepting coauthored dissertation chapters. New faculty members, in particular, may have a broad, interdisciplinary, and community-based perspective on what successful scholarship entails. Scholars who can successfully build productive collaborations naturally remain engaged, because the social aspect of being part of a partnership dovetails with the goal of a thriving research agenda. Having the overarching perspective of an administrator, you can invest in connections among campuses and coordinate these connections based on faculty interest.

Connecting faculty to each other and providing support for research relationships is a straightforward way for an administrator to encourage good scholarly work. To do this, you will need to know what people are working on, where their strengths lie, and how to provide support without being overbearing or directive. If your campus rewards interdisciplinary research, there may be connections across campus you can forge that will lead to strong, engaged collaborative research. Oftentimes funding commuting costs to a nearby research university or flights back to their graduate campus is sufficient to maintain a faculty member's link to coauthors and engagement with cutting-edge scholarship in their discipline. State systems and regional consortia are another avenue for productive collaborations. In addition, for those campuses where student-faculty research is highly valued, it is worthwhile investing in memberships for faculty in organizations like the Council on Undergraduate Research (CUR) to expand grant writing that will fund student-faculty research.

This general connection strategy is one that increases in value as relationships grow, so the benefits may not arrive for several years. For the faculty member who is currently feeling frustrated, quicker action is necessary, and fortunately these academic relationships have short-run benefits as well. Nearby universities provide valuable venues for research presentations, where the faculty member can get helpful feedback on works in progress, so it is worthwhile keeping up contacts with their departments and programs. Frustrated faculty members also may be stuck in a rut regarding the mode of disseminating their work, wanting to publish in a particular journal, or present at a specific national conference. If you have previously developed constructive connections with faculty scholars on your own campus, then you have a group of mentors who can provide practical research advice. Ask one of them to serve as a scholar's consultant to help a frustrated faculty member see the bigger picture of academic publishing. Discussions with faculty at other institutions also can provide the impetus to break through the faculty member's frustration and give a broader view of the possible direction and impact of his or her scholarly output.

EMPOWERING AND SUPPORTING

Empowering faculty via internal and external grant funding is an important aspect of any faculty development program. *Wait,* you might be thinking, *aren't grants by definition extrinsic motivation?* Yes, but the rules surrounding those grant programs determine the extent to which they support the goal of moving faculty back toward healthy intrinsic motivation within their research agendas. For internal funding programs, the greater the flexibility and choice a faculty member has regarding the use of research funds, the more intrinsically motivated the resulting research tends to be. The accounting requirements for reimbursement of research expenses provide accountability, ensuring that the expenses are related to research. Limits on buying the latest tech gadgets or on meal and hotel expenses may be necessary, but resist the urge to implement overly complicated rules or to try to legislate to avoid abuses by a small fraction of the faculty. Instead, help faculty understand basic accounting principles, college or university policies meant to provide fairness and transparency, and the importance of good financial record keeping, particularly because institutions are regularly audited. When new mission-related professional development funds become available to support university initiatives, try to ensure that those resources are over and above previously available funds and that the method of implementation incorporates faculty voice along with resources to promote the kind of connectivity described above. Extrinsic motivational levers will be more effective when they lay the groundwork for the social aspect of scholarship that encourages the internalization of the goals of the new initiative.

Getting external grants has become more difficult recently due to greater competition, but forging ahead with grant activity is still worthwhile. Coordinating gatherings of people who are working on similar topics will help facilitate intellectual community and eventually lead to good grant proposals. Buying lunch is usually all it takes to get a conversation started. Providing funding for small groups to attend grant-writing workshops is another good investment in the intellectual life of the campus. Having an energetic grants professional dedicated to faculty working either in academic affairs or the advancement office provides support and connectivity to faculty who are searching for funding. The good news is that these strategies for increasing grant activity both inspire faculty in the short run and provide community and resources in the long run.

RECOGNIZING AND CELEBRATING

Make sure all good work gets recognized, and find appealing ways to celebrate faculty accomplishments. An annual research award to a faculty member who has done particularly good work is a nice gesture, but it does little to build community or provide motivation. Highlights on the website or in the alumni magazine are good, but events that draw the community together have greater impact and generate less cynicism on the part of faculty. Events that I have seen work well include wine-and-cheese events where colleagues review each other's work, student-faculty colloquia over the lunch hour, and book parties where the entire campus is invited. Sending college-wide e-mails to congratulate a colleague gets the word out, but consistency is important, and people may resent having lots of e-mail in their in-boxes. Better yet, send a personal letter from the president or dean to congratulate a faculty member on a major milestone, perhaps inviting him or her to lunch or coffee if you have time.

Many schools use self-reporting mechanisms by which faculty members can list in a Google Doc (or in other software) an important scholarly accomplishment that they want to have publicized among their colleagues. Although this method is efficient, it is not reliable—the people doing the most engaged work may also be the busiest or most modest, and so you will miss out on great opportunities to promote interesting research if you rely on self-reporting. If you have too many faculty members to keep track of yourself, then enlist division or department chairs to keep up with what people are working on, and meet with them periodically to find out what good work is being done. Simply asking chairs to follow people's scholarship has the potential to build community and support engaged scholarship.

Fostering engaged research by enhancing the intellectual community for faculty members will allow intrinsic motivation to thrive on campus. Of course everything you can do to make the personnel process more transparent and consistent will go a long way toward alleviating the fearful negative energy surrounding scholarship for faculty on your campus. But taking for granted institutionally determined rules and processes designed to exert extrinsic motivation, there are still ways to help faculty regain the excitement that they felt at the start of graduate school—a period when the sheer joy of thinking about their scholarly work kept them going through the tough times.

Consider three key steps to take in order to support engaged research on your campus:

- Devote resources to creating research connections between faculty members on campus and with those at nearby institutions.
- Identify faculty members who can be scholarship consultants or research mentors for other faculty on campus.
- Design a celebration of scholarly work that is inclusive and broad based, involving numerous faculty interest groups, as a way of creating community and recognizing good work.

Reference

Boyer, E. L. (1990). *Scholarship reconsidered: Priorities of the professoriate.* Princeton, NJ: Carnegie Foundation for the Advancement of Teaching.

CHAPTER FIFTY-SIX

Engaging Faculty in Service and Community Work

Stephen J. Kreta
California Maritime Academy, California State University

> The new dean pauses as she eyes the stacks of binders of her young faculty seeking retention, tenure, and promotion reviews. She reflects on her own process, as she mentally establishes a strategy for review that will combine fairness, compassion, toughness, and leadership, knowing the stress this process takes on the faculty.
>
> How difficult can this be? Teaching standards should be obvious; the dean expects to see excellent peer and student evaluations, clearly established course learning outcomes, and rubrics with data to show their students are learning and enjoying the process at the same time. Scholarship should be quite clear as well: peer reviewed journal and book entries, presentations at prestigious conferences around the world, a scholar in the true sense, one who makes the university proud. And yes, of course there must be service. The dean ponders the evaluation of service: Does the university have standards for service? How does service advance the individual, the college, the university, or the profession? Have I as dean established clear expectations? "Well," she decides, "maybe we'll just see what they say—teaching and scholarship are what we do."

Most, if not all, tenure and promotion policies seek to review and evaluate faculty in three areas: effectiveness in teaching, accomplishment in scholarship or research, and engagement in service to the campus or community. Yet it is hard to imagine a faculty member not earning tenure due to insufficient service. He or she may be denied tenure for poor teaching, or poor scholarship, but poor service—not likely. What does this tell our faculty about the relative importance of service? That it is perfectly acceptable to concentrate on teaching and scholarship only. The service box must be checked off to be sure, but there is no requirement for it to be of true benefit to anyone. If one is a strong enough teacher or researcher, then one's service contribution, or lack thereof, generally is given little weight in the evaluation process. The question must be asked, is this view what the university promotes, advocates or expects? And, perhaps more disconcerting, is this what the university accepts? The expectation of faculty service must be championed by the university's executive leadership at its highest levels, and indeed, it is the dean's responsibility to implement this standard and hold faculty accountable for such engagement. But if the university is not getting the kind of faculty service that it desires, how can the environment be changed to make service to the campus or community an integral part of faculty life?

WHAT IS SERVICE, AND WHY IS IT IMPORTANT?

Service to the university community can be defined as one's contribution to the effective administration of the university's many tasks outside the classroom and research arenas. Examples include participating in faculty governance; serving as department chair or director of a center; actively participating in the leadership of curriculum design, assessment, accreditation, strategic planning; and serving (with interest and commitment) on committees such a diversity, retention, budget, and hiring.

Service to the college or university is as critical to the mission of the university as is effective teaching and research. This is because it allows the many important roles of the institution to stand alongside teaching and scholarship, resulting in a stronger college or university. If the faculty do not provide leadership and input to this work, who will? Administrators and staff members certainly can make decisions, but if these decisions are not made in harmony with the existing pedagogies and philosophies of the academic departments, then chaos and uncertain direction for the university can result. Without direct and open communication and dialog on important issues among all stakeholders of the campus, success is unlikely.

"THESE ARE THE DECISIONS WE WANT TO MAKE"

Anna Neumann and Aimee LaPointe Terosky (2007), in "To Give and Receive: Recently Tenured Professors' Experiences of Service in Major Research Universities," summarize the faculty view of service in four ways:

- Broad-ranging, eclectic, variable, and thereby underdefined
- Increasingly prominent in faculty careers but underappreciated and underresearched
- In tension between content and context perspectives
- Comprising "new work" for professors at (or approaching) midcareer, a stage that is itself expansive and underdefined.

If these are the faculty views of faculty service, then we are a long way from an environment of volunteerism. And I don't think we want to suggest volunteerism—instead, how about: environment of committed and engaged service that is recognized and integral.

However, in an article written for *The Chronicle of Higher Education*, "Tenured Professors Feel the Weight of Service Work," Audrey Williams June (2012) discusses the increased service load for tenured faculty as the ranks of lecturers and contingent faculty relative to the tenure-line core increases. June quotes Barbara Ching, English department chair at Iowa State University: "I have not found people trying to get out of doing what needs to be done," she says. "These are decisions we want to make." Professor Ching's statements encapsulate the desired faculty attitude toward service—faculty should want to make the decisions. Deans can create an environment where faculty freely volunteer to serve, without the use of coercion ("It will look good in your tenure file.") or intimidation ("Remember, you are up for promotion soon.").

MAVERICKS: "RIDING THE WAVE" TO FACULTY SERVICE

There are numerous ways a dean can signal the importance of engagement on a campus and provide opportunities for faculty to be involved in creative initiatives and even decision making. One key is ensuring that tenure and promotion criteria explicitly state the importance of service; annual faculty activity reports or plans can also provide an important guide to encourage faculty into campus service. As one example, I developed such an opportunity modeled after a world-renowned surf competition held off Half Moon Bay in California called "Mavericks." This special event, held with only a few days' notice, brings the best big wave surfers from all over the world, along with tens of thousands of spectators. The Mavericks Big Wave Surf Competition occurs only when the super waves are sure to form. Everything—the winds, the tides, and the currents—must converge perfectly to form the super waves, or there is no competition.

Inspired by the Mavericks Competition process, and in an attempt to test the waters of faculty engagement and interest, I would on occasion call a "Mavericks" session. This occurred when a particular issue was burgeoning, information was coming from all directions, rumors were rampant, and it looked as if there would be a massive storm on the horizon. We either could grab a board and ride the waves (to continue the analogy) or wait to have them come crashing down upon us. Fortunately, on our campus, faculty and staff were willing to come together on very short notice to handle the issue and move on. All were invited, but no one was specifically requested to be present.

This gathering brought people together solely to discuss an important issue of the day. Based on established rules, a Mavericks session might be called once a semester as the dean saw appropriate. Often participants agreed to continue the conversation and take the issue to another level, sometimes forming a committee, task force, or partnership to delve deeper into the issue because they felt it important to do so for the university. Topics have included current news events, interdisciplinary research, disruptive student behavior, and faculty-student advising.

There are few rules to the Mavericks sessions, but they are important to follow to be effective:

- Subject matter can vary, but topic must be "hot"
- One topic and one topic only
- No one person leads the conversation
- No presentations
- No handouts
- No scheduling issues—the gathering is called no more than a few days out, and those who can make it make it do so; those who cannot, do not get to ride this wave
- The session happens at lunch so participants can bring bag lunches and informally discuss the topic
- No minutes, no votes, no Robert's rules—only basic rules of civil engagement

This is the essence of a program and environment that fosters engagement with the community that might not have happened otherwise. It is this level of interest and commitment to an issue that will draw faculty and staff together to solve problems. This is the atmosphere that we, as deans, need to make pervasive on campus.

WOULD FACULTY VOLUNTEER FOR SERVICE IF IT WERE NOT REQUIRED?

Faculty will volunteer for service to the campus community when the environment is right. The challenge for deans is to create that environment. Indeed, we know many of our faculty volunteer for service in the surrounding community, their churches, or professional organizations. They do so for a variety of reasons:

- To make a difference
- Because they believe in the cause

- To come together with others of like mind
- To advance personal satisfaction
- To advance their professional careers
- To network
- To give back
- To put unused talents to use
- Because it feels good to do so

Simply put, an environment that fosters faculty engagement is one where faculty members want to serve. Anything less becomes just more work. In *College Deans: Leading From Within*, Mimi Wolverton and Walter H. Gmelch posit academic leadership as "the act of building a community of scholars to set direction and achieve common purposes through the empowerment of faculty and staff" (2002, p. 33). An academic dean's primary role is to provide leadership to the academic community of the university, and to assist in obtaining the resources that are needed to enable the faculty to be most effective. It now should be clear that none of this can be accomplished without the engagement of the faculty, and that if the faculty are not committed to providing input with enthusiasm, the building of a university community will be incomplete. Only when the dean creates an environment in which the faculty willingly and constructively engage in all aspects of university decision making will the campus community fully benefit from the synergy of faculty talents.

Simple Steps Deans Can Take to Engage Faculty in Service

Getting faculty to serve is one thing; keeping them is another. Here are some steps for engaging faculty:

- Welcome them, and acknowledge their busy schedules. Whether or not folks are as busy as they claim, the reality is that the time given to this initiative is time otherwise given to some other function. Verbal acknowledgment is not enough; it must be accompanied by a true sense of time management and efficiency.
- The project must be meaningful. Again, service is about giving time. The project outcomes must be important enough for those involved to willingly devote their time and energy. Team members must be assured that this project will result in something better than the status quo.
- Each volunteer brings *something* to the table. It is the role of the leader to allow that strength or talent to be used.

- Get to know each other. When folks from across campus come together for a common cause, there are more opportunities for synergy in the future. Allow personalities to be revealed and interests to be known. This allows faculty members who may not have other opportunities to work together to learn more about each other. This in turn may lead to interdisciplinary professional work in the future. We know that our faculty members look to outside organizations for professional growth and networking; we must encourage this on university grounds as well.
- Respect your faculty members' professionalism. This means: be prepared. Have an agenda, a time line and keep minutes. Once a decision is made, record it and move on. Be a steward of everyone's time, and give your faculty reason to respect your professionalism as well.
- Thank them. Thank them in person and thank them in writing. Include a "cc" to their supervisor. Remember, although they may volunteer for many reasons, faculty members are still subject to review. Memos in their files outlining specific contributions to the project are always welcome and appreciated.

There is one *Do Not* that must be added to the list of *Dos*. If we are working toward an environment of engaged service, we simply cannot treat our faculty as if they have to be there, or that their participation on a committee simply relieves us of the effort. This will be met with nothing but hostility and resentment. Abraham Lincoln once said, "If you would win a man to your cause, first convince him that you are his sincere friend. Therein is a drop of honey that catches his heart, which, say what you will, is the great high-road to his reason, and which, when once gained, you will find but little trouble in convincing his judgment of the justice of your cause." Working with people in any walk of life is about developing and fostering positive relationships.

References

June, A. W. (2012, September 26). Tenured professors feel the weight of service work. *The Chronicle of Higher Education*. http://chronicle.com/article/Tenured-Professors-Feel-the/133293/

Neumann, A., & Terosky, A. L. (2007, May/June). To give and receive: Recently tenured professors' experiences of service in major research universities. *The Journal of Higher Education, 78*(3), 282–310.

Wolverton, M., & Gmelch, W. H. (2002). *College deans: Leading from within*. Westport, CT: American Council on Education, ORYX Press.

CHAPTER FIFTY-SEVEN

"The War of the Worlds"

Assessment of Student Learning Outcomes of Academic Majors

Karen Doyle Walton
DeSales University

Orson Wells caused a panic in 1938 when he broadcast his infamous announcement that the United States was being invaded by monsters from Mars. Unfortunately, some chief academic officers regard the visiting team from their regional accrediting agency as extraterrestrial aliens. Fear not! Wells's demons were fictional, and chief academic officers' fears are merely nightmares that can be made to disappear if four achievable steps are followed.

Each of the six regional accrediting agencies requires their member institutions to provide evidence that they are accomplishing the expected student learning outcomes (SLOs) of their academic programs. The word *assessment* can be a monster from another planet that frightens the faculty. Alternatively, assessment can be regarded as a helpful and necessary tool to verify that the institution is fulfilling its mission. The challenge for faculty members is to think of assessment as "doing the right thing for the right reasons" and to regard the visiting team as colleagues from peer institutions who are volunteering their expertise to provide constructive recommendations.

PROVIDE LEADERSHIP

The assessment of individual academic majors needs leadership, and because the chief academic officer (CAO) is responsible for the institution's academic programs, the CAO is the appropriate leader. Muffo (2010) explains:

> An understanding of disciplinary assessment is important to a senior leader, particularly one with major academic or academic support responsibilities

> . . . especially if the assessment program in place is mandated externally, for example, by the state or federal governments or by professional or specialized accreditation. . . . Thus, comprehending the assumptions behind the processes and methods employed in disciplinary assessment and the related area of disciplinary accreditation can only enhance one's effectiveness as a senior leader in higher education. The fact that many decisions resulting from these processes have major budgetary implications . . . only heightens the importance of assessment. (p. 16)

Many institutions that have found it difficult to design and implement an effective assessment plan for their academic programs have hired one or more administrators to address the problem. These professionals hold titles such as director of institutional research (IR) or director of assessment and usually have advanced degrees in statistics, educational measurement, or similar fields. They have the experience and expertise to design and administer surveys for students, faculty, and administrators. However, they frequently face a wide chasm between their positions and the faculty who regard assessment as threatening, intrusive, or, even worse, irrelevant and unnecessary. The director of assessment can provide data, but the most important need is to turn the data into information. Much of the data generated by IR is ignored at institutions because it cannot be interpreted by the faculty. Too often, such data is presented without context or an answer to the question, "What does this information tell me about what students are learning?" or "How can I use this data to improve my program, or student learning in my program?"

The ideal situation is for the CAO to show strong leadership with respect to assessment of the academic programs. The CAO can arrange and, if possible, attend meetings between the director of assessment and the faculty members of each academic department or major. Because the CAO is responsible for and knowledgeable about all academic programs, he or she can facilitate the process of turning the data provided by IR into information that is useful to the faculty.

SUGGEST A MODEL

The faculty at DeSales University have regarded assessment favorably since they developed the university's first formal assessment process in 1987. However, the greater emphasis that the Middle States Commission on Higher Education (MSCHE) now places on assessment demands far more rigorous assessment methods than in the past. Linda Suskie (2006), formerly a vice president at MSCHE, states in "What is 'Good' Assessment? A Synthesis of Principles of Good Practice" the following five characteristics of good assessment: (1) there are clear and important goals, (2) the process is cost effective, (3) it is valued by the entire community, (4) the results are reasonably accurate and truthful, and (5) the results are used for improvement purposes. Suskie's 2009 book, *Assessing Student Learning: A Common Sense Guide*, especially its lists of examples of direct and indirect evidence of student learning, is an excellent resource for CAOs. Bers and Swing (2010) also provide extensive examples of direct and indirect assessment methods that provide qualitative and quantitative data. These examples include capstone courses, course-embedded assessment, culminating projects, curriculum and syllabus analyses, focus groups, exit interviews, portfolio assessment, rubrics, and others.

The MSCHE publication titled *Student Learning Assessment, Options and Resources* (2007) asks the question "What is the Assessment of Student Learning (Standard 14)?" and gives the following answer:

1. Developing clearly articulated *learning outcomes*: the knowledge, skills, and competencies that students are expected to exhibit upon successful completion of a course, academic program, co-curricular program, general education requirement, or other specific set of experiences;
2. Offering courses, programs, and experiences that provide purposeful *opportunities for students to achieve those learning outcomes*;
3. *Assessing student achievement* of those learning outcomes; and
4. *Using the results* of those assessments to improve teaching and learning and inform planning and resource allocation decisions. (p. 55)

Faculty can find those four activities to be daunting. However, if they are given a list of steps to accomplish those goals and examples of academic majors that are following the steps and achieving their goals, the faculty can regard the challenge as achievable.

The following outline for an assessment report for each academic major was drafted by the CAO of DeSales University and shared with the university's Academic Oversight Committee, which is composed of the heads of the four academic divisions (Business, Liberal Arts and Social Sciences, Performing Arts, and Science and Healthcare), the dean of undergraduate education, the dean of graduate education, the dean of lifelong learning, and the provost/vice president for academic affairs (CAO). The CAO welcomed suggestions for revisions to the draft. The Academic Oversight Committee expressed approval and support of the document, as well as appreciation for the guidance provided by the model. Having taken ownership of the assessment report, the four division heads then shared the following model with the departments within their divisions.

Assessment Report
Major, Department, Division, Data

I. DeSales University Mission

A. Academic Affairs Mission

B. Undergraduate Education Mission

II. Division Mission—consistent with the University's mission

III. Department Mission—consistent with the division's mission and the University's mission

IV. Major Mission—consistent with the missions of the department, division, and University

V. Student Learning Outcomes for the Major—the knowledge, skills, and competencies that students are expected to exhibit upon successful completion of the major

VI. Courses and Experiences—that enable students to achieve each particular student learning outcome of the major

VII. Data—from the direct and indirect assessment of student achievement of the learning outcomes; students' results from the last five years

VIII. Analysis of the Data in VII

IX. Student Satisfaction Survey Data—senior majors' responses from the last five years

X. Analysis of the Student Satisfaction Survey Data in IX

XI. Alumni Survey Data—results from the most recent year in which the alumni majors were surveyed (every five years)

XII. Analysis of the Alumni Survey Data in XI

XIII. Report on the jobs and graduate school attendance of recent graduates, including scores on GRE, MCAT, LSAT, NCLEX, and other standardized tests

XIV. How the assessment results have been used to improve teaching and learning

XV. How assessment results have been used to inform planning and resource allocation decisions

In addition, each major conducts a comprehensive self-study every five years and hosts a three-member visiting team of outside evaluators.

The CAO encouraged the division heads and department chairs to meet with her, enabling her to provide suggestions, guidance, and support as they developed an assessment report for each academic major. She prefers to oversee assessment of DeSales's academic programs herself; hence she is the de facto director of assessment. Every institution undoubtedly has majors that are accredited by professional agencies that demand rigorous assessment of their particular disciplines. For example, many university business programs are accredited by the Association to Advance Collegiate Schools of Business (AACSB International, formerly the American Association of Collegiate Schools and Programs), the Association of Collegiate Business Schools and Programs (ACBSP), or the International Assembly of Collegiate Business Education (IACBE). Other disciplines with outside accrediting agencies include nursing, education, and social work. Each of these accrediting agencies demands rigorous and comprehensive assessment for the academic program to maintain its accreditation. Any new academic initiative needs supporters. The department chairs and faculty of majors that are accredited by agencies particular to their disciplines can be effective supporters of the CAO's leadership in the assessment of academic majors, especially those majors that do not have particular accrediting agencies. As Muffo (2010) states:

> Large disciplinary areas such as English, foreign languages, the biological sciences, physics, history, sociology, and so on, have professional societies but no accreditation. . . . Consequently, they are unlikely to have formal site visits, disciplinary criteria developed by professionals in their own field, formal reviews with written reports, and a determination of pass or fail along with a series of recommendations for improvement. . . . This means that such disciplines will likely continue to be more difficult to work with, on average, in doing assessment, since they will have less experience and guidance from their own discipline. This is unlikely to change soon, though leadership in some of these fields could help by providing models to assist their colleagues in moving forward. (p. 173)

Astin and Antonio (2012) state that "Faculty involvement [in assessment] is necessary for obvious reasons. Any change in the curriculum or instructional methodology obviously must involve the faculty" (p. 14).

CLOSE THE LOOP

Todd Bricker, chair of the DeSales social sciences department, whose specialty is criminal justice, has developed an assessment program that "closes the loop" and shows how the criminal justice faculty use assessment results to improve teaching and learning, to inform academic planning, and to facilitate resource allocation decisions.

The following are excerpts from the criminal justice assessment report, beginning with the student learning outcomes that are consistent with the criminal justice mission statement.

V. Criminal Justice Major Student Learning Outcomes

Upon graduation from DeSales University, a student who has majored in Criminal Justice will be able to:

1. describe and apply key concepts from the criminal justice system;
2. recognize and define the elements of a criminal offense;
3. research, write, and/or present findings concerning significant issues in the criminal justice field; and
4. analyze and discuss criminological theory and its applicability to society.

VI. Courses and Experiences of Criminal Justice Majors

Courses: Criminal Justice faculty assess student achievement in each course by evaluating oral and written communication skills, as well as critical thinking and problem solving skills, through direct and indirect assessment mechanisms. These mechanisms include objective and/or essay examinations, written assignments, oral presentations, class participation, comprehensive examinations, and the Educational Testing Service (ETS) Major Field Test in criminal justice. Courses also were mapped in order to show which courses satisfied the criminal justice student learning outcomes, as table 57.1 identifies:

Table 57.1 Criminal Justice Student Learning Outcomes

	Student Learning Outcomes			
Required Courses	*1*	*2*	*3*	*4*
CJ109	X (AD)			
CJ160		X (AD)		
CJ250				X (ABC)
CJ260	P (ABD)			
CJ280	P (ABD)			
CJ350			X (AB)	
CJ365			P (C)	
CJ453	P (CEF)			
CS105				
SO109				
SO203				
PS109				

Key: X = Satisfies the learning outcome; P = Partially satisfies the learning outcome

Assessment Mechanism: (A) = Objective/Essay Exams, (B) = Written Assignments, (C) = Oral Presentations, (D) = Class Participation, (E) = Comprehensive Exams, (F) = Major Field Test

VII. Data from Direct Assessment of Senior Criminal Justice Majors

XIII. How Assessment Results Have Been Used to Improve Teaching and Learning

XIV. How Assessment Results Have Been Used to Inform Planning and Resource Allocation Decisions

The 2010 criminal justice visiting team's recommendations included increasing the quality control oversight of the criminal justice major offered by the DeSales ACCESS program, an evening degree program for nontraditional students. ACCESS seniors' results on the Criminal Justice Major Field Test were lower than those of the traditional day students. Consequently, a full-time social sciences department faculty member is released from one course per semester to serve as the social sciences ACCESS coordinator with the responsibility of evaluating every aspect of the ACCESS criminal justice program and to make appropriate improvements.

Julie Himmelberger, a junior faculty member, enthusiastically took on the challenge of designing and implementing an assessment program for the chemistry and the biochemistry/molecular biology majors. Her faculty colleagues in those majors collaborated, and they chose to use the American Chemical Society examinations, which provide national norms. The following are excerpts from the chemistry assessment report, beginning with the "Courses and Experiences of Chemistry Majors" that are consistent with the student learning outcomes of the major.

VI. Courses and Experiences of Chemistry Majors

A. Courses—[A matrix like the one used for criminal justice is used to show how the courses required for the chemistry major satisfy the student learning outcomes.]

B. Experiences—The chemistry assessment report includes tables that document the following experiences outside the classroom that contribute to the accomplishment of the student learning outcomes for chemistry majors over the last five years:

   1. Chemistry internships
   2. Employer evaluations of chemistry interns
   3. Presentations of chemistry majors' research projects at American Chemical Society (ACS) meetings
   4. Chemistry Demonstrations Program—[Students prepare educational and entertaining scientific demonstrations and present them during approximately 10 shows each semester to visiting local elementary school, middle school, and high school students.]

VII. Data from the Direct Assessment of Senior Chemistry Majors

The American Chemical Society examinations are used as direct assessment tools for the accomplishment of the student learning outcomes. In order to ensure that each student completes the test seriously, the ACS scores are calculated as a percentage of the student's grade in the appropriate course. The chemistry assessment report includes DeSales chemistry majors' results on American Chemical Society examinations compared with national norms, and a comparison between DSU students' ACS exam percentiles and their final grades in the corresponding courses.

IX. Satisfaction Surveys Data from Chemistry Seniors

Most items on the survey correspond directly to the chemistry major student learning outcomes. Examples of three items are the following:

1. How satisfied are you with the basic knowledge of fundamental principles and concepts you developed in the chemistry program? [A 5-point Likert scale from Dissatisfied to Extremely Satisfied is used for each of the following chemistry courses: analytical, organic, physical, and inorganic.]
2. How satisfied are you with respect to your achievement in the following skills? [A 5-point Likert scale from Dissatisfied to Extremely Satisfied is used.]
   a. Ability to search and use scientific literature?
   b. Ability to clearly communicate technical information in all areas of chemistry?
   c. Ability to conduct independent, analytical, and creative scientific research?
   d. Ability to understand and appreciate the ethical responsibilities of scientists in obtaining and reporting scientific results?

In both the criminal justice and chemistry cases described above, the faculty who teach in the major took ownership of the assessment process. Muffo (2010) states that "the engagement of faculty in something that they care about deeply is the key to successful assessment of learning outcomes."

ACKNOWLEDGE SUCCESS

Any new academic initiative needs nurturing, and the faculty who have been "pioneers" should be congratulated. The chairs and directors of all of the majors and academic programs, both undergraduate and graduate, at DeSales University have developed assessment reports, and their efforts and accomplishments are acknowledged. The CAO chose to highlight the report developed and implemented by Todd Bricker, a senior faculty member who was experienced in assessment from his service at another university prior to joining the DeSales faculty, and the report developed and implemented by Julie Himmelberger, a junior faculty member who completed her PhD and joined the DeSales faculty just one year prior to designing and implementing the assessment report for the chemistry major. The criminal justice assessment report illustrates that senior faculty members are receptive to the assessment of academic programs. The chemistry assessment report illustrates that junior faculty members can be leaders in the increasingly important area of assessment of student learning. Both junior and senior DeSales faculty members have developed and implemented outstanding assessment programs for their majors and are certainly deserving of acknowledgment and praise.

While working with individual faculty members, the CAO has given them copies of Bricker's and Himmelberger's assessment reports, and she has suggested that the faculty seek their colleagues' help, if they choose to do so. The CAO made a presentation at the August 2012 Assessment Workshop of the Association of Independent Colleges and Universities of Pennsylvania (AICUP), and she asked professors Bricker and Himmelberger to be copresenters. Consequently, a chemistry professor from another institution who was impressed with Professor Himmelberger's assessment report was responsible for her being asked to make a presentation at the 46th Annual MAALACT (Middle Atlantic Association of Liberal Arts Chemistry Teachers) meeting, which she did. Thus Professor Himmelberger's success with assessment techniques earned this young teacher-scholar early recognition in her academic discipline.

As is the case at most universities, DeSales University faculty are evaluated annually in the areas of teaching, professional growth, and service, and annual merit salary increases and contract renewal are based on those evaluations. If faculty members include in their annual reports evidence that they have used assessment to improve teaching and learning, their success is acknowledged and rewarded. In addition, when a faculty member applies for promotion, tenure, or sabbatical leave, the Rank and Tenure Committee is receptive to documentation that the faculty member has used assessment to improve teaching and learning and has "closed the loop" by using assessment results to inform planning and budget allocation. When considering a faculty member's request for a reduced-course semester, funding for research, or a travel grant to make a presentation at a professional meeting, the CAO considers the faculty member's use of assessment to improve his or her courses. She also takes into account a faculty member's success in using assessment to improve academic programs when she is considering administrative appointments such as department chair and division head.

The CAO makes presentations about assessment once or twice each year at faculty meetings or at the one-day faculty workshop at the end of the academic year. In her presentations she acknowledges particular faculty members for their success in specific parts of their assessment reports, encouraging other faculty members to ask them for advice or help in replicating their successful practices. Two or three times yearly, the CAO publishes "Faculty Professional Activities" to the university community in which she briefly lists and describes faculty members' presentations at professional meetings (podium, poster, and panel presentations), publications of articles in academic journals, published poems, chapters published in books, book publications and reviews, faculty offices in professional organizations, honors and awards, and similar academic activities reported to the CAO by individual faculty members. The "Faculty Professional Activities" also are placed and saved on the DeSales University website and are available from November 1, 2004, to the present. The first "Faculty Professional Activities" announcement for the 2012–2013 academic year acknowledges Professor Bricker and Professor Himmelberger's presentations at the 2012 AICUP Assessment Workshop and Professor Himmelberger's presentation at the 46th annual MAALACT meeting.

In *Planning and Assessment in Higher Education*, author Michael F. Middaugh (2010), former chair of the MSCHE Commissioners, eschews the idea that assessment is a "strategy du jour" like zero-based budgeting, total quality management, and continuous quality improvement have been in the past. In Middaugh's opinion:

> assessment has become an essential tool for demonstrating the ongoing effectiveness of colleges and universities to those public and private sources that fund us. But more important, assessment has become the primary tool for understanding and improving the ways in which students learn and for developing and enhancing those institutional structures and programs that support student learning. Accreditation agencies—both at the institutional and the programmatic level—are now operating in a "culture of evidence" that requires institutions to qualitatively and quantitatively demonstrate that they are meeting student learning goals and effectively marshaling human and fiscal resources toward that end. . . . Institutions are explicitly required to demonstrate the use of systematic strategic planning, informed by a comprehensive program of assessment, to support teaching and learning. Because accreditation is a prerequisite to institutions receiving Title IV federal student aid, this culture of evidence is not likely to disappear anytime soon. (p. ix)

The chief academic officer, with the support of the president, can provide the leadership and support that nurtures a "culture of evidence" that enables the institution to accomplish its mission.

Here are three ideas to keep in mind:

- A culture of assessment must be created and then its principles should be regularly articulated by both the president and the dean.
- Any assessment must invite faculty to be participants in the development process, with a feedback mechanism built in to allow for further revision.
- Assessment success stories should be collected and widely shared so that faculty can learn from each other.

References

Astin, A. W., & Antonio, A. L. (2012). *Assessment for excellence: The philosophy and practice of assessment and evaluation in higher education* (2nd ed.). Lanham, MD: Rowman & Littlefield in partnership with the American Council on Education.

Bers, T., & Swing, R. L. (2010). Championing the assessment of learning: The role of top leaders. In G. L. Kramer & R. L. Swing, (Eds.), *Higher education assessment: Leadership matters* (pp. 3–26). Lanham, MD: Rowman & Littlefield in partnership with the American Council on Education.

Middaugh, M. F. (2010). *Planning and assessment in higher education.* San Francisco: Jossey-Bass.

Middle States Commission on Higher Education. (2007). *Student learning assessment, options and resources* (2nd ed.). Philadelphia: Middle States Commission on Higher Education.

Muffo, J. A. (2010). Assessment in the disciplines. In G. L. Kramer & R. L. Swing (Eds.), *Higher education assessment: Leadership matters* (pp. 161–177). Lanham, MD.: Rowman & Littlefield in partnership with the American Council on Education.

Suskie, L. (2006). What is "good" assessment? A synthesis of principles of good practice. Retrieved from http://www2.acs.nscu.edu/UPA/assmt/resource.htm#suskiegood

Suskie, L. (2009). *Assessing student learning: A common sense guide* (2nd ed.). San Francisco: Jossey-Bass.

CHAPTER FIFTY-EIGHT

Effectively Working with Student Media

Patricia S. Poulter
Joe Gisondi
Eastern Illinois University

The student newspaper at your college is chasing a story that will reveal details about a tragic incident at your school, the death of a band member from a hazing ritual. Unfortunately, the student-journalists mistakenly cite the wrong person as the assailant, which prompts a libel lawsuit. The newspaper immediately retracts the story and issues a correction.

In your opinion, the newspaper has not been doing a professional job, covering the campus unevenly, perhaps even sloppily at times. As an administrator, you are not impressed by how the adviser to the student-run newspaper has guided and trained the staff. You believe the libel lawsuit is the last straw, and this student media needs a major shake-up.[1] So when the newspaper makes this mistake, what should you do?

(a) Invite the adviser or the student-editor (or both) to a meeting in order to learn how the newspaper made this mistake so you can help the staff develop a more rigorous method of verifying information for all future stories.

(b) Evaluate curriculum to ensure students have an opportunity to take courses in communication law, ethics, copyediting, and news writing. If these courses are absent, you determine to help them and to fund campus workshops and travel to journalism workshops.

(c) Suspend the newspaper, fire the editors, and remove the adviser.

If you selected *c*, you have decided to infuriate students, incense faculty, rile alumni, enrage professional journalists, and detonate an explosive public relations fiasco—no matter how much you claim the decisions were made to improve the program and to better educate students. Conversely, if you selected both *a* and *b*, you more fully understand education, student media, and public relations. You realize that a student newspaper staff is only as good as the resources the university supplies. Without the proper education, student-journalists will not always make the best editorial decisions. However, education will not solve everything. The college newspaper is where students train to become journalists, frequently spending thirty or more hours a week on this extracurricular activity. Clearly, the students care.

As a dean, you'll be a key source for student journalists, asked to comment on new initiatives, challenging or unpopular decisions, and personnel changes. And serving as a source is not always easy, so we offer several best-practice suggestions for working with student media to ensure respectable, high-quality journalistic output. This discussion is limited to student media that, regardless of structure (online, print, broadcast), is supported by institutional resources. Autonomous, independent, off-campus publications are not addressed. For issues related to such publications, we urge you to consult the Student Press Law Center's resource guide.[2] In addition, these actions model for students your understanding of the role—and importance—of a free press in a democracy.

PROFESSIONALISM

Modeling and expecting professionalism from your faculty, staff, advisers, and students is imperative for development of a robust and thoughtful student media.

First, you must familiarize yourself with the professional organizations that govern, guide, and serve as watchdogs for journalistic ethics, integrity, and student media. The primary agencies are the Society of Professional Journalists (SPJ), the Student Press Law Center (SPLC), and College Media Association (CMA). Each organization has extensive and contemporary resources online. If you are unsure of how to handle a situation or have questions about ethics or professional comportment, then contact someone in the organization. If your journalism advisers, faculty, and students are not part of these organizations, offer to fund their membership. This is a small investment with great return. Hold the students, advisers, and faculty in the student media courses and working with student media accountable to professional ethics.

Simultaneously, one must recognize that student media is a lab setting for classes in newsgathering and reporting, writing, communication law, ethics, written and visual communication, design, critical thinking, analysis, and research. Moving students from novice to expert is a slow process. Student-run media is akin to publishing homework for public consumption. Allow for errors, and be willing to engage in thoughtful and productive dialogue with advisers and student journalists using the professional ethics and guidelines to frame the conversation.

Familiarize yourself with the First Amendment and what it means for media outlets. Your campus legal counsel is an excellent resource for this, in addition to the professional organizations previously listed.

If your campus does not have in-house counsel, assist your student journalists and advisers in establishing a publication board. This board should consist of professional journalists, both journalism and nonjournalism faculty, and students. The board approves budgets and bylaws, appoints student editors in chief, mediates policies that govern student media, serves as a liaison between student media and campus members, and offers general guidance. Members may serve anywhere from one- to three-year terms and be appointed by student government, faculty senate, the director of student media, or by some combination of these three. Administrators should attend at least one publication board meeting a semester, if for no other reason than to understand the process and to meet key members. At first, simply listen during the meeting and review documents that are distributed, such as agendas and financial budgets. Stay afterward to chat, asking questions of the professional and student journalists. By attending a meeting, you can learn how student media operates, understand its challenges, and develop a relationship with key members. Student media is an integral part of the campus experience. The more you understand, the more you are likely to support the important student development inherent in student publication experiences.

There are different laws governing administrative latitude at private and public institutions (see the SPLC website for additional information.) However, we encourage administrators at private institutions to abide by the same stringent standards as those of public institutions. Again, this models for students your understanding of the role of a free press and prepares them for experience in the journalism profession.

PRIOR REVIEW

Student media should be able to produce their publications and broadcasts without interference from those in power. Attempting any sort of prior review is viewed as censorship by student media and professional journalists.

The mayor of a local town or the president of your institution would never be allowed to determine content or to write and edit stories for any professional media. On a college campus, you are that person in power, which means that you or anybody hired by the university is prohibited from altering content. Can an adviser affect coverage? Certainly, but he or she should do so without an agenda, such as preserving the college's reputation or personal gain. Advisers suggest story ideas, offer ways to improve content, provide education, and serve as both ethics and legal counselors. Advisers should abide by the College Media Advisers (CMA) Code of Ethics, which disallows modification of student work, reversal or alteration of student decisions, and staff selections by the board. In addition, the Code requires advisers to teach without censoring. According to the CMA Code, a university's public interests are not always compatible with the news goals of the student media. Remember, student media is not supposed to serve as the university's public relations publication. As a result, according to the code, "Student media must be free of all external interference designed to regulate content" (College Media Association, n.d.).

TRANSPARENCY AND ACCESS

Although there will be instances when you cannot share specific information with student journalists, recognize that student media should be treated no differently than public sector media outlets.

Provide regular and open access to student journalists. The fundamental philosophy driving our nation's constitutional government is to serve its citizens, which means, by policy, that state and federal governments must fully disclose information regarding their affairs and actions to all residents. Therefore, clearly, your college's legal counsel should offer student media the same access to information as professional journalism organizations and individuals receive. Just as important, foster a professional relationship with student media by regularly meeting for informal, off-the-record discussions where both sides can speak candidly and frankly about campus issues, news coverage, and upcoming events. At some campuses, leaders of the student media meet with presidents and vice presidents every three to four weeks. Consequently, on these campuses student media are better able to offer more informed reporting on ideas they might never have considered, and administrators are able to publicize important information and respond to editorial content. Ultimately, these meetings can help diminish strident stances by each side.

CURRICULUM

There are critical curricular components required for student journalists. Even if your program is not accredited or if it is part of an interdisciplinary experience, student journalists deserve academic preparation and grounding for appropriate development.

Do all students participating in student media have access to courses in communication law, ethics, copyediting, news writing, photojournalism, and visual communication (design)? Are these courses required for student editors and directors? As with all courses, expect clearly articulated learning goals and assessments of student learning in all syllabi. Invite professional journalists to review student work samples as an excellent means of authentic and meaningful assessment. Encourage, and facilitate when possible, this added assessment component in order to enhance pedagogy.

Faculty, staff, and advisers should receive ongoing professional development in their respective fields. An informed and engaged mentor is an effective and trusted mentor. Support professional memberships, scholarly engagement, creative activity, and service to the profession. Modeling lifelong learning will benefit the students and the program.

Student media and college administrators are not always going to agree, but that does not mean the two sides can't develop a relationship built on respect, trust, professionalism, transparency, and empathy. By applying the best practices outlined above, student journalists and administrators can better understand the challenges each faces. Ultimately, if these practices are employed, you will have more educated students who should act far more professionally.

ENGAGEMENT

Your presence at—or absence from—key events related to student media will be noticed.

Attend and support as many events (e.g., journalistic speakers, colloquia, contests) as possible that are held on your campus. Your presence is a clear indication of your belief in the free press. Seeing students interact with professionals in the field and wrestle with difficult ethical issues is enlightening. You might even learn something such as the challenges faced by student editors or the reasons behind key news decisions.

Editors and reporters working at campus media also are your students. They are not rivals or villains, just young adults who want to know you care enough to help them succeed and to support them during difficult times, such as a libel suit or a student organization stealing newspapers from campus racks. You know this, so prove it. Stop by the student media offices to chat in the newsroom, congratulate students on awards and recent coverage, attend journalism functions, and converse with advisers. This might not solve all your student media challenges, but it can mean a great deal to students, who, like you, frequently face major challenges on campus. Moreover, it can mean even more when a major problem arises on campus.

To best support student media, here are four points to remember:

- Model and expect professionalism from all parties engaged in student media.
- Student media should produce their publications and broadcasts without interference from those in power.
- Student media deserve the same treatment as public sector media outlets.
- Attend key events related to student media.

Notes

1. This situation arose on the campus of Florida A&M University in December 2012 as a result of a story that ran in the *The Famuan* in December 2011. The decision was made to "suspend the newspaper, fire the editors and remove the adviser" (choice *c* in the opening scenario). In response to the issues this situation raised, Dean Ann Kimbrough of Florida A&M's School of Journalism and Graphic Communication, stated: "We are working to balance students' rights to a free press through this process while also ensuring that *The Famuan* has the proper support from the School of Journalism and Graphic Communication" (SPLC, 2013). We acknowledge that we do not know the kind of pressures put upon Dean Kimbrough to address the situation at her university. Nevertheless, the public does not usually care about such pressures. Instead, the public focuses on the related issues and conflicts. These issues are moderated through the media, which will empathize with student journalists, not administrators. Kimbrough's decision was condemned in letters and editorials from the Society of Professional Journalists, the Student Press Law Center, the College Media Association, and numerous other professional journalists and college newspapers across the country. Dan Reimold, a columnist for *USA Today*, called FAMU's actions "stop-start censorship," (Reimold, 2013 January 14) and SPLC executive director Frank Lomonte likened the school's actions to a hostile takeover. "From the standpoint of the law, only one fact matters," Lomonte wrote in a special column for the *Tampa Bay Times*. "A newspaper was prevented from publishing by order of the government. That fact alone should send a shiver up the spine of anyone who cares about government accountability" (Lomonte, 2013, February 10).
2. Student Press Law Center's resource guide, "Law of the Student Press," https://www.splc.org/store.asp.

References

College Media Association. *CMA's code of ethical behavior.* http://www.cma.cloverpad.org/Default.aspx?pageId = 1111735

Lomonte, F. (2013, February 10). At FAMU, a jarring turn in journalism. *Tampa Bay Times*. Retrieved from http://www.tampabay.com/opinion/columns/at-famu-a-jarring-turn-on-journalism/1274467

Reimold, D. (2013, January 14). My take: FAMU campus paper shutdown a big FU to students & a downright "noxious form of censorship." College Media Matters. Retrieved from http://collegemediamatters.com/2013/01/23/florida-am-fires-student-newspaper-editor-in-chief-for-publishing-negative-stories/

SPLC. (2013, January 9). Florida A&M student paper's publication suspended, adviser removed. Available from http://www.splc.org/news/newsflash.asp?id = 2507

CHAPTER FIFTY-NINE

Managing Student Relationships

Handling Student Complaints

Adelia Williams
Pace University

The provost of Eastern College has received an e-mail from a student complaining about the online Sociology 101 course she took in the spring semester. Soc 101 fulfills the social sciences distribution requirement in the general education program at Eastern. The student claims that the instructor, Jerry Black, associate professor of sociology, was unorganized and unresponsive. She states that exams and assignments were not returned to students. In addition, the student is dissatisfied with her final grade of C–. She believes she has earned a significantly higher grade, though she does not indicate what she thinks her grade ought to be.

The provost forwards the e-mail to Dean Josh McGuire of the College of Arts and Humanities. She points out that this is the second complaint she has received about Professor Black and that she wants the case investigated and settled immediately. Dean McGuire is aware that the faculty member has, in fact, received numerous similar complaints in the past in both face-to-face and online courses. Because the sociology department chair is on vacation, the dean decides to call in Professor Black to discuss the student's e-mail.

The meeting takes place in the dean's office. Professor Black denies the allegations. Although the course syllabus he produces for the dean does not include a grading policy or information on assignments and examinations, Professor Black explains that each of the four exams or assignments is worth 25 percent of the final grade, and that he announces this to students in his first e-mail to the class. His grade roster shows that the student received the following grades on her assignments and tests: 70 percent, 67 percent, 72 percent, and 71 percent; the average is 70 percent or, C–.

The dean asks Professor Black to write to the student with his explanation and adjourns the meeting. A few days later the student responds to the dean to say that she was never informed of the grades she earned, had no opportunity during the semester to contest the grades, and could not improve her subsequent work without this information. When the dean e-mails Professor Black for further clarification, he receives an "out of office" message indicating that Professor Black will respond to e-mails after September 1.

Unable to reach either the chair or the professor and feeling pressure from the provost to resolve the situation as soon as possible, an eager-to-please Dean McGuire telephones the student and asks her to resubmit her assignments to him. He will identify another sociology instructor to review the work and regrade it. The new professor determines that the average of the assignments is 84 percent, a grade of B. The student is satisfied with the new grade; the matter is closed. Dean McGuire reports to the provost that all has been straightened out, the student is satisfied, and that the issue has been put to rest.

The above situation is an example of what has become a prevalent area of a dean's ever-growing array of responsibilities: receiving student complaints that require attention and a prompt solution. Students increasingly see themselves as paying customers. Whether brought to their attention from the upper administration or directly from students, or often from parents, academic deans handle complaint scenarios that are often complex and time consuming to untangle.

Unfortunately, in his haste, and perhaps to please the provost, who has been vocal about his dislike of receiving such student complaints, Dean McGuire overstepped his bounds, even though he knows that Professor Black's teaching has a checkered history, and even though the student is pleased with the resolution.

Although we can assume that Dean McGuire meant well, he made numerous errors in his handling of the complaint, most of which pertain to ignoring protocol and due process. Like most institutions, Eastern University has a grade appeal policy in its undergraduate catalogue. The policy enumerates the steps a student must follow in order to begin a grade appeal. These include such common actions as

1. The student must first contact the professor to seek a resolution.
2. If the professor and student cannot agree on a grade, the student appeals to the department chair in writing. The written appeal must include a numerical calculation that shows the grade the student believes she or he has earned.
3. The chair investigates the claim, reviews documentation, interviews the student and professor, and arrives at a decision.
4. If the student wishes to take the matter further, she or he may forward the materials to a university grievance council composed of students, faculty, and deans. The council's deliberations include review of the documentation and statements by the student and faculty member. The council's determination is final.

It is quite possible that Dean McGuire has justifiably lost his patience with Professor Black's behavior. Still, deans must follow consistent protocol, including referencing written policies, and respecting lines of responsibility and chain of communication. For example, he did not refer the matter to the chair, as required by the policy. Most universities have formal policies and procedures for complaints, academic concerns, and grievances, which, in some cases, include preprinted student complaint forms and templates.

As students are increasingly viewed as revenue generators, deans face mounting demands to handle student complaints quickly, and often to the satisfaction of the student, and frequently of parents. In addition to grade appeals, deans are asked to intervene in academic issues, such as curriculum and curricular policies, assignments, exams, course offerings, prerequisites, required course work (especially general education), homework, reading, papers, and textbooks. As a result, deans must understand FERPA (the Family Educational Rights and Privacy Act[1]), a federal law that protects students' privacy. Deans must ensure that their staff and faculty are educated about the law as well, through workshops and regular means of communication.

Student complaints, of course, reach beyond the academic. Students grumble about tuition, fees, closed classes, crowded classes, boring professors, incompetent professors, other students, staff members, unhappiness with course offerings, class times, advisement, food, financial aid, and other areas over which the dean has minimal jurisdiction. Especially serious are legal issues, such as student allegations of sexual harassment, which require prompt and appropriate responses. The dean must know when to delegate to associate deans, chairs, and advisers, when to consult with university legal counsel, and when to refer issues to the appropriate unit, such as grievance, affirmative action, counseling services, the dean of students, or judicial compliance officers. The dean must act swiftly, judiciously, and fairly, ever cognizant of university process and protocol.

Deans also should be aware that the Internet has produced a plethora of sites where students can air their grievances publicly, including College Prowler, College Confidential, Students Review, RateMyProfessors.Com, and even Facebook and LinkedIn. Universities and colleges can counter the deleterious opinions that are rampant on these sites, and, in some instances, even have them removed. Many prospective students and their parents consider these sites when selecting a college, so their influence is not negligible and can offer noteworthy perspectives. Although deans should not act directly on these anonymous posts, they can acquire valuable insights into students' perceptions of their institutions.

As a general rule, the dean must ensure due diligence in investigating student complaint cases and know when to refer the concern to the appropriate office or staff member. Here are some questions the dean must ask:

- Have all sides been heard?
- Is all information documented?
- Is protocol being followed? Have the appropriate channels for resolving particular student complaints been contacted?

The dean should also be sure to

- use discretion and consistency;
- not rush to judgment, by carefully and thoughtfully considering the complaint; and
- let the process play out, no matter how obvious the outcome of the situation may appear.

Note

1. FERPA is explained at http://www2.ed.gov/policy/gen/guid/fpco/ferpa/index.html

CHAPTER SIXTY

Establishing an Effective Academic Advising Program

Craig A. Almeida
Stonehill College

As an academic dean you realize that it can be difficult and at times daunting for students to navigate the waters of a college education for a wide variety of reasons: unfamiliar territory due to being the first in the family to go to college, indecision about career and therefore uncertainty in selecting a major, academic challenges due to a disability, and inability to balance the demands of school, athletics, work, family, and personal commitments and issues, to name a few. A critical factor in student achievement is having a strong academic advising program in place that actively (1) seeks to identify and work with students who are struggling with their course work, and (2) trains faculty on their role in working with academic advisees so that they are able to effectively recognize students who are struggling and provide them with the appropriate support and resources that will assist them in getting back on track.

The success of a college is due in no small part to the success of its students. A critically important factor in student achievement is effective academic advising. There is no one-size-fits-all model for academic advising, but what is in place needs to satisfy the unique needs of the college or university. This chapter will discuss a number of factors that need to be taken into consideration when developing an academic advising program that serves the students and faculty well. Deans, and other senior academic leaders, need to fully understand their students and their campus culture in order to develop an advising program that is best suited for success at their college or university. Because they have a wider-angle view of the campus constituencies, it is crucial that deans ask several important questions and articulate a clear philosophy regarding advising.

WHO IS YOUR STUDENT POPULATION?

Who your students are and what they have going on in their lives while taking classes plays a large role in determining their needs and how they interact with the college. All students are not the same; their needs vary and can be quite complex and very specific depending on whether they are attending college on a part-time or full-time basis, live on campus or commute short or long distances, are of traditional or nontraditional age, do not work at all or have a forty-or-more-hour a week job, or are first-generation college students or come from families in which attending college is the norm.

WHO IS DOING THE ADVISING?

One advising model has full-time faculty who serve as academic advisers of students who have declared majors or minors in their disciplines. Full-time faculty have many competing interests for their time—primary among them are the areas in which they will be evaluated for tenure and promotion: teaching, scholarship, and service to the department and college or university. Where does advising fit in among them? Academic advising often is not explicitly addressed in the tenure and promotion criteria, although it can be (discussed later in this article). Advising is often considered a service to the department (if majors are being advised) or to the college or university (if undeclared students are being advised). Typically, faculty advisers are supported by professional staff in an advising office, who serve as a resource for both students and faculty (see the "Services" section). An alternate model has full-time professional staff in an advising office serving as the academic advisers. In either of the models, part-time paraprofessionals or student peer advisers (or both) can also be used.

TRAINING OF FACULTY ADVISERS

Academic advising is much more than simply helping students pick their courses for the following semester. It requires a commitment on the part of the adviser to invest in getting to know each advisee as a unique individual—a person with a specific background, abilities, skill set, talents, capabilities, interests, and goals. Creating a schedule that includes classes that satisfy particular requirements for general education and the student's major and minor can be a challenge in and of itself, but when work, athletic, home, and volunteer commitments are added to the mix, it can easily be a monumental task that requires a great deal of thought and planning.

It should not be assumed that simply because faculty were once undergraduates and now teach that they will naturally know how to advise. Faculty advisers need to be equipped with the knowledge and resources to best assist advisees regardless of whether they are in their first or final semester of college, are on probation or have a 4.0 GPA. Faculty need, want, and appreciate a strong academic adviser training program that does the following:

- Introduces new advisers to the college's curriculum and to the mission or philosophy and goals of the advising program
- Reviews and provides updates on the college's curriculum and to the mission or philosophy and goals of the advising program to current advisers
- Educates faculty about when to send students to disability services, the counseling center, or health services
- Provides resources that will be helpful to an adviser during a meeting with an advisee in order to respond to his or her specific needs (e.g., sheets that list the college's general education and major requirements, contact information for offices that provide a variety of services to students such as writing, tutoring, counseling, academic coaching)
- Shows how advising software can be used to track graduation requirements that have been satisfied to date, determine those that still need to be satisfied, and possibly, depending on the software, create "what if" scenarios (e.g., what requirements will be satisfied and not satisfied if an advisee was to switch from one major to another)
- Guides the adviser through a discovery process in order to better understand each advisee:
  - What is his prior academic preparation?
  - What courses did he like and not like or do best and worst in while in high school?
  - What does he anticipate will be the biggest challenges he will face in college?
  - What GPA does he hope to attain at the end of his first year?
  - What does he want to major in and why?
  - Does he know what he wants to do for a career? How confident is he in that choice?
  - What extracurricular activities does he want to participate in while in college?
  - Will he have to work during the academic year and if so, how many hours a week?
  - What is occurring in his life that may negatively affect his academics?

PHILOSOPHY OR MISSION

An effective academic advising program incorporates both prescriptive and developmental advising. Prescriptive advising provides information that students can use when making decisions; it assumes a more active role by the adviser and a more passive role by the student. The developmental advising approach has the objective of getting advisees, over time, to be active, to have the desire and ability to seek out, process, and use information and resources in order to make well-informed decisions and choices regarding their academics and preparation for what is planned for after graduation.

PHYSICAL SPACE

Academic advising is often coordinated out of either an advising office or center with space sufficient for individual offices for each professional so that private conversations can be had with students, faculty, and parents. Desk space in a central reception area for an administrative assistant and, if possible, a work-study student is another common feature. Some advising offices focus on individual advising only, and others are more multipurpose programs that advise also on other topics, such as postgraduate fellowships and graduate school applications.

SERVICES

Regardless of size, advising offices and centers typically work with students and faculty by offering the following:

- Walk-in advising (especially valuable when a student's adviser is unavailable)
- Regular communication with faculty to identify and conduct outreach to students who are struggling in class, attending class sporadically or have stopped coming completely, or are disruptive
- Outreach to students who have received more than one midsemester grade deficiency
- Some form of "back-on-track" program that works with students who are either on or have just come off of academic probation
- Workshops on reading, note taking, study and time management skills, and coping with test-taking anxiety

- Coordination of academic integrity violation hearings
- Information to help appropriate academic committees develop and revise academic policies that relate to academic achievement

PROXIMITY TO OTHER OFFICES

On most college campuses space is at a premium, but it is convenient, if possible, for particular offices that work closely with an advising office, such as the registrar's office, career services, international programs, intercultural affairs, and student aid and finance to be adjacent to one another. This fosters the development in a more natural way of a closer, more collaborative working relationship among the staff in those offices. It allows a student to experience a more comprehensive and cohesive experience by being able to get something done by visiting more than one office without having to travel from building to building or halfway across campus and back.

EVALUATION AND RECOGNITION FOR EFFECTIVE ACADEMIC ADVISING

If effective academic advising is something that faculty are expected to do and do well because of its critical role in connecting students to the academic, professional, and personal developmental goals of the college, then faculty should be evaluated on their role as academic adviser. The form in which that evaluation takes place will certainly convey the degree to which the senior academic leader values the role of advising and is likely to carry the greatest weight if it is included in the rank and tenure evaluation process.

Traditionally, teaching, scholarship and professional development, and service are the three principal areas in which faculty are assessed when applying for tenure and promotion. It could be required that faculty must discuss, either in the teaching or service sections of the dossiers or in an entirely separate advising section, the approaches taken toward advising. This could include personal philosophies, tactics used, materials developed or adapted for advising purposes, ways in which currency has been maintained on graduation requirements, and technology used in the advising process. Additionally, advisers could be asked to comment on their knowledge of college resources for those (a) struggling in the classroom or with personal, psychological, or medical issues, (b) whose plans upon graduation include graduate school, work, military service, and volunteer service, and (c) who intend to apply for nationally prestigious scholarships, fellowships, and awards. Alternatively, a distinguished Academic Adviser Award could be established for which there are clearly defined criteria and a nomination and selection process.

From a dean's perspective, the following should be considered when setting up or revamping an academic advising program:

- What issues are your students dealing with that are often at the root of academic struggles?
- What role are faculty expected to play in academic advising?
- What is the role of professional staff in the advising program?
- Who is responsible for directing the academic advising program, and does that person have the respect of faculty and the authority to coordinate adviser training?
- What would be the ideal location for an advising office, and is the space sufficient for the range of services offered by the office?

CHAPTER SIXTY-ONE

Faculty Mentoring and Evaluation

A Model

Susan Thompson Gorman
Stevenson University

"You're simply not doing a good enough job for us, Professor Newbie, and I cannot recommend you for promotion," says the dean. "Your department chair has given you some low marks on your annual appraisal, which tells me that you have some performance issues to address."

Professor Newbie, in a burst of understandable frustration, exclaims, "How am I supposed to know what to address when I don't even know exactly what is expected of me? And besides, my chair has it out for me, so I may as well just quit now because I'll never get promoted as long as he's here."

Sound familiar? Job performance is one of those things that often falls into the intuitive category of "I'll know it when I see it," which is fine as long as performance is good and raises and promotions are awarded. On the other hand, if performance is lacking and change is necessary, then intuition and subjective feelings are not going to stand up to a challenge. Essentially, in the end, decisions about retaining or promoting faculty cannot be made intuitively—the legal framework of higher education will not allow that kind of subjectivity. Although these human resources truths may seem self-evident, they are not necessarily tied to common practice in academic circles, particularly where faculty performance is concerned.

One reality of academia, tacitly acknowledged by colleagues and explicitly discussed by students, is that there are great teachers, adequate teachers, and those teachers who should probably be in another line of work. Also relevant to this discussion is the mantra *academic freedom*, which permeates faculty culture and characterizes the ideal life of an academic: the engaged scholar, free to think and pursue lofty ideas, and the engaging teacher, free to foster learning and shape the minds of students. It is not uncommon for attempts to define and evaluate how well a faculty member is performing to be met with indignation, self-righteous justification, and even, perhaps, hostility.

It also is helpful to keep in mind that traditional faculty culture is now subject to more modern rules of engagement. In particular, as the public scrutiny of higher education has grown and questions about value and student learning have intensified, colleges and universities have struggled to define, measure, and demonstrate student learning outcomes. The academy is, if you will, trying to prove its worth in a climate of disappointing achievement statistics and a weak economy.

Although it can be argued that every employee at a university, from those in student affairs to the housekeeping staff, is responsible for educating students, it is the faculty who bear the primary responsibility for doing so. This point, then, brings us back full circle to the question of what exactly it is that faculty should be expected to do, how their roles should be defined, what guidelines should be used to assess their performance and, how their contribution to student learning at the university is either validated and rewarded, or not.

Although there are clear and substantial differences between mentoring and evaluating, and indeed, at many colleges and universities these are two distinctive processes, at Stevenson University we use an integrated approach to faculty work, mentoring, and evaluation. This approach works for us and has become a model "best practice" that is now being implemented across all six of our schools. In short, the School of the Sciences, collectively and in full communication with faculty governance, developed a faculty job description, promotion standards, and faculty mentoring and evaluation committees (FMECs). All of these components were designed to support faculty in an effort both to stimulate improved performance and to create faculty evaluation processes that was fair and objective. With clear job expectations and established performance standards, as well as the provision of a peer mentoring group for support, this initiative has been embraced by the faculty, who recognize it as an effective process that facilitates personal and professional growth and development. This initiative also is appreciated by all supervisors who value improved and well-defined standards and processes.

Stevenson University was founded in 1947 as Villa Julie College. Prior to the year 2000, faculty autonomy was high, but engagement with the administration of the college was low. In 2001–2002, a new president facilitated the creation of an initial faculty governance structure centered on a faculty council that empowered faculty to share responsibility for running the college. Shortly thereafter, in 2004, an appraisal instrument was designed by the faculty and implemented by the academic administrators to evaluate faculty performance on an annual basis. The only assessment available before that time was the Student Evaluation of Instruction survey, which remains at best an inadequate measure of overall faculty performance.

Implementing a formal evaluation process for college faculty where none existed before has been a bit of a bumpy ride. From "How dare you presume to tell me what to do?" to "I don't care what you think, I am my own boss!" and other variations on this theme, the initial responses ranged from defiance, to disregard, to resigned acceptance of yet another blow to "academic freedom." And, as the annual appraisals were completed for the first time, a myriad of questions emerged regarding what was being evaluated and how it was being measured. Disagreements between faculty perceptions and supervisor ratings were common and not easily addressed because there was no set of clear expectations against which to measure performance.

In an effort to improve the situation, the faculty of the School of the Sciences undertook a major project that was designed to define clear standards and objective measures of performance that would supplement the "fuzzy" expectations and remove as much as possible of the "I'll know it when I see it" aspects of faculty evaluation. In 2006–2007 the science faculty engaged in the creation of a faculty job description, followed shortly thereafter by the creation of documents that detailed expectations for each level of faculty rank, all of which were to be used in clarifying promotion expectations, as well as to measure annual performance against mutually agreed upon standards.

The faculty job description project was a collective effort afforded due process and adequate time to complete. The initial charge and discussions were held at the School of the Sciences level, and more detailed discussions were held at the department level. Once each department had formulated and summarized its thoughts and recommendations, a draft job description document was crafted and circulated for review and revision. After several iterations, the faculty voted to adopt faculty job descriptions in May 2008 and reaffirmed its support in May 2010. As part of a regular, self-imposed cycle of review and revision, the faculty of the School of the Sciences again reaffirmed its support of faculty job descriptions in January 2013. It is important to note that the process of crafting and implementing the faculty job description was carried out in full communication with the faculty council; in fact, the chair of the Faculty Welfare Committee of the council at that time (2006–2007) was a member of the biology department. The document, then, was consistent with the university's faculty policies; it simply provided more specific guidelines and examples intended to assist the faculty member and the department chair in planning and implementing faculty roles and responsibilities.

As part of crafting the job description, it became apparent that the process would need to address the different expectations of faculty depending upon the rank held, as defined by the university's policy. A professor, for example, is expected to demonstrate superior and sustained performance in teaching, scholarship, and service, whereas an associate professor is expected to show sustained effort toward and high level of success in teaching, scholarship, and service. For this reason once the job description was adopted, the next project moved on to drafting and adopting the "rank expectation" documents. The process for this effort was similar to that described for the job description, and School of the Sciences faculty voted to adopt the rank expectation documents in May 2008, May 2010, and January 2013. These documents are now referred to as "promotion standards," and they are used to guide faculty in their efforts to advance their academic career and faculty rank.

Arising from these discussions of faculty work and expectations was the idea for a committee approach to faculty growth and development. Along the lines of "it takes a village," the consensus was that faculty would benefit greatly from an environment in which collaboration and shared responsibility for success was the norm. To this end the science faculty created faculty mentoring and evaluation committees (FMECs), the purpose of which is to provide each full-time faculty member in the School of the Sciences with a small group of colleagues who are invested in supporting, guiding, and mentoring the faculty member through his or her process of academic growth and professional development. The commitment to mentoring during this process is key, because it allows us to work with new faculty during their probationary years in a formative, developmental way. And this mentoring needs to go beyond just making new faculty aware of tenure and promotion requirements. The FMEC document was adopted and revised along the same time line as the job description and the rank expectation documents. Published guidelines define and describe the structure and function of the FMEC.

In brief, each promotion-eligible faculty member in the School of the Sciences is required to have an FMEC, and all other faculty members are encouraged to have one. In addition to the faculty member's department chair, the FMEC must include two faculty peers with at least one of them from another department in the School. Minimum expectations for committee meetings and individual responsibilities are described in the guidelines. For the first time in the spring of 2010, FMEC letters substituted for the department chairs' letters in faculty applications for promotion, resulting in both acclaim for the process and success for the faculty. Questions and concerns about the fairness, accuracy, and reliability of department chair evaluations evaporated. Candidates for promotion, buoyed by a recommendation from their peers, sailed through the process with ease and widespread success. Others, having received "you're not ready" feedback from their FMECs, avoided the waste and embarrassment of failed applications.

The leadership team and faculty of the School of the Sciences believe that the FMEC process is a collegial, constructive, fair, and efficient one that supports each faculty member in a meaningful way. The process minimizes difficulties that might arise between any given individual and his or her department chair, providing a more collaborative environment for professional academic growth and development. The role of mentoring is combined with the role of evaluating, giving the FMEC important responsibility for determining the individual faculty member's academic progression. The faculty and academic administrators in the School of the Sciences have worked collaboratively over many years and put considerable effort into crafting a mechanism consistent with university policy that defines and supports the faculty. Although time consuming and, at times, frustrating, the process of defining faculty work and clarifying expectations while also providing a mechanism for support and guidance has yielded benefits that far outweigh the extra effort and added hours of negotiation. The guidelines are inclusive and allow faculty in all disciplines, not just the sciences, to be recognized and rewarded for engaging in research or other scholarly pursuits with students, for pursuing innovative teaching strategies, for service, and for engaging in the scholarship of teaching and learning, all with excellence in student learning as the ultimate goal.

Just as colleges and universities are being asked to "prove" that students are learning something, so too, are administrators being asked to ensure that the faculty are doing their jobs effectively. Although staff and administrators have a history of more routine engagement with standard human resources practices, faculty job descriptions and annual performance evaluations are perhaps less common. If you wish to explore this idea, the following steps may be of help:

- Work collectively to create a job description for full-time faculty members that clearly defines expectations in each category that they are asked to perform (teaching, scholarship, and service). Ensure that the faculty job description is consistent with all governing bodies and aligned with the core vision and mission of the institution.
- Work collectively to develop rank and promotion standards that enable each faculty member to understand what is expected at each rank and what behaviors or accomplishments he or she will need to demonstrate in order to achieve that rank. Promotion success is not guaranteed by any means, but having a clear understanding of responsibilities and expectations certainly facilitates improved relations and minimizes the potential for surprises.
- Put in place expectations of what good mentoring looks like, beyond simply informing faculty of tenure and promotion criteria. Hallmarks of good mentoring include a safe, confidential conversational space separate from those in evaluative positions; support for pedagogical innovation and risk taking; and guidance in finding resources to support research, scholarship, and creative work.
- Teamwork is now arguably a "new" gold standard for twenty-first century employers, but it is a concept as old as civilization. Curricula are increasingly shifting

toward engaging students in group learning exercises, team-based activities, and the like in an effort to enhance learning and to promote "soft skills" that will prepare students for success in the global marketplace. It is in this spirit of shared responsibility and community relationships that you are encouraged to develop a team approach to faculty mentoring, development, and evaluation such as the FMEC described in this chapter.

Taken together, these four steps have enhanced faculty satisfaction in the School of the Sciences and built community within and among the departments. The success demonstrated in the sciences has led the faculty council to mandate adoption of similar practices in the other five schools of the university by the end of the 2012–2013 academic year. While embracing academic freedom and respecting individual faculty giftedness, the existence of clear expectations and guidelines for shared responsibility serve to catalyze positive relationships, build trust, and, ultimately, to enhance student learning, which is, after all, our raison d'être.

Faculty Mentoring and Evaluation Committee

Each faculty member in the School of the Sciences (SOS) eligible for promotion is required to have a Faculty Mentoring and Evaluation Committee (FMEC) and all other faculty members are encouraged to have one. The composition of the committee as well as guidelines and expectations for the process are outlined herein. We believe that the FMEC process is a collegial, constructive, fair, and efficient one that supports each faculty member in a meaningful way. The process minimizes difficulties that might arise between any given individual and his or her department chair, providing a more collaborative environment for professional academic growth and development. The role of mentoring is combined with the role of evaluating, giving the FMEC important responsibility for determining the individual faculty member's academic progression.

Faculty Mentoring and Evaluation Committee (FMEC)

Purpose: The purpose of the Faculty Mentoring and Evaluation Committee (FMEC) is to provide each full-time faculty member in the School of the Sciences with a small group of colleagues who are invested in supporting, guiding, and mentoring the faculty member through his or her process of academic growth and professional development.

- A Faculty Mentoring and Evaluation Committee (FMEC) will be established for each full-time faculty member in the School of the Sciences who is promotable in terms of faculty rank. (Promotion eligibility is defined in the University's policy manual.)
- A Faculty Mentoring and Evaluation Committee (FMEC) may be established for each full-time faculty member who is not promotable in terms of faculty rank upon his/her request. (Promotion eligibility is defined in the University's policy manual.)

- The FMEC will consist of two faculty members from the School of the Sciences (SOS) plus the appropriate department chair. The faculty members on the committee may be from any department in the SOS, but the department chair is determined by the individual's departmental appointment (biology, chemistry, mathematics, or nursing). (Note: At least one of the faculty members on the committee must be from outside the individual's own department.)
- At least one of the faculty members serving on the FMEC must be at or above the rank being sought by the applicant.
- The Faculty Mentoring and Evaluation Committee (FMEC) will be selected by the following process:
  - The department chair and faculty member will meet together to generate a list of faculty members best suited to serve on the committee. The department chair will then send this list to the dean.
  - The dean will coordinate the final selection process in order to balance requests made of faculty members. The dean contacts faculty members, in writing, with the request to serve. Given the importance of the FMEC to faculty development and the care with which assignments are made, the faculty member is expected to accept this request. Permission to decline a request may be sought from the department chair and dean.
  - Once the FMEC is established, the individual is notified by the dean. The responsibility for convening the FMEC and following through on the process rests with the individual faculty member.
- At the first meeting of an FMEC the chair of the committee is selected. (Note: the department chair may not serve as the FMEC chair.)
- The FMEC will meet with the faculty member in mid-fall semester and mid-spring semester, annually. The faculty member will permit his/her FMEC to review assessment results, including, but not limited to, student evaluations, the annual performance appraisal, the annual professional development plan, and the annual updates to the Promotion Evaluation Form. The FMEC chair will provide a written summary of (or minutes from) each meeting to the faculty member, the committee, and the dean.
- If the faculty member is applying for promotion, then the FMEC will meet with him/her more frequently. The FMEC will review the application. It is expected that the FMEC will hold a lengthy meeting with the faculty member early in the fall semester, followed by at least one additional meeting prior to the date that the promotion application and portfolio are due to the department chair (FMEC). The FMEC chair will draft a letter to the promotions committee, relying on substantive input from all committee members, which will evaluate the faculty member's qualifications for promotion when the faculty member is applying for promotion. Final approval of the letter that is to be included in the promotion materials will be by majority vote of all committee members.
- It is important to ensure the integrity and value of this process; therefore, honest, open, and forthright communication among members of the FMEC is imperative. To this end, it is also necessary and important to keep all materials strictly confidential.

- Those who serve on the Faculty Mentoring and Evaluation Committees will understand their responsibilities. They will be expected to prepare for the meetings and to offer substantive mentoring and evaluative feedback.
- The FMEC process is explained to all newly hired faculty at the University's New Faculty Orientation program offered each fall. The annual deadline for establishing the Faculty Mentoring and Evaluation Committee (FMEC) for faculty without an FMEC is 01 November. This deadline applies to newly hired faculty, faculty members who are newly eligible for promotion, and faculty members who are not required to but wish to avail themselves of the opportunity to have an FMEC.
- Note: The FMEC process will be reviewed by the full-time faculty in the School of the Sciences every two years, or earlier by request of faculty members. Revisions will be made as warranted.

(Approved 2008; Revised May 2010; Revised January 2013)

CHAPTER SIXTY-TWO

Learning How to Work "In Between"

Advice for Associate Deans

James M. Sloat
Colby College

Dear Associate Dean:

Welcome to a life of being perpetually "in between." As an associate dean,[1] you will often be caught in between the faculty and the administration, in between academic affairs and other divisions or units of the institution, in between a faculty career and a possible administrative career. Life "in between" can occasionally be disorienting, so let me offer an insider's introduction to the work of serving as an associate dean.[2]

Take an initial set of snapshots: As you prepare for your work as associate dean, take an initial inventory of the institution as you see it. What is working really well? What is doing "just fine" but could be better? What is broken? What is disastrous? This initial inventory (like a set of snapshots before a home renovation) can guide one's work to make the institution better.

Make the full jump: The transition from faculty to administration can be jarring. Although it is tempting to hold on to the vestiges of your faculty identity, such an effort is both futile and unhelpful. Your faculty colleagues will see (and treat) you differently—in spite of your protests. It is better to make the full jump into administration quickly. Develop (and employ) an institutional perspective; learn about the pressing issues in higher education; go to administrative conferences (such as those convened by the American Conference of Academic Deans); update your wardrobe, if necessary; begin to use an online calendar; get used to attending (and calling) lots of meetings. As you make this jump into administrative work, you need not (and should not) sell your faculty soul. In fact, your quick transition into an administrator will increase your opportunities to do good for both faculty and students. (Quick tip: No whining about working during the summer, 8 a.m. meetings, or "no break for me" during spring break. This is just what administrators do.)

Serve the dean: For academics who value autonomy, the associate deanship can feel like an abandonment of one's values. You have traded being "the authority" in your classroom and scholarship for a "boss"—perhaps the first one in your career. You have entered a hierarchy of authority, and you are not at the top of that hierarchy. Your authority (such as it is) comes from the dean, and your primary job is to serve the dean in ways that enhance his or her success. Coming from the faculty you have a valuable perspective, but you are not the representative of the faculty. Instead, you are the representative of the dean and must work to advance the vision of the dean.

It is possible that you will face some unpleasant moments in this hierarchy. The dean may occasionally give you assignments that do not make good sense (to you). Even worse, you may find yourself in the position of arguing against a particular course of action only to be overruled and then sent out to "sell" the idea to your former peers. You may take some solace in the recognition that the dean may also be in the same position—having to implement a policy that he or she did not advocate. (Quick tip: Even if you have argued against a course of action, once you leave that meeting with the dean, you are on the same team and need to advocate the policy publicly in ways that support the dean's decision.)

This is not to say that you will have no influence as an associate dean. You will have greater access to decision makers than you had as a faculty member (or as a director). You will have more opportunities to make the case to senior decision makers, even if you are rarely in the position to make the call. This access carries a significant responsibility. You are expected to provide the dean with all the information that he or she needs to make decisions and respond to inquiries (especially in public forums). Additionally, one must choose carefully which cases to advocate—always keeping the dean's interests primary.

Work quickly for the "best possible" outcome: Your work for the dean will likely include multiple projects that may not have much in common—other than the need to be well managed, appropriately collaborative, and completed quickly. The volume and pace of projects may require some adjustment, because the extended attention necessary for faculty scholarship is very different from the efficient turnaround of multiple projects required of the associate dean. Given the volume and pace of projects, you must make peace with decisions and actions that are imperfect—but which represent the best possible decisions under the constraints of limited time and resources. Instead of finding "perfect" solutions that satisfy all concerns, you may have to dispense "half loaves" to colleagues who are asking for three loaves and convinced that they deserve two loaves. Even more frustratingly, you may even have to make a knowingly bad decision because it is better than the alternative. For example, you might have to concede office space to a bullying faculty member who is going over your head—simply in order to get the issue off the dean's desk. (Quick tip: Some battles cannot be won—and should not be fought.) More often, though, good organization and communication will lend tractability to even the most difficult problems.

Develop a thick skin—and don't fight back: As an administrator who makes or communicates difficult decisions, you will need to develop a thick skin. You will hear (or hear about) faculty comments that are not always kind. Ranging from benign references to "the dark side," to dogmatic assertions, to "knowing" assurances, to malicious claims, most of these comments will reflect an ignorance of the complexity involved in making difficult trade-offs. Although you might be tempted to fight back, to reveal confidential information, or to match the intensity of language coming at you, resist these urges—knowing that the high road will most often produce the most durable good. Remember that the temperature of faculty responses often radiates from a furnace of perceived mistreatments aggregated over time. This is not to say that faculty are accurate in their perceptions—or right to turn to incivility. It is helpful, though, to know that the attacks are not really personal—even if the words are. You are hearing (and feeling) the response because of your position as a member of the administration.

Look for mutual wins: Many of the issues you will face (particularly those related to staffing, budgets, and facilities) may be framed initially in zero-sum terms with clear winners and losers—hence the fierce competition for limited resources. You are in the position to help colleagues look for mutual wins by means of creative solutions. As faculty begin to articulate their real needs—as contrasted with their perceived "needs"—it may be possible to find cross-departmental solutions that benefit both (or all) parties. By bringing people together, you have the opportunity to help them see both each other's legitimate needs as well as your interest in mutually beneficial outcomes.

Bridge the gap—learn to translate: Your unending project load as associate dean will require you to establish a new network of administrative colleagues in other institutional divisions. Student life, public safety, physical plant, career services, development, admissions, alumni—offices which could safely be ignored as a faculty member—will suddenly become essential to completing your work on projects like commencement or summer school or internships. Take the opportunity to meet the colleagues in these areas and to understand their work. Not only will you gain a valuable education in how the broader institution works, you also will find a dedicated set of colleagues who share the same passion for student growth and development. In these new relationships, you will often have the opportunity to serve as a bridge between the faculty and administrative offices. Many administrative colleagues do not understand what matters to faculty, and many faculty have no sense of the challenge and value of administrative work. As you help translate from one group to the other, you will provide the institutional "glue" that helps colleagues from different worlds come to see their shared vision and purpose.

Plan for your future—cultivate new and old networks: In the midst of all your work supporting the dean, reaching out to faculty, and bridging gaps, take some time to reflect on your work and think about your future. Administrative conferences and annual performance reviews can be valuable prompts toward reflection. As you consider your future options, draw on the wisdom of your new network of administrators at other institutions. While you are exploring potential administrative options for the future, be sure to "keep the home fires burning" in your academic discipline by attending occasional conferences, reading article abstracts and book reviews, and making connections between your administrative work (with its attendant literature) and your teaching and scholarship. Once you have reached clarity about your preferences, have a conversation with the dean to explore the options that may be available. Although it may not always be possible to *do* what you want, it can help to *know* what you want before engaging the conversation of what the options might be—a common response to the question of "What are my options?" is some version of "What would you like to do?"

Pull out the photo album: Life as an associate dean is often complex and conflicted, but it can also be very deeply rewarding. You will have the opportunity to influence policy more directly than in your previous work. You can develop efficient systems that can be sustained over time. Furthermore, you can effect multidimensional change by moving multiple projects toward a common end. You will also get to work with colleagues from across the institution—meeting new people and finding new friends in unusual places. And occasionally, though only very occasionally, people may appreciate the way that your hard work has allowed others to thrive. More often, you will be able to quietly take great joy in the success of faculty and students whom one has served in invisible ways. As you leave your position (whether to return to the faculty or to another administrative post), you will be able to see the difference that you have made by referring back to those initial snapshots that you took at the beginning of your term.

With best wishes for your success,
Your Predecessor

P.S. Make the full jump—become a full administrator. Embrace the new role and accept the new challenges. Remember that you work in the service of (and for the good of) the dean.

P.P.S. Be the best sort of bridge. Help connect different departments to each other. Help connect faculty with the dean. Help connect faculty with other administrators. Help create peace by charitably translating to different parties in ways that clarify shared goals.

P.P.P.S. Care for the people as you take care of the projects. Your role is one of service; serve other people well. Pay attention to those with whom you work. Say "How *are* you?" "Thank you," and "I'm sorry" very often.

Notes

1. For the reader's convenience, we will use *associate dean* as a proxy for the full range of titles (e.g., assistant dean, associate dean, assistant provost, associate provost, associate vice president of academic affairs) that report to the dean or provost.
2. This article is informed by a series of associate dean workshops over the past few years held in conjunction with the ACAD annual meeting. These workshops have been facilitated by a number of different associate deans (with particular thanks to Kathleen Harring) and attended by many associate deans. Many of the observations from this article come from those workshops.

CHAPTER SIXTY-THREE

Supervising Faculty

Legal Issues for Deans

Jon K. Dalager
Wayne State College

Dean Marshall has had an academic year he'd like to forget. Allegations of harassment and hostile work environments surfaced in the fall, and some questionable teaching practices and classroom speech came to his attention in the spring. And this was in addition to the too-often-usual complaints of department members' bickering and students concerns with difficult classes. He's glad the year is over and now hopes that he's handled each of the situations that's come his way carefully, ethically, and legally.

The senior academic leader's role is not an easy one, and there are many situations that arise in the day-to-day operation of the office that may raise questions about legal concerns and potential liability. Several scenarios of common situations that deans, provosts, and other academic leaders confront follow, with responses that will help deans recognize legal issues and avoid becoming embroiled in litigation.

Q: *Two common issues: First, a tenured faculty member has told his graduate assistant that she is unfit to be a scientist because she is female and her brain doesn't function properly. He also criticized her angry response to this announcement as her being "too emotional" because she "must be having her period." The student claims this is unlawful sexual harassment and a hostile work environment. Can she sue the professor and university? Second, one of my younger professors has started dating a student in one of his classes. He says that it's okay because she consented to date him.*

A: These issues are related, but let's address them separately. In the first instance, the ability to sue is not an issue, because anyone can bring a lawsuit at any time. Whether the plaintiff will be successful is the real question. In this case, the student has *not* experienced unlawful sexual harassment. Under the federal definition and most state laws, sexual harassment is defined as follows:

> Unwelcome sexual advances, requests for sexual favors, and other verbal or physical conduct of a sexual nature constitutes sexual harassment when
>
> 1. submission to such conduct is made either explicitly or implicitly a term or condition of an individual's employment,
> 2. submission to or rejection of such conduct by an individual is used as the basis for employment decisions affecting such individual, or
> 3. such conduct has the purpose or effect of substantially interfering with an individual's work performance or creating an intimidating, hostile, or offensive working environment. (Sexual Harassment, Title 29)

The professor was sexist but not sexually harassing his graduate assistant. The "hostile work environment" is covered by section 3 and related to the defined conduct. However, the professor's sexist behavior may provide grounds for an action under several other statutes. Title VII of the Civil Rights Act of 1964 prohibits discrimination in employment on the basis of race, color, religion, sex, or national origin. The professor is treating his graduate assistant differently because of her sex. Title IX of the Education Amendments of 1972 provides that "no person in the United States shall, on the basis of sex, be excluded from participation in, or denied the benefits of, or be subjected to discrimination under any educational program or activity receiving federal aid" (US Department of Education, 1998). Assuming the graduate assistant's employment status has been affected negatively, she will be able to seek a remedy under these provisions. The dean should attempt to mediate the situation with the professor and his student, and inform HR and legal counsel as soon as possible.

In the second instance, much will depend on college or university policy. The relationship may indeed be consensual, but relationships do change. As long as the professor has a position of power over the student, there is a cause for alarm. It is recommended that the student transfer to another section and that the professor be advised on the permissibility of such a relationship under university policy.

Q: *Although Professor Jones has brought a lot of money to the university, she is a real jerk. She bosses people around, calls them names, and has targeted Professor Newbie, a new member of her department, for special abuse. When Professor Newbie speaks, Professor Jones rolls her eyes and coughs, snorts, or makes other noises. Jones has told Newbie that she should never have been hired and is wasting the taxpayers' money.*

Newbie comes to you and complains about Jones and threatens to sue for the hostile work environment.

A: The "hostile work environment" is a legal term applicable to cases of unlawful sexual harassment. Newbie doesn't have a valid claim on those grounds. What really is happening is that Jones is a workplace bully. Neither the federal government nor any state has adopted a law protecting the victims of such bullying tactics, even though such laws have been introduced. The dean should check the university policies to determine if there are any provisions applicable to this situation. Some universities have adopted policies requiring faculty and staff to be collegial, or require cooperation with other university employees. If such a provision exists, then both parties need to be so advised. In either case, the dean needs to meet with the parties, separately at first and then together, to mediate the situation before matters escalate.

Q: *Professor Snape loves to scare his students by excessive workloads and poor classroom behaviors. Although it sometimes motivates them, it also has caused problems. The dean has been contacted by students' parents complaining about the workload and the name-calling that occur in the classroom. You have talked to Snape about the complaints, but he says he has academic freedom and doesn't need to change. What to do?*

A: Academic freedom permits the faculty to teach classes in a manner that they choose, but the protection is limited. Student abuse is not within the protection of academic freedom. In *Mills v. Western Washington University* (2011), the university attempted to discipline a professor for a series of behaviors that included verbal abuse of students, faculty, and administrators, threats to kill students and others, and display of guns and knives in the classroom and on university property, among others. The court properly determined that such behavior was not protected by the First Amendment because the activities complained of were not pedagogical.

In addition, your university may have adopted a Student Bill of Rights that offers some protections for the students. These provisions typically prohibit unfair treatment and abusive tactics in the classroom, and can be used to restrain the professor's behavior.

Q: *I have two faculty members that constantly fight and cannot get along. The junior faculty member has applied for tenure, and the tenured full professor has convinced the other faculty to recommend denial of tenure based on collegiality. Is that sufficient to end the junior professor's career?*

A: It may be, depending on the promotion and tenure criteria published in the university's policy manual or collective bargaining agreement. Note that the "1940 Statement of Principles on Academic Freedom and Tenure" (American Association of University Professors, 2006; 1940) rejects using collegiality as a separate criterion but suggests that it is part of the trifecta of teaching, scholarship, and service. The courts, however, have upheld university decisions to deny tenure based on collegiality, unless the term was used as pretext for a discriminatory reason. If the junior faculty's teaching, scholarship, and service were otherwise excellent, I would try to find a way to mediate the dispute so that the university could retain an outstanding faculty member.

Q: *I just learned that a member of the faculty posted a threatening comment on her Facebook page. She said she can't stand her English Comp students and would like to kill them all. Can I do anything about this personal post, or is she protected by academic freedom?*

A: By all means you need to take action. It may have been just a sign of frustration after a tough day, but academic freedom is not intended to protect that sort of threatening commentary. Call campus security and Human Resources, meet with the faculty member and get to the bottom of the posting as soon as possible. In similar cases, the courts have upheld the institutions' actions despite claims of free speech by the teachers. Student safety outweighs academic freedom.

Q: *A professor in my school teaches higher education administration. He tends to use real-life examples in class, and frequently criticizes the decisions of our university administration. One day, during a lecture on higher education and the state of the economy, he criticized the leadership provided by the university president, claiming that he is leading the school "down the toilet." The president called me and demanded that I fire the professor. Isn't the professor protected by the First Amendment and his academic freedom?*

A: This is why you get the big bucks. In the recent case of *Garcetti v. Ceballos* (2006), deputy district attorney Ceballos wrote a memo critical of his supervisor and was reassigned and denied promotion. He claimed retaliation for engaging in protected activity—First Amendment right to free speech. The Supreme Court held that when public employees make statements pursuant to their official duties, the employees are not speaking as citizens for First Amendment purposes, and the Constitution does not insulate their communications from employer discipline. This would imply that the professor is not free to criticize his employer. But, Justice Kennedy notes:

> Justice Souter suggests today's decision may have important ramifications for academic freedom, at least as a constitutional value. . . . There is some argument that expression related to academic scholarship or classroom instruction implicates additional constitutional interests that are not fully accounted for by this Court's customary employee-speech jurisprudence. We need not, and for that reason do not, decide whether the analysis we conduct today would apply in the same manner to a case involving speech related to scholarship or teaching.
> *Garcetti v. Ceballos* (2006)

The Supreme Court has not addressed academic freedom issues since this case, although lower courts have gone both ways. Your professor may make a stronger case for protection because of the nature of his speech—he is discussing a subject that lies within his expertise and is related to the topic of the course. According to the AAUP's "1940 Statement of Principles on Academic Freedom and Tenure," that sort of speech is within the protection of academic freedom.

Q: *A student in our anthropology program has claimed that he has a learning disability and that his teachers have repeatedly refused to give him special accommodations to complete tests or papers. Despite his claims of discrimination, he has remained in the program and has received poor grades. The department has now voted to dismiss him from the doctoral program. Will the refusal to accommodate his disability be a problem?*

A: Yes. The Americans with Disabilities Act (1990) prohibits colleges and universities, among others, from discriminating against anyone on the basis of disability, including learning disabilities. A dean first needs to address the issue of whether or not the student has a verified disability; your campus's disability services office can provide enormous assistance and expertise. Once the disability is verified, the department needs to understand that by refusing to accommodate the student's disability and perhaps retaliating against him for his complaints, the department faculty have placed the university in jeopardy. In *Carlos Bayon v. SUNY at Buffalo* (2006), the jury awarded the student $601,000! As a dean, I would suggest that the student's course work be reviewed by independent faculty and the decision to dismiss him from the doctoral program be reconsidered. If the department faculty discriminated and retaliated against the student, then the situation must be remedied.

Each of these scenarios represents real issues faced by deans on a daily basis when supervising faculty. In order to understand the implications of these issues, here are three points to consider:

- *Academic Freedom*. Be familiar with what is covered and not covered by the principle. Many in academia think it is an absolute immunity for their behavior, but it is not. Become aware of the principle and educate your faculty. This understanding may prevent future problems.
- *Faculty Handbook, University Policy, and Collective Bargaining Agreement*. In days gone by, a dean could make decisions by the seat of his or her pants, using the years of academic experience and tradition to make the correct decision. But we live in the Age of Rules, and as deans, we are the keepers of the rules. You need to know them well and inform your faculty. Full disclosure and constant communication serves as excellent preventive medicine.
- *The University Counsel and Human Resources Office*. When you do hear about threats to people's health and safety, or discriminatory behavior of any kind, you need to report it to the HR office or university attorney so that the matter can be handled promptly through the appropriate channels. Such behavior may involve practices in hiring, ADA issues, and Title IX implementation, so deans should be well versed in legal issues in all such areas. There have been many cases in which the administration had knowledge of improper behavior and failed to take immediate action. These cases usually lead to disastrous results.

Deans don't need to be lawyers, but with a sharp eye and an understanding of the applicable rules and policies, they can be effective supervisors of faculty and avoid litigation.

References

American Association of University Professors. (2006; 1940). 1940 Statement of principles on academic freedom and tenure. In *AAUP Policy* (10th ed.). Retrieved from http://www.aaup.org/file/principles-academic-freedom-tenure.pdf

Americans with Disabilities Act of 1990, 42 U.S.C.A. § 12101 *et seq*.

Carlos Bayon v. SUNY at Buffalo, Reported in F.Supp.2d, 2006 WL 1007616, 32 NDLR P 169, W.D.N.Y., April 13, 2006 (NO. 98-CV-0578E(SR).

Garcetti v. Ceballos, 547 U.S. 410 (2006).

Mills v. Western Washington University, 246 P.3d 1254 (2011).

Sexual Harassment, 29 C.F.R. § 1604.11(a).

Title VII, Civil Rights Act of 1964, 42 U.S.C. § 2000e–2.

Title IX, Education Amendments of 1972, 20 U.S.C. §§ 1681–1688.

US Department of Education. (1998). *Title IX and sex discrimination*. Retrieved from http://www2.ed.gov/about/offices/list/ocr/docs/tix_dis.html

THE CONTRIBUTORS

Craig A. Almeida has taught in the biology department at Stonehill College since 1995 and is currently an associate professor. Between 2000 and 2008 he served as the first director of Stonehill's biochemistry program. In July 2008 he assumed the role as Stonehill's first dean of academic achievement, which is responsible for the coordination and delivery of all academic resources to Stonehill students to ensure their academic success across the continuum of ability and achievement.

Laura L. Behling is the vice president for academic affairs and dean of the college at Knox College. Prior to this, she served at Butler University, as associate provost for faculty affairs, and at Gustavus Adolphus College, as a faculty member in English, department chair, and director of the John S. Kendall Center for Engaged Learning. Behling has taught in the Czech Republic as a Fulbright Scholar and serves as a member of the Board for the American Conference of Academic Deans.

Alison Benders serves as the vice president for academic affairs and dean of the faculty at Ohio Dominican University. She has a BA in philosophy from Yale University, a JD from the University of Virginia, and a PhD from Boston College in systematic theology. Her administrative experience has included positions as graduate dean, dean of professional programs, and academic vice president at two institutions. Here, her areas of expertise are in strategic planning, employment issues, and assessment of student learning; Benders's scholarly work relates to personal identity and moral formation.

Charlotte G. Borst is professor of history and vice president for academic affairs and dean of the faculty, Whittier College, California. She has twelve years' experience as an academic leader. Her administrative accomplishments include building interdisciplinary programs, fostering internationalization through on-campus and study abroad programs, advocacy for faculty development, and support for faculty teaching and research. This experience also includes oversight of risk assessment processes within academic affairs, including setting best practices for tenure and promotion.

Frank Boyd is associate provost at Illinois Wesleyan University (IWU). He has served in a variety of positions at IWU including associate dean and interim provost. Boyd is a Senior Teagle Scholar at the Center of Inquiry in the Liberal Arts at Wabash College and has served on the Illinois Board of Higher Education's Faculty Advisory Council.

Mark J. Braun is provost and dean of the college at Gustavus Adolphus College. He has responsibility for the academic program, including academic strategic planning and facilities planning. He also represents the academic program to both internal and external constituencies and works with institutional advancement to secure resources. He was previously senior vice president and dean at Augustana College (South Dakota). Braun has published a book and several articles on decision making for new communications technology standards.

Jeffrey R. Breese is a sociologist, having focused much of his scholarship on the applications of role exit theory. He has been at Rockhurst University (Kansas City, Missouri) since 2009, where he served as the dean of the School of Graduate and Professional Studies. Since March 2012 he has been serving as the interim vice president for academic affairs at Rockhurst.

David W. Chapman is a professor of English and dean of the Howard College of Arts and Sciences at Samford University. He played a key role in the development of Samford's interdisciplinary core curriculum and in the Problem-Based Learning Initiative funded by a one-million-dollar grant from the Pew Charitable Trusts. He is the director of the International Organizing Committee of the Pan-American Network for Problem-Based Learning and former director of the Birmingham Area Consortium of Higher Education.

Katie Conboy is provost and senior vice president at Simmons College. For twenty-six years, she worked at Stonehill College, where she led three strategic planning processes and a complete revision of the general education curriculum. She has served as chair of the CIC-CAO Task Force, as a member of the advisory board to the National Institute for Technology in Liberal Education (NITLE), and as a member of the board of directors of the American Conference of Academic Deans.

Virginia Coombs retired in 2013 from the Council of Independent Colleges as vice president of annual programs. In that position she planned and conducted the annual Chief Academic Officers Institutes and Workshops for Department and Division Chairs. Prior to working for CIC she served as provost/vice president for academic affairs at Central College, Oklahoma City University, University of Wisconsin-River Falls, and Keuka College. Elected to the ACAD board in 1995, she served as chair from 2004 to 2007.

Jon K. Dalager received his PhD in political science from the University of Illinois and his JD from the University of Minnesota. He has been admitted to the state and federal bars in Minnesota, North Dakota, Illinois, and Kentucky. He is a board member of the American Conference of Academic Deans and *The Department Chair* newsletter and is a peer reviewer for the Higher Learning Commission. He regularly presents at national conferences for deans and department chairs.

John T. Day is provost, academic vice president, and professor of English at John Carroll University. He served in similar roles at Roanoke College. At St. Olaf College he was English department chair, associate dean for interdisciplinary studies, and assistant vice president for academic affairs. He has expertise in early modern British literature and modern Irish literature. John attended Holy Cross and Harvard, and also served as an ACE Fellow at Holy Cross.

Kent A. Eaton serves as provost and professor of cultural studies at McPherson College in Kansas. He has degrees from Texas Christian University (BA), Dallas Seminary (ThM), La Universidad de Barcelona (diploma in Hispanic studies), and the University of Wales at Lampeter (PhD). He has written widely on Christianity in Spain, having lived there for twelve years. Kent has been active in community service through leadership in the not-for-profit sector.

Frank Eyetsemitan holds a PhD in organizational psychology and is currently the associate dean for social sciences and professor of psychology at Roger Williams University in Bristol, Rhode Island.

Stephanie Fabritius is vice president for academic affairs, dean of the college, and professor of biology at Centre College, where she has developed a robust undergraduate research program, expanded faculty development, and refined the hiring, mentoring, and evaluation of faculty. Previously, she was professor, associate provost, and director of the Paideia program at Southwestern University, and an ACE Fellow at Bowdoin College (2002–2003). She holds a BS in biology from Pepperdine University and a PhD from Purdue University.

Joseph Favazza serves as provost/vice president for academic affairs at Stonehill College, Easton, Massachusetts. He holds a PhD in religious studies and has published and presented on issues from ritual practices of forgiveness to academic leadership and pedagogy. Previously, he served as dean of general education and dean of the faculty at Stonehill, and as associate professor of religious studies and director of the Program of Interdisciplinary Humanities at Rhodes College in Memphis, Tennessee.

Larry J. Frazier is dean of the School of Arts and Sciences and professor of theology at LeTourneau University in Longview, Texas, serving in this role since July 2011. Prior to this appointment, he served as associate provost, dean of the School of Arts and Sciences, and professor of religion and philosophy at Chowan University in Murfreesboro, North Carolina.

Eugenia Proctor Gerdes recently retired from Bucknell University, where she began teaching social psychology and psychology of women in 1974, became dean of the College of Arts and Sciences in 1989, and returned to the faculty in 2006. In addition to developing courses on liberal arts education and the commercialization of higher education, her recent interests have included leadership in higher education, particularly the dean's role and the progress of women leaders since the 1970s.

Joe Gisondi, professor of journalism at Eastern Illinois University, is the author of *The Field Guide to Covering Sports*, published by CQ Press. He has served on several committees for the College Media Association and as president for the Illinois College Press Association. His student publications have won several national awards. He worked as a journalist for twenty years at several Florida newspapers. Gisondi has an MFA in creative nonfiction from Spalding University.

Philip A. Glotzbach became the seventh president of Skidmore College in 2003. His appointment followed eleven years at the University of Redlands in California, serving first as dean of the College of Arts and Sciences and then as vice president for academic affairs. Previously, he had been associate professor of philosophy and chair of the philosophy department at Denison University, where he taught for fifteen years. He has a BA from the University of Notre Dame and a PhD from Yale University.

Susan Thompson Gorman is the founding dean of the School of the Sciences at Stevenson University, Stevenson, Maryland. She earned her BA in physics at Kenyon College and her PhD in physiology at Johns Hopkins University and has served as both a faculty member and academic administrator for over twenty-two years. Gorman's professional expertise includes building and sustaining academic units, conceiving and launching new programs and initiatives, mentoring, and fostering service and community outreach.

Linda Cabe Halpern is vice provost for university programs at James Madison University, overseeing numerous large academic programs, including the general education program. Prior to that, she was dean of university studies (2006–2013) and dean of general education (1996–2006), leading JMU's general education program through a successful reform effort and establishing it as a national leader in general education outcomes assessment. Halpern has served on the board of directors of ACAD and was board chair from 2009 to 2011.

Darla S. Hanley, dean of the professional education division at Berklee College of Music, holds a PhD and MM in music education research (Temple University) and a BM in music education and vocal performance (dual major) (University of Massachusetts-Lowell). She is an experienced arts leader who specializes in administration, vocal jazz, music for children, and creative movement. Hanley works with teachers and students all over the world and enjoys facilitating the education of others.

Susan S. Hasseler is the senior vice president for academic affairs at Augustana College, Sioux Falls, South Dakota. Hasseler has served in multiple academic leadership positions, including dean of the School of Business, Education and Social Sciences at Messiah College, Grantham, Pennsylvania, and the associate dean for teacher education at Calvin College, Grand Rapids, Michigan. She was awarded a PhD from Northwestern University. Her scholarly interests include inclusive excellence and higher education leadership.

Robert Holyer is a senior consultant for AGB Search. He served as the chief academic officer at Lyon College, Randolph-Macon College, and Presbyterian College. He is a graduate of Bethel College (Minnesota), Yale Divinity School, and the University of Cambridge and taught at the University of Virginia, Converse College, and Lyon College. Some of the material for his article was contributed by ACAD colleagues in preparation for the ACAD workshop he led, "Becoming a CAO."

Lisa Ijiri, PhD, is associate provost for academic programs and resource planning at Lesley University, where she leads initiatives including globalization, accreditation, grants, and program planning. Previously she served as associate dean for academic affairs at Curry College and as director of its renowned program for students with learning disabilities. Ijiri has been active in NERCHE think tanks and on the executive board of Massachusetts ACE National Network for Women Leaders in Higher Education.

Bonnie D. Irwin serves as dean of the College of Arts and Humanities at Eastern Illinois University. A professor of English, she has also served as dean of the Honors College. She earned her PhD in comparative literature from the University of California at Berkeley; her scholarly research area is medieval Spanish and Arabic literature and oral storytelling traditions. Irwin is a member of the board of the American Conference of Academic Deans.

Adrianna Kezar serves as professor for higher education, University of Southern California, and codirector of the Pullias Center for Higher Education. Kezar is a national expert on non-tenure-track faculty, change, governance and leadership in higher education. Her recent books include *Embracing Non-Tenure Track Faculty* (Routledge, 2012) and *Understanding the New Majority of Non-Tenure-Track Faculty* (Jossey-Bass, 2010).

Carol Kochhar-Bryant is senior associate dean in the Graduate School of Education and Human Development at the George Washington University.

A former department chair and professor, she has developed advanced graduate and doctoral programs in special education and disability studies. She has consulted and conducted evaluation with public school districts and state departments of education, the US Department of Education, and the National Association for Public Administration and has collaborated in international special education research with the World Bank, Asia Technical Division.

Stephen J. Kreta currently serves as vice president for student affairs at the California Maritime Academy. Prior to this position, he held the positions of associate vice president for academic affairs and academic dean and holds the rank of professor in the engineering technology department. He holds a BS in marine engineering technology from the California Maritime Academy and an MS in industrial and systems engineering from San Jose State University.

Mary L. Lo Re serves as professor of finance and department chair at Wagner College. She entered academia with seventeen years' business experience, nine years in technology and eight years in executive management. She earned her PhD in economics from City College of New York Graduate Center specializing in monetary theories and policies and international trade. She has served on the faculty tenure/promotion personnel committee and as director of MBA programs, director of assessment, and chair of the Department of Business Administration. Her research interests include EU/EMU policies and civic engagement. She recently authored *Experiential Civic Learning: Construction of Models and Assessment* (North American Business Press, 2012).

Maria Maisto has taught English on contingent appointments at two Ohio colleges, including Cuyahoga Community College. She cofounded and leads New Faculty Majority and its affiliated foundation, national nonprofits working to improve the quality of higher education by improving the working conditions of the majority of its faculty. She has a BS in Foreign Service (humanities) and an MA in English from Georgetown University and is ABD in comparative literature at the University of Maryland. She is a former administrative director of American Conference of Academic Deans.

Thomas W. Meyer, PhD, dean of the Willis Holcombe Center at Broward College, has over twenty-two years' teaching and training experience, serving thirteen years in academic management and administrative roles. In addition to college-level teaching experience, Meyer has served as a department chair and as an associate dean and has spent time working in the private sector as a management consultant in the area of organizational development and leadership training.

Pamela Monaco serves as vice president at Southwestern College of Professional Studies. She holds a doctorate in English from The Catholic University of America. Prior to her current position, she served in leadership positions at Brandman University, the University of Massachusetts Amherst, and the University of Maryland University College. She has taught in online programs for over a decade. Her research interests include modern American theater, trends in Baltic theater, and generational issues in the workplace.

Carl O. Moses is the provost and dean of the faculty at Susquehanna University and professor of earth and environmental sciences. He earned an AB in chemistry from Princeton University with a certificate from the program in science in human affairs and his MS and PhD in environmental sciences from the University of Virginia. Before coming to Susquehanna, he was a faculty member and academic administrator (associate dean, interim dean, and deputy provost) at Lehigh University.

Kathleen Murray is provost and dean of the faculty at Macalester College. She joined the Macalester administration in 2008 after spending three years as provost at Birmingham-Southern College and nineteen years at Lawrence University in Wisconsin. She holds degrees in piano and piano pedagogy from Illinois Wesleyan University, Bowling Green State University, and Northwestern University.

Laura Niesen de Abruna is provost, vice president for academic affairs, and professor of English at Sacred Heart University. She holds an AB from Smith College, an MA from the University of North Carolina at Chapel Hill, a PhD from the University of North Carolina at Chapel Hill, and an MS from the University of Pennsylvania. Her many awards and achievements include Fulbright Fellowships and the ACE Fellowship.

Kerry Pannell is currently the associate vice president for academic affairs and associate dean of the college at Agnes Scott College. In 2012, she completed a three-year term as dean of the faculty at DePauw University, where she was also QG Noblitt Professor of Economics and served as department chair and as a Great Lakes Colleges Association Teagle Pedagogy Fellow.

Ross Peterson-Veatch is associate vice president for academic affairs at Goshen College and director of the master of arts in intercultural leadership. He is also the director of curriculum, teaching, and faculty development for Goshen's Center for Intercultural and International Education. In that role he is responsible for providing leadership for academic program assessment and revision, and leading workshops and seminars that support faculty in transforming their pedagogical practice to serve all students.

Patricia S. Poulter, EdD, is associate dean of the College of Arts and Humanities, and professor of music at Eastern Illinois University in Charleston, Illinois. She is a graduate of the HERS Institute (Bryn Mawr). Her research interests include creative processes, arts advocacy, and higher education faculty development. Poulter is active as a guest conductor, soloist, and clinician and has presented at national ICFAD, AAC&U, and ACAD/PBK conferences.

Peggy Rosario has been dean, Division of General Education at the Pennsylvania College of Health Sciences since 2004. She received her doctorate in education in higher education administration and a certificate in community college leadership from the University of Nebraska-Lincoln, her master's in health education from Pennsylvania State University, and a baccalaureate in sociology from Wittenberg University. She holds a certificate of mastery in prior learning assessment and is also a certified health education specialist.

Marc M. Roy has served as Goucher College's provost since 2007. He previously served as the vice president for academic affairs and dean of the faculty at Coe College in Cedar Rapids, Iowa. He began his career as a biology faculty member at Beloit College, Beloit, Wisconsin. Marc earned his BA from Lawrence University and his PhD in neuroscience from the University of Wisconsin-Madison.

Mark Rush served as dean of the College of Arts and Sciences at the American University of Sharjah (United Arab Emirates) from 2010 to 2013. He is the Stanley D. and Nikki Waxberg Professor of Politics and Law at Washington and Lee University, where he has served as head of the Department of Politics and director of the international commerce program.

Karen Ryan is currently dean of the College of Arts and Sciences at Stetson University in DeLand, Florida. She taught at the University of Virginia from 1989 to 2012, where she served as chair of the Department of Slavic Languages and Literatures; as associate dean of the arts, humanities, and social sciences; and as interim dean of the College of Arts and Sciences. She is a specialist on Russian literary satire of the twentieth century.

James M. Sloat is assistant dean of faculty for academic development at Colby College in Waterville, Maine. Prior to this position, Sloat was at Washington and Jefferson College (serving as associate dean for assessment and new initiatives and director of the Center for Learning and Teaching) and at Dickinson College. He received his training in political philosophy at Washington and Lee University and Duke University. Sloat has facilitated several workshops on the work of associate deans.

Elizabeth A. Throop has an MSW from the University of Illinois at Chicago and an MA and PhD in psychological anthropology from the University of California, San Diego. She is dean of the College of Liberal Arts and Education at the University of Wisconsin-Platteville and has been in academia since 1990. She has considerable experience in the nonprofit and business sectors as well. Throop has published two books and several book chapters on psychological issues cross-culturally.

David Timmerman is dean of the faculty at Monmouth College. He taught rhetoric at Wabash College for sixteen years prior to arriving at Monmouth, also serving as department chair and chair of the humanities and fine arts. He coedited, with Todd McDorman, *Rhetoric and Democracy* (Michigan State

University Press, 2008) and coauthored, with Edward Schiappa, *Classical Greek Rhetorical Theory* (Cambridge University Press, 2010). He has published essays in *Philosophy and Rhetoric, Rhetoric Society Quarterly, Rhetoric Review,* and *Political Communication*.

Donald Tucker is provost at Malone University, Canton, Ohio. He earned his doctoral degree in higher education (with distinction) from the University of Pennsylvania. He is an active member of the Christian College Consortium-Chief Academic Officers Association, the Council of Independent Colleges-Chief Academic Officers Association, the American Conference of Academic Deans, and the Association for the Study of Higher Education.

James R. Valadez is dean of the School of Education at the University of Redlands. Valadez received his PhD in educational psychology from the University of California, Santa Barbara. He has been on the faculty at North Carolina State University, the University of Washington, and California Lutheran University. Valadez has published widely in the areas of multicultural education, community college education, and issues related to access to higher education.

Karen Doyle Walton serves as provost and vice president for academic affairs at DeSales University. She has degrees in mathematics from Vassar College, Harvard University, and the University of Pittsburgh and a doctorate in higher education administration from Lehigh University. She served as a visiting scholar at Cambridge University, a Fulbright Administrative Fellow at La Sainte Union College of Higher Education in England, and chair of two universities' mathematics departments. Walton has served on fifteen visiting teams of the Middle States Commission on Higher Education and on its Substantive Change Committee.

Michael K. Wanous is associate academic dean and professor at Augustana College in Sioux Falls, South Dakota. He has also served as natural science division chair and chair of biology at Augustana. Wanous has served as the director for a large faculty and student research grant and as the project shepherd for a new science building. As a faculty member, he taught in the area of genetics and involved many students in undergraduate research.

Adelia Williams is professor of modern languages and cultures, and associate dean for academic affairs in the Dyson College of Arts and Sciences at Pace University. She served as chair of the Department of Modern Languages for eight years. She teaches French, Italian, and interdisciplinary humanities, both online and in the classroom, as well as international travel courses. Her research interests are in cross-disciplinary nineteenth- and twentieth-century studies, and in current trends in higher education.

ACAD

AMERICAN CONFERENCE OF ACADEMIC DEANS

MISSION

Founded in 1945, the American Conference of Academic Deans (ACAD) is an individual membership organization dedicated to the professional development of academic leaders. Recognizing that provosts, deans, and other academic administrators undertake academic leadership as their "second discipline," ACAD's mission is to assist these leaders as they advance in careers dedicated to the ideals of liberal education. Through meetings and workshops relevant to the current and future directions of higher education, ACAD facilitates professional networking across institutional types in order to promote collaboration, innovation, and effective practice.

VISION

The American Conference of Academic Deans will be recognized as a leader in promoting the effective practice of academic leadership in higher education. Our professional development and networking opportunities will not only expand the expertise of academic leaders, they will also advance inclusive excellence in order to meet the changing needs of students, faculty, staff, and society and to foster their success. To these ends, we will also partner with other organizations whenever such partnerships serve the needs of our constituency.

VALUES AND GUIDING PRINCIPLES

In fulfilling its mission, ACAD will be guided by certain values. We will:

- Uphold the highest ethical standards in our work and promote ethical development in our academic communities.
- Foster and support academic freedom.
- Promote within academic communities equity, diversity, and respect.
- Encourage innovation by faculty.
- Promote responsible stewardship of resources.

For more information about ACAD visit us at www.acad-edu.org.

INDEX

Page references followed by *fig* indicate an illustrated figure; followed by *t* indicate a table.

A

D

E

F

L

M

N

O

P

T

U

V

W

Z

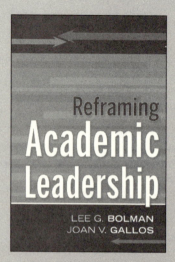

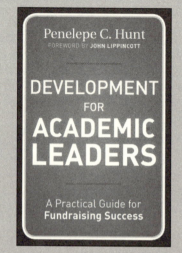

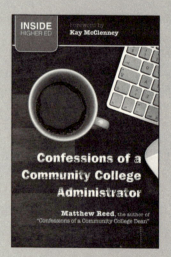

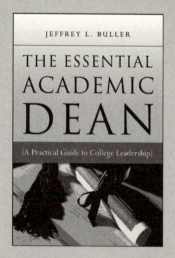